MAGNUS
MAXIMUS

Britannia fertilis provincia tyrannorum
'Britain, a province fertile in usurpers'

St Jerome, 415

MAGNUS MAXIMUS

A NEGLECTED ROMAN EMPEROR AND HIS BRITISH LEGACY

MAXWELL CRAVEN

AMBERLEY

For Peggy & Reg Withington, Deganwy, Llanrwst & Kentchurch

Half-title page: Piperatorium from the Hoxne Hoard, Suffolk, *c.* 400, just over 4in (10cm) high. (Trustees of the British Museum)

Title page: 'Empress' steelyard weight. It may depict an empress of the Theodosian dynasty, 379-450. (Metropolitan Museum of Art)

First published 2023

Amberley Publishing
The Hill, Stroud
Gloucestershire, GL5 4EP

www.amberley-books.com

British Library Cataloguing in Publication Data.
A catalogue record for this book is available from the British Library.

ISBN 978 1 3981 1136 3 (hardback)
ISBN 978 1 3981 1137 0 (ebook)

1 2 3 4 5 6 7 8 9 10

Typeset in 10pt on 13pt Sabon.
Typesetting by SJmagic DESIGN SERVICES, India.
Printed in the UK.

Contents

Sculptor Philip Jackson's 1998 bronze statue of Constantine
outside the Minster at York. (Leila Craven)

List of *Stemmata*

Maps

1. The Western Roman Empire *c*. 385 showing dioceses and provinces. Valentia is here shown as being coterminous with Wales, not in the north, as suggested below.

2. Late Roman Britain. The provinces of the diocese of the Britains, with Valentia positioned as suggested in the text.

3. Post-Roman Britain.

Preface

There may be sins of omission and commission in this work which sharper eyed readers may notice and for which I would crave their indulgence. Nevertheless, thanks to the librarians of the Universities of Nottingham and Leicester, of the Roman Society and of the Society of Antiquaries of London amongst others, I have, I hope, covered most of the bases.

I grew interested in Magnus Maximus and his era as a result of a childhood and early youth spent living in north Wales, scampering over the remains of *Arx Decantorum* (Degannwy Castle) with my cousins there, one of whom (learning the subject at school) tried to teach me the rudiments of Welsh. Later, with these same companions, then living in the Herefordshire-Monmouthshire border country and encouraged by their bookish parents, I read the *Mabinogion*, Geoffrey of Monmouth, and some of the other legendary material, and visited Caerwent, Cardiff Castle and various inland forts. I became closely familiar with the countryside of what had once been the 'Dark Age' kingdom of Ergyng. The incomparable topography and ambience of these locales added to the romance and piled fuel on the fires of enthusiasm. Years later, I wrote a minor dissertation for my first degree on Roman history, moderated by John Rich of the University of Nottingham.

Having been appointed to Derby Museums, I plunged in deeper, studying under Peter Wiseman at Leicester before the local authority for which I worked decided that such arcana were not going to give them value for their money, and ordered me to switch to museum studies. Nevertheless, these academic forays had relocated my interest towards the power structures of the early empire. I continued to squirrel away prosopographical material for about four decades, before publishing *The Complete Imperial Families of Ancient Rome 49BC-AD602* in 2019. The two intriguingly different Magnus Maximuses of history and legend continued to tantalise me, the apparent dichotomy between ancient sources and insular legend being brought home to me not so long ago when, valuing a collection of Roman coins at my present place of work at Bamford's auctioneers, I became re-acquainted with the issues of Magnus Maximus.

Acknowledgements

I owe a debt of gratitude to so many people. The libraries upon which I have more recently relied and the two tutors who were so encouraging during my rather chaotic studenthood have been deservedly acknowledged above. The librarians of the National Library of Wales, Aberystwyth, and of the university libraries of Leicester and Nottingham have also all uncomplainingly accommodated my requests. Others have been most supportive over many years, especially Terence Westgate whose early IT skills allowed me to think more logically, Tom Glaser's presence always allowed optimism to triumph over opposing forces, not to mention a handful of much valued friends who have since died, notably my friend and kinsman, HSH Prince Michael Grousinski, and Roy Hughes FSA under whom I worked for seven enjoyable years at Derby Museum. To the originators (where copyright owners could be identified) of the sources of the illustrations I am especially grateful, and where the originators could not be identified and anyone has not been duly credited, please let me know and we will correct on reprint. The encouragement and indeed tolerance of my family deserve especial mention, particularly the hospitality and stimulating company of the late Peggy and Reg Withington, and above all, my long-suffering wife Carole; the first couple for encouragement in my younger days and the latter for driving me around Britain to look at associated places which allowed me to take photographs, not to mention proof reading and much other assistance.

Introduction

The Roman emperor Magnus Maximus is most commonly dismissed as an ephemeral usurper but, in a largely unchallenged and near-universally acknowledged reign of at least five years (possibly more, as suggested below), his legitimacy while he lived was as strong to contemporaries as were the credentials of most other rulers of the later empire. Like a considerable number of his predecessors, successful or otherwise, he started out as an imperial claimant, an aspirant to supreme power, and from Britain, as had Constantine I, whom he may well have regarded as having set a valid precedent. Maximus's reputation, though, *post mortem,* was enduringly savaged by a disinformation campaign waged on behalf of his nemesis, Theodosius I.

When one talks of usurpers, one enters a terminological minefield. Most people tend to rely on the accepted canon of emperors as found in the better reference books as an inventory of the 'legitimate' or recognised ones, but these lists, with their subtle variations, are a modern (or at least post-imperial) construct. One might argue that acknowledgement by the senate conferred legitimacy, whatever subsequently befell the beneficiary, but there are obvious exceptions to that, too, especially as one moves through the uneven annals of third-century turmoil. What therefore, *is* the difference between an usurper and a 'legitimate' emperor? This is no abstract concept. The final arbiter was the harsh reality of military success; in the words of Adrastos Omissi, 'some men were made tyrants by the victories of others.' Thus, Maximus legitimated himself by dethroning Gratian and winning acknowledgement from the surviving emperor, Theodosius, but his defeat five years later by the same, backed up by the subsequent panegyric delivered before the victor, instantly deprived him of the legitimacy he undoubtedly enjoyed while alive.[1] On this basis, there is plenty of room for grey areas; the list of 'legitimate' emperors will always be subjective to an extent, and malleable. J. F. Matthews has written, in this context:

At various times ... usurpation had met needs for local defence and financial and legal administration when legitimate emperors were too distant or too harassed to attend to them. It is therefore a sort of diagnostic test of the natural divisions of the empire at times when these did not coincide with the conventional ones ... on the other side, that of legitimate emperors, an overriding sense of the integrity of the imperial office had led to the determined suppression of usurpations, even to the apparent detriment of provincial communities which the pretenders ... were better able to protect.[2]

It was the fate of Maximus to enter one of these grey areas between accepted legitimacy and being an usurper from the moment of his defeat in 388. Thus, there are two criteria which mark out the usurper: being declared emperor while another is still ruling without having gained the support of the incumbent and taking power in the wake of an assassination in which the usurper himself played (or was perceived to have played) a crucial role. The most cursory knowledge of imperial power politics reveals that usurpation and legitimation are remarkably fluid concepts.

Yet there are two, very different Magnus Maximuses. The one described above, who was a Roman emperor, reasonably well documented in contemporary or near contemporary sources; the other in most ways seemingly a wholly different Maximus, who is a fixture in British and Welsh legend, genealogies and histories, and one who occupies an almost bafflingly prominent place in them. This book seeks to lay before the reader all that is known about both manifestations of Maximus: to set out a considered account of the Roman Maximus and then examine all that can be gleaned about the *Maxen Wledig* so prominent in later British and Welsh sources. In so doing, fresh insights are hopefully offered into the life, career and potential achievements of the Roman emperor, with the caveat that what was written about him in later, insular, sources, will inevitably be of questionable value. Yet the fact that this material exists at all requires an explanation, and in that may lie the key to understanding both man and phenomenon.

In considering these later sources, I have tried to use the term 'British' over 'Welsh', for while what has come down to us are largely Welsh sources, they reflect British post-Roman events and people, and none of the sources, except Gildas and St Patrick, really fall provably within that earlier period. Yet it was only after the fracture of Britain, when the north and the south-west were finally severed from what was to become Wales, and all of them from any form of notional central control, that these enigmatic sources were assimilated within the literary tradition of the surviving British polity, Wales. These semi-legendary sources have thus long been mainly embedded in Welsh annals, poetry and literature, despite their wider British origin.

We seem to perceive two Maximuses, the man and the myth. But having looked at what we can glean about both, how much of the man is there lurking within the myth – if any – and what circumstances led to the creation of the myth? If the answer to the former is not very much, then how can the discrepancy be explained? Furthermore, are we able to adduce any reasonably reliable additional information about Roman Maximus and the condition of Britain during and in the aftermath of his reign from these sources? What was it about the Roman man that later propelled the British *Maxim Wletic* to such prominence in the legends and stories of those he left in Britain in 383? The man departed our shores in what one might call a cavalier fashion, driven by the expediency of personal aggrandisement, or, in a kinder view, by the necessity to secure the Rhine frontier of the empire.

There is also the suspicion that Maximus could have been the junior partner in an elaborate scheme devised with the future emperor Theodosius to eliminate the two youthful survivors of the dynasty of Valentinian and replace that house with a new dispensation, led by experienced commanders, members of an aristocratic Spanish dynasty. At the time, a step-change was perceived as urgently required in the tumultuous times in the aftermath of the catastrophic defeat of the Eastern Emperor Valens at the hands of the Goths at Adrianople in 378. Certainly, there must have been a reason, and what follows is an attempt to tease it out.

A third element arises from the British mythologizing of Maximus. This may have been emphasised at an early date by Gildas claiming that Maximus was the 'first independent ruler of Britain', which fact, as understood by later generations 'had a profound effect on later Welsh (British) writers'.[3] Furthermore, how was it that Constantine III, who arose in Britain just over two decades later, and was similarly acclaimed emperor there, was apparently so much less prominent in the history, legend and mythology of the Britons he left behind? After all, like Maximus, did he not cross to the Continent to sort out problems in Gaul and similarly fail to return? Yet his legacy in British and Welsh historiography is vanishingly small, although there are certainly a few echoes of his career, as well as of his traitorous lieutenant, Gerontius.

Although an account of Constantine III's imperial career might seem superfluous, some reference to it is required, if only to determine whether he indeed left a similar legacy amongst the Romano-British he left behind him in 407, or whether his career only flourished because of the success of Maximus in stabilising Britain. That the collapse of direct imperial administration in Britain in Constantine's wake had been a traumatic event for most of those in Britain is widely accepted. But why the actions of Maximus – a man arguably single-mindedly pursuing a personal agenda, to the apparent detriment of the Romano-British population of the diocese of Britain – left so powerful a legacy amongst them, cries out for explanation.

In the wake of his defeat and death, Maximus's name came to be vilified by the victors, as typified by the panegyric delivered before Theodosius in front of the senate in Rome by the Gallic senatorial rhetor, Pacatus, in 389. Later opinion was more favourable, although much of it emanated from Gallic or Hispanic sources, more likely to have been sympathetic, including Sulpicius Severus and Orosius. Sulpicius Severus said Maximus was

> ... a vigorous and honest man worthy to be Augustus, had he not risen to power by usurpation ... a man whose whole life would have been praiseworthy, if he could have refused the diadem thrust upon him by a mutinous army and refrained from waging civil war. But a great empire cannot be refused without risk or retained without fighting.[4]

Orosius, writing nearer the time, albeit still a generation after the event, similarly wrote that Maximus had been a man whose qualities of leadership and soldiery would have entitled him to the highest honours, had he not allowed himself to be acclaimed emperor, ending with the telling phrase that he 'was made emperor almost against his will'.[5] The similarity of these remarks suggests that they might derive from a common source, perhaps a lost late Roman history, like that of Sulpicius Alexander (much quoted by Gregory of Tours) and certainly of north-west European origin. Maximus was, after all, 'the last soldier-emperor to conduct effective government from Trier'; indeed, he was the last to rule the whole of north-west Europe effectively, for in his wake nothing was ever the same again.[6]

Either way, the general impression seems to be that he was competent and well-liked, although when all was said and done, had come by the empire through non-legal means. So did many of his predecessors, although those that did so and managed to enter the canon of recognised rulers, escaped, by and large, the opprobrium of their initial usurpation. Who now would tar men like Vespasian, Septimius Severus, Diocletian or Constantine with the same brush? With regard to his *pronunciamento* in Britain, however, it is worth asking whether Maximus was a victim of the enthusiastic regard of his troops, or a devious plotter and ambitious opportunist.

What follows is an attempt to put on record the life of a semi-successful Roman emperor, to record his appearances in subsequent writings (mainly insular) and to explain the longevity of his memory amongst his former Romano-British subjects and their posterity. It will be argued that he was a far-sighted strategic commander who required an armed, personally loyal, retinue – a *comitatus* – and managed to create one without actually weakening the seemingly porous frontier regions of Britain at all; indeed, that he actually strengthened these vulnerable regions by recruiting local groupings and those from further afield to do the job for him.

It will be further argued that he set them up almost as were the client kings of the early empire, and that the scheme was effective and durable. It was amongst these same people whom he thus empowered that the collective memory of him was cherished, endured, flourished and which enabled the indigenous identity of post-Roman Britain to re-emerge.

It will be argued, too, that there survived a more Romanised post-Roman central administration with a strong link in British genealogical tradition to Maximus, which was only gradually overwhelmed by the decline of the money-based economy (at that time chiefly export-driven by the profitable re-supply of the Rhine army) and expanding Germanic control of lowland Britain from the early sixth century. These changes led to the extinction of the records and traditions of this post-imperial central authority, only disjointed fragments of which were assimilated into traditions of the surviving polities securing the periphery, probably at second-hand and rapidly mutating into legend. Hence in time they passed into the much more enduring historical and legendary traditions of these less Romanised frontier areas of the former diocese, thereby losing touch with their probable origin in post-Roman lowland Britain. In association with this, the possibility that Maximus was acclaimed three years earlier than conventional history allows is also taken into account. If such a radical proposition could be accepted, then it would amply provide Maximus with the time required for such a settlement to be proposed, negotiated and officially settled.

What will emerge in the process of examining these factors is that Roman life and Roman ways most emphatically survived the empire's loss of control of the diocese for a considerable time, much longer than many would have us believe. Post-Roman Britain, politically at least, carried on beyond full imperial control in the *modus vivendi* to which it had been used for nearly four centuries, in a manner that all could recognise, but one that was irreversibly mutating into something wholly different.

Marble bust of Clodius Albinus (detail), Vatican Museum, Rome. (M. Craven)

PART I
Roman Maximus and Late Roman Britain

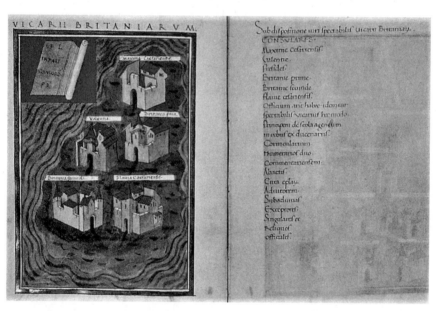

The *Notitia Dignitatum*, west, XXIII (Bodleian Library copy). Diploma of office of the vicarius of the Diocese of Britain, with the provinces, shown as fortified cities. Clockwise from top: Maxima Caesariensis, Britannia Prima, Flavia Caeariensis, Britannia Secunda and Valentia. (Oxford, Bodleian Library Canon.Misc.378 roll 186B frame 15)

1

Britain before Maximus

St Jerome's dismissive comment that Britain was a 'fertile ground for tyrants' was written with good reason, although one might point to other highly militarised provinces like Syria or Pannonia as having produced more claimants (successful or otherwise) to imperial power over the centuries. Britain's position at the north-western edge of the empire would, one might think, have limited the practicalities of becoming a *tyrannus* (usurper), although its cohesion with the provinces of Gaul and Spain as a unit of control was certainly a practical proposition, as events were to establish more than once. Another problem was the failure of Cn. Julius Agricola to conquer the entire island of Britain (not to mention Ireland) in the 80s. Whether even he would have managed to pull off such a feat is a matter for debate. Yet, without having the entire island secure, there was always going to be a problem with whatever borders (*limes*) were arrived at. And so it proved, causing Britain to require a far bigger military establishment than it might otherwise have warranted. Hence, there were perpetual troubles, from raiding to full-scale incursions. At so turbulent and unpredictable an outpost, the potential for trouble was ever-present. As far as the potential to encourage attempts at supreme power went, the rot seems to have set in with the declaration of D. Clodius Albinus in 193.

Clodius Albinus and Septimius Severus

Albinus as governor of Britain seems to have declared himself a contender to succeed the murdered Pertinax in 193. Presumably, he was acclaimed *imperator* either by his soldiers, as had apparently happened (abortively) twice in Britain during the reign of Commodus, or by his entourage. Two other commanders, Pescennius Niger and Septimius Severus, had made similar declarations in other parts of the empire, but the latter reached Rome first and appointed Albinus Caesar in early April 193, in order to secure his flank against his potent rival, Niger. Albinus, on agreeing, took the style D. Clodius Albinus Caesar and we may assume that the senate ratified this state of affairs as soon as Severus's pre-eminence had been acknowledged, and these same conscript fathers no doubt granted him, with Severus, the tribunician and proconsular power by then normal in an acceding emperor and without which no emperor could legitimately govern without destroying the delicate post-republican balance between ruler and senate.[1]

Although apparently not necessarily acclaimed by his troops (as became the norm in the third century for those grasping at the purple), he probably acquired an imperial acclamation from them. June 193 probably also marks the change in his style to D. Clodius Septimius Albinus Caesar, the addition of 'Septimius' being to set out the more clearly his position as notional heir of Severus.[2] Although already of consular rank, he was (ordinary) consul again with Severus for 194.[3]

It is thought by modern scholarship that his previous posting, to Lower Germany – although only recorded in the unreliable *Historia Augusta* (*HA*) – is likely, and that it would have immediately preceded his appointment to Britain in 191, thus falling in 189/190, enabling us to date his first suffect (that is, additional to the pair elected to start each year) consulship to 187 or 188. If the German governorship is rejected, the consulship can be safely re-allocated to 190, in which year there were, in addition to the two ordinary consuls, no fewer than 22 *suffecti*, of whom only about eight are identified for certain. Through most of his subsequent period in power he was effectively ruling and administering the northern European provinces: the Gauls, the Germanies, Britain and Spain, a prophetic forerunner of the Gallic Empire that arose under Gallienus in 260, and of that ruled by Magnus Maximus from 383.

Nobody can tell what Clodius Albinus's true intentions were when he heard about the murder of the short-lived but rather admirable emperor Pertinax in April 193. His mother was from Hadrumetum (Sousse, Tunisia) in Africa, from whence some of the family of Pertinax's venal and ephemeral successor, Didius Julianus, also hailed, which might have inclined Severus (also African, of Phoenician Carthaginian descent) to believe him unreliable. Another consideration was that the proconsul of Africa at the time, Asellius Aemilianus, who had swung his considerable influence behind the other imperial claimant, Pescennius Niger, was (according to the *Historia Augusta* at least) related to Albinus. To drive a wedge between them might have been prudent for Severus; more to the point, it might even open Aemilianus to offers.

Judging by the speed of events, little discussion through messages passing along the *cursus publicus* (postal system) can have taken place. The likelihood is that Severus sent a message saying that he had been proclaimed and offering Albinus the role of junior colleague and eventual successor; perhaps he had heard that he had been poised to throw his helmet into the ring. This would have been perfectly convincing, bearing in mind that Severus's two sons were then but five and four years old respectively and that infant mortality was high. On the other hand, there must always have been the fear that Severus would eventually dump his fellow African, an eventuality for which Albinus doubtless prepared over the years of their partnership. Initially, however, while Severus advanced rapidly on Rome and then moved east to deal with Niger and the Parthians, Albinus held northern Europe for him.

Albinus was apparently regarded as a good-natured man and seems happy to have remained in Britain as Caesar for the two years following his appointment, although in regular contact with Rome (and presumably Severus) for administrative purposes; in the capital, too, he was receiving quite a bit of support from senators who preferred him to Severus. Had he any serious suspicions of his senior colleague he would surely have crossed the Channel and marched on Rome himself, a relatively safe option, for Severus was a long time away in the east, following up his victory over Niger with a punitive expedition against Parthia.

In the middle of this campaign, however, about May 195, Severus announced that he was the 'son of the Divine Marcus' (that is, Marcus Aurelius who had died in 180) and at the same time proclaimed as Caesar his elder son Bassianus, renaming him, in accordance with his bizarre self-adoption, sanctioned neither by an adoptive parent's ritual nor testamentarily, into the Antonine dynasty, M. Aurelius Antoninus Caesar. Albinus's position had suddenly become exceedingly precarious.

Yet Severus still could not risk a war against Albinus while advancing on Nisibis, the Parthian capital; perhaps he wanted the news that there was another official heir to force Albinus's hand so that, by the time he was back in the west, he had a ready-made *casus belli*. He had apparently already attempted to have Albinus assassinated. Albinus could thus either resign (and hope to be allowed to retire), or fight. He chose the latter. Crossing the Channel, he declared himself Augustus in opposition to Severus. This provoked Severus to call upon the senate to declare Albinus a public enemy, which they pusillanimously did on 15 December 195; this was his 'official' deposition.

Severus arrived back in Rome by the end of August 196, having taken measures to bottle Albinus up in northern Europe, although one general, Virius Lupus – ancestor of a long line of senators – had already been dealt a drubbing by Albinus's forces. Nevertheless, by autumn, Severus had gone north again and was heading a campaign to finish the matter. When Albinus assumed the purple on his own account, he styled himself Imperator Caesar D. Clodius Septimius Albinus Augustus, which seems surprising, as one might in the circumstances have expected him to have dropped the 'Septimius' element of his style pretty quickly, yet it appears on three versions of his coinage titulature before eventually being dropped. It is possible, in the light of the savagery meted out to over sixty senators after his fall, that the senate may – at least for a time – have recognised him as co-emperor, but this would have ceased before Severus returned to Rome in May 196.[4]

Despite heading a much superior force against Albinus, however, it took Severus until February 197 to bring the matter to a resolution. Even then, Severus came within an ace of losing the final battle outside Lugdunum (Lyon) in Gaul on the 19th, before fortune swung his way. Albinus's forces were eventually crushed, the city burned, plundered and the corpse of his unfortunate former colleague brought before his vanquisher to be humiliatingly mutilated and thrown into the Rhône. The *Historia Augusta* claims the empress and those of his children who were present also died, but there is a suspicion that his wife may have died prior to his elevation, otherwise she would have appeared on coins; neither do the authors Dio Cassius or Herodian mention her.[5]

In the course of these events, it is conventionally assumed that a considerable number of troops must have been removed to bolster Albinus's efforts to maintain his position, but when one bears in mind the resources available to him on the Continent, this is not by any means a given and indeed, it was not until 208 that Severus felt obliged to go north again on campaign to Britain. He also instituted a major change in that he divided the province into two, essentially to decrease the amount of military support the governor of either could call upon in the event of a further imperial declaration, bearing in mind the overall effectiveness of Albinus. Whether he did this in the immediate aftermath of the defeat of Albinus or when he came to Britain in 208 is unclear. Thus, there emerged Britannia Superior in the south and west including the legionary forts of Isca (Caerleon) and Deva (Chester) governed as before by an ex-consul, and Britannia Inferior, which included the legionary base at Eburacum (York) and the northern frontier, under the governorship of an ex-praetor. So Superior had two legions and Inferior only one, but it was supported by a considerable number of auxiliaries. Furthermore, the Deva unit was well-placed to intervene in the north if required. The campaign was still live, however, when Severus fell ill and died at York on 4 February 2011.

Most sources depict the unpopular Caracalla, Severus's elder son, as having thereupon patched up a quick settlement with the Caledonians, against whom their father had been fighting, thought to have been aimed at finalising the Roman frontier in the far north so that he could return quickly to Rome and encompass the doom of his younger brother and co-emperor, Geta. More recent research has concluded that Caracalla, no mean general himself, actually completed his father's campaign to a point where a mutually agreed treaty could be concluded without loss of face for either side, before returning. This possibly included a scorched earth approach north of the Forth; certainly, there was no further trouble for a century or so.[6] A new thirty-two acre fort was one product of this sequence of events, established by Severus at Carpow, Perthshire, on the confluence of the Tay and the Earn.[7] While its permanent occupation may have ended with Caracalla's treaty, its very existence would have aided any form of pacification required over the following decades.

The turbulent third century

However that may be, the two British provinces seem to have remained relatively quiescent despite the upheavals of the third century, which saw a continuing crisis of constant barbarian incursions along the Rhine, the Danube and the eastern frontier with Parthia, then newly rejuvenated as Sassanid Persia. These crises lead to frequent changes of emperor and equally numerous more ephemeral claimants to imperial power, mainly beginning with the fall of the last of the Severan dynasty, Severus Alexander, in 235 but presaged by such events in 217, 218 and 231.[8]

In Britain meanwhile it was mainly coastal raiders causing trouble, using Britain's vulnerable east coast especially as a source of easy pickings when it came to plunder, and later, Irish attacking the western seaboard. This indeed may have begun even before Clodius Albinus's time, for the instability which began to affect the boundaries of empire can probably be traced back to the plague of the later 160s that weakened the ability of the Imperial government to recruit soldiers and placed little-understood pressure from the east on the tribal groupings abutting the empire's frontiers. Britain had long had a fleet, the *Classis Britannica*, with which to keep these predatory attackers at bay and inflict upon them the occasional salutary lesson. Yet at some point in the third quarter of the third century, this problem having continued and perhaps increased, the *Classis Britannica* was gradually phased out and a series of strongly defended forts built adjacent to the important estuaries – the Wash, the Yare and the Thames initially – by which the raiders previously had access to the interior by boat. The first appear to have been Branodunum (Brancaster, Norfolk), Garrianum (Burgh, Norfolk) and Regulbium (Reculver, Kent). These appear to have been garrisoned in a less than formal way by auxiliary troops and, when needed, also acted as supply bases and *entrepôts*.[9] They are presumed to have had auxiliary naval units as part of their garrisons to replace the *classis*. To these forts, more were added over the last few decades of the third century.

Britain was only caught up in the shifting instabilities of the third century when, as a result of an unprecedented incursion of German tribes across the Rhine and into Gaul, which was accompanied by much destruction and looting, M. Cassianius Latinius Postumus, was acclaimed emperor there in 260.[10] He was swiftly acknowledged throughout Gaul, and at its height, the Gallic-based polity so created encompassed the three Gallic provinces, the two Germanies, the two British provinces, Belgica and all the Spanish ones.

After the first decade, though, most of Spain had been lost, as had Gaul south of the Alps and east of the Rhône. The reason for the relatively long endurance of this mini-empire was that none of its rulers were willing to chance their arm on making a bid to occupy Italy or take Rome. Once this became obvious to the acknowledged ruler, Gallienus, he was able to let the Gallic Empire get on with securing the German frontier, confident that he would experience no stab in the back from that quarter while active elsewhere (there may indeed have been an unrecorded arrangement concerning this); it suited his strategy in damping down the unrest the capture of his father by the Persians in 260 had caused. By 266/267, he could claim that there was 'everywhere peace', a fact he put on the reverse of one of his coin issues of the time. For this he certainly owed a good deal to the Gallic Empire.[11]

This state of affairs lasted until the Emperor Aurelianus (*restitutor orbis*, as he declared himself – 'restorer of the world') had consolidated his position and was able to bring the whole breakaway polity back under his central control. Its very existence, though, had set something of a precedent, and the experiment was to be repeated more than once in the future. Yet none of these events seem to have caused any known perturbations in Britain, about which we have very little information in any case, save for the evidence of archaeology which appears to demonstrate a generally settled picture, although it is known that some towns at least acquired masonry walls at this time.

Bearing in mind that this period was marked by a plethora of unsuccessful usurpers or imperial claimants (and of course a number of successful emperors who had begun so), it was inevitable that a British one might arise. There is a clear reference in Zosimus' *New History* to an usurper in Britain (probably Britannia Superior) around 280, put down with apparent ease by the man who had recommended him for the post, one Victorinus, allegedly a relative. Regrettably, he is not named.[12] Yet the only one imperial claimant of British origin was the highly ephemeral Bonosus, also in 280, unless he was part of the upheaval Zosimus mentions. Hence, at some stage in the reign of Probus, two Rhine commanders, Proculus and Bonosus, had themselves proclaimed emperor, most probably in spring of that year. Bonosus was commander of the army on the Rhine and the acclamation took place at Colonia Claudia Ara Agrippinensium (Cologne). Quite how Proculus fitted in is obscure; perhaps he was sent to Britain. They may have commanded the armies in the two Germanies and thought to make their bid jointly.

To confuse matters, fourth-century author Aurelius Victor omits Proculus entirely, although he is mentioned by Eutropius and may thus be taken as more than a flight of *Historia Augusta* fantasy.[13] Most of our information, however, comes from that very work and is not therefore to be entirely relied upon. Included is the fact that Bonosus was a career soldier, said to have been of British descent, son of a schoolmaster or similar, who had married a Goth and settled in Spain, thus covering most of the bases.[14] This pair were also quickly suppressed and killed by the efficient Probus, so probably their reign lasted something like a month or six weeks; there was apparently no time for any coins to be minted, for instance.[15] There is the possibility that the unknown British claimant's *coup*, if not identifiable with it, was linked to those of Bonosus and Proculus, either in accord with them or, more likely, in opposition to them.

Nor had trouble in the British provinces died down completely, for we find that the emperor Carinus assumed the honorific *agnomen* Britannicus Maximus around 285, which implies a victory in Britain, although it is nowhere mentioned specifically.[16] Furthermore, his successor, Diocletian also so styled himself, implying more trouble, although Birley suggests that it may have been the conclusion of the same affair, or even that Diocletian merely assumed the title from his overthrown predecessor.[17]

Carausius and Allectus

The next *tyrannus* to come out of the two British provinces was a much more notable figure, Carausius. He had been born in the low countries, of a people called the Menapii, and became an experienced mariner. He also proved himself a capable soldier, too, serving under Maximian against a bandit with imperial ambitions called Amandus. At some stage, he had received a commission to equip a fleet and suppress the Germanic pirates, predators in the Channel and North Sea – the very same raiders as had led to the building of the three forts at Brancaster, Burgh-by-Yarmouth and Reculver. There is some suggestion that this may have been a commission promulgated by Carinus, Diocletian's predecessor who, as we have seen, styled himself as the victor over some enemy in Britain, but if not, it would have been under Maximian. His exact position cannot be determined, despite plentiful contemporary references to him; he may have been prefect of an *ad hoc* British Fleet and then have had a wider brief as *dux* (general), but the original *Classis Britannica* had almost certainly been disbanded by then (no doubt encouraging the marauders), so the latter seems more likely.[18] He was also allocated detachments from about six legions stationed in Britain, Germany and even Moesia to augment the resources available to him.[19]

It was certainly under Maximian – who is said to have owed his promotion as co-augustus to Carausius's competence against Amandus – that his admiral, operating out of Bononia (Boulogne), cleared the seas of pirates and recovered much booty, but instead of returning the stolen property either to those from whom it had been taken or to the imperial fisc, kept most of it himself, lavishly rewarding his men for their efforts in aiding his enrichment. News of this behaviour soon reached the ears of Maximian, who ordered his immediate extirpation. Having been tipped off about his impending arrest for this piece of *lèse majesté*, he thereupon declared himself independent of the empire, with the result that he was acclaimed emperor in 285, seizing control of northern Gaul and the whole of Britain.[20] It may even be that this *coup* was the spur that led Diocletian to promote his junior colleague Maximian from Caesar to Augustus in April 286, in which case Carausius's acclamation may have taken place in autumn 285. The new imperial claimant's name is not wholly clear; it is given (in its fullest form as appearing on a milestone at Gallows Hill, Carlisle) as M. Aur[elius] Maus[ ] Carausius, where the 'Ma[ ]' element may or may not be expanded to the Gallic name Mausaeus, although Maius, Magius or Marius are all possible.[21] The name Carausius itself seems to be of Celtic origin, and in him it makes its first appearance on the pages of history.

The claimant's style appears to have been Imperator Caesar M. Aurelius ... Carausius Pius Felix Invictus Augustus, and he probably assumed the 'M. Aurelius' element on his acclamation, as Carus also had. Whether he assumed the title of *pontifex maximus* is not clear, but he did award himself two consulships during his seven years in power.[22] He also rather cheekily attempted to gain acceptance as co-ruler with Maximian and Diocletian, presumably before the former mounted an attempt to dislodge him, which failed, possibly due to the weather in the Channel (his excuse), but more likely because Carausius, as a master of naval warfare, had outwitted him. Whether the upstart's overtures were accepted (presumably to buy time in which to regroup and mount another campaign) we do not know, for the sources are universally hostile after the event, but the British claimant did produce a famous issue of coins bearing the profiles of himself, Maximian and Diocletian with a legend *Carausius et fratres sui* ('Carausius and his brothers').[23] He certainly seems to have believed that his regime would usher in better times, marking some of his silver coin issues with the cypher RSR, recently identified as an abbreviation for the Virgilian phrase *redeunt saturnia regna* – 'the golden age returns'.[24] In any case, it would appear that during his reign Britain was quiet, and like Magnus Maximus later, local memories of him must have been most favourable, for one finds British aristocrats bearing his name in the fifth and sixth centuries, most notably on an inscription from remote Penmachno in North Wales.

The spectacular sequence of additional stone-built and multi-towered shore forts, stretching from Cardiff to Caister-on-Sea (Norfolk) may well be partly a legacy of Carausius's reign, although whether built as part of the campaign against the German pirates or as a security measure after his Britannic empire had come into existence is not wholly clear. Three, as we have seen, were already in existence, but the remainder form a coherent strategic pattern, and the balance of evidence is in favour of them have been built at this period.[25] Nevertheless, another five *could* have been the work of Aurelian, following the collapse of the Gallic empire: Bitterne, Portchester, Lympne, Richborough, and Bradwell-on-Sea. However Portchester and Bitterne have been thought by some commentators to have been established a little later and thus Carausian; Pevensey and Walton (Suffolk) are certainly considered to be so.[26] Despite replicating these forts on the coasts of Gaul, too, his loss of the continental port of Boulogne to the Caesar Constantius *c.* 292/293 may have been the trigger for the seizure of power by his lieutenant Allectus, which resulted in Carausius's murder in the latter year. Then again, the panegyricists would have us believe that the ambitious subordinate believed he would be recognised in some way by Constantius and the senior Augusti if he rid the island of the tyrant. Perhaps he believed he would be made Caesar. In the event, of course, he was deluding himself. Strangely, nothing is known of Carausius's family, nor of any wife or children – unless of course the survival of his exceedingly rare name implies progeny.

While the assassination of Carausius may well have been the result of the loss of that ruler's continental possessions, Allectus, his nemesis, continued to control the British provinces, then still probably two in number, for it is not known when Britain was further subdivided from the two provinces into which it had been divided in *c.* 213 into the four recorded in *c.* 314. This division could indeed have happened under Postumus, or as part of Diocletian's empire-wide re-organisation, although that probably had not occurred until after 285, so would not have affected Britain, thanks to Carausius. Again, we do not know Allectus's other names, for no inaugural minting of coins (for use as a donative to the troops) has turned up, which as tradition tended to demand usually incorporated the ruler's full imperial style.[27] We do know he was Carausius's chief ally and his *rationalis summa rei* (chief financial officer). The two of them had attempted to reform their currency to match that being undertaken in the wider Empire.

That he survived for as long as three years is down to the fact that Constantius and the other Tetrarchs had to be sure that the Germanic tribes to the east of the Rhine would not rise to support him or take advantage of an attempt to end the secession by invading Gaul. Furthermore, there having been an unsuccessful attempt to dislodge Carausius earlier, in *c.* 289, no chances could be taken, and a sufficiently powerful force had to be readied. The fact that Allectus had to be dislodged at all, suggests that there was little opposition to his *coup*.

Allectus held a consulship (of his own devising and not recognised beyond the limits of his control, needless to say) in 294 and, despite the loss of Bononia

(Boulogne) by his predecessor, seems to have still had control of some parts of Gaul. He seems also to have continued work on the Saxon Shore forts begun by his predecessor, and have begun the construction of an imperial palace beside the Thames in the south-west angle of the City of Londinium (London).[28] When the invasion did come in 296, the Caesar Constantius sent two fleets, one led by his praetorian prefect, Julius Asclepiodotus, the other by himself.[29] Allectus seems to have been wrong-footed by being under the impression that only one fleet had arrived, the other having evaded his own experienced fleet in a channel fog near Insula Vectis (Isle of Wight), and hurried to meet the invaders. The second fleet outflanked him and he was killed in battle, in which he was allegedly supported by Frankish mercenaries, who took the most casualties. Constantius then arrived in London and set about restoring the provincial organisation, striking a very fine gold medallion to mark the occasion.

The Dynasty of Constantine

The aftermath of the deposition of Allectus seems to have been at first quiet in the provinces of Britain, and it was most likely at this point that Britain was re-divided into four provinces in the wake of Constantius's settlement rather than in the somewhat less probable third century. Again, the thought was that by sub-dividing the provinces, even fewer troops would be available to a governor to use in any attempt at the purple, but if that was the idea, it was out-of-date; usurpers were no longer relatively lowly civilian *praesides* governing the provinces, but henceforth tended to arise from amongst the military commanders, for reforms carried out slightly later by Constantine himself had seen a division between the civilian, administrative, sphere and the military; governors no longer commanded troops. Another reform was a move in taxation from the collection in cash to payments in kind related to the requirements of the army, a proportion of soldiers' pay being henceforth also rendered in kind. An exceptionally comprehensive census in 296 allowed the value of every process, agricultural or manufacture, to be gauged and tax levied accordingly. This enabled tax to be exacted much more fairly, so that the quality of land, say, was taken into account. Collection was also devolved from the bureaucrats to the *decuriones* (councillors) of the towns against the requirements of the military, assessed by the praetorian prefect, a new official with responsibility for whole sectors of the empire. This system enabled the population to come into contact with the administration of the *civitates* and provinces much more than previously, a move that was on the whole to have a cohesive effect.[30]

Constantius, however, was obliged to return to Britain in 305, having the previous year been campaigning on the Rhine frontier after an incursion by Germanic tribes.[31] Constantius was soon afterwards (on 1 May 305) promoted to the rank of co-Augustus, replacing the retiring tetrarch, Maximian. He was embarking at Bononia (Boulogne) for Britain when he was joined by his son Constantine who, having been kept by the eastern emperor Galerius very close to his side (as a measure of control over his western colleague by using his son as an hostage) managed to escape and reach him, probably in October 305.[32] The reason for the expedition to Britain appears to have been that the northern border had begun to give trouble. With Constantine appointed as his *comes* (essentially close companion and colleague), they set about restoring order, campaigning particularly successfully against the Picts. It is possible Constantius was attempting to complete what Caracalla had declined to do on Severus's death almost a century before: the conquest and integration of the whole of northern Britain. Having come back to Eboracum (York) after the conclusion of this campaign, Constantius, like Severus, became ill and died there on 25 July 306, in only his second year of extraordinary powers.[33] Very little is known of the events that followed, certainly no coherent narrative, but the late fourth century anonymous *Epitome de Caesaribus* adds a detail:

> While a young man, being held as a hostage by Galerius in the City of Rome on the pretence of his religion, [Constantine] took flight and, for the purpose of frustrating his pursuers, wherever his journey had brought him, he destroyed the public transports and reached his father in Britain; and by chance, in those very days in the same place, ultimate destiny was pressing upon his parent, Constantius. With him dead, all who were present, especially Crocus, King of the Alemanni, who had accompanied Constantius for the sake of support, were urging him on, he took *imperium*.[34]

It is easy to over-interpret the role of this unexpected German aristocrat. The epitomator was perhaps influenced, in emphasising Crocus' presence, by the pre-eminence of German generals when writing nearly a century afterwards – some of whom will be encountered later. We should bear in mind that prior to his son's arrival, Constantius had been campaigning against the Alamanni amongst others, so it is perfectly plausible that a contingent of auxiliaries, headed by the prince, should have been recruited and included within the emperor's expeditionary force. Another possibility is that Crocus was already stationed in Britain, probably on the northern frontier in command of a unit of ethnic auxiliaries. As far back as the late 270s, the emperor Probus had been settling Burgundians and Vandals in Britain and later on Valentinian I transferred a whole tribe of Bucinobantes to Britain.[35]

Having been acclaimed and now technically an usurper, Constantine led the *cortège* at his father's funeral in York, where he was presumably buried, before returning to his capital Augusta Treveriorum (Trier). An interesting coda relates to Constantius's death, for according to legend, he was supposedly buried in Wales. After his defeat of the last ruling prince of Wales, Llewellyn ap Gruffydd in 1282, King Edward I had the emperor's supposed monument drawn to his attention and, the following year, the remains within were taken to Caernarfon (previously Roman *Segontium*) and there re-buried in the church. The author of the ninth-century *Historia Brittonum* indeed mentions the burial: '... et sepulchrum illius monstratur juxta urbem quae vocatur Cair Segeint ut litterae quae sunt in lapide tumuli ostendunt...'[36] How much credence we may give to either the *Historia Brittonum* account or the identification of the remains re-buried in 1283 is impossible to say, except that considerable cynicism would seem to be in order. There may well have been a late Roman funerary monument somewhere in North Wales to a person named Constantine, who was perhaps merely *assumed* to be either Chlorus, Constantine, or Constantius II, but was in reality some forgotten officer, administrator or post-Roman warlord of that name. After all, as Constantius died in York, he would hardly need to be buried 150 miles away in Wales!

Constantine returned to Britain again in 307, the information deriving mainly from the interpretation of his coin issues from the mint which Carausius had established in London, and several other visits are relatively certain, whereas their dates are not.[37] This period of quietude must have been interrupted in 314 or 315, for in the latter year Constantine assumed the honorific *agnomen* of 'Britannicus', indicative of a military victory in the diocese, although not necessarily one in which the emperor personally led troops.[38] It also appears that Britain had definitely been split into its four provinces by 312/314 at least, according to the so-called Verona List of that date, which presents us with the first evidence for the arrangement, but as we have seen, this *could* have occurred as early as the time of the Gallic empire or as late as Constantius's post-Carausian reconstruction.[39] The latter must be the more favoured, if only because Britannia Inferior became divided as Britannia Secunda and Flavia Caesariensis and the prefix of the latter, deriving as it does from Flavius, a favoured *nomen* of the rising dynasty of Constantine, strongly suggests that the later date is the more likely. Likewise, calling another new province (carved out of Britannia Superior) Maxima Caesariensis – thus deriving its name from the senior (western) tetrarch at the time, Maximianus – would seem to emphasise the likelihood.

These new provinces of Britannia Inferior were governed from Lincoln (Lindum Colonia) and York (Eburacum) respectively, while the former southern province, Britannia Superior, divided as Maxima Caesariensis and Britannia Prima, were governed from London (Londinium, henceforth Augusta) and Cirencester (Corinium).[40] That Maxima Caesariensis was (at least as recorded decades later)[41] governed by a man with the rank of ex-consul, outranking the *praesides* in charge of the remaining three, is taken to confirm that this was the province of the capital. This empire-wide subdivision meant that these smaller provinces had to be grouped to allow administrative oversight, which was achieved by allocating them to dioceses. The diocese of Britain included all four of the new provinces with the man in charge, the *vicarius*, exercising central authority from London; a similar situation pertained throughout the empire.

Dioceses themselves were grouped into yet wider administrative units, called praetorian prefectures, overseen by a praetorian prefect of senior rank (whose role was in no way related, except in name, to the all-powerful post of the first three centuries of the empire, being civilian). The diocese of Britain was thus lumped together in the dioceses of Gaul and Spain as one praetorian prefecture in control of all of NW Europe north of the Alps from the Rhine to the Atlantic. As John Wacher has pointed out, this must have vastly increased the number of bureaucrats required to administer everything – no economies of scale here! He further speculated that this might even have been done to provide a decent career structure for the élite, bearing in mind that the senatorial *cursus honorum* had been severely curtailed by the reforms of the Emperor Gallienus half a century before.[42] Whatever the precise consequences of this massive re-organisation, Britain for the remainder of Constantine's reign appears to have remained calm, whatever upheavals transpired elsewhere in the empire; archaeology, furthermore, supports a dramatic rise in prosperity in the fourth century.

On top of all this re-organisation, there were the consequences of the Edict of Milan of 313. This recognised Christianity and allowed it to organise. London seems to have become the seat of a bishopric and one of the three Bishops from Britain who attended the Council of Arles in 314, Restitutus, was bishop or archbishop of London.[43] The conference had been called by Constantine to enable the church to debate the Donatist problem, and Britain sent a delegation of five, the three bishops attended by a priest and a deacon.[44] While Christianity is thought to have spread relatively slowly outside the cities, its rise became an important element in the unfolding story of the final decades of Roman Britain and the reign of Magnus Maximus.

It is not wholly clear what military arrangements pertained in Britain under the Constantinian dispensation. The three original legions were still in place at this period, but are thought to have been reduced to an establishment of about 1,200 each. They were henceforth charged with the defence of their original base and its region, being titled *limitanei* (border troops), and by this time, too, were allowed to marry and start families, limiting their mobility in conducting either aggressive or defensive deployments beyond the sphere assigned to them. For troubleshooting purposes, auxiliaries were beefed up and merged with other élite units as either *milites* (infantry) or *equites* (cavalry) and collectively called *comitatenses,* which were highly mobile and stationed near the diocesan capital or wherever the *magister militum* (general i/c) or emperor (if present) deemed it necessary for them to be. When the emperor was in the diocese, then they were where he was.[45]

The subsequent presumed tranquillity in Britain seems, however, not to have outlived Constantine's death in 337. His son Constans was given control over the Gallic prefecture of the empire when his father died, and after some five years in power, felt obliged to visit Britain in winter 342-343, although for what reason is not entirely clear, but doubtless in response to some trouble, especially as he felt obliged to cross and campaign in winter, an exceptional step for a commander, even though the climate was somewhat milder than we are used to (so far) today.[46] The visit could have been the spur to the re-commissioning of Anderida (Pevensey Castle, Sussex), for one of his coins was found in the constructional putlog holes.[47] It would seem that Constans (or, conceivably, the emperor Julian seventeen years later) also strengthened the defensive walls of the diocesan capital, Londinium/ Augusta, adding something like twenty-two bastions for much improved defence, which would imply that whatever upheavals had occurred prior to the emperor's visit may have affected the capital directly.[48]

To confuse matters further, a fifth province was added at some stage. It first comes to notice at the time of the so-called 'Barbarian Conspiracy' of 367, for Ammianus Marcellinus wrote of the suppression of this trouble by the *comes* Theodosius, father of the future emperor of that name:

> The restoration of a province, which had fallen into the hands of the rebels, to such a pristine state that … it now had a lawful governor, and the emperor, treating the matter as a triumph, declared that it should in future be called Valentia.[49]

This has long been taken to mean that a new province was thus created, for both the early fifth-century *Notitia Dignitatum* and the calendar of the mid-fifth century Gallic writer Polemius Silvius mention a fifth province. It is now thought (and seems implicit in the above text) that the fifth province was already in existence in 367 (under a name that has been lost to us) and that it was merely re-named after its restoration by the triumphant Valentinian. In view of the fact that Ammianus makes clear that it had been trashed in the uprising, it was presumably a province in the north and Birley points out, supported by archaeology, that it must have included Hadrian's wall.[50] The *Notitita* also tells us that it was, like Maxima Caesariensis, governed by a man of consular rank, which certainly emphasises its importance. This has inclined people to view its capital as having been at York, but Carlisle seems much more likely, and it may well be that the province included a considerable tract both sides of the wall, perhaps as far north as the by this time long unmanned line of the Antonine wall, as the pattern of post-Roman events and polities seems to indicate. The most convincing explanation would appear to be that it was created as a result of Constans' campaigning in Britain and that it was created as a sub-division of Britannia Secunda by him as early as 343. Its later re-naming in the wake of Theodosius's successful suppression of the revolt of 367 has perhaps served to throw sand in our eyes.[51]

Constans, once he had returned to the Continent, was not destined to survive long. Having taken control of the whole of the west at the tender age of 20, he ruled from his return without major upset, although was increasingly criticised for his immorality. He also suffered from arthritis, despite harbouring an overwhelming penchant for the chase. Playing on these supposed grievances, and while the eastern emperor's attention was diverted by a hard campaign against the Persians, in mid-January 350 the unmarried emperor was murdered in the palace as a result of a conspiracy organised by his army commander Magnentius, who promptly declared himself Emperor in his place.

More usurpers

Constans' nemesis was Magnus Magnentius, a professional soldier who had risen high in imperial service. The sources are united in calling him a barbarian (and attributing to him in consequence, numerous negative qualities) but differ in whether he was the son of a German or a Briton. The latter might seem the more likely, however, for this tradition asserts that he was born at Ambianum (Amiens, France) and that his mother was Frankish – hence no doubt the assertion that he was German; he was probably born in 303. His earliest soldiering was done as a member of an infantry regiment (probably one of the old legions) on the north-west borders, but soon he advanced rapidly, becoming a *protector* (officer in the Imperial guard). At the time of his bid for the throne, he was *comes rei militaris* that is, imperial military advisor/commander, with the *Ioviani* and *Herculani* (field army regiments constituted under the first Tetrarchs) under his command in Italy.[52]

On being proclaimed on 18 January, he at first hoped that he would obtain recognition from Constantius II in the east, especially as the latter was hard pressed, and to underwrite this charm offensive he adopted the additional name of Flavius.[53] Whether he managed to obtain recognition by the senate at Rome is doubtful, for Constantius, who needless to say was quite unwilling to grant him any recognition, would surely have wreaked a terrible revenge upon its members in consequence. Indeed, at Rome, Constans' assassination had gone down very badly, and a clique of senatorial grandees thought that, with a grandson of Constantius Chlorus himself amongst their number, there might be a chance of dislodging the usurper, or at least keeping him pinned down until Constantius II could intervene. Their candidate Flavius Julius Popillius Nepotianus's father, an ex-consul called Virius Nepotianus, had married Chlorus's daughter Eutropia. He also issued coins in the name of Constantius as well as in his own and in one account made his son Nigrinianus *caesar* (heir apparent).

But the attempt to thwart the hardened general inevitably failed. After attempting to resist, the Prefect of the City, Fabius Titianus, a supporter of Magnentius, fled, leaving the new ruler to establish his position. But Magnentius quickly dealt with the situation by sending a force under his *magister officiorum*, Marcellinus, and in the ensuing one-sided encounter on 30 June, the hapless Augustus was killed, his head put on a lance and paraded around the city *pour encourager les autres*. His mother Eutropia, possibly a prime mover in the matter, was also killed the day afterwards, along with his son and other members of the Constantinian family in the capital. A large number of other people involved, most of them senators, were also liquidated. In this respect, Magnentius managed to burn his boats *vis-à-vis* any *rapprochement* with Constantius; killing much of his family was hardly going to endear him to his intended ally.

The rough usurper then appointed Magnus Decentius, apparently his younger brother, as his deputy with the rank of caesar to hold the west while he moved against Constantius II.[54] In September 351 he unsuccessfully fought a bloody battle at Mursa (on the River Drava, Croatia), which was a Pyrrhic victory for the Eastern emperor, for the imperial claimant, although defeated, remained in the field with some of his forces intact. He retreated to Gaul and effectively once again recreated a secessionist Gallic Empire, managing to hang onto it until the opening of the campaigning season of 353, when Constantius II came after him again, defeating him, like Clodius Albinus, near Lugdunum (Lyons).[55]

It has been suggested that Magnentius or Decentius must have stripped troops from Britain to support their régime (or to make up the catastrophic losses of Mursa), but the idea that every western usurper in the later fourth century removed forces from Britain seems to have become almost a trope, which, if wholly true, would have left the diocese undefended for decades, which was patently not the case. While there must be an element of truth in many of these instances, to keep the island secure numbers would certainly have been made up subsequently, even if quality was perhaps uneven. It is also thought to be the case that the replacement units included a substantial portion of Germans, for which Crocus in 306 was an attested avatar.[56] Also, about the time of Magnentius's usurpation, a unit called the *areani* was created to maintain intelligence gathering north of Hadrian's Wall, which was seen as a preventative measure.[57]

Magnentius, meanwhile, committed suicide on 10 August 353 to avoid being handed over to his nemesis. He left a widow, a young woman of senatorial ancestry called Justina, who soon afterwards married the future emperor Valentinian (I). It is probable that, with the Eastern emperor advancing towards Gaul in spring 353, Decentius was appointed co-ruler with his brother; had he declared himself augustus only after his brother's death, it is unlikely we would have the one inscription reflecting that enhanced rank, for after Magnentius' death, he had escaped chaotically with some military units in the hope of recovering the situation, but realising that his position was too far gone, he took his own life near Agedincum (Sens) eight days later.[58]

The collapse of Magnentius's régime would appear to have provided the context for the mysterious appearance of yet another claimant to imperial power, Carausius II. This shadowy person is relevant to Britain, partly because his name evokes that of his namesake of the late third century, and partly because the only context in which so illustrious a name could have had sufficient resonance would have been in Britain. Carausius II is known from a coin found at Richborough of a familiar *fel[icium] temp[orum] reparatio* ('return of happy times') type that could only date from the mid-350s, but the authenticity of which was long doubted.[59] The recent discovery of about twenty other examples, some from primary deposits, and all from Britain, suggests that this man and his possible successor Genceris represent events which have entirely eluded Roman sources; after all, Ammianus Marcellinus's history, so important for the years 354-378, does not survive for the preceding reigns and would appear to have missed this enigmatic Briton by a whisker, despite describing the baleful influence of the *notarius* Paulus Catena (Paul 'the Chain') who, on being sent to Britain by the emperor to arrest some officers who had been adherents of Magnentius, proceeded to go ape all over Maxima Caesariensis (implied but not stated) rooting out all manner of other people and extracting confessions by torture and engrossing their assets. While it would not appear that this reprisal was diocese-wide, it was severe enough for the *vicarius* Martinus to fall victim too, essentially for trying to temporise with the vengeful and unscrupulous bureaucrat on someone else's behalf.[60]

The likelihood is that Carausius II was acclaimed in Britain in the wake of the elimination of Magnentius. If so, he was not the only pretender to have arisen in the aftermath, for the *magister peditum* left in charge of the Rhine defences by Constantius prior to his departure once again for the east, Silvanus, also had himself acclaimed emperor on 11 August 355.[61] Indeed, Silvanus may have made his attempt as a result of whatever events surrounded the emergence of and suppression Carausius II across the Channel. The latter's coins themselves read:

DOMINO [NOSTRO] CARAUSIO C[A]ES[ARIS]

A unique way of styling an imperial claimant, or even a recognised emperor for that matter. The lack of the style 'augustus' in inexplicable, although the use of 'caesar' suggests that he was appointed by an emperor with full authority, as Decentius had been by Magnentius. Could he have been made Caesar by the latter in his brief period ruling Gaul alone, or was he a true usurper, or *tyrannus*? The name Carausius is redolent of what some optimistic historians have characterised as British secessionism, and it may be that, by this date, there was latent admiration for the British claimant, or even that people looked back on his seven years in power as a golden age. As regards secessionism, this is a concept quite alien in Roman history. As John Drinkwater emphasises:

> One of the constants of imperial history was the strange absence of true nationalism. Though local leaders might be tempted or forced into usurpation for local reasons, with the purple they accepted a claim on and hence responsibility for the whole empire – in short, they became Roman Emperors, and their local backers became Roman officials. This gave the Empire enormous moral strength, but at a price that was very high and indeed, ultimately unbearable.[62]

Of course, the name of this particular usurper might suggest either a descendant, perhaps a grandson, of Carausius I, but it might just as well be that an ambitious general in the diocese assumed that name in lieu of (or in addition to) his own for just this reason, once his *coup* had been successful. That coins were minted at least suggests that the episode lasted more than the five weeks of Silvanus's fleeting pre-eminence, when Trier's mint was closed to him. In either case, it seems to suggest that here was a British imperial claimant who wished to go it alone, as had been the case in 286. Yet the reverse inscription would seem to run counter to this, for it presents a familiar bronze type of Constantius II coin with the emperor holding a phoenix and *labarum* standard on the prow of the vessel, the rudder of which is held by Victory. The inscription, uniquely, reads DOMINO/CONTA/NO, suggesting an attempt at 'domino Con[s]tan[ti]o' which, contrary to any successionist ideas, might betoken a claimant rebelling against the other usurpers and proclaiming his support for Constantius II. Several more coins have the legend altered. Carausius has also been furnished with a wife, Oriuna, and daughter Flavia, but these are highly speculative; after all, the claimant himself is still clouded with doubt. Yet Carausius II appears also to have had a deputy or successor, called Genceris. The name is known from a single variant of the coins noted above and may represent the name of a caesar. Neither is named in any other context, most notably in Ammianus Marcellinus. Their absence from his pages is the most telling argument against (if not entirely conclusive in view of the fact that his narrative has only survived from his account of events from October 354). The most recent overview of the subject is by P. J. Casey, who does not quite commit himself.[63]

All this seems to emphasise that the Praetorian Prefecture of the Gauls was in chaos from 350 to 355 and that state of affairs might have extended to Britain, too. Carausius II could have been acclaimed in Britain by the locally based senior officials who, noting the turmoil on the Continent during the melt-down of Magnentius' régime, wanted to keep the provinces of the island clear of the consequences, and it may be that an appeal was made to Constantius II for recognition, which might explain the oddity of the coins. It may even be that his situation was similar to that of the usurper Vetranio, who was acclaimed in Illyria in the wake of the murder of Constans in March 350 but who was spared after handing himself over to Constantius as few months later, once the latter had marched west to retrieve the situation.[64]

In around 500, a person of some consequence, possibly a priest, was buried near Penmachno, in North Wales. A memorial was erected to him, which was found on the site of the ancient church there and is now affixed to a wall in its Victorian successor, St Tydglyd's.[65] Beneath a looped cross of the period, it reads:

CARAVSIVS/HIC IACIT/IN HOC CON/GERIES LA/PIDVM[66]
('Carausius lies here in this heap of stones').

Clearly the name must have retained its mystique two centuries after the demise of Carausius II for it to have been given to a man born in all probability a generation or two after the collapse of Roman imperial control over the diocese. Either that, or the name marks a belief entertained by the parents that there existed a line of descent from the late third century usurper or even his mid-fourth-century namesake. Strangely, despite the many names in the Welsh king-lists and other genealogical tracts, neither the name nor any obvious form of it appears even once, unlike that of Magnus Maximus.

The Barbarian Conspiracy

Constantius appointed his cousin and brother-in-law Julian to the rank of Caesar and sent him to the Rhine to sort out the chaos left by Magnentius, Decentius and Silvanus. His efforts, leading an army of only 13,000 men, met with considerable success, and it would be reasonable to assume that in the aftermath he made sure numbers in Britain were restored as far as possible to establishment strength.[67] No doubt he also sorted out Carausius II and Genceris, or accepted their submission; perhaps even spared them. Indeed, such a conclusion may explain why we hear nothing of them in any other context. Had they fallen foul of the *notarius* Paul, who was sent with Julian to keep an eye on him by Constantius, Ammianus would have surely told us about it.

A period of quiescence thereafter seems to have descended upon the diocese, especially when one looks at the military situation in, say, Wales, where most of the minor forts show little evidence of mid-fourth-century occupation; nor does the legionary base at Caerleon, suggesting the withdrawal from thence, perhaps by Magnentius, of the occupying legion, leaving just two in the diocese.[68] Things were to change later, but for all the upheavals, it would seem from the archaeological evidence of both town and country there was continuing prosperity. It is also clear that the post-Magnentian settlement must have included a treaty with the Picts to the north of the Forth-Clyde valley and the Scots of Ireland (the name *Scotti* meaning something like 'bandits'[69]), both peoples with a record for opportunistic raiding by sea. In the case of the former, the preference for seaborne raiding was to avoid the wall and the Roman allied tribes to its north. We know that there was a form of treaty thanks to Ammianus expressly telling us that the two groupings broke it in 360, not long before the death of Constantius.[70]

This latest upset suggests that there was more opportunism amongst those living around the periphery of empire like Britain than during the century before, when the aggressors seem to have been Germanic raiders, hence Carausius. Ammianus says that the Picts and Scots 'laid waste the country near the frontier, leading to alarm amongst the people of the province', meaning, presumably, the northernmost province, which by this time is thought to have been created. There also seems to have been a serious breakdown in security on Wales, too, always vulnerable to attacks from across the Irish Sea. That there were Irish elements involved seems confirmed by the number of distinctive 'door knob' spear butts found in the south-east of Britain from this period.[71]

Julian, lodged at Lutetia Parisiorum (Paris) for the winter of 359-360, was coming to the end of his pacification of the German frontier. The caesar felt that the situation in northern Gaul was insufficiently settled to allow him to go to Britain to attend personally to the troubles, and despatched the *magister equitum* Flavius Lupicinus to restore the situation, either by negotiation or by force.[72] A peaceful Britain meant uninterrupted corn supplies for the armies that Julian commanded could be guaranteed.[73] Lupicinus took with him, initially to London via Richborough, units of lightly armed Herulian and Batavian auxiliary cavalry, along with two units of Moesians as his *comitatenses,* to shore up the shattered forces of the governor of the border province.

Julian could have done without this added problem, for Constantius had dealt him a very poor hand by issuing a decree demonetising much of the western currency, partly to remove all references to the hated Magnentius and partly to keep Julian short of cash in case he used it to bribe his troops on the German frontier into acclaiming him emperor. The usurpations of Carausius (II) and Silvanus (if we can accept the they really happened) would have left the troops demoralised, a situation exacerbated by the lack of cash to pay them.

Yet Julian was a far superior general to his cousin (who had been slogging away at the Persians with very mixed results on and off since his accession) and soon brought the Rhine and related border areas to order, gaining much popularity in the process, which only increased Constantius's distrust. As a result, both his remit and powers were reduced, which led to much dissatisfaction and in early 360, not long after the departure of Lupicinus, he was acclaimed emperor by his troops in Paris. Julian was alert to the possibility that, should the news of his elevation reach Lupicinus in Britain, the general would attempt a counter-coup, ostensibly in Constantius's name. The fact that this should worry Julian at all strongly suggests that Lupicinus – *homo superbae mentis et turgidae* ('an arrogant, cocksure man') – had met with rapid military success, otherwise the possibility of his acclamation would not have arisen.[74] As the intervening time was only about two months, we may infer that the emergency on the northern frontier had been relatively easy to deal with. Therefore, in order to neutralise the threat of Lupicinus mounting a *coup*, Julian sent a senior bureaucrat to Boulogne to prevent anyone crossing to Britain with the news, with the result that shortly afterwards Lupicinus returned, a job well done, to be surprised on his arrival to find Julian as emperor.

Following these events, Constantius died in November 361, Julian succeeded him but also died in the midst of a successful campaign against Persia and was briefly succeeded by Jovian when he died of an infected wound in June 363. By February 364, Jovian, too, had died and been succeeded by Valentinian I, who later appointed his torpid brother Valens as co-ruler. Valens was allocated the eastern half of the empire to rule (not wholly competently) while Valentinian himself took control of the west. In late May 367, Valentinian received news of a major incursion of barbarians in Britain, and hurried toward Ambianum (Amiens) to deal with it. This time it was apparently a 'concerted attack', which had affected all the provinces of the diocese, which had been 'reduced to ruin', although a Gildasian note of rhetorical exaggeration can be detected in Ammianus's words, especially as the situation was saved in the event by Theodosius, father of the future emperor whom the author especially admired and under whom he wrote.[75]

Nectaridus, the *comes maritimi tractus* (commander of the maritime approaches), had been killed. This post is assumed by most commentators to be the close equivalent of the *comes littoris Saxonici* (commander of the Saxon Shore) of the *Notitia Dignitatum*, but it has been plausibly suggested by Roger White that it was actually a separate command, obsolete by the time the *Notitia* was compiled, responsible for the western coastline of the diocese, from Cornwall to the Solway.[76] Also in trouble was the general Fullofaudes (probably the *dux Britanniarum*, the overall military commander of the British diocese) who had been 'surprised and surrounded' in the crisis, although many commentators translate this as 'captured' which, although perhaps implicit is not what is stated.[77] One cannot imagine the raiders actually bothering to capture someone; they would surely, going by other such outbreaks (and the example of poor Nectaridus) have dispatched any Roman grandee unfortunate enough to have fallen into their clutches. Indeed, what this German-born commander was cut off *from* is not entirely clear either, but the obvious interpretation is that he was out of touch with the continent of Europe and thus with supplies, reinforcements and cash. As for Nectaridus, as *comes*, one wonders if he met his fate on the southern shore of the Channel at the hands of the Saxon and Frankish groups raiding the Gallic coast, or at the hands of a diversionary foray by the Picts and their Irish allies in the north, the wall having been by-passed by sea, though the general tenor of Ammianus' account seems to focus more on London and not so much on the north. Somehow, this raid had not been predicted, possibly through a failure of the enigmatic intelligence gathering units called the *areani*, the leaders of which may have been bribed or made complicit by the attackers – hence perhaps the 'conspiracy' element in Ammianus's description.[78]

Be that as it may, Valentinian was shocked and worried at this news, especially as in 360 it would mean that corn supplies (it was late August) might be curtailed through the chaos across the Channel with a knock-on effect on supplies affecting his own efforts to secure the Rhine frontier. His immediate response was to send his *comes domesticorum* (guard commander) Severus to Britain to assess the situation and respond to it as appropriate, but soon afterwards he was recalled, no doubt armed with a report on the situation, which was presumably helpful, for he was duly promoted to *magister peditum* (infantry general), a post he held until 372. His replacement in Britain was the Gallic senator Flavius Jovinus, then serving as consul in tandem with being *magister equitum* (cavalry general), who immediately on arrival sent for strong reinforcements.[79]

To complicate matters, while these developments were taking place, Valentinian suffered a near-fatal illness in August 367, which resulted in the newly returned Severus being canvassed as a possible successor, but in the end Valentinian appointed his young son Gratian as co-ruler instead, so that he could succeed him should something similar happen again. On hearing from Jovinus, more troops – apparently hardened ones – were detached from the forces available to the emperor and rapidly despatched to Britain under the well-regarded Spanish *comes rei militaris* (senior staff officer) Flavius Theodosius. One of this man's senior officers was the general's own son, Theodosius the younger (the future emperor); another was also a Spaniard and seemingly a kinsman, Magnus Maximus.[80]

Quite what the situation actually was is not really clear from Ammianus. What he does is to enumerate the hostile tribes of the Picts – the Dicalydones (presumably the Caledonii of Tacitus) and the Veturiones – together with the Attacotti and the Scotti from Ireland. He tells us that they were causing serious devastation almost everywhere.[81] Of these, the Scotti are well attested, but the Attacotti had only first been mentioned a few decades before. The name appears to derive from the Celtic *aithechthúatha*, a term applied in Irish to a grouping of lower-status tribes.[82] Ammianus adds that the Franks and Saxons were at the same time raiding those coastal areas of Gaul nearest to their own territory. This suggests that the activities of the Picts from north of Britain's fifth province and the Scots and Attacotti from Ireland were seriously affecting the beleaguered diocese, possibly in abrogation of a formal treaty previously struck to replace strife and looting with trade. The German tribes were abroad and raiding but this was not affecting Britain, although no doubt such attacks were making the Channel a much less secure place.[83] So collusion between the Germans and the Celts is not explicit. Furthermore, bearing in mind the author's partiality to the future emperor Theodosius, it is always possible that in describing the crisis as a *barbarica conspiratio* he was over-egging events in order to burnish the lustre of the future emperor's attainments.[84]

Ian Hughes, a recent biographer of Valentinian, has suggested a different sequence. While agreeing that the Saxon raids were directed at the Gallic coast (as Ammianus says) he rejects the idea that either Severus or Jovinus crossed to Britain, but instead in sorting out the Germanic raiders (who, he suggested, had already neutralised Nectaridus and Fullofaudes) only *then* heard that Britain was in chaos. Somehow, this alterative narrative seems out of step with what the Roman account actually presents to us.[85] Supporting evidence for the entire episode comes from pro-Theodosian sources, which serve to emphasise what a splendid job Theodosius did in restoring order.[86]

Nevertheless, the crisis was clearly serious, and Theodosius quickly crossed from Boulogne to Richborough with vexillations (detachments) of Valentinian's field army, probably no more than 2,000 men, called the *Jovii* and *Victores* along with further detachments of Batavians and Heruli, just as Lupicinus had done seven years before. From thence he marched to Londinium, otherwise now called Augusta.[87] En route, it appears that they encountered roving bands of barbarians and other opportunists still raiding but who were apparently overburdened by their ill-gotten gains. He countered these by subdividing his force into small, highly mobile units and managed to round up the lot, recovering large quantities of loot that he returned to the various owners, less a percentage with which he rewarded his troops.

He thereupon entered London in triumph before resting his men over the winter and spending some time gathering information about the disposition of the remaining enemy. The fact that he felt obliged to issue an amnesty to all deserters suggests that the situation was more than just a concerted barbarian attack. It is made clear that the deserters were Roman soldiers (if, perhaps, British manned local militia units), and that the majority seemed to have returned to the colours. The element of desertion undoubtedly links the entire affair to an attempted usurpation. Having decided upon a strategy of stealth and surprise, Theodosius sent word to the emperor to replace the *vicarius* of the diocese, of whose fate we are not informed, and also to request the services of a colleague-in-arms, Dulcitius, a man of proven military prowess. Ammianus actually says that Theodosius asked for one Civilis to be appointed *vicarius*, but it would seem unlikely that the emperor would have allowed him to make such a specific demand for a particular senior civilian official.[88]

If the chaos Theodosius encountered was indeed the result of an attempted usurpation, then the account of Zosimus is relevant: 'About this time, a person named Valentinian [*sic*] for some offence was banished to the island of Britain, and endeavouring there to render himself absolute, was at once deprived of his life and his hopes.'[89]

Quite how closely this was linked to the barbarian rampage is not known, but there certainly seems to have been a link or at least an overlap. Maybe this chancer, emboldened by his impeccable connections, was hoping to stir unrest and then triumphantly put it down, seeking to benefit by claiming credit for his actions; more probably, the rebellion was already manifest and he sought opportunistically to gain advantage from the tumult. Somehow, one cannot imagine why he would make his pitch for the purple with a charismatic *dux* already in the diocese with plentiful fresh troops, effectively putting matters to rights. Yet Valentinus's rebels are said to have obtained the support of the army in Britain, and it is more likely that in the chaos of the Barbarian Conspiracy that troops dispersed by defeat (or merely deserters), may have seen in him a possible lifeline to avoid being butchered by the invaders and were easily suborned, the chaos and looting guaranteeing a good pay-out. This is supported by Theodosius's clemency towards those associated with the *coup*, keen to keep everyone who could help on-side during the campaign to extirpate the various barbarian bands and their leaders and restore the diocese. It is not made clear if Valentine was actually styled Augustus or not. It would seem very unlikely that any rising would have worked if he hadn't, and the use of the word *tyrannus* to describe him strongly supports it. There are no coins, however, so his time in the sun must have been short; either that or he had no access to a mint, London being the only one in the diocese. Yet we do not need to disbelieve Ammianus when he tells us that once Theodosius was present, Valentinus was captured with the other ringleaders and handed over to the newly appointed Dulcitius for execution.[90]

The man's name was Valentinus (= Valentine), and Zosimus links this attempted *coup* with the emperor Valentinian's sudden illness, which would put into much more cohesive context the outbreak of chaos in Britain. Ammianus, on the other hand, expressly states that the problem arose *while* Theodosius was dealing with the rebellion in Britain; this could easily be a distortion to increase the reader's regard for the general. Nothing is known of Valentinus's background except that he was a Pannonian; the likelihood is that he was a senior official of some sort, promoted by the emperor Jovian, or one of his successors. He had apparently committed some serious offence and his brother-in-law Maximinus, then a praetorian prefect (about whom Ammianus is especially uncomplimentary), persuaded the emperor to exile him to Britain rather than have him executed, where, with other exiles, he plotted a rebellion.

After the revolt of 367, it is widely supposed that many, if not all, town walls and those of a number of important forts were strengthened by the addition of bastions as platforms providing enfilading fire from *ballistae* mounted thereon. Defensive ditches were also improved and re-cut, although some or indeed much of this reconstruction might well be attributable to the efforts of Maximus a decade and a half later; archaeology can rarely be that specific. Indeed, as the archaeological record for the Barbarian Conspiracy is so slight, it may well be that much of these works do in fact stem from a later period, that of Maximus as emperor.

In the context of the fifth century, admittedly, Frere noted that Germanic forces had 'almost total incapacity' to capture a fortified town if any effort was being made to defend it. Towns can be seen as part of a planned scheme of passive defence in depth.[91] The various Celtic tribes who had just allegedly inflicted such damage upon the diocese of Britain were no more accomplished at siege warfare than their German counterparts on the Continent. Walling round cities and strengthening forts, therefore, would have been a valuable defensive exercise and one no doubt calculated to maintain morale amongst those thus protected. The re-fortification of the cities and strongpoints made good strategic sense. If Ammianus was not exaggerating, the majority of towns, despite what was said before about the efforts of Constans to strengthen them, must still have been undefended. Yet this is not necessarily the message of the archaeology, so again, the seriousness of the revolt of 367-368 has probably been tweaked by Ammianus in Theodosius's favour. Nevertheless, Theodosius clearly did undertake some substantial improvements and specifically the security of the frontiers. For instance, it is thought that it was as a result of the upheavals that the strategic intelligence gathering *areani* were abolished for having failed to predict the attacks; or they had been fatally overwhelmed in the uprising. Salway suggests that this strategy was replaced by making treaties with the tribal leaders north of the wall, with the chiefs endowed with new powers on imperial behalf to keep the peace.[92] For the purpose of this, the abolition of the *areani* must have been viewed as a positive step. It does seem doubtful, though, whether this was necessarily a policy of Theodosius; it certainly seems to have occurred, but on balance it is more likely that this quite drastic reform came later.

It was a strategy that must then have occurred to the young Magnus Maximus. In serving under Theodosius, he and Theodosius's homonymous son, a kinsman and comrade-in-arms, must have been in a position to get to know tribal leaders on the frontiers and befriend them in the process of post-conspiracy reconstruction. Some of their clansmen were even recruited into the army, the example of four units of Attacotti being salutary. In the *Notitia Dignitatum*, we find the *Atecotti* [sic] stationed in the Balkans under the *magister militum* there, and independently attested by an inscription. We know the eastern section of the *Notitia* was complete by 395 (unlike the more fluid and probably later western section) and it is thought that from its simple name it was the earliest unit of Attacotti to have been raised, some time between 368 and 395. Additionally, stationed in Gaul under the *magister peditum praesentalis* (C-in-C infantry) were the *Honoriani Attecotti Seniores* and *Iuniores* (raised after emperor Theodosius's son Honorius was made co-augustus in 393, or re-named at or after that time) as well as the *Attecotti Iuniores Gallicani*.[93] This suggests that after 368 these regiments had been raised from this Irish grouping following their having been re-settled after the Barbarian Conspiracy.

It was on the completion of his endeavours that Valentinian officially declared that the fifth province 'which had fallen into enemy hands' should bear his name and henceforth be called Valentia.[94] On his return to court, the *comes* Theodosius was promoted to *magister equitum* in place of his predecessor, Jovinus.

Some forces, apart from the two legions of ancient foundation still stationed in the diocese – II Augusta based at Rutupiae (Richborough, Kent) and VI Victrix in Eburacum (York) – along with the *comitatenses* or field army, were *laeti*, first noted in Britain with Constantius Chlorus.[95] Legally, at this time, these troops were *dediticies,* defeated men granted liberty to settle but excluded from the provisions of Caracalla's decree of 212, which made all free people living in the empire full Roman citizens. Thus, the men in Constantius's train in 305 may have been Picts and Scots defeated by him and enlisted following the defeat of Allectus in 296. They may have been settled somewhere in Gaul – Armorica (Brittany) not excluded – on his return; settled, but without full 'civil rights' and probably remaining as border guards. Hence the later use of the term *laetavii* for Armorican Bretons.[96] In support of which it is worth remembering that Magnentius (350-353) was allegedly the son of a British *laetus* and a Frankish princess.[97] It has been suggested that under him a military unit called the *Seguntienses* – thus raised in and around Segontium (Caernarfon) – had been transferred as Palatine auxiliaries to the Continent, presumably as the usurper's bodyguard.[98] Nevertheless, the size of the Roman army in Britain in the later fourth century is still reckoned to have been between 12,000 and 30,000 men.[99] There were also German auxiliaries in Britain from about this time, as was suggested before. For example, Ammianus reports the appointment of the young German prince Fraomar as a military tribune to command a unit of these in Britain in 372, just as Crocus had been so appointed under Constantius I.[100]

In the religious field, troubles were also piling up. Gratian was the first emperor to renounce the position of *pontifex maximus,* until that time normally bestowed upon newly elevated emperors.[101] This was originally granted to him by the senate (in the persons of the *quindecimviri sacris faciundis*) on his accession. He issued an edict of religious toleration in 375, but it came with a rider, insisted on by Pope Damasus I, that declared the primacy of the See of Rome, which did not go down well in either Constantinople or Alexandria. Furthermore, there was a tendency in the east towards Arianism. This deviation from the Nicene creed's version of Christian belief (to which Gratian was faithful) was simple: the Nicene Creed declared that God the Father and God the Son were of one substance, whereas the Arians believed that, while similar, the two were not the same. This dichotomy was to have important consequences in the years to come. As most Germanic peoples living beyond the borders of the empire were evangelised by eastern missionaries, they, too, if Christian, tended to be Arian. Arianism is barely noticeable in the record of Roman Britain, although it played an important part in the tragedy of Magnus Maximus.

We can see, over the preceding century, that the diocese of Britain was largely turbulent and because of this, inclined to encourage *tyranni*: men prompted by events to make a bid for supreme power. This, then, is the context in which Magnus Maximus the Roman emperor was to make his entrance in the unpredictable world of the later western empire and into the little-understood events unfolding in the British diocese.

2

Magnus Maximus:
Before Empire

The family of Magnus Maximus, we are told, came from Gallaecia (Galicia) in Spain, and was related to that of Theodosius – the text says *adfinitate iactans,* which essentially says just that: they were related – although how is by no means clear.[1] John of Nikiou's assertion (made centuries later) that Maximus was of British descent can safely be ignored, although it may reflect the possibility that he had been acclaimed in Britain somewhat earlier than conventionally accepted.[2] Maximus had an uncle (whose name is not known) so his father was unlikely to have been the elder Theodosius's younger brother, or else the sources would have mentioned it. Yet it was a close enough relationship for Maximus to presume upon it and for him to have risen through the army alongside the future emperor under the elder Theodosius's command. Probably they were uterine first cousins, as the names borne by Maximus's family are not found amongst Theodosius's. This is paralleled in the career of Flavius Claudius Antonius, a senator who served as praetorian prefect of Italy 377-378 and was by all accounts made consul in 382 by Theodosius, entirely through their relationship to one another – his sister Maria married the emperor's brother Honorius, thus introducing the name Maria into the Imperial family.[3] It may well be that Maximus was the product of a similar alliance, perhaps between an aunt of the elder Theodosius and his own father or grandfather; it is argued below that the name Antonius is detectable amongst Maximus's known kin, so this alliance may well have strengthened the ties of kinship between Maximus and Theodosius.

Maximus's date of birth is not known, but having had a relatively young family on his acclamation – his son Victor was proclaimed co-emperor with his father 'in infancy'[4] – it may reasonably be assumed that he must have been born around 340/345 and so would have been about the same age as the future Emperor Theodosius.[5] Under Maximus's rule, one of the Spanish provinces was granted enhanced status, being given a governor of superior rank, a *consularis*, which may reflect this connection. Any fine-tuning of the date that can be applied arises from the actions of the two kinsmen as the drama surrounding Maximus's life is played out. The suggestion of Pacatus, the panegyricist, that he was 'low-born' is a typical slur made to denigrate his memory and may be disregarded; on the contrary, it arises from contemporary sources that Theodosius's family owned an estate in their native Spain and were thus of some standing. The merciful and indeed generous treatment by Theodosius of Maximus's mother and daughters after his fall would seem to reinforce further the likelihood of a relatively close kinship. After all, his mother, granted a pension, may have been the Emperor's aunt.[6]

The relationship was probably fairly close, as the future emperor's first recorded military posting was to serve under the emperor Theodosius's father in Britain in 367-368, when it has been suggested that he was the officer who suppressed the imperial claimant Valentine, although this remains unproven.[7] The most reliable source, Ammianus Marcellinus, relates that the punishment of Valentine was entrusted by Theodosius to Dulcitius, but that does not preclude Maximus's participation as a senior officer under the general. This may not, however, have been his earliest posting for he would undoubtedly have served a few years earlier as a military tribune, as did his contemporary and namesake who fell in heroic circumstances when fighting under Julian against the Persians in 363. It is possible that both he and the younger Theodosius were serving on the Rhine as officers in the units which were transferred in haste to Britain in 367.[8]

Military career

Maximus and the young Theodosius were therefore in all likelihood friends, undoubtedly colleagues-in-arms, knew each other well, and served together again in the war in Africa against the imperial claimant and Mauritanian prince, Firmus, a few years later.[9] The son and heir of Nubel, King of the Moorish people in Mauretania, Firmus was a thoroughly Romanised member of a large and influential local tribe. He fell out with the *comes* of Africa, Romanus, who was subsequently exposed as corrupt and consequently went to considerable lengths to deny Firmus a hearing at court over his grievances. In the end, the Moor's restraint collapsed and with the backing of several allied peoples and two important military units, he declared himself emperor late in 372 or early 373, being also acknowledged in the surrounding provinces.[10]

The elder Theodosius, fresh from his travails in Britain and following previous campaigning on the Rhine, arrived in 373 at the head of reinforcements. He refused to treat with Firmus but co-operated with the claimant's loyal brother, Gildo, in a raid to arrest Vincentius, an associate of the *comes Africae*, Romanus.[11] After a series of sanguinary encounters over an eighteen-month campaign, Theodosius's efforts paid off and Firmus was defeated, following which the prince committed suicide. He seems to have issued no coins, probably because his area of influence did not include a city with a mint.

So Maximus and Theodosius's son fought alongside each other in these theatres of war, no doubt forming the sort of close bond which shared danger and difficulties invariably bring. Maximus was still on hand when operations had been satisfactorily concluded, which, significantly, included the settling of allied tribal groupings on the southern frontier under the general supervision of Roman *praefecti*, a policy which may well have presaged the subsequent settlement of the border peoples of Britain, postulated here as a policy pursued by Maximus a decade later. This policy in Africa is indicated by epigraphic evidence for the appointment of such administrators, usually high-ranking subordinates of the provincial governor, to indigenous *gentes* (tribal groupings).[12] In the process, Maximus will of course have made other friendships and acquaintanceships along the way, which were likely to be of great value to him later on, too.[13]

At just that point, on 17 November 375, Valentinian, notorious for his volcanic temper, suddenly died of a seizure while bawling out a barbarian envoy. The death of an emperor is always a time of peril for powerful men, for the transition of power frequently led to people being sidelined, sometimes terminally. This appears to have been the case with Theodosius *père*, for he was unexpectedly liquidated at Carthage, probably shortly after the emperor's demise. Unfortunately, nothing is known of the precise circumstances of the commander's execution, but Birley suggests that it was ordered by Valens, acting on the memory of an oracular prophecy that he (Valens) would be succeeded by someone whose name began with 'Theo-'.[14] This was part of a hoary imperial Roman trope: to neutralise in a pre-emptive strike any successful general who might present a perceived danger to a succession. It is possible that Maximus himself was somehow involved in these events, or that he was perceived to have been, in which case it might explain why he may have felt passed over, as several sources allege, when his former comrade-in-arms was later elevated to the purple. This is not, however, by any means proven or even especially probable.

From the unfortunate events in Carthage, several commentators have identified Maximus with a man of that name who had been posted shortly afterwards to that perpetual trouble spot, the Balkans, although not all are agreed. This was the officer called Maximus who assisted the incompetent *comes rei militaris* Lupicinus (not the man of the same name whom we have already encountered in Britain) in trying to re-settle the Goths on the south-west bank of the Danube in 377, during the run-up to the Battle of Adrianople and which ended in the uprising from which that calamity inevitably flowed.[15] This Maximus is called by Ammianus *dux exitiosus* ('the pernicious general') and adds other denigratory epithets (eg. 'a man of flawed character'), strongly suggesting hindsight, for he uses the same type of language about this Maximus as that of the panegyricist Pacatus in his paean of praise of Theodosius delivered in the wake of Magnus Maximus's death – hence the possibility for confusion. Indeed, Pacatus' language is far more inflammatory, calling Magnus Maximus 'insatiably greedy, a flesh-eater and a despoiler of the public realm', suggesting that both he and Ammianus were writing from the same post-Maximus standpoint. By that time, it would hardly have been politic to do anything else but denigrate the fallen emperor.[16] But Pacatus never mentions the Danubian debacle, which he most gleefully would have latched on to had Magnus Maximus been one and the same man as the Maximus so involved.[17]

Nevertheless, Magnus Maximus may have been on hand in the aftermath of the Battle of Adrianople, when the eastern emperor Valens was killed by the Goths and his army very nearly annihilated. Competent surviving senior officers would have been essential to help in the stabilization of what was probably a fairly desperate situation after the most disastrous defeat suffered by any Roman army since the *clades Variana* in the Teutoburger forest in AD9. He may well have been that rarity, a surviving commander who actually fought in the battle, but this is by no means certain. Theodosius was there because after a stint as *dux Moesiae*, his father's death had inclined him to discretion and he had retired to his Spanish *hacienda*. Western emperor Gratian had recalled him, however, as a competent replacement commander, possibly as *magister militum*, in the wake of Adrianople, while in all probability Maximus was either already there or was also drafted in from a posting somewhere else, perhaps even at his former comrade-in-arms' request.

The frustration is that we do not know quite what he was up to following the campaign in Africa and the elder Theodosius's demise. The clear implication is that he had received a relatively senior appointment in the forces hastily mustered to counter the Goths' uprising after the battle. Certainly, Maximus must have been part of the faction that elevated Theodosius to the purple, accomplished without even consulting Gratian, the surviving co-emperor.[18]

In the post-Adrianople commotion, Gratian had been obliged to hasten to the east to treat with the Gothic commanders and patch up a truce followed by a settlement.[19] If Maximus really had been fighting at Adrianople, his presence may have been the more valuable for any insights he might have had to aid such delicate negotiations, which were being undertaken by the surviving *magistri militum* and the western-based advisers of a very youthful emperor from a position of relative weakness.

It was from these deliberations that Maximus's old commander's son – and, as we have proposed – probable cousin, Flavius Theodosius, was raised as the new emperor of the east to replace the fallen Valens, on 19 January 379. As Maximus was a fellow countryman and comrade-in-arms of the new *augustus* (not to mention a kinsman) it has been speculated that he would have been expecting appointment to one of the highest military offices of state and must have become bitterly disillusioned he didn't get it. The shrill laudations of Pacatus mendaciously refer to him at this stage as an exile and a fugitive. But he was certainly not overlooked. The suggestion nevertheless is that he was to some extent damaged goods, perhaps as having been perceived as having been involved somehow in the execution of Theodosius's father. In that respect, his candidature for imperial favour at the highest level may have been out of the question, whatever the personal relationship between Maximus and Theodosius. Here we enter into a lacuna in which Theodosius's initial dispositions are opaque.

In the outcome, he was appointed to a very senior post in Britain, probably having military responsibility for the *comitatenses*, the mounted field army, of the diocese which included what were by this time five separate provinces: hence the Roman sources calling the island the 'Britains' rather than the 'Britain', to which we are far more accustomed. It might well be that, far from coming away from the re-ordering of the Empire a disappointed man, he was happy to have received his own important independent command. Furthermore, to preserve imperial propriety Gratian would have had to have been consulted – unless the appointment was made over the young western emperor's head, which is not impossible; for it looks on closer examination that the elevation of Theodosius was indeed made over the head of Gratian.[20] Whatever occurred, proprieties were probably maintained, for with Maximus in Britain, he would have been answerable to Gratian; the fact that he was a kinsman of the new emperor must have been discomforting. There is no reason to think that he was pushed off to a remote backwater with a middling appointment. It would seem far more likely that the emperors agreed to give him a highly responsible command with the prospect of being made *magister militum* (master of the soldiers or C-in-C) in due course. Of course, we should not lose sight of the possibility that there might also have been an unspoken agreement between Maximus and Theodosius to dispense with Gratian in the medium term, and that this appointment was part of a carefully worked-out scheme to achieve such an end without drawing down any opprobrium upon the heads of the principals involved. Although this might seem, on the face of it, unlikely – too Machiavellian by half, one might think – by the time all the circumstances of Maximus's years in the sun have been reviewed, nothing really emerges to refute the notion entirely.

We have no certain idea what Maximus's British role actually was, nor do we know the exact date the responsibility was bestowed upon him. It makes perfect sense that he would have been given his British command immediately after the post-Adrianople negotiations were completed, the position in Thrace stabilised and Theodosius duly acclaimed. Thus, the appointment would have begun fairly early in 379. Unfortunately, all we know for sure is that he had been there for at least a while before he was acclaimed in 383 (if indeed that was when his acclamation occurred) but that is all. To obtain more precision, we have to risk delving into the domain of the second part of this work to resolve the question.

A British legendary source tells us that he was in Britain for seven years prior to his usurpation, making possible an appointment from 377 onward. If that were so, he would have missed the Battle of Adrianople, which would certainly have left him out of the picture with respect to the negotiations that took place in the wake of the battle, which seems unlikely. Apart from the complete unreliability of any apparent fact to be encountered in a work such as the *Mabinogion*, this would appear startlingly concise – unless the legend conflates his two or three years in Britain from 367 with his later years there, which is by no means impossible.[21] On the whole, it would seem safe to assume that he was sent to Britain in the aftermath of Adrianople and the elevation of his kinsman to the purple, but the *possibility* that he was there beforehand and was caught out of the loop following the events of 378 needs to be borne in mind. As we shall see, if he had been *en poste* only for a year or two before his elevation, much of the activity in Britain here proposed for him would simply not have been possible.

British commander

The actual designation of Maximus when he was assigned to Britain is another problem. Edward Gibbon thought that he had been given a minor function, and many concur.[22] Further, had he been appointed, say, a *consularis*, this would have been anomalous, as it was junior senators at this period who were appointed to this sort of office, which was a civilian and administrative one, not something which a fairly senior army officer not yet of formal senatorial standing would have been expected to assume.

Birley has suggested that he was appointed *dux Britanniarum* (General in [the diocese of] Britain) in charge of a rather motley collection of inferior troops, guarding the northern frontier. An alternative mooted is that he was appointed *Comes Littoris Saxonici* (C-in-C of the maritime sphere, including the Channel coast of Gaul). Neither of these seems quite to fit, given subsequent events. As a former comrade-in-arms of the new Emperor, the likelihood is that he was appointed a *comes* – literally a companion, translated into the modern idiom as 'count', although such appointments were not hereditary under the Empire.[23] A *dux* – a leader, thus a general, the root of 'duke' – was of lesser standing. It may very well be that his previous (unknown) posting was as a *dux*: the next would inevitably have to have been a step up. The most likely explanation is that he was sent to Britain with a specific brief as a *comes rei militaris* – an imperial advisor of superior military authority.[24]

That Maximus is thought to have had some judgement about naval matters and might have been Count of the Saxon Shore (or possibly of the maritime tract, the western shores) arises from the reference in Zonaras to his remarkably rapid crossing to Gaul after his acclamation.[25] The events surrounding his final campaign, too, have inclined some to think that he may well have had this command, but this is not supported by the fact that once appointed he appears to have inflicted a heavy defeat on the Picts and the Scots, presumably in northern or western Britain, a long way from the Saxon Shore; although raiding could by the time of his arrival have spread further south, encouraged by news of imperial weakness following Adrianople. Such northern operations would normally have lain within the remit of the *Dux Britanniarum*. But there is some debate as to whether the position of the superior appointment of *comes Britianniarum* actually existed at this time, for it has been plausibly suggested that it was created later, perhaps by Stilicho, the imperial general whom a later panegyric avers conducted (or sent) an expeditionary force again to restore order in Britain in the late 390s, an intervention which may well have happened. It could also have been much inflated in importance for the purposes of subsequent praise, an inherent trait of panegyrics.

Yet the reported fact that Maximus achieved a great victory against the Picts and the Scots, presumably north of Hadrian's wall, (Gregory of Tours says he was 'victorious over the Britons' following the Chronicle of 452, on which see below) would suggest that he was most probably appointed *comes* to resolve a particular situation, as Theodosius *père* had been in 367.[26] Maximus then, was sent in 379 as an imperial appointee with superior authority to sort out some kind of break-down of order or barbarian incursion in the diocese of Britain. It would seem far more likely that, as *comes*, he would have conducted the campaign against the Picts and the Scots as such a special appointee, as Theodosius had twelve years before, aided by the officer *en poste*, the *dux Britanniarum*. As for this campaign in the north, the Gallic *Chronicle of 452* says that '*incursantes Pictos et Scottos Maximus strenue superavit*' ('Maximus strenuously overcame an incursion of the Picts and the Scots').

The outcome was obviously a notable victory and may indeed have been the spur to his acclamation. Exactly how serious this threat was in the first place is open to question, bearing in mind Frere's judgement that after 368, 'prosperity returned and continued to the end of the century.'[27] Nevertheless, the fact of his appointment suggests that affairs were certainly perceived as serious and the campaign had been successful enough to inspire the absolute confidence of the military units serving under him, perhaps heightened by previous acquaintance in some cases. While therefore it was still apparently a serious outbreak, it was probably put down soon enough not to interfere with the economic and civil life of the bulk of the diocese, unlike the so-called Barbarian Conspiracy, in which the diocese had been allegedly reduced to chaos. Having done so, there arises the possibility that he spent some time building alliances and indulging in a root-and-branch re-organisation of the frontier regions to make them much more secure and stable, a step invisible in the classical sources, but strongly implied by the post-Roman and later insular evidence (such as it is). To this aspect of Maximus's tenure in Britain, we return in Part II.

Acclamation

We are uncertain what impelled Maximus to make a bid for the throne. Because much of the contemporary comment is *post facto* and hostile, the waters have become muddied. Zosimus wrote:

> ... the [British troops] were encouraged by Maximus, a Spaniard, who had been a fellow-soldier of Theodosius in Britain. He was offended that Theodosius should be thought worthy of being made emperor, while he himself had no honourable employment. He therefore cherished the animosity of the soldiers towards the emperor.[28]

In favour of this supposition is human nature and the fact that another of the new emperor's relations (arguably by marriage) Fl. Claudius Antonius, had already been made consul (for 382 with the aristocratic Gaul, Fl. Afranius Syagrius), by imperial favour and just prior to Maximus's elevation, certainly a *possible* cause of a sudden swell of resentment against the emperor.[29]

Yet there are other reasons for a man to suddenly find himself leading a revolt. Spontaneous acclamation by the troops after the successful campaign in the north might, as implied by Sulpicius Severus, just as plausibly have been the trigger, as it had been with so many claimants to the imperial office in the previous century, in the succession of Decius, Gallus, Aemilianus and Valerian in just the four years between 249 and 253.[30] In support of this suggestion, Gregory of Tours in an enigmatic assertion, claimed that '*Maximus vero cum per tyrannidem oppressis Brittannis sumpsisset victoriam, a militibus imperator creatus est.*'[31] ('But Maximus, when he had gained a victory, the Britons having been oppressed by a usurpation, was created emperor by the soldiers.')

Thus, success over the barbarians was followed by a spontaneous acclamation. But what did he mean by 'the Britons having been oppressed by an usurpation'? An alternative translation might be: 'the Britons, who were oppressed by tyranny', but, as we have seen, the meaning is hardly divergent. We know of no other usurpation in 379-383 in Britain. Stevens argued that the strange sentence referred to Maximus's suppression of the usurper Valentinus when he was serving with the future emperor Theodosius under the latter's father in 367, but that is certainly not what the text says, as the elevation clearly followed the victory, although the lapse of two centuries between the event and Gregory's text might well allow for the sequence to get scrambled. Apart from the elusive and unlocated usurper Servatus, no name obtrudes either.[32] Had an usurper arisen in Britain then, it certainly might add weight to Maximus having to be sent there, perhaps as *comes*, but on the whole, his arrival earlier with a mandate to roll back the Picts and the Scots seems the more credible.

If spontaneity was not the prime mover, then his elevation was possibly a combination of the euphoria of victory and general dissatisfaction amongst the troops of the diocese and indeed on the Continent, with the rule of Gratian and Valentinian II, aptly described by J. F. Matthews as a '*dilettante* youth and a child', both under the firm control of barbarian officers and women, particularly the Arian empress Justina, the widow of both the British usurper Magnentius and subsequently of the elder Valentinian.[33] British troops might perhaps have nursed a grievance for having been overlooked in this distribution of rewards, donatives and honours. In the event, under Maximus as emperor just as many barbarian generals were employed under his command, and indeed, he later boasted to St Martin of the 'many thousands of barbarians who fight for me and take their *annonae* (pay in kind) from me'.[34]

Yet with the diocese duly returned to order, he may well have sought, perhaps echoing mess conversations with the younger Theodosius in earlier times, to return the western empire to firm military rule in the mould of the elder Valentinian. One can reasonably infer from the panegyric delivered before Theodosius in 389 that it was that emperor's neglect of Gaul which may have sparked the resentment that fuelled the revolt (and was to do so again).[35] Contemporaries felt that the spontaneity aspect was valid, though: Maximus had not assumed power willingly. Gratian in 383 had been preparing for war against the Alemanni with the support of the Alani, barbarian mercenaries bribed with special favours and over-promotion, which went down very badly amongst the more traditional military establishment at Trier, and this disgust at preferential treatment for such people, who were perceived to have done little to deserve it, may well have manifested itself in Britain, too. Sulpicius Severus, quoting St Martin, who later spent an uncomfortable time under Maximus's sway, mentioned that Maximus had taken on the *regni necessitatem* ('rule of necessity'), supreme authority having been thrust upon him by the cheering soldiery through, inevitably, divine will, and this is to some extent supported by Orosius.[36] One notable adjunct to his elevation to the purple is that Maximus immediately underwent Christian baptism, going, as he told Pope Siricius, 'straight from the font to the throne'.[37] If his words are to be taken literally, then this might preclude any acclamation that was strictly spontaneous. On the whole, one is persuaded that his elevation was a longer-term aim and that any re-ordering of the diocese was quite probably done at least partly with that aim in mind, so regular frontier troops could be safely withdrawn without the risk of yet another outbreak of looting.

The usurpation is normally accepted as having taken place in spring 383, following an incursion across the Rhine of Alemanni (Bucinobantes) under their leader Fraomar, back amongst his people on the Continent. As we have seen, this German prince had been transferred to Britain carrying *potestate tribune* (the authority of a tribune) at the head of a unit of his fellow tribesmen, the *numerus Alemannorum,* in 372, and somewhere along the line he may even have been befriended by Maximus, perhaps just prior to the Barbarian Conspiracy. His tribune's authority certainly echoes in later events.[38] Fraomar's return to Germany and incursion was conceivably engineered by Maximus's Gothic lieutenant, Andragathius to provide an excuse for the planned *coup.*[39] Birley suggests that Maximus had crossed to Gaul *before* being acclaimed. In contrast, Grunel has suggested that Maximus was acclaimed in Britain much earlier, in autumn 382, but this has attracted little subsequent support.[40] There is in fact little actually to contradict it, and Jones and Casey have gone to the trouble of analysing more closely the sequence set out in the *Gallic Chronicle of 452*:

> Gratian, year III: *Maximus tyrannus in Britannia a militibus constituitur.*
> [Maximus was put in place as an unauthorised ruler in Britain by the soldiers.]
> Gratian, year IIII: *Incursantes Pictos et Scottos Maximus tyrannus strenue superavit.'* [Maximus strenuously overcame the invading Picts and Scots.][41]

First of all, this places the acclamation of Maximus *before* the victory over the Picts and Scots, which flies in the face of all other sources. The sequence also seems to have been based on three different calculations, making the establishment of a precisely dated sequence difficult. The telling computation and the most convincing one is that of regnal years, here of Gratian, which were not calculated from the year a particular emperor was raised to the purple, but on the year in which he became *senior emperor*; hence Gratian is here only counted from 378 (as a whole year) when he became the senior ranking augustus, not from 367 when he was first accorded this rank. Thus, Maximus's acclamation in Gratian's year III has to be 380 (years were counted from one not nought), his victory over the Picts and Scots was in

Gratian year III (IV) thus 381, while his crossing to the Continent is correctly listed as Gratian year VI (383), suggesting that there was no casual error there, enhancing the veracity of this rather startling sequence.

Yet this exercise delivers a sequence which begins with Maximus's acclamation in 380, followed by his campaign and victory against the Picts and Scots in 381, with the crossing of the Channel and deposition of Gratian in 383, the year to which both the first and last of these events are usually attributed. It also provides for the finalising of a treaty between Maximus and Valentinian II in 383, too. Casey adds that 'the inconvenient entry for 380 ... will simply not go away' and that the alternative must be that the date of the usurpation or the 381 date for the victory over the Picts has to be wrong, but that the most likely conclusion must be that both are correct.[42] Casey also suggests that the numismatic evidence for Magnus Maximus and his *comitatus* in Britain (the mintmark AVG issue) could be a confirmation of this early date, too. The *solidi* issued show Maximus, diademed and cuirassed, with a reverse showing him as *restitutor reipublicae* ('restorer of the state') a well-known slogan for recently acclaimed emperors.[43] Silver *siliquae* are also known, this time with the reverse VOT V/MVLT X, a formula frequently employed during the first five years of a reign (as Valentinian I) and by this date no longer indicative of the passage of five regnal years.[44]

Nor is this sequence of events undermined by the archaeological evidence relating to the Wall either, with coin finds locating Maximus there, not to mention the contemporary renovation of Corbridge, where a hoard including a good number of his early issues was found. On this dispensation, the establishment of the east coast signal stations also fall neatly into place. This, in turn, would explain the refurbishment and garrisoning of the fort at Malton (Yorks.) by the *Numerus Supervenientium Petuariensium* clearly transferred from Petuaria (Brough on Humber) as attested by the *Notitia Dignitatum*. The latest coin from that place is also one of Maximus's issues.[45] Similarly, the abandonment of inland Welsh forts and the provision of new sea defences there instead, with Caernarfon as the possible centre of command, would seem to be another consequence of this post-campaign reconstruction, where the western coasts and the difficult country north of the Wall both seem to have been strengthened and with ties to the empire reinforced. The suggestion is that this was also underpinned by formal arrangements struck with indigenous British (and Irish) groupings as further proposed below.[46]

It is thus possible to adduce evidence that the *coup* was premeditated and even may have had Theodosius's tacit support, despite the eastern emperor having appointed his infant son Arcadius his co-ruler on 9 January 383, just prior to the conventional date for Maximus's elevation. Had Maximus been in power in Britain since 380, however, this act on Theodosius's part may have been a counter to Maximus's elevation instead of a cause of it.

The situation would have resembled the position in which Clodius Albinus found himself in 193. The lack of other references to this date for Maximus's elevation mean that having him in sole power in Britain for three years is impossible to substantiate. It may be that Theodosius was happy to have him, Carausius-like, in Britain, but was less impressed when the events on the Rhine frontier caused him to cross the Channel and assert control over all the north-western dioceses. Was the raising of Arcadius to the purple the straw that broke the camel's back, threatening Maximus's long-term future? Or was Theodosius merely ensuring the future of his dynasty in his own sphere of influence? Could he, indeed, have been aiming in the medium term at a revival of the Tetrarchy?[47] In this respect, Theodosius was in a strong position in Constantinople, but the west was divided between two callow youths. It is tempting to think that he might have evolved a long-term plan to remove them in a manner that did not redound to his discredit, using his trusted lieutenant and kinsman to eliminate these two youngsters, catspaws of their generals. This is a very coherent if somewhat Machiavellian stratagem. The allegation emerges after Maximus's capture in 388 via the panegyric delivered to the victorious emperor the following year and, for Pacatus, the panegyricist, to have even mentioned it (if only to ridicule the entire suggestion) accords it an underlying persuasiveness, bearing in mind various precedents.[48] Certainly, Theodosius seemed in no hurry to move to depose his kinsman, as emerges from some rather weasel words used by Pacatus to explain this in his peroration.[49]

Moving forward to 383, another underlying cause of Maximus's sudden need to try his luck on the Continent was almost certainly discontent there arising from Gratian moving his court away from Augusta Treverorum (Trier), where its presence was a physical guarantee of the Rhine frontier, to Mediolanum (Milan), at some stage prior to or in 381, at least partly to be nearer the northern Danube, where there was also border trouble.[50] This left those officers and functionaries remaining in Britain feeling neglected and disconcerted, especially as many were members of the Gallic upper crust, recruited to court and civic service in the wake of the rise of Gratian's influential former tutor Ausonius. Those who did not stay either retired to their estates or went to Constantinople to continue their careers under Theodosius who was, after all, himself a westerner. In 383, Trier was still the capital of the Gallic prefecture after having been the location of the western court for a considerable time, but now found itself somewhat cut off from the seat of power. The troops or, more especially their officers, as ever reliant on imperial patronage, no doubt considered themselves snubbed and disadvantaged.

It seems highly likely that after having defeated the Picts and the Scots in Britain, Maximus had devoted a good deal of time, thought, diplomacy, and effort into putting in place a new dispensation in the frontier zones north of the Wall, in Wales and even perhaps in western Dumnonia, which would have enabled the release of some extra units for disposition elsewhere. It would seem highly likely, too, that in doing so he adopted the system put into operation in Africa by the *comes* Theodosius alluded to above, for by this time it would have been reasonably apparent that such a system was perfectly viable and produced stability. He seems also in this process to have had dealings with the Irish (see Chapter 8), not all of whom were disposed to raid the diocesan coasts, and if so, it was surely he who raised three regiments from the Irish Attecotti, as we have seen, further details of which may be found below.[51] These measures might not necessarily show that he was planning to challenge Gratian all along; it was more likely an inspired solution to a long-standing security problem facing the diocese, and as such stands to his credit as a general, diplomat and a fairly visionary administrator. It will be argued below that the later, semi-legendary British sources strongly suggest by implication that this is exactly what did happen, and that it was Maximus who was the instigator. In either case, however, in crossing the Channel Maximus initiated a series of events which were to bring him into much sharper focus and, in the longer term, to encompass his demise.

Seizing power

Whatever the date of his acclamation, the new claimant to the purple styled himself [Imperator Caesar] Dominus Noster Magnus Maximus [Britannicus Maximus] Pius Felix Augustus. The style is attested by the coinage he minted in London celebrating his elevation[52], although the *Britannicus Maximus* element only appears in a damaged inscription from Pisaurum (Pesaro, Italy):

D[ominus] N[oster Ma]gnus M[aximus/Brita]nnicus M[aximus/Pi]us Felix [Augustus/Nobili]ssimii [   ].[53]

He then appears to have struck gold and silver coins at the London mint to emphasise his position and with which to pay a donative to his loyal troops. The style, bearing the AVG mintmark for London, seems not to echo the prevailing issues of Gratian but deliberately to hark back to the issues of Valentinian I: a message perhaps dissociating himself from Gratian.[54] If the issue was really in response to an acclamation in 380, of course, replicating the style of issues of Valentinian closer to their period of issue would make perfect sense.

The emphatic assertion in later sources that Maximus wholly or partially denuded Britain of troops is unlikely to be entirely true, especially as two of those who came after him, Stilicho (possibly) and Constantine III are also said to have removed substantial levies from the island; if Maximus took them all, what was left for the other two?[55] The *comitatus,* perhaps strengthened by units released by the success of Maximus's suggested frontier settlement, would have returned to the Continent with him, but further speculation is unproductive. If units were withdrawn when the move to the Continent occurred, they were surely to some extent replaced, newly stabilized frontier zone notwithstanding, and as attested by the relative peace which descended on the diocese after 383. Dornier supports this when she says that he 'was not abandoning Britain but trying to augment his empire and so would not have left such a valuable frontier region without garrisons'.[56]

The thorough re-ordering of the frontier regions proposed above must, though, have played a significant part in allowing him to use units that otherwise would have been required in the island. There seems to be no evidence that Hadrian's wall was stripped of its garrison at this time, for instance, nor in 407 to aid Constantine III.[57] Graham Webster speculated whether Maximus may have removed *Legio* XX from Deva (Chester) at this time (perhaps as part of a settlement of the frontier in this region), or whether this was the legion pulled out on the orders of Stilicho, if indeed, the latter's intervention in Britain was not simply a rhetorical flourish, as the source is a panegyric delivered to Stilicho himself in 400 by Claudianus.[58] This last speculation rests rather heavily upon the date at which the *Notitia Dignitatum* was compiled too, for it clearly states – whether anachronistically or not – that there was only one of the original three legions still in Britain at the time: *Legio* II at Rutupiae (Richborough, Kent), not an obvious locale for a frontier unit, but it is possible that it supplied vexillations as garrisons for the Saxon Shore fort there and those adjoining, at Reculver, Dover, Lympne and even Pevensey. If the twentieth legion was pulled out of Chester, it must have been done before the *Notitia* was compiled, so Maximus's expedition across the Channel is about the final possibility, although it *could* have been done by Constans as early as 343, by Magnentius in 350 or even the *comes* Theodosius in 368. If any garrison troops (*limitanei*) were included in Maximus's expeditionary force, it has been suggested that they were the regular units from the Saxon Shore forts, not only as being to hand, but because in the *Notitia,* we find the *Anderitani* and *Abulci* (from Pevensey), the *Secundani* (from Richborough) and the *Exploratores* (from Portchester) all by then stationed on the Continent.[59] Casey argues that most of the vexillations sent to the Continent to support Maximus there in 383 would have been brought back when the emperor made a return visit the following year (see Chapter 3), adding that the account by Gildas in this context is 'unacceptable as an historical source'.[60]

Nevertheless, Maximus would have crossed from Rutupiae (we know it was from here from an insulting epithet used about him later) with sufficient forces to confront Gratian, and most of these troops would surely have been mobile units (*comitatenses*), not the former legionaries, by this time long relegated to garrison duty.[61] Having arrived on the Continent, Maximus managed to repel the invading barbarians and establish control without serious bloodshed, the first emperor to have stabilised the Rhine frontier since Julian in 360. At first, Gratian must have been ignorant of his general's elevation (or intention to leave Britain) for he had left Verona after mid-June to campaign against the Alemanni in Raetia; had he been informed at this juncture what had happened, he would surely have postponed the expedition.

If the revised chronology of Maximus's elevation is accepted, however, he must have complacently felt secure that Maximus would remain in the island, or have even received assurances that he would. Once the emperor had been tipped off, however, Maximus had then to confront Gratian's forces, suddenly diverted from the campaign in Raetia. Maximus, presumably, was confident of any outcome of such a clash. For Gratian, the first blow was that his *magister peditum* (C-in-C infantry) a Frank called Merobaudes, then serving for the second time as consul, had gone over to the pretender, under whom he was promptly preserved in office.[62]

At some time shortly after the 16 June, Gratian's forces faced those of Maximus near Lutetia Parisiorum (Paris) in a five-day stand-off, only ended by the desertion to him of Gratian's Moorish cavalry, probably a pay-off from Maximus's years in Africa supporting Gildo and putting the rebellious Firmus in his place. Gratian himself, his army fatally weakened, bowed to the inevitable and fled, but was caught and killed by Andragathius at Lugdunum (Lyons) on 25 August, the deed being achieved thorough an act of deception which plagued Maximus's reputation thereafter and indeed may have done so throughout his subsequent reign. Having captured the young emperor, the Master of the Soldiers is alleged to have invited him into a closed carriage in which his beloved new wife, Laeta, was supposedly seated, away from the stares of the uncouth soldiery. Having climbed in, he was promptly run through and despatched with a sword by a waiting assassin.[63]

This story is not the only account of Gratian's demise, however, and it emerges from the letters of St Ambrose that Maximus had not intended to have Gratian killed, but rather had planned to send him to Theodosius at Constantinople. If this were true of course, it would further deepen the suspicion that Theodosius was prepared at the very least to tolerate Maximus's acclamation and rule as means to a comprehensive settlement of the empire. According to the assassination account, Gratian only died because Andragathius had exceeded his orders.[64] A likely story, some might say, yet it is by no means inconceivable. Zosimus continues:

The reign of Gratian being thus terminated, Maximus, who now considered himself imperially secure, sent an embassy to Theodosius, not to intreat pardon for his treatment of Gratian, but rather to increase his provocations. The person employed in this mission was the imperial chamberlain (for Maximus would not suffer an eunuch to preside in his court), a prudent person, with whom he had been familiarly acquainted from his infancy. The purpose was to propose a treaty of amity and alliance against all enemies who should make war on the Romans and, on refusal, to declare against him open hostility. Upon this, Theodosius agreed that Maximus should become co-ruler along with the trappings of statues and imperial style. Nevertheless, he was at the same time privately preparing for war and endeavouring to deceive Maximus by every species of flattery and observance. He gave instructions to Cynegius, the prefect of his court, whom he had sent into Egypt in order to shut down all pagan worship, and to close the temples there, that he should shew a statue of Maximus to the Alexandrians, and put it up publicly, declaring to the people that he was associated with him in the empire. This Cynegius did, closing the doors of the temples throughout the east, Egypt, and Alexandria, and prohibiting all their ancient sacrifices and associated rituals.'[65]

It is interesting that Zosimus states Maximus had been 'familiarly acquainted from his infancy' with his imperial chamberlain, as it supports the view that his parents were moving in fairly elevated circles for this acquaintanceship to have come about, which in itself reinforces the likelihood of Maximus's family being related to that of Theodosius, at that time in exactly the same sort of *milieu*. The chamberlain would have surely been also well known to Theodosius. There is no evidence of Theodosius 'privately preparing for war' even had he wished to; he had his hands full elsewhere.

3

Emperor in the West

A New Gallic Empire

At this point, with the German Merobaudes as *magister militum*, the murderous Andragathius as *magister equitum*, and the Gallic grandee Flavius Evodius as Praetorian Prefect, Maximus settled his court at Trier, in control of what was effectively a revived Gallic empire, probably from fairly early on also including at least part of Africa but excluding Italy, where the young Valentinian II still held sway.[1] As we saw at the end of the preceding chapter, he thereupon sent an embassy to Theodosius led by the unnamed *praepositus sacri cubiculi* (head of the imperial household) in 383, proposing an accord between them; he seems to have offered no excuse or apology for his actions, either – he was clearly confident. Zosimus, oddly, does not tell us of the result of this diplomatic offensive, and some commentators suggest that recognition only came in 386, after Theodosius had settled a dispute over the partition of Armenia with the Persian king Sharpur III.[2] Yet this would seem an odd point at which to offer recognition, despite Theodosius facing another serious problem with the Goths in Thrace, which might have made him keen to acknowledge Maximus to secure his rear. It seems far more likely that, although the occasion of recognition has escaped record, it must have occurred early rather than late; after all, Maximus's consulship for 384 appears to have been recognised, which would surely imply that his status had been duly acknowledged in 383 and not two years afterwards.[3] Furthermore, the consulship of Maximus's right-hand man at Trier, Evodius, was designated for (and served in) 386, and he would have been appointed consul designate in good time before that. If the recognition had been only in 386, Evodius could only have assumed a suffect consulship for that year. Theodosius, who although apparently discomforted by the murder of his western colleague, was probably not unduly bothered by it, perhaps even secretly pleased, if disapproving of the way in which Gratian was allegedly dispatched. In any case, he was busy with the Goths and various Persian perturbations on his eastern frontier. Thus, he was obliged, no doubt after a period of consideration, eventually to accept his old comrade-in-arms' *de facto* position and acknowledged him as co-emperor with himself, Arcadius and Valentinian II, who, although technically senior to Theodosius, found his area of responsibility duly reduced to Italy, Africa and part of the Balkans, an arrangement that Casey thinks may have emerged from a conference between the two sides' embassies. Valentinian seems to have been given Dacia and Macedonia in addition, to save face, a gesture only Theodosius could have made, emphasising his complicity in the arrangements, willing or otherwise.[4]

Theodosius seems at this point to have been unsure of the solidity of his own position, although, as we have seen, he may have covertly welcomed Maximus's intervention. In a *quid pro quo,* Maximus was obliged to recognise the position of Valentinian II and the integrity of those parts of the west in which his writ nominally ran.[5] Maximus duly received the recognition he sought from his eastern colleague and kinsman. As a result, apart from his statues being exhibited in the east and the recognition of consulships, Theodosius had coins struck bearing Maximus's image at the mint of Constantinople.[6] It would seem that with the Spanish diocese having acquiesced in Maximus's takeover, generally people and officials welcomed the change of régime and a sense of normalcy appears to have prevailed.

Henceforth, the new augustus' name began to appear upon inscriptions coupled with those of his new colleagues, as in Tripolitania,[7] put up by a local luminary:

QUINTO FL[AMINI] P[ER]P[ETUO] SAC[ERDOTALI] PROV[INCIAE]
SALVIS AC TOTO ORBE VIN[CEN]TIBUS
DDDD.NNNN. FFFFLLLL
VALENTINIANO THEODOSIO
ARCADIO ET ~~MAXIMO~~ SEM[PER] AUGUST[I]
OB MERITUM MAGNIFICE LEGATI
ONIS QUAM PRO VOS TOTIUS
PROVINCIAE EXECUTUS EST ET [PER
EG]IT QUINTUS VIR LAUDABILIS
SACERDOTALIS HUIC CAPIENSE
CONPETENTIBUS MERITIS
RESPONDERE TOTIUS PRO
VINCIAE CONSILIO AD[QUE]
DECRETO ORD[INIS]
N[OSTR]
I PO
S[ITA] P[ECUNIA] P[UBLICA]

In this instance, once Maximus had met his end it is noticeable that his name was duly struck through, reflecting the imposition of a formal decree of *damnatio memoriae,* imposed upon him by a pliant senate acting in the shadow of an imperial visit by the victor.

St Ambrose – the senatorial former provincial governor, fundamentalist orthodox Christian and strong-minded Bishop of Milan – sems to have brokered the deal whereby Maximus agreed to respect the realm of Valentinian II in Italy and the Balkans. Ambrose would probably have been pleased to do this, as a strong Nicene Christian emperor in the north would have seemed to him an ideal counterbalance to the Arian-dominated court of Valentinian and his mother Justina in Milan, with whom Ambrose's relations were equivocal to say the least. In return, it would seem, Valentinian's court allowed Maximus's brother Marcellinus to go north to join him, for which action St Ambrose was soon berating Maximus, in a letter urging him to return the body of the murdered Gratian to the bosom of his family – that is to the court at Milan, as a *quid pro quo*:

> Look too at the man (Marcellinus) who now stands at your right hand, whom Valentinian, when he had the opportunity of avenging his grief, sent back to you loaded with honours. He had him in his own territory, and yet restrained his hand: even when he received the tidings of his brother's death, he restrained his natural feelings, and abstained from retaliation ... compare for yourself therefore the two actions. He sent back your brother alive; so you should restore his brother to him at least now that he is dead. Why do you refuse to him his relation's remains, when he refused not to you those who would assist you against him?[8]

A precious fragment, albeit possibly a fiction, is that Marcellinus ended up standing on Maximus's right hand, suggesting an important but unrecorded role, but probably no more than as an unspecified *comes*. Despite the asperity of St Ambrose's remarks, the bishop must privately have welcomed the presence of a strong ruler of zealous orthodox Christian views. The Council of Nicaea had long before (in 325) settled the potential schism caused by the followers of Arius, which undermined the unity of the Godhead. Although formally settled, the heresy still embraced the majority of Christians amongst the barbarians. With Justina bringing up the young Valentinian II in a court dominated by Arians therefore, Ambrose can have been far from happy.

Circumstantial evidence suggests that although he did not control Italy, Maximus managed to obtain some degree of recognition then (certainly later) from the senate in Rome, amongst the members of which in later decades, his memory appears to have been held in some respect, in contrast to the scathing words of the panegyricist Pacatus (himself a senator) in 389 and some of the chroniclers of the fifth century. In the light of this, it would seem wrong to regard Maximus as a mere usurper; the imperial claimant had arrived, established himself in a manner very similar to that of the Gallic emperor Postumus over a century before, had been officially recognised and had begun to rule what in effect was a revived Gallic Empire, unchallenged for five years. That Theodosius failed to move against Maximus after his elevation (in 380 or 383) has been considered strange by some commentators. However, even if Theodosius's inclinations had been firmly for it, logistics were against it, especially as there was so much going on in Theodosius's own eastern part of the Empire.[9] It has also been suggested that the shadowy events surrounding the demise of Theodosius's father in Africa in 375/376 had been authorised by Gratian or done in his name. His ruling clique may have been manoeuvred into giving the orders for his execution, along with a number of other eminent people.[10] If so, it may be that Theodosius's nose was not so put out of joint, as long as his kinsman restricted himself to the west. It was also suggested by Orosius (followed by Jordanes) that it was Valens who ordered the death of Theodosius *père,* which would amount to much the same thing as far as Theodosius was concerned and indeed, may have had much to do with Gratian's acknowledgement of his acclamation as emperor to replace the fallen Valens, who, by any measure, was not his elder brother's match as a ruler.[11] Theodosius, therefore, was by no means free of imputations of collusion in Maximus's *coup,* which, if true, may well have circumscribed his subsequent relationship with his co-rulers.

Nevertheless, despite the accord which secured him recognition, both sides took precautions against a possible push south by Maximus: Valentinian's *magister militum* Bauto fortified the Alpine passes against a surprise attack, while for his part Maximus set out his stall by naming his young son Flavius Victor as co-Augustus, probably in 384, perhaps also as a riposte to Theodosius' naming of his own elder son as co-emperor the year before. Victor is called Magnius Victor Maximus [*sic*] on one clumsy inscription from Numidia:

DDNN MAGNI
O MAXIMO MAXCI
MO ET MAGNIO
VICTORE MAXIMO
SENPER
AUGUSTIS

This perhaps reflects Victor's full name prior to elevation to the rank of Augustus, the name Flavius being assumed then. The misspelling of *semper* though suggests that the intrusive 'i' in both iterations of 'Magnus' may represent a blunder; perhaps the inscription had been set up immediately after the son's proclamation and before notice of his official style had reached the province.[12] The lad probably took his name from Maximus's *comes* Victor, who had been sent to meet St Ambrose at Mogontiacum (Mainz) and later went to Milan to broker a peace settlement. Victor would seem to have been a kinsman of Maximus, possibly (see the suggested *stemma* below) an uncle.[13] Hostile contemporary sources call the younger Victor a child, including Sulpicius Alexander, quoted by Gregory of Tours, who says that Maximus entrusted his 'infant son' to the Rhine generals Nannienus and Quintinus, yet his coin portraits seem to show a youth in his early teens and Zosimus, in describing his fall, calls him a youth.[14] Somehow, given the clemency Theodosius showed to the other surviving members of Maximus's family, one suspects that if Victor had really been too young to appreciate his position, he would have been spared and perhaps tonsured, whereas a 'youth' might have become the focus of a counter-*putsch* had he been allowed to live. Had he been young enough to have been born in Britain (that is, nine or younger), British legend would have surely made something of it; as it is, there is barely any trace of him is those sources.

Father and son adopted the style:

D[OMINI] N[OSTRI] MAGNUS MAXIMUS ET FLAVIUS VICTOR
INVICTIS ET PERPETUIS AUGUSTI.[15]

This is confirmed by a clutch of milestones in Italy, one of which, near Brixia (Brescia) is typical and reads:

DD NN
MAGNO MAXIMO ET F[L] VIC
TORI INVIC
TIS PERPETUIS
AUGUS
TIS
BONO REI PUBLIAE NATIS
IIIIII[16]

There is no mention here of the other three emperors, which suggests that these stones were perhaps put up after the final breach with Theodosius late in 387. No doubt Maximus had been granted the tribunician and proconsular powers, probably from a provincial council-cum-senate, and these must most certainly have been confirmed by the senate at Rome once the accord between him and Theodosius had been agreed. There is no suggestion that the position of *pontifex maximus* was conferred, for Maximus – with the zeal of the newly baptised – had become an exceedingly keen Christian and probably took the same line as the unfortunate Gratian about this pagan office and declined it.

Return to Britain

Once the Germans had been put back in their box and the situation on the Rhine frontier stabilized, Maximus appears to have made a return visit to Britain. We know this by inference from numismatic research. Since a reform of Valentinian I in 366/367, the ruler and the *comitatenses* – effectively the Imperial court – issued cash in bullion, gold *solidi* and silver *siliquae*, to pay the army, and mints, instead of striking coins on a regular basis, tended to be activated only when the court was nearby. As we have seen, Maximus's first coin type, minted in London in silver and gold only, demonstrated a break with the past in that instead of continuing the issues of Gratian, the issue reverted to a type that was demonstrably pre-Gratian, an issue which preceded the new Augustus and his court crossing to Trier.[17] A second coin issue, of a type also minted at Trier, Maximus's headquarters, not long after the accession but after recognition by Theodosius, was also issued in limited quantities from the re-opened London mint (the mint mark being slightly different from his first British issue: AVGPS, AVGOB or AVGOP instead of AVG) and this probably happened at some stage in 384. Casey has argued this clearly implied a temporary move back to Britain accompanied by his *comitatus*.[18]

Precisely what Maximus accomplished in Britain is lost to us, although some suggestions may be made, mainly implicit in the archaeology and bolstered by the suggestions made above. It has been proposed that the chief legacy of this visit was the building of London's seemingly exceptionally grand metropolitan cathedral, the vestiges of which were unexpectedly discovered on Tower Hill in 1995. This was built certainly after 350 on a small hill, levelled off, and astride one end of one of the main east-west roads across the city. The proposition that it may have been built at his instigation, especially as it was based in plan on that dedicated to St Thecla at Milan, seat of the hectoring St Ambrose – but at 330ft (100m) by 160ft (50m) somewhat larger – is highly persuasive. Excavations by David Sankey of Museum of London Archaeology have established that the thick exterior walls of this previously unknown church were constructed on a concrete base out of re-used stone taken from other buildings, and embellished internally with a veneer of black marble and with properly glazed windows.[19] It was built before 400, but the preponderance of evidence tends to indicate a later rather than an earlier date after 350, and the link with Magnus Maximus has been convincingly argued. Significantly, the church is thought to have been dedicated to St Paul.[20]

It has to be remembered that within a year of the Edict of Milan, Britain appears to have had a fully developed ecclesiastical hierarchy, even to having metropolitan bishops, that of London having attended a church council at Arelate in 314.[21] Bearing in mind that the emperor's return visit to Britain was within a year or eighteen months of his move to Trier, the idea that he might have been the driving force behind this out-doing of Ambrose becomes an attractive one. Interestingly, a Welsh Triad (written down by Iolo Morgannwg at least seven centuries later) tells us that an archbishopric of London was created 'through the favour of the Emperor Maximus'.[22] Coincidentally, the incumbent bishop at Trier when Maximus arrived as emperor was called Britannius, which might suggest an ecclesiastic of British descent or connections, perhaps even one who had urged him on in his devotion.[23] Other works carried out in Londinium at this period included a new stretch of river wall, 10 ft 6 ins (3.2 metres) wide at the base abutting the south-east angle of the city walls, which were also strengthened, gates altered and further bastions added. In some respects municipal life within London's walls was more vigorous than in many western cities at this time.[24]

Other measures known to have been taken in the later fourth century in Britain may well have been on his initiative but in most cases, we cannot be sure, for the *comes* Theodosius might have beaten him to it in some instances. If Maximus made a return visit in around 384, one must ask why this should be. Most obviously it might have been to consolidate whatever arrangements he had made prior to moving across the Channel on his acclamation, possibly even in the frontier regions, which some of the legendary material implies. Recently, it has been proposed that Maximus 'enrolled mercenary Saxons from the North Sea coast' to garrison Britain, on the assumption that the previous establishment had been eviscerated by the emperor's *coup*.[25] This would appear to be an ingenious way of explaining the presence of Saxons open to revolt in Britain much later. This will be shown to be unlikely, although Maximus's dispositions on the frontier areas were certainly a case of 'thinking outside the box', and like those made by his old commander in Africa a decade earlier, appear to have worked well.

Generally, town walls were given added bastions, each to carry a *ballista* to deter a close siege, combined with the improvement of the associated ditch systems. As has been emphasised, though, Germanic and indeed Pictish and Scottish forces were notable for their inability to undertake sieges.[26] The north-west was certainly reinforced, most probably at this time, including the late Saxon Shore type fort at Lancaster. In Wales, the fort at Canovium (Caerhun, Caernarvonshire/Clwyd) guarding an important crossing in the Conway valley was re-commissioned, and Segontium (Caernarfon, Gwynedd) was re-occupied and much strengthened at some stage in the third quarter of the fourth century, acquiring a secondary one-acre fort with a stone wall on nearby St Peblig Hill and a probable signal station, too.[27] On Anglesey, Caer Gybi (Holyhead) was built, while Holyhead mountain gained Caer y Twr, a watchtower, *pharos* or signal station, and other similar hill-top look-outs, now lost, eroded or undiscovered, may have been set up, all probably in line with Cardiff, Lancaster and Segontium, and with locally based defence against the Irish (Scotti) in mind.[28]

A digression: Segontium

In the probable re-commissioning and strengthening of the Welsh forts under Maximus, the re-occupation and ambitious up-grading of Segontium (Caernarfon, Gwynedd) finds resonance in much later British tradition. Maximus's of course, enjoys a legendary connection with Segontium, but this supposed linkage, first aired in the *Breudwyt Maxen Wledig* ('The Dream of Maxen Wletic' in *The Mabinogion*), is essentially a topic for the second part of this work, for it is mentioned only there and has no known confirmation in Classical sources whatsoever. It is, of course, *possible* that the emperor's acclamation took place in North Wales, for the Scots (from Ireland) and Picts could have been finally ejected by Maximus from the Seiont estuary in 381 or even before. Furthermore, having dealt with the incursion, we put forward above the suggestion that Maximus set about strengthening the northern defences and re-organising those in Wales, too. Thus, it could be that his acclamation *did* arise in Segontium, and not somewhere more obvious. Indeed, if the year was 380 and not 383 as proposed by the re-evaluation of the *Chronicle of 452*, then his being there seems all the more likely. That so powerful was the memory of this that it survived in however garbled a form to be incorporated in the *Dream*, might seem that much less surprising. Nonetheless, most scholars consider it became the prime locale of the *Dream* in order to flatter the then ruling house of Gwynedd, whose links with Arfon were strong. Whatever distant memory caused this place to be incorporated in the tale, it lies well beyond proof.

Without doubt, though, the site is not without interest in connection with what Maximus may have been able to achieve in Britain either before his acclamation or even in 384. A potential clue lies in the stray unit of *Seguntienses* mentioned in the previous chapter. This unit could, instead of having been transferred away from Britain by Magnentius, have been part of the *comitatus* (mobile field army) created by Maximus prior to crossing to Gaul. After Maximus's defeat at Aquileia, the unit could hardly be permitted to be repatriated, so could possibly have been incorporated into his own army by Theodosius. This unit of (*pedites*) *Seguntienses* (infantry of/from Segontium) were, it seems, drafted to Illyricum in the Balkans and out of harm's way. They were recorded as such in the *Notitia Dignitatum* which was compiled some years later, but the transfer of such units (in both directions) was entirely normal in the third and fourth centuries, and we have no evidence that the *Seguntienses* had not been in Illyricum for decades.[29] Their very existence, however, has tended to reinforce Maximus's legendary personal link with Segontium, and it would not contradict any (admittedly risky) supposition that this unit had actually been instrumental in acclaiming Maximus there, had been consequently included in his *comitatus* and hence moved as far away as possible by Theodosius after the debacle at Aquileia.

Latent memory of this might have become a distant inspiration for the later emergence of Segontium (in the *Historia Brittonum* included in a list of post-Roman *civitates* as *Cair Segeint*) as the legendary place of association with Maximus in the *Breudwyt Maxen Wledig*.[30] In response to Gildas blaming Maximus for stripping the island of its defensive forces, a competent commander would have sent such vexillations back once he had taken over command of Gratian's forces and secured Gaul. While the accusation undoubtedly had force in some later accounts, it overlooks the fact that prior to crossing the Channel, it is here proposed that Maximus made a successful settlement of the frontier regions which well outlasted him, and which enabled him to release this and other units to serve with him elsewhere.

As for Segontium, itself, it does have resonance in the late and post-Roman period. The fort had been established in *c.* 78 by Agricola to house a unit of 500 part-mounted auxiliary troops, the unit in possession in the time of Septimius Severus having been the *Cohors I Sunicorum* (first company of Sunici, a grouping from Roman north-western Germany) which left an inscription on an aqueduct, by which time the fort had been rebuilt in stone.[31] It was served by a Roman road from Tomen-y-Mur (Trawsfynydd, Gwynedd) to the south-east and by another running north-east to Caerhun, both being connected to the main Welsh north-south road, the Sarn Elen (named after Maximus's fabled wife in the *Mabinogion*, Helen of the Hosts).[32] It was enlarged in the mid/late fourth century, and the regular coin sequence continues until 394, including issues of Maximus, but also including a clipped *siliqua*, suggesting a longer duration, with use continuing into the fifth century.[33]

The fort continued in use, with its extensive *vicus* (with separate baths) into the fifth century, supplemented by a late-fourth-century fortlet, almost a miniature Saxon Shore fort, measuring 237 by 171ft (72 by 52m) called Hen Waliau ('Old Walls'), strongly walled indeed, including bastions, near the shore, 164 yards (150m) north-west of the main fort, much resembling the site at Holyhead (Caer Gybi) and quite possibly part of the arrangements put in place to defend against the attacks of the Scots (Irish), as with probable refurbishments to the Saxon Shore-type forts at Cardiff (built late 3rd century) and Lancaster (of *c.* 330/350). This would have been also to defend the port facilities in both locales, here ascribed to the efforts of Maximus.[34]

Evidence is beginning to emerge of considerable Roman settlement on the spur to the north of Hen Waliau, that upon which a Norman motte was built followed by Edward I's castle, its walls marked by Roman-style horizonal banding; could the site of the castle and walled town have been that of another shore fort?[35] It may thus be, therefore, that a matching fort may have been built there and that the brick banded walls may have been the direct inspiration for Edward I's masons to create a similar visual effect. They might, indeed, have incorporated portions of the surviving structure, if such can eventually be established to have existed. Not only that, but nearby was an exceptionally stout timber bridge across the Seiont, the remains of which were rediscovered in 1817, and adjacent to the extra-mural cemetery of the main settlement was the ancient church of St Peblig, significantly built on top of a Mithraeum.[36] The dedicatee (allegedly in 433) was a legendary grandson of Maxen Wletic/Maximus, bearing the Roman name of Publicius.[37] A Roman pagan altar was discovered in the south wall during an 1894 restoration of the present mainly 14th-century fabric.[38] While later churches in Roman forts – like Caerhun, Caergybi, Carmarthen, Llandough villa in Wales, and any amount in England – certainly imply continuity, they do not necessarily prove it.[39]

Five miles south-west was another fortlet, Dinas Dinlle, at Llandwrog (also with associations with *The Mabinogion*), seemingly a re-used Iron Age stronghold, which may have been adapted to defend a Roman *Pharos* or a signal tower.[40] Strategically, if one's potential enemies were likely to attack across St George's Channel, then Segontium was defensively very well placed and, in the later fourth century, was certainly equipped with the necessary military infrastructure. Thus, by this period in which Maximus briefly flourished, Segontium was a place of no small significance, which may well have owed something of its re-fortification and expansion to the frontier re-organisation scheme of Maximus, legendary associations aside.

Dispositions elsewhere

In the south of Wales, equally exposed to Irish sea-borne raiders, the nine-acre Saxon Shore-type fort at Cardiff was re-commissioned or indeed, re-built, for very little evidence to date it positively has so far emerged as most of the internal archaeology was lost before the mid-19th-century alterations there made on behalf of the Marquises of Bute, who 'restored' the Roman walls. It, too, may also have been supported by signal stations, as on the north-east coast, along the north side of the Severn Estuary, but any evidence of such will have long been eroded away on this exposed littoral, although such suspected sites can be identified at Martinhoe and Old Burrow in Somerset on the opposite side.[41] Collins and Breeze speculate that there must have been a late-fourth-century military command in west Britain, perhaps under a *comes tractus maritime per Britannias* following the hints given by Ammianus Marcellinus.[42] As will be seen in Part II, this might not have appeared so necessary, given the arrangements for these frontiers Maximus appears to have put in place, although some kind of supervisory command may have continued with a small, probably maritime force to make maximum strategic use of the coast defences. In this respect, activity at *Deva* (Chester) was renewed, and military activity there seems to have continued to the end of the century and beyond, for coins of Arcadius have been found both inside and outside the fortress, this despite the withdrawal southwards of Legio XX Valeria Victrix probably at this period, if not earlier.[43] The simultaneous abandonment of some of the forts of the Welsh interior may be linked with Maximus's presumed settlement, for they represented defence in depth, with units originally stationed inland for 'police' duties being re-deployed elsewhere, possibly in Maximus's *comitatus*. If, on the other hand, Maximus had set up some kind of locally based and locally led militia defence in northern England and Wales, as the legendary sources might seem to confirm, then the local levies upon which such a settlement may have depended will have had no need of the interior forts; in either case, the threat was plainly external, thus coastal, not interior.

Nor was York neglected. The fortress underwent a late-fourth-century refurbishment, eight bastions being added; the *principia* here was also rebuilt, along with other works, setting the scene for what appears to have been an extensive sub-Roman phase as a strong point and probably a dynastic centre.[44] Probably at the same time, the forts at Olicana (Ilkley) and Virosidum (Bainbrigge), both Yorkshire, were also rebuilt, while the north-east coastal signal stations were likely built as part of the same campaign of defensive improvements.[45] Of these, one has given us the name of the *praepositus vexillationum* (detachment commander) in charge, Justinianus, whom we presume to have been the first appointee after building, and his vexillation of auxiliaries (could they have been Germans?) were probably responsible for the entire stretch of coast. It has been suggested that this was the same man who just over two decades later was appointed *magister militum* by Constantine III, in which case we shall encounter him again.[46] Such measures, if indeed undertaken under Maximus's command in Britain and not by the *comes* Theodosius, hardly betoken a strategy that would include a significant and permanent weakening in defensive military capability. On the assumption that these measures, if we can accept Maximus's responsibility for them, were initiated just before or after his elevation, then the return visit to Britain was quite probably to ensure that they were complete and satisfactory and to undertake any fine-tuning.

With all these improvements, how were these defences manned, especially if the standard establishment really had been weakened? Militia troops, independent of the military high command, mainly consisting of local levies, and barbarians drafted in and billeted in towns are attested in Gaul, but not directly in Britain, but are nevertheless a possibility. The measures outlined suggest that some kind of similar arrangement may well have come into being, but not necessarily in an urban context, especially if one bears in mind the so-called 'Germanic' belt fittings and other military-style ornaments discovered in urban sites all over the diocese. While these are today considered elements of a near universal late Roman attire and accoutrements worn by civil servants, imperial officials and senior military officers, there remains the possibility that some of the levies protecting town walls, the Saxon Shore forts and the north-east coast signal stations were perhaps of barbarian origin, as was so frequently the case in the late Roman army.[47] It is in relation to all this that the key to Maximus's lasting, largely legendary fame may lie. Leslie Alcock wrote:

> It is thought that he [Maximus] handed over the responsibility for defence to native chieftans, who founded the local dynasties of the fifth and later centuries. The case for this rests partly on the fame which he acquired in Welsh folk-tale and poetry, and partly on a number of royal genealogies which trace their line back through Maximus ... If Maximus really was responsible for some or all of these arrangements he deserves great credit ... no imperial action was necessary in Britain until 396-8.[48]

If that was the case, this arrangement probably owed its origins to the settlement by the *comes* Theodosius in 367-368 (following the disbandment of the *areani,* whose activities can hardly have been productive or confidence-building) with the British chieftains north of the wall and elsewhere; Maximus may even have met and befriended some of them during the negotiations, in which he may well have been involved and which he may have taken a stage further in his settlement of 383/384 or prior to 383. As Salway says, 'There is no certain evidence that the rule of Maximus had ... been deleterious to the security of Britain,' and that evidence for troop withdrawals is 'extremely thin', mainly resting upon post-Roman British legendary material and Gildas's *de Excidio.*[49]

Appointments in Trier

There was still plenty of sorting out to be done at Trier, too, either in 383 or during the year following. There appears to have been a purge of barbarian officers, much favoured by the unwarlike Gratian. Maximus's own high command was, as we have seen, itself hardly free from barbarian appointees at the highest level. The difference was, no doubt, that those he put in place were *his* barbarians, doubtless bound to him in a later imperial version of the tradition of Roman *clientelae,* and not Gratian's. The convention of *largitio* – the distribution of bullion in cash to supporters through the dispossession of defeated opponents – no doubt came into play too, as indeed is alleged by Pacatus in 389. This must have been in part responsible for Maximus's posthumous reputation for avarice.[50] Meanwhile, the aristocratic Gallic poet, former tutor to Gratian and friend of Pacatus, Ausonius, was still (just) in residence there but quickly sent his son home to Aquitania, presumably for his own safety, while his brother Decimius Hilarianus Hesperius retired to Italy, probably at the urging of his friend, the prominent senator Q. Aurelius Symmachus (who quickly dropped him after Maximus's arrival in Trier). Indeed, the latter may have been instrumental in keeping open a line of unofficial communication between Valentinian's court at Milan and that of Maximus in Germany.[51] Yet pursuing a court career at the feet of a man perceived as an usurper was to run a risk, and such purely personal channels were essential; at this level of discourse, few people were not known to each other in some way or another.

As for Ausonius, the move of the court to Milan, followed by the death of Gratian, had more or less ended his long career and he, too, was allowed by Maximus to retire to his native Burdigala (Bordeaux).[52] The possibility of a violent purge with the coming of a new ruler, although increasingly rare at this era, but with the example of the mysterious demise of Theodosius I's father on the death of Valentinian I in mind, retirement was the prudent option.[53] In 383, higher ranking officials would have had the Theodosius *père's* fate still in mind, armed as they were with the true story behind it, now lost to us. Ausonius, despite this exercise of moderation, did not fail to put the boot in once out to grass, thereby missing the consulship for 384, and his predecessor, Flavius Manlius Theodorus, also took himself off to retirement, in his case to Milan, which was to remain the core support base for Valentinian II, the remaining member of the dynasty, by this time no doubt feeling increasingly insecure, the more so with St Ambrose snapping at his heels.

Yet on the whole, there appears to have been little or no serious fall-out in the sense of blood-letting from the change of régime at Trier. Maximus's pretty solid support in Gaul was, from the outset, probably a combination of relief at having a competent commander and imperial claimant on the spot to trouble-shoot when required, and the natural instinct to close ranks behind the nearest effective contender for power. Furthermore, Maximus's Christian fervour must certainly have struck a chord amongst the Gallic bishops, and it cannot have harmed his standing at the court of Constantinople either. On the whole, the only negative views of him can be securely dated to the years following his death; as Sivan has perceptively commented, 'Gallic expressions of protest against Maximus were only uttered when he was safely out of the way for good.'[54]

Hence, Maximus appointed a number of eminent Gauls, untainted by close association with Gratian and outside the closed circle of Ausonius's friends. Taking a wider view, Maximus's régime also gave the Gallic nobility a considerable boost in opening up careers and restoring their self-esteem, much more so because, on the whole, Maximus was seen positively. While the revival of the Gallic Prefecture under Constantine III in 407 probably had a similar effect, by the time that dispensation and its somewhat ephemeral successors had been snuffed out, the world had changed irreversibly, especially in north-west Europe; worse, Constantine had established his court at Arelate (Arles), not Trier, a city that was from 407 virtually untenable as a seat of government.

Maximus appears to have appointed to his staff as *comes* the senator Sextius Rusticus Julianus, who had been proconsul of Africa back in 371-373 (where he had been branded as harsh – shades of Firmus's revolt) and whom Maximus made Prefect of the City of Rome once his court had moved south in 387. Although thought to have been a Gaul, in some ways he was an odd choice, for although he was according to Symmachus an *arriviste* amongst the ranks of the senate, he was also a keen pagan, being the leading light amongst the worshippers of Mithras in Rome, in contrast to the new Emperor's zealous Christianity. He had also, according to Ammianus Marcellinus (who would have known him), been suggested as emperor himself by the Gallic courtiers in 367, when Valentinian I had fallen suddenly and perilously ill, normally the sort of career check that an existing emperor might take as an opportunity to send someone rapidly into exile; perhaps Julianus was too valuable a person to have on-side to dismiss. He was in a way fortunate in that he died in office at Rome in 388 before the fall of his patron.[55]

Another appointee was Claudius Lupicinus. Like Ausonius an Aquitanian, he was given the governorship of the new province Maximus had created in Gaul and he was remembered on an inscription possibly from his estate, that he had been patron of three cities in the province, Senones (Sens), Autissiodurum (Auxerre) and Aurelianorum (Orléans).[56]

Another provincial governor, although this time presumably of Spanish descent, was Antonius Maximinus. His appointment appears to have been to an entirely new Spanish province, a creation of Maximus, and it is not unlikely that he was a near kinsman, perhaps a first cousin of the new emperor and thus a son of Victor, the uncle who served Maximus as *comes* in various capacities.[57] That his *nomen*, Antonius, also appears amongst the family of Maria, the wife of the emperor Theodosius's brother Honorius, might represent reasonably close kinship, and if so, it may contain a clue as to the real link between Maximus and his eastern colleague. The *stemma* represents an attempt to suggest how this link might have worked.

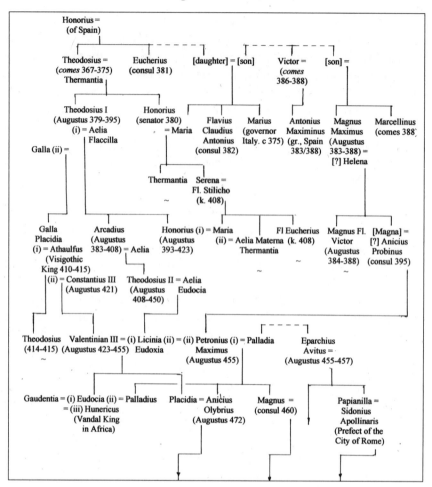

Stemma 1. Theodosius and Magnus Maximus.

Marinianus, Maximus's *vicarius* of the Spanish provinces, seems to have been inherited from Gratian's régime; he was in office in the May of 383 and is thought to be identifiable with an unnamed holder of the same office later that year.[58] At this time, too, Maximus re-graded the standing of the governor of Tarraconensis from *praeses* to a *consularis*, an honour that may well have been bestowed to mark a link with his family's origins.[59] To one of his dioceses, Maximus appointed one Desiderius, who was certainly in office by July 385, when he received a rescript (ruling) from the Emperor from Trier. Birley puts forward the suggestion that he might well have been Maximus's *vicarius Britanniarum*. He also draws attention to the silver chalice (subsequently lost) discovered in 1760 in the Tyne at Bywell, near Corbridge, Northumberland, inscribed *Desideri vivas* – 'Desiderius, may you flourish.'[60]

Two other diocesan *vicarii* are known, but again, the location of their actual appointments is not wholly clear: Marcellinus and Marcianus were both *en poste* in March 383 and seemingly kept on under the new dispensation. The latter developed a penchant for serving unsuccessful imperial claimants for, after serving Maximus, he pops up a decade later as Emperor Eugenius's appointee as proconsul of Africa, from whence he was rusticated by Theodosius, saving his neck by repaying his salary to the treasury. As if that wasn't enough, in his declining years he was appointed prefect of the City of Rome in 409 by the Visigothic *magister militum* Alaric's puppet emperor Priscus Attalus; one gets the impression of a second-rater obliged to take office under chancers like Eugenius and Attalus in order to kick-start a languishing *cursus honorum*. Perhaps Marcianus was appointed to Britain and managed to achieve some renown, which might account for the recurrence of the name amongst several later British princes, although for those whose births might be datable to the mid-fifth century, the eastern emperor of the time is a more likely source.[61] If Marinianus was in Spain in 383, then these two perhaps held office over the dioceses of Gaul and Britain, Desiderius presumably succeeding whichever of the two was *vicarius* of Britain.[62]

Birley also draws attention to two other former *vicarii* of the Britains, Chrysanthus and Victorinus. The former died in old age in Constantinople in 419, but had been *consularis* (governor) of an Italian province 'under Theodosius, after this having been appointed *vicarius* of Britain.'[63] Given that he was old by 410, his period as *vicarius* might easily have fallen under Maximus, especially as he received no other apparent preferment for more than two decades prior to being elevated to *comes* after 411 (which bestowal allowed him to be styled *vir illustris*); a period of disgrace or self-effacement might be suggested here, which might also accord well with someone who had served under a deposed emperor. The belated appointment as *comes* may indeed have been made through his making a smarter call, remaining loyal to Honorius during the reign of Constantine III.

Victorinus, on the other hand, was a friend of the poet Rutilius Namatianus, who called upon him in 417 and in a complimentary poem pointed out that he had served as a well-regarded *vicarius* of the Britains in earlier, happier days.[64] Again, this could mean under Maximus, but it depends upon whether these elderly grandees would have regarded that period as being particularly happy, bearing in mind the way it ended. It is even possible that Victorinus was a relation of Maximus's probable uncle, Victor, if the diminutive of the latter's name is accepted as a possible indication of kinship; unfortunately, both names were then fairly common. However, Victorinus might just as well have served *after* Maximus and before another 'less happy' interlude, the usurpation of Eugenius. Either way, once Maximus had returned from Britain in 384, he would have needed a reliable man in place there as *vicarius*, so it is unfortunate that we cannot name him.

Two provincial governors are known to have been serving in this part of the Empire at about this time but, again, their provinces are unclear:

Leucadius, serving as a *praeses* 383, and Bonosus, only a *palatinus* (guard officer) in 384 but known to have governed two provinces before 387.[65] Leucadius – if a forebear of the Leucadius who was serving somewhat later as a *primicerius domesticorum* (senior guard commander) and who married a Nonita, memorialised in Tarragona – might well have been Spanish too, but he required the services of St Martin to avoid trouble when Maximus took over from Gratian and dispensed with his services, conceivably from a British province. The name of Bonosus evokes the unfortunate and supposedly British-born imperial claimant who was put down by Probus in Gaul in 280; that he, too, was a Gaul is not unlikely, although any relationship seems speculative in the extreme.[66] An ex-provincial governor and *vicarius* of Spain was Marius Artemius, who is probably to be identified with Artemius, an envoy sent by Maximus on a mission to Spain later in his reign. Gregory of Tours mentions him because he fell ill en route at Augusta Nemetum (Clermont), was cured by the bishop there and, in gratitude, forsook fiancée, mission and fortune to be ordained on the spot, eventually becoming the next bishop.[67]

The supreme military appointment of *magister militum* (master of the soldiers) is one for which we can supply four candidates. Adragathius and Merobaudes we have already met as *magistri in praesenti* (at court), but two others are known, both Romans rather than Barbarians, Nannienus and Quintinus. The former had distinguished himself, probably as Count of the Saxon Shore in 372 and again elsewhere. Both were appointed by Maximus, Nannienus as *magister militum* to command in Gaul but who refused to participate in a rash punitive cross-Rhenish campaign undertaken by Quintinus, which ended in disaster.[68]

As regards praetorian prefects, the most senior administrative position, only Flavius Evodius is known, serving in 385 and 386, the year he served as ordinary consul (and thus gave his name to the year). However, it may very well be that he was succeeded by Flavius Afranius Syagrius, of whom his descendant, the Gallic senatorial man of letters, Sidonius Apollonaris, wrote that he had served *three* prefectures, but of which only two are known for certain: his prefecture of the city (of Rome) in 381 and that of Italy in the same year as his consulship, 382. As Sidonius is generally considered to be entirely reliable, the third prefecture may well have been that of Gaul (including Spain and Britain) under Maximus, most probably prior to the appointment of Evodius as, had he been *en poste* when Maximus fell, he might well have suffered the consequences. As it is, he may have served as Maximus's *comes sacrarum largitionum* (controller of the public purse) in 387 before retiring (it is assumed); he died in retirement and was buried at Lugdunum (Lyons).[69] It is also possible that either he or his probable cousin and namesake, Flavius Syagrius (consul in 381), was married to a sister of Theodosius.[70]

One interesting character who became involved with Maximus's régime was Maternus Cynegius, another person of Spanish origin and conceivably also a relation of Maximus and Theodosius. His parentage is unclear, but we know he was related to Florus, who was Theodosius's Praetorian Prefect of the East when Maximus seized power and whose grandson also bore the name Cynegius. Maternus Cynegius was Theodosius's *Quaestor Sacri Palatii* (attorney general would be the nearest equivalent) when Maximus was acclaimed, but succeeded Florus as Praetorian Prefect in 384; he was clearly held in high esteem by the eastern emperor. Having acceded to office, we have already encountered him travelling to Alexandria in order to display portraits of Maximus, whom Theodosius had just recognised as a colleague. The fact that one of Cynegius's two (known) daughters bore the name Antonia Cassia might suggest that the Western emperor's possible uncle or cousin Antonius Maximinus, who governed a province in Spain for him, may have enjoyed some degree of kinship with him, too, given that they were both of Spanish origin, underlining that on his accession Theodosius was quick to draft in fellow countrymen to bolster his régime, Maximus and Maximinus included.[71] Although Zosimus claims Cynegius died on his way back from getting Maximus's statues raised in Egypt, we in fact later find him at the pinnacle of his career as western consul with Maximus in 388.[72] The possibility of his being a kinsman of both Maximus and Theodosius needs to be borne in mind too, and he seems to have co-existed with both men without any known friction.

Another family, this time Gauls, which attained preferment under Maximus was that of the emperor's *comes sacrarum largitionum* (finance minister), Florentinus. Son of a retired provincial governor from Trier, Maximus's capital, Minervius, Florentinus was one of three brothers. He had been appointed by autumn 385 and was still in office the following December. He probably had a promotion the following year (to what is unclear) for one Licinius had succeeded him by 387. Whatever Florentinus's subsequent position, it seems to have left him unscathed after the end of Maximus's rule, for we find him serving as Prefect of the City of Rome in 395-397 with a young son, another Minervius, just beginning his career, and he later retired to Gaul. Nor did Maximus's fall incommode the careers of Florentinus's brothers Minervius and Protadius; they later served as *comes sacrarum largitionum* and Prefect of the City respectively under Theodosius's son, Honorius, and the former left issue in Gaul who flourished well into the fifth century.[73]

These dispositions seem to suggest that the north-west was in competent hands aided by experienced ones, although inevitably, most were closely bound to the new augustus by kinship, service, origin or background – as was the norm, then as later. Here was a general in power of proven competence, political acumen and armed with sufficient diplomatic skills to enable him to flourish and ensure his segment of the empire would remain stable.

Trier: the interior of the Constantinian basilica (*Aula Palatina* – palace
hall) in which the trial of Priscillian took place in 384, now the
Church of the Redeemer. (The late P. J. R. Withington)

4

Trier, Rome and Aquileia

Religious perturbations

St Martin of Tours was in Trier from 384.[1] He had been an officer in the army under Constantius II and Julian, and probably served somewhat longer than his biographer, Sulpicius Severus, was prepared to admit. A Christian from the age of ten, he sought discharge while serving under the pagan Julian.[2] Having been appointed Bishop of Caesarodunum (mutating to Civitas Turonum at this period, but subsequently Tours) in *c*. 370, he came to Trier to plead with Maximus for the ascetic Spaniard Priscillianus, accused of heresy. He also successfully persuaded the emperor to free numerous prisoners and restore confiscated property generally.

The train of events of which this was part had begun before the accession of Maximus, but the working out of the crisis devolved upon him and his administration. Priscillianus was a man who failed to toe the line with regard to the religious orthodoxy of his day and his divergence from this manifested itself as a sort of asceticism leavened by esoteric theism. He was, apparently, an eloquent man with a keen intellect. His *origo* was probably a bit close to home for both Maximus and Theodosius, being Gallaecia; he was also said to be from a noble family, so could well have been well known to both, which might well have made his sudden rise to notoriety uncomfortable for Maximus, at least.[3]

His deviation from fourth-century Catholic norms on the surface hardly went further than the avoidance of church-going in Lent and of fasting on Sundays. Yet the bishop's adherents' beliefs were actually much more divergent than that. They considered that the Trinity was 'a name devoid of personality ... a simple Christ and human beings were part of the divine' and lived by an order which ran, 'swear, foreswear but do not reveal your mysteries,' from which one might well infer that it included a Gnostic element within its rather opaque precepts. St Jerome added that their sexual practices

83

were also at odds with conventional belief, whether Christian or not: he contended that they believed marriage to be derogatory; that they consorted in lonely houses at night with loose women; that they prayed naked and ended *inter coitum amplexusque*, justifying their sexual embraces by quoting Virgil, no less. Their beliefs were branded by Maximus as Manichean, a term which subsequently gained much traction in this context.[4]

Priscillianus himself had been appointed Bishop of Abela (Avila, Castile & Leon) in about 380 and was summoned to the Council of Caesaraugusta (Saragossa) the same year but failed to turn up, getting himself excommunicated for his pains (or lack of them), a verdict promulgated by Bishop Ithacius of Ossonoba (near Faro, Portugal) and underwritten by a decree of Gratian, which excluded his followers from both churches and towns. He thereupon appealed to Pope Damasus I in 381 but was refused an audience (St Ambrose also refused to see him), and the pope exiled him for his deviant practices.[5] However, Macedonius, Gratian's *magister officiorum*, granted Priscillianus a mandate of restoration to his see in 382. Once back in Spain, the wayward cleric proceeded to sue Bishop Ithacius in the civil courts, who himself thereupon travelled to Trier to appeal to the praetorian prefect. The latter issued a warrant for Priscillianus's arrest but once submitted to Gratian for endorsement, the emperor vacillated over the matter for some while until finally turning the whole situation around by instead issuing a warrant for the arrest of Ithacius – a *volte face* in contrast to the position adopted by the pope and supportive of Macedonius's position. It was more or less at this point that Gratian's regime fell and Magnus Maximus assumed power.

Thus, Maximus, soon after having established himself, was faced with having to deal with an increasingly complicated ecclesiastical rift. This was exacerbated by St Martin, who was notoriously difficult and absolute in his fundamental approach to Christianity, no doubt born of his military training. Nevertheless, the recently converted Maximus seems to have taken to him; arriving in 384, aside from his efforts to get prisoners freed, he managed successfully to protect two over-zealous defenders of the interests of the late emperor Gratian, Narses and Leucadius, from the rigours of his successor's mopping-up operations. He is said also to have persuaded Maximus not to send troops in to Spain to extirpate Priscillianus's adherents, fearing an unnecessary bloodbath. There is a caveat here: it has been argued that settlements of Britons on the northern coast of the Spanish province of Gallaecia between Ferrol and the Eo, served by a see later called Santa Maria de Bretoña, were perhaps founded by British *laeti* (barbarians settled by treaty to defend a frontier) sent by Maximus to help suppress some of the more turbulent adherents of Priscillianism. Their presence may explain the long resistance put up by the Romans of Gallaecia to the invading barbarian Sueves two decades or so later.[6] Interestingly, Mailoc, 'bishop of the British church', attended a church synod at Bracara (Braga, Portugal) in 572, which might well be a legacy of this settlement, unless he attended from Britain (or more likely perhaps, Brittany).[7]

Maximus turned out to be much more absolute about Priscillianus's form of heresy than the previous régime. Overreacting to the crisis, he threatened to treat almost anyone with ascetic tendencies as a Priscillianist, especially if St Martin, himself no stranger to asceticism, continued to demur. He overturned the warrant against Ithacius, the chief persecutor of Priscillianus who had been forced out of Spain, who then petitioned the emperor. Ithacius found Maximus, as a fellow Iberian, sympathetic to his pleas that the divergent beliefs of Priscillianus be crushed. He was also lobbied for action against the sect because Priscillianus had made converts in Aquitaine, which had mobilised the Gallic bishops against him.

Felix, Britannius's newly appointed successor as Bishop of Trier, was also induced to persuade Maximus to intervene, while powerful voices outside Maximus's sphere of influence like Saints Ambrose and Martin were opposed and formed an anti-Felician faction that wanted the matter dealt with by the Church, without interference from the civil arm, then a fairly revolutionary concept. Constantine I had followed a relatively hands-on approach to the newly emancipated faith from 313. Martin, while in Trier, initially refused to attend Felix's consecration or take communion with the bishops who had been the drivers of Priscillianus's persecution. As Maximus had retorted that he would treat all ascetics like him as heretics if he refused, Martin swallowed his principles and took part.[8] His emollience might have earned a rebuke from fellow ascetics, but it kept channels of communication open between him and the emperor. This resulted in a council of the church being held at Burdigala (Bordeaux) in 384, to which Priscillianus and his followers were summoned.

Meanwhile, in Trier, Ithacius's accusations were heard in court by the praetorian prefect, Flavius Evodius, in 384. The case was interrupted by Martin, who averred that the followers of Priscillianus must be judged by the Bishops at Bordeaux, not by the civil courts. This caused Martin to be accused once again of Priscillianist leanings and the case was sent for re-trial, with the result that Evodius recommended the death penalty for the miscreants. This seems to have arisen not from the nature of Priscillianus's beliefs, but from the wayward bishop being accused of other misdeeds – probably falsely laid – leading Evodius to suspect magical practices and adultery (shades of Virgil). The upshot was that all the accused were convicted, but the implication of the verdicts was such that Maximus decided to re-hear the case yet again, this time presiding in person. In the end, though, he confirmed them and wrote to the new Pope, Siricius, to inform him.[9] The verdicts meant the execution of Priscillianus on a charge of *maleficium* (magical practices) along with four other priests, a lady called Euchrotia, her daughter Procula, and a Spanish senator and author called Latronianus, supposedly for adultery and allied misdemeanours. This caused some consternation in Gaul, as Euchrotia's late husband, Attius Tiro Delphidius, a prominent rhetor and senior ex-official, had been well-connected and a friend of Ausonius, while *his* father, Attius Patera, had been a prominent Gallic grandee too.[10]

Of the others, Instantius, a priest and leading disciple of Priscillianus, was exiled to the Isles of Scilly: 'in Sylinancim insulam, quae ultra Britannias sita est, deportatus', with another upper-crust Spaniard, Tiberianus, from the province of Baetica.[11] Strangely, these sentences, being unprecedentedly harsh, had the effect of uniting Saints Ambrose and Martin, who thereupon made efforts to lighten them, hence Martin being credited with having persuaded Maximus out of taking punitive military action against the dissidents in Spain. Rather than have other followers of Priscillianus killed, Martin successfully counselled that they should merely be expelled from communion with the Catholic Church.[12] Pope Siricius also criticised Maximus for his harshness and went so far as to excommunicate the bishops involved in Priscillian's persecution, despite the fact that he himself was strongly opposed to his followers' practices; this equivocal stance might suggest that the Arian court of Milan was trying to cause mischief for the northern court.

The matter also raised the important problem of what, if any, imperial control could or should be exercised over bishops. The situation of course was thoroughly inconsistent, as the previous pope and Ambrose had both refused to see Priscillianus, thus abdicating their episcopal responsibility (which they now attempted to defend) to the civil power. Not only were Ambrose and Martin now united against the exercise of imperial authority over the church, they were also united in their detestation of Arianism, too.

Yet Arianism was again to reawaken the Kraken of civil interference, the Arianism of Valentinian II's court providing the stimulus a couple of years later. The two saints were, in fact, keen to assert the autonomy of the church unless it suited their purposes to do otherwise, a significant avatar of future disputes.

St Martin was then seen as a divisive figure, but he had impressed through his working (against his will) with a bishop accused of murder in order to free two condemned men.[13] As we have seen, he had also made it his business while in Trier to see to it that Maximus 'set free the imprisoned, restored those who had been exiled and secured the return of property which had been confiscated.'[14] In the longer term, the unrelenting orthodoxy of Maximus probably won over the equally absolutist Martin. They were able to sit down to supper together in 376 and Maximus was able to boast to him that he had large numbers of loyal barbarian troops amongst his continental forces, indicating an amicable relationship.[15]

None of this seems to have reflected particularly badly on Maximus, for the blame mainly fell upon Ithacius and the bishops for recommending so dire a sentence, which was taken up on their imperative by the Praetorian Prefect. Maximus excused himself in a letter to the pope and a generation later St Jerome seems to have considered the matter entirely justified. Prosper of Aquitaine, writing three-quarters of a century later, clearly regarded both Maximus and Theodosius as strong defenders of orthodoxy bestowing benefits on the state through the suppression of heretics and the defeat of barbarians. Normally a strong supporter of what might be viewed as 'legitimate' emperors, he made a notable exception of Magnus Maximus, who, for him, came close to the ideal.[16] Nevertheless, Maximus has gone down in history for being the first Christian ruler to execute someone accused of heresy – a dubious accolade.

A less harsh side of the emperor was displayed in the visit of the saintly old Bishop Illidius, who was summoned from Augusta Nemetum (Clermont) in the hope that he could cure the emperor's daughter from what was identified as demonic possession. Maximus was 'very troubled by the unhappy plight of his daughter' in the words of Gregory of Tours, and his complete faith in the ancient confessor was triumphantly rewarded after a night of prayer. Illidius refused all rewards offered by the relieved and grateful Maximus but obtained instead the commutation of the taxes of Augusta Nemetum.[17]

Despite the difficulties Martin had encountered in his dealing with the emperor, Sulpicius Severus nevertheless left us with an account of Maximus (also described by him as 'in other respects a good man') at supper with him, his wife waited silently on the saint 'like a servant'.[18] It may be that it was on just such an occasion, possibly earlier, that Martin had warned Maximus not to attempt to depose Valentinian, predicting that he would succeed but would later, not long afterwards, be killed.[19]

Under Maximus the Alemanni were put in their place and his good relations with several barbarian leaders ensured peace, during which the economy prospered; he also remitted taxation to some extent and built up good relationships with the senatorial nobility within his *imperium* and beyond. He also streamlined the provincial administration, subdividing one of the provinces of Lugdunum. Ancient authors were however highly critical, the roll-call of calumny itemised in Pacatus's panegyric to Theodosius being particularly lurid, if understandably so, bearing in mind his audience. Yet, as we have seen, opinion was by no means uniformly hostile, Orosius and Sulpicius Severus giving us a much more favourable picture of him.[20]

Uneasy co-existence

Despite his accord with Maximus which secured him recognition, both Theodosius and Valentinian II took precautions against a push south by Maximus. Valentinian's Frankish *magister militum* Bauto fortified the

Alpine passes against a surprise attack. After his return visit to Britain in 384 Maximus seems to have assumed the title Britannicus Maximus, although this could possibly have been actually earned before 383; the interpretation of the relevant but somewhat damaged inscription at Pisaurum is not entirely secure. Nevertheless, it is entirely likely, based on most precedents of the era.[21] Whoever Maximus appointed as *vicarius* of the British provinces, perhaps Desiderius, must have been a success, for there was no further minting of bullion at London thereafter, suggesting he did not need to return and pay *comitatenses*; we can presume all was quiet and that whatever settlement the emperor had made to secure the province was holding.

Meanwhile, Theodosius, having granted Maximus recognition as co-augustus, was having troubles in the east, faced with a serious invasion of Scythians on the Danube and other troubles in the diocese, not to mention Illyricum; the last straw was a tax protest at Antioch which resulted in the deposition of Theodosius's statues and those of his consort, to which he took the gravest exception; only a delegation from the city led by the philosopher Libanius succeeded in calming a vengeful ruler.[22] These, the historian Zosimus claims, were the reasons why Theodosius did not make any immediate effort to depose Maximus.[23] The logistics and possible cost in lives, equipment and goodwill were also a daunting prospect, as the campaign against Magnentius thirty years before had dramatically demonstrated. Setting aside for a moment the supposition that Maximus and Theodosius were in covert collusion, one might feel entitled to suppose that at this juncture the latter saw no necessity to depose his kinsman, even had he wished to. Even the sceptical Matthews agrees: 'Since Gratian's overthrow in 383, Theodosius' attitude to his surviving senior colleague in the west had been cautious but by no means unsympathetic.'[24]

Little else apart from the Priscillianus affair is reported from the historical accounts relating to the period while the court remained at Trier, which argues *ex silentio* for a period of peaceful and settled government. All we do learn is of the passage of envoys as Maximus sought to neutralise the boy emperor Valentinian at Milan so that he could bloodlessly extend his control over Italy, Africa, Pannonia and Illyricum. As we know, St Ambrose had travelled north as early as autumn 383 to try and negotiate some kind of *modus vivendi* with the court at Trier, while at the same time the *comes* Victor had travelled south with a similar proposition, albeit much more to Maximus's advantage. With the Milanese bishop to hand, Maximus urged him to persuade Valentinian I's widow Justina to come to Trier with her son 'as a son to his father', which sounds like an invitation to a traveller to lodge overnight with a certain Transylvanian count. Ambrose, of course, had not the power to do this, even if he had the inclination. The clear implication, if not seemingly fatal to Valentinian II, was that the government of the remainder of the west should be henceforth vested in Maximus. Ambrose, in a parting temporisation, declared that with the onset of winter, passage across the Alps would not be advisable for a youth and his mother.

Unfortunately, we do not know what pitch Victor was making simultaneously in Milan, but it ran no doubt along the same lines. In either case, with winter drawing in, there was little more that could be done until the following spring made communications easier. During the winter months both sides would have garrisoned their side of the Alps, as we know that Valentinian's generals did.[25] A supposed expedition to oust Maximus from Constantinople got no further than Beroea in Thrace; some doubt has been cast upon its real purpose, despite the recorded presence of Valentinian II at Aquileia, on the doorstep of the Balkans, the normal route from east to west. It was presented at Constantinople as having such a purpose, but in reality, the entire thing seems to have been window dressing.[26] Maximus's jittery reaction not long afterwards to a military expedition led by Flavius Bauto to turn back an incursion of Iuthungi in Raetia (mainly part of Switzerland) suggests that he did feel threatened, or alternatively that he was pretending to do so in order perhaps to establish a *casus belli* to move against the court at Milan. Again, Ambrosius temporised, pointing out that had such an incursion got out of hand, originating where it did, it would have been as much a threat to Italy itself as to Maximus's area of authority. Ambrosius's correspondence clearly suggests efforts being made on both sides to reach a mutually acceptable accommodation.[27]

Thereafter, matters settled down, but communications still remained open between the courts of Trier and Milan. In 386, the *comes* Marcellinus, Maximus's brother, travelled to Italy on a diplomatic brief and returned, his mission apparently accomplished. Ambrose had returned to Trier as well. Maximus's aim was probably to exploit the religious antagonisms at Milan between their fiercely Orthodox bishop and Valentinian's dedicatedly Arian mother and her Gothic supporters, who garrisoned the city on her behalf. At one stage, Ambrosius had been barricaded in the *Basilica Portiana* following a disputed move to allow freedom of worship for the Arians, only resolved by the Empress Justina backing down; resentments were certainly simmering there, and no doubt Maximus saw in them a possible opportunity. Also, Ambrosius had form, having come unexpectedly into his see in 374 while trying to subdue a similar outbreak of religious factionalism.

Reuniting the west

A further exchange of envoys took place in 387, when the eastern senator Domninus was sent by Valentinian II to negotiate military assistance from Maximus for an expedition against some barbarians in Pannonia who, again, could have threatened both spheres of influence if left unchecked.[28]

However, we do not hear of any resolution to this proposal, only that according to Zosimus an advance-guard of Maximus's troops was allowed to escort Domninus back, thus allowing Trier intelligence of the preferred route south over the Alpine passes, the guard temporarily being lifted for the passage of the envoy and his large entourage. Thus, late in the year, Maximus took the opportunity offered and moved against the régime in Milan, having gathered 'vast forces of Britons, neighbouring Gauls, Celts and the tribes thereabouts', this force possibly including the *Seguntienses* and new units of Attacotti, duly mediatized through what has been suggested as Maximus's earlier efforts in securing Britain's frontiers.[29]

If the Attacotti really were included in this force, then their presence might suggest the possible source of the 'vast host' of Welsh deployed by the legendary Maximus in his assault on Rome as set out in the *Dream of Maxen Wledig*. Whatever the truth in Zosimus's slightly unlikely tale, there was clearly some kind of skulduggery, as there had probably been when Maximus left Britain for the Continent in 383; yet everything went unbelievably smoothly. Young Victor, the co-augustus, was left nominally in charge in Trier under the care of the two *magistri militum* Nannienus and Quintinus, although the latter's catastrophic punitive expedition against the Franks across the Rhine left Nannienus to cope with the fall-out in Maximus's absence in Italy. The losses and remedial measures necessary to repair the damage this had caused no doubt deprived Maximus of any hope of essential reinforcements from Trier, once the campaign to oust him by Theodosius got under way in earnest.

We have only Zosimus's explanation as to how Maximus, deploying the desire to rid the government of Italy and its surrounding provinces of Arianism as a *casus belli*, managed to fall upon northern Italy with such unsettling speed. This element of surprise ensured that little resistance was encountered and there were few casualties.[30] Needless to say, Valentinian's court was quite unprepared for the sudden onslaught, and decamped with all speed to Aquileia. Unfortunately for them, Maximus's forces were hot on their heels and Justina and her daughters Galla and Valentinian were obliged to take ship, making landfall in Salonica where they threw themselves on the mercy of Theodosius. Here, Theodosius, far from promising an immediate expedition to reinstate the boy emperor, did very little for quite some time, although the lateness of the season was perhaps a factor against immediate action, if not promises of it.

Maximus was now in control of all Valentinian's part of the empire except most of Illyricum. He swiftly had his position re-confirmed by the senate in Rome, which he visited in person, and extended his reforming government to his new dioceses, although his court remained at Milan. Here he assumed his second western consulship for 388, duly recognised in the east, and was pleased to welcome Ambrosius's old friend Symmachus to join in the celebrations and for him to compose and deliver a panegyric before him, which, unfortunately, is lost or destroyed – although that perhaps is no surprise in view of subsequent events.[31] It would have shed much light upon his dispositions in Britain, origins, family and relationship with Theodosius, had it survived.

The fact that this distinguished senator delivered it at all suggests that the western senatorial order generally was in favour of their new emperor, which might explain the alliance one of his daughters seems to have contracted, probably once the dust of Maximus's defeat had settled, with Anicius Probinus, a senior (but then still extremely youthful) member of the impossibly grand and powerful Anician family, as reported by Procopius. That such an alliance must have followed Maximus's deposition is clear from the uniquely distinguished career of the girl's prospective father-in-law, Sex. Claudius Petronius Probus, which reflected his loyal adherence to the cause of Theodosius.[32] That aside, it may be that for nine or ten months governance of the west proceeded smoothly with no reported upheavals, bar the trouble Quintinus had provoked on the Rhine, which appears to have been sorted out satisfactorily.

In consolidating himself within his enlarged polity, we can identify very few of his new appointees. Ragonius Vincentius Celsus may have been made suffect consul, perhaps even when negotiations were still under way between Trier and Milan, and was thereafter installed as *praefectus annonae* at Rome 387-388.[33] As Maximus probably appointed him to both, he may have served him in some other capacity at Trier or in the north-western dioceses before the *drang nach süden*, gained his consulship in recognition, and was felt to be a reliable man to take on the post at Rome, where a shortage of supplies at the wrong moment could so easily tip the balance of events. He was in any case a Roman, coming from a family that had gained their first consulship in the late second century, and had also produced an ordinary consul, in L. Ragonius Quinctianus, under the Tetrarchs in 289.[2][34] Celsus's brother (or cousin) L. Ragonius Venustus may also have had a brief flirtation with service under Maximus.[35] One Sallustius, probably a Gaul, was prefect of the city (of Rome) at the same stage too, being in office when he received a rescript from Theodosius, Valentinian and Arcadius in June 387, but he must have been replaced by Maximus's ally Sextius Rusticus Julianus fairly rapidly after that. A new proconsul of Africa was also appointed, but unfortunately, the name is lost to us.

Maximus may have been confident, even then, that his position was secure. On having received Justina and Valentinian Theodosius seems at first to be struck with inertia. Zosimus says that

> ... arriving at Thessalonica, they sent messengers to the emperor Theodosius, intreating him now at least to revenge the injuries committed against the family of Valentinian. He was astonished at hearing of this, and began to

forget his extravagance, and to lay some restraint on his wild inclination for pleasure. Having held a consultation, it was determined that he, with part of the senate, should proceed to Thessalonica. This journey they performed, and there again consulted what measures to adopt. It was eventually agreed, with the unanimous assent of those present, that Maximus should receive the punishment due to his offences. Their opinion was that such a person was undeserving of life, who had not only murdered Gratian and usurped his dominions, but after having succeeded in his usurpation, had extended his progress, and also deprived the brother of Gratian of the territory which had been allotted to him. Though Theodosius was highly incensed at these actions, yet his natural effeminacy, and the negligent habits of his former life, rendered him unwilling to undertake a war. He therefore pointed out to them the inconveniences which unavoidably arise from civil discord, and that the republic must of necessity receive fatal wounds from both parties. He therefore stated that it would be better to send an embassy first, and that if Maximus would surrender the empire to Valentinian and remain at peace, the empire should be divided between them all as before, but if he should yield to his ambition, they would without delay go to war against him. None of the senate dared to speak in opposition to this, because it appeared to be calculated for the public advantage.

Meanwhile Justina, who was a person of great experience, and knew the best manner of conducting her affairs, knew that Theodosius was naturally inclined to amorousness, introduced into his presence her daughter Galla, who was extremely beautiful. Then, embracing the knees of the emperor, she made supplication with great humility that he would neither suffer the death of Gratian to pass unrevenged, to whom he owed the empire, nor for them to remain neglected and destitute of all hope. As she spoke these words, she shewed him her daughter, who was in tears, lamenting her misfortunes. As Theodosius saw and heard her, Galla's beauty struck his eyes and stole his heart. Yet he prevaricated while meanwhile raising their hopes.

With his lust for Galla daily growing more urgent, he begged Justina her daughter's hand in marriage, his former wife Flaccilla having died two years before. To this demand she replied that she would only agree if he would make war on Maximus to avenge the death of Gratian and restore her son. Resolving, therefore, to obtain her consent, he exerted himself in preparing for war. Being thus impelled by his passion for Galla, he not only conciliated the soldiers by augmenting their pay, but was roused from his negligence in other affairs, resolved to make provision of affairs of state in his coming absence.[36]

While one must bear in mind that this was written almost a century after the event (although deriving much from the mainly lost account of the period by Eunapius) and requires some caution, it does provide a reasonably credible version of events. Yet two matters obtrude. Why, for instance, does Zosimus claim that Theodosius was '*astonished to hear* of the indignities inflicted upon Justina'? Here, one can only conclude that Maximus's descent on Italy and the flight of the Milan court were so precipitate that news had somehow failed to reach Theodosius. The alternative is that he was making a pretence of not knowing, which if true might well strengthen the possibility that he was in cahoots with Maximus all along. Zosimus also accuses Theodosius of being prone to extravagance, natural effeminacy, negligent habits, and an inclination to amorousness.[37] While it has already been said that he had troubles pending and in progress on a number of fronts, including lengthy negotiations with the Persians over a settlement of the eastern frontier, all these matters were placed in the hands of competent officials and commanders, and in the end all were sorted out satisfactorily, not least Petronius Probus's annihilation of the 'Scythians', as Zosimus calls the Greuthungi from the northern bank of the Danube.

One might therefore ask if Zosimus's insights into the emperor's character are a lot closer to the truth than his biographers are prepared to acknowledge.[38] That he was plagued by such personal shortcomings would certainly explain Justina's effective deployment of her daughter's charms before the recently widowed emperor.[39] It is, after all, a train of events pivoting upon one person's human frailty, as played out more than once in history. It cannot be taken as certain that prior to this unexpected turn of events, Theodosius had any intention of deposing Maximus.

There were dynastic considerations which must have followed swiftly upon his being so smitten: by marrying Galla, he would be linking himself to the previous dynasty, although if that had been really important to him previously, one might have expected him to have made overtures to Justina before; if he had, they would have surely been recorded. The young princess's potential charms may indeed have brought about a change in policy, therefore. Furthermore, through Justina, Galla was descended from the Neratii and the Vettii Sabiniani, both old senatorial families, which over two centuries had accumulated much prestige of the kind that neither the Valentinians nor his own family enjoyed.[40] Matthews is highly sceptical of the story of Galla, however, preferring to see Theodosius as a calculating, risk-averse, careful operator playing cat-and-mouse with his rebellious kinsman.[41] Yet to ignore the effect of Galla on the emperor as a motivation for the deposition of Maximus is to ignore the vagaries of human nature; it certainly looks as though such realities were not lost on Justina, who had herself survived being the widow of a usurper.

Meanwhile, the united West seems to have enjoyed a tranquil period. Maximus would have replaced some, but probably not all Valentinian's senior officials and military leaders, his own nominees probably including some of those named above. Yet, with Theodosius suddenly besotted with Galla, things were unlikely to remain peaceful. Turbulence threatened, although Maximus at that stage is unlikely to have lost too much sleep over the prospect of an attempt to dislodge him.

Endgame

With the end of winter came the beginning of the campaigning season, signalling the window of opportunity for Theodosius to set out to eliminate his kinsman, whilom comrade-in-arms and possible former collaborator. It is widely accepted that Theodosius made dispositions for the smooth running of the East while he was away, as Zosimus specifically stated and, if we can accept his word on that then there is no real need to doubt those other aspects of his narrative that have been challenged. There had indeed been problems, for it was claimed that early in 388 Maximus's agents had been at work suborning Germanic levies stationed in Macedonia in the hope of turning their allegiance. Worse, there had been a riot and other demonstrations of loyalty to Maximus in Alexandria, where the church was particularly orthodox and pro-western. This was hardly encouraging. Once set on his course of action Theodosius was obliged to strengthen security through his forces in Egypt to prevent a recurrence, or even the prospect of a second front opening in his rear.

A large force was assembled, much strengthened by Goths, Huns and Alans, and assigned to the command of the former *magister militum* of Valentinian II, the Frank Flavius Richomeres (who had been eastern consul in 384), with Promotus as *magister equitum* and Timasius as *magister peditum*. Also involved was Arbogastes as *magister militum in praesenti* (senior commander in attendance); he was Richomeres' nephew and a newly promoted *magister militum*. In a subordinate role as *comes domesticorum* was another Romanised barbarian, Flavius Stilicho, whom we have already encountered in his supposed oversight of the British diocese a decade later. In order to try and dominate the Adriatic and possibly open up a second front in Maximus's rear, a fleet was fitted out and set sail for Italy.

Maximus, having gained intelligence of Theodosius's preparations, began to prepare as well, moving to Aquileia, where he commissioned Andragathius to command his forces to move to defend the approaches to the Julian Alps; a detachment was also sent to Siscia (Sisak, Croatia) on the Sava in order to block any attempt to advance into Italy from that direction. The main force was sent to Noricum (a province occupying portions of eastern Austria and Slovenia) under Maximus's brother Marcellinus. These constituted a perfectly sensible set of dispositions, and no doubt Maximus was looking to advance his forces from these positions to intercept Theodosius's army as it advanced through the trickier terrain of the middle Balkans. He also detached Andragathius to prepare a fleet to intercept any potential crossing of the Adriatic to Italy – Zosimus claims that this manoeuvre was in fact Justina and Valentinian II crossing back to their 'rightful' place in the west, but their journey was in fact undertaken later, once the situation had stabilised. Instead of finding the enemy fleet, dealing with it and returning to resume overall command, the two passed each other, leaving the barbarian *magister militum* cruising fruitlessly round the Adriatic trying to locate his quarry.

Unfortunately for Maximus, the advance of the eastern forces was conducted at unexpected speed, thanks chiefly to Promotus's barbarian cavalry (who were probably well acquainted with the terrain) and such was Theodosius's progress that Maximus was caught with his preparations incomplete, instead of the reverse. When Promotus's forces arrived at Siscia, defence works were still unfinished, and battle was joined outside the city walls with the defending forces in some disarray, with the result that they were comprehensively defeated. Simultaneously, the *comes* Marcellinus moved south and east to Poetovio (Ptuj, Slovenia) where the two main armies met in another set-piece battle. It turned out that the two sides were pretty evenly matched in this instance. In the end the Theodosian forces won, but at a heavy cost in casualties, for even Theodosius's panegyricist Pacatus had to admit that the defence 'fought with the desperation of gladiators, not yielding an inch but standing their ground until they fell'.[42]

The survivors were either dispersed or (perhaps like the *Seguntienses* and the Attacotti) included amongst the ranks of the winning side. Some of Marcellinus's forces seem to have escaped north-west towards Italy, although he himself appears to have been killed in the engagement. Thus, buoyed by two convincing successes, Theodosius's forces pressed on with all haste, with Maximus falling back on Aquileia where he hoped to make a stand while reinforcements from Italy and Gaul could have time join him. But again, his legendary flair deserted him and his luck ran out. It was probably becoming increasingly obvious that his cause was lost, and that would have caused defections amongst his non-core units and dissension amongst others. Theodosius, meanwhile, approached Emona (Ljubljana, Slovenia), the inhabitants of which bowed to the inevitable and welcomed him, allowing the emperor to advance into Italy.

When Theodosius's van reached Aquileia, again with quite unexpected rapidity, Maximus was apparently attempting to repair the loyalty of his remaining forces by issuing a *largitio*; one source claims he was in the act of so doing when the opposing side entered the city and he was taken prisoner. At that stage, more than just the advance guard must have arrived, for we find Theodosius present, encamped at the third milestone outside the city to the east, and before whom the captured Maximus was brought. His last loyal troops – his Moorish cavalry – had been captured and slaughtered to a man. The defeated emperor may have had some reasonable hope of having his life spared by Theodosius, who enjoyed a reputation for clemency, but the only evidence for this is Pacatus's panegyric, which sought to portray the victorious emperor as a paragon of *clementia*. We are asked to believe that when brought before the eastern emperor Maximus emphasised that he had sought and obtained his acquiescence in his position initially and had only moved into Italy in the interests of orthodoxy and the good of the empire.[43]

In the world of *realpolitik*, it is doubtful whether Theodosius had any option but to kill him. He may have wavered, but whatever he had decided to do was forestalled by his officers, who took Maximus and executed him. It was 28 July, and the event was celebrated annually thereafter, for Procopius (no less) remarks upon it nearly two centuries later. This subsequent celebration of his fall may explain the number of much later insular sources citing his death 'at the third milestone from Aquileia'.[44]

Not that this was the end of the matter. For a start, Andragathius was still fruitlessly cruising the Adriatic. Eventually, news of Maximus's fate reached him, and he did a Robert Maxwell and threw himself overboard. Maximus's original polity, consisting of the four dioceses of Spain, Gaul, Viennensis and Britain, were yet to be neutralised. The *magister militum* Arbogastes was despatched north to deal with the youthful co-emperor at Trier. Whether Victor's protector Nannienus managed to put up a fight and was defeated, or whether he merely slipped away into exile, we are not told by any source. Arbogastes entered Trier to find that Victor had managed to escape, but only for a few days. When he, too, was taken, he was summarily executed despite his tender years, no doubt along with the majority of the people with him, the remnants of his court and *comitatus*.

Aftermath

Having achieved his objective, Theodosius sent Maximus's head on a grand tour of the empire and the pliant senate ordered a *damnatio memoriae*, as evidenced by a number of inscriptions.[45] A good few former acquaintances, precariously placed by the speed of events, rapidly wrote to distance themselves from Maximus. St Ambrose, for instance, was quick to claim that God had been on Theodosius's side all along, thanks to his own intercession, writing to the emperor:

> The very usurper of thy empire I so bound, and so fettered his mind, that although he had the means of flying from you, he shut himself in with all his followers, as if fearing in case any should escape you. His lieutenant [Andragathius] and his forces on the other element, whom I had before

dispersed to prevent their combining to make war on you, I now called together again to render thy victory complete. Thy army, an assemblage of many fierce nations, I caused to keep faith and peace and concord, as if they had been but one nation. And when there was imminent danger that the treacherous plots of the barbarians should penetrate the Alps, I gave you victory within the very barrier of them, that your victory might be without loss. Thus, I enabled you to triumph over your enemy…

Was it not the very reason why Maximus was abandoned, that before he set out on his expedition, hearing that a synagogue had been burnt at Rome, he sent an edict thither, acting as if he were the guardian of public order? Wherefore the Christians said, 'No good awaits this man. That ruler has become as a Jew; we have heard of him as a protector of order, but Christ, who died for sinners, shortly after put him to the proof.' And if this was mere rhetoric, what will be said of actual punishment? Hence he was soon defeated by the Franks and by the Saxons, in Sicily, at Siscia, and in every part of the world.[46]

It is generally agreed that 'in Sicily' is a copyist's error for 'in Siscia'; unless Andragathius had suffered an unrecorded reverse in the Mediterranean, the correction would appear essential to the meaning. The incident of the Synagogue in Rome (Jewish religion having protected status) was the result of a perfectly humane ruling by Maximus, objected to by St Ambrose, revealing an unpleasantly intolerant attitude amongst Roman Christians to the Jews.[47] Ausonius wasn't going to be left out, writing in *Ordo Urbium Nobilium*:

> But enhanced by recent services, you, Aquileia, shall be hailed as ninth among famous cities, an Italian *colonia* facing the mountains of Illyricum, very celebrated for your walls and harbour. But what stands out more is that in these last days Maximus, a merchant posing as a gentleman, chose you to receive belated expiation when the five-year term was completed. Happy are you, joyful spectator of so great a triumph, who have punished with Ausonian arms the Rutupian brigand.[48]

The belief seems to emerge that part of the British garrison was taken to the Continent when Maximus seized power, but (mainly later) accounts differ. They say that he virtually denuded the diocese of men, but as we have seen, this seems highly unlikely in view of his military experience. However, it is likely that in his time in Britain he had radically overhauled the island's defences, replacing regular troops with levies or settlers controlled by native grandees, supervised by senior officials responsible to the *vicarius* in the north, Wales and possibly the West Country, securing these mainly coastal frontiers by treaty-like arrangements, and allowing him to reduce the establishment of the diocese without risking its security. In Chapter 3 it was noted that in setting up such arrangements – which we shall largely attempt to expand upon from the patchy, late and mainly unsupported insular evidence in Part II – he also withdrew garrisons from inland military infrastructure but built or strengthened others in the coastal areas. We do not know what elements of his former British-stationed troops he employed when he advanced south to dethrone Valentinian II, or what elements of them were deployed in the attempt to block Theodosius's campaign to oust him. The stationing, as recorded in the *Notitia Dignitatum,* of the *Seguntienses* in Illyricum might suggest that some were present at Poetovio or Siscia, although as we have also seen, these might just as well have been transferred to south-east Europe at an earlier time. Nevertheless, if this was a contingent from North Wales, then it might explain the semi-legendary sources' insistence on Maximus's withdrawal of troops, while explaining the focus of the *Dream of Maxen Wledig* on Segontium as a pivotal location in its romantic version of Maximus's legend. The evidence for the re-settlement of troops in Armorica after 388 is perilously thin on the ground, and we only have very late or legendary attestation for that, too. Yet the third milestone from Aquileia seems uncommonly well known to later and insular sources (Procopius's note about the subsequent celebration of the events of 27 August 388 notwithstanding), pointing to oral 'history' handed down from those tumultuous events and picked up by later chroniclers, in however garbled a form.

Not that this swift victory was without its consequent problems. Theodosius had to ensure that the western provinces would remain loyal to him, having spent between eighteen months and five years (or more) loyal to Maximus. This could only be realistically achieved by the judicious exercise of clemency, especially where the Spanish, Gallic and British élites were concerned, who had backed him *ab initio*. People like Symmachus (who at first had thoughts of seeking sanctuary in a church – and him a convinced pagan!) were without doubt feeling apprehensive, even those who had not delivered resounding panegyrics in honour of the late ruler. Another problem for Theodosius, if contemplating using the stick rather than the carrot, was that apart from the elimination of Gratian, Maximus had ruled effectively and without uncalled-for harshness. Making an example of leading players would certainly not reap any rewards. Thus, most of Maximus's appointees were allowed to retire honourably or just quietly vanish like Evodius ('one of the most righteous men that ever lived' according to St Martin, *l'affaire* Priscillian notwithstanding).[49] Those who were deemed to have remained loyal to the ousted Valentinian were mostly reinstated. His *clementia* he proclaimed in the senate following his triumphal visit to the ancient capital of the empire the following summer; the senators responded with repeated acclamations, as well they might, having experienced a close shave. Their *damnatio memoriae* is expressed in the total lack of surviving sculptural images of the deposed emperor.[50] They had to listen to Pacatus's panegyric, which went out of its way to belittle Maximus's qualities and exaggerate those of his nemesis, excusing Gallic enthusiasm for him as having arisen in the belief that he had enjoyed Theodosius's support (which he clearly had). Panegyrics have been condemned as 'linguistic bankruptcy'. Drinkwater observed that 'praisers, praised and audiences were all aware that what was being said was rarely honest...'[51] The emperor also paid visits to the houses of a number of leading members of the senate in his efforts to build bridges. Yet in celebrating a triumph on 13 June 389, rather than an *adventus*, as some of his immediate predecessors had done, the emperor committed a solecism (as in a 'breach of good manners'), for such things were only, by the precedent of centuries, to be celebrated over foreign or barbarian foes, not over the defeat of a Roman rival in a civil war. There is the suspicion that once the relief at being effectively pardoned had worn off, the senate may have remembered this with the strongest disapproval. To their refined and largely patrician outlook it must have smacked of failing to tip the staff at the end of a house party, or the Roman equivalent: the fellow was obviously not top drawer.

Maximus's family

Nevertheless, Theodosius's treatment of Maximus family was a model of restraint, compared, say, with the wholesale elimination of the family of Gallienus 113 years before, the killing of poor Victor aside.[52] Other senior kin, like Marcellinus, probably died in the Poetovio campaign. Had there been other sons, things might have been different but, later insular traditions aside, it is probable that Victor was the only surviving son. The daughters and Maximus's mother, as we learn from Pacatus, were taken in by members of the Imperial family.[53] We also hear little of an empress, which we would have expected to have done had he had a widow, yet Sulpicius Severus, without naming her, describes her as a pious woman who, as mentioned earlier, waited silently upon St Martin while her husband entertained him to supper, and enjoyed spiritual discourse with him at Trier. The absence of coins or inscriptions seem anomalous, although lack of mention of her on the part of Pacatus suggests she may have died before Aquileia (unless she was killed with her husband, which no source even suggests).

Maximus's mother was alive (also not named, nor, it would seem, made Augusta, as often was the case) as were certainly one, perhaps two or more daughters. Not only are they mentioned by St Ambrose (but again, unfortunately not by name) as being entrusted to a relation of Theodosius after the death of Maximus, but we have seen that one at least was apparently cured by St Illidius before 385.[54] The suggestion that a daughter made a glittering senatorial marriage is to some extent confirmed by a remark of the Byzantine historian Procopius, who mentioned *en passant* that the unfortunate successor to Valentinian III, the Anician Petronius Maximus (reigned only from 17 March to 31 May 455) was a descendant of Magnus Maximus.[55] An otherwise persuasive argument for this, illustrated by a *stemma* and proposed by Mommaerts and Kelly, has too many generations between Magnus Maximus and Petronius Maximus, who was born *c.* 390. The former's daughter must have been born *c.* 368 and cannot have married much before 385 or 386 (and probably somewhat after 388, her husband Probinus being very young), which would make her the mother, not the grandmother, of Petronius Maximus. Mommaerts and Kelly suppose Maximus's daughter might have married an Ennodius and that a resulting daughter *then* married Probinus, the emperor's father, interposing an extra generation which requires too much to have happened in too short a time.[56] In genealogical terms, however, it leads to the same result, that Petronius Maximus was in all probability Maximus's grandson; why else introduce the name Maximus into a family that had not previously used it but which revived it again thereafter?

This possible outcome has an added poignancy insofar as in 455 this putative grandson, after a most distinguished career which would not have shamed one of the heroes of the middle republic, organised the deposition and murder of Valentinian III, the grandson of his grandfather's nemesis. One is tempted to speculate that Petronius Maximus might well have had this slight at the forefront of his mind when he hatched his plot, brought about allegedly to avenge the murder of the successful marshal Aëtius at the hands of Valentinian III. None of the chroniclers record it – but human nature being what it is, the possibility would seem to be one worth bearing in mind.[57]

Maximus's anonymous wife, who is mentioned in the context of St Martin's visit to Trier, must have been a Christian of sufficient conviction and knowledge to engage him meaningfully in conversation.[58] If she felt able without discomfort to help serve him at supper, then she was probably of modest disposition and elevated social origin. Knight suggests this account may have inspired the later legends of Maxen Wledig and Helen of the Hosts.[59] She is, however, never named, but only in later insular tradition as a British woman (or a Roman woman living in Britain) called Helena, which commentators dismiss as a double for St Helena, the mother of Constantine I. Yet, if we remember that the emperor spent as much as a couple of years in Britain in 367-369, when he was probably in his late 20s, and thus at a most suitable age to be wed, his marriage to a British resident is not quite as unlikely as it might seem and, of course, the name of the Augusta Helena was by then sufficiently revered as to have inspired the nomenclature of numerous female infants.[60] And while the events of Maximus's reign, not to mention those of his early fifth-century successor Constantine III, have highlighted the enthusiasm with which the Spanish and Gallic nobility espoused their cause, we hear little or nothing of the Romano-British aristocracy, who would have been just as powerful in their sphere and just as well-connected, with ties across the Channel. Indeed, if anything emerges from the analysis in Part II, it is that there would seem to be persuasive circumstantial evidence (albeit of a late and largely unreliable kind) for the existence of several such families in lowland Britain. Unfortunately, whether insular tradition was correct in so naming Maximus's empress, we shall, short of a miracle, never know.

The striking late Roman silver gilt *piperatorium* (pepper/spice pot) discovered amongst the Hoxne treasure unearthed in Suffolk in 1992, and which is now on display in Room 49 of the British Museum, is modelled as the upper half of a late Roman empress, princess or noblewoman. The date is around 385/405, and she is shown richly attired, pointing to a scroll in her left hand and wearing a jewelled head-dress or diadem. Whoever Maximus's wife was, this delightful object gives us a splendid general idea of what she would have looked like. The image itself and its treatment bears a close affinity with a group of early fifth-century steelyard weights, which are also thought to depict empresses, and which wear a diadem of exactly the same type.[61] If insular tradition, as transmitted through the centuries to the writer of the *Breudwyt Maxen Wledig*, was sufficiently admiring of the empress as of her spouse, then perhaps she *was* called Helen. If so, it is doubly unfortunate that she gets so intermixed with St Helena in the Triads and genealogies.

Constantinople, the circus: contemporary relief showing Theodosius and his court receiving tribute. (Griffindor/Wikimedia Commons)

5

Aftermath

Those that fail to learn from history...

If Theodosius was hoping to return to his pregnant new wife in Constantinople once he had eliminated Maximus, he was to be disappointed. Leaving a restored Valentinian II, now aged nineteen, as western emperor (his scheming mother now recently and conveniently deceased) with only the newly appointed *magister utriusque militum* Arbogastes to guide him, was to invite an inevitable repetition of previous events, those of five years before. Theodosius was obliged to remain in Italy for quite some time in order to oversee the settlement and to ensure that any anticipated pitfalls could be allowed for. In the end it was only a serious spat between his new wife and her elder stepson Arcadius that made his return to the eastern capital essential, in spring 391. He thus installed Valentinian II and his court at Trier under the tutelage of Arbogastes, through whom Theodosius expected to be able to exercise power in the western empire as well as the east. The late Empress Justina's entreaties had been met, as far as he was concerned, although longer-term prospects, with the possibility of Valentinian marrying and having heirs, and his own two surviving sons being, or about to become, co-augusti, the potential for conflict looked high. And indeed, as Valentinian matured, disagreements between him and Arbogastes increased alarmingly.

The barbarian marshal successfully campaigned against some of his own kin on the Rhine, and restored control over Colonia (Cologne) and its *pagus*.[1] A year later, Arbogastes hotly and rather publicly declined a direct order from his emperor and within days Valentinian was dead. It was 15 May 392, and the young ruler was almost 21; officially it was suicide, but others had their doubts.[2] If Theodosius had been hoping that Maximus would deal with Valentinian for him, to secure 'their' dynasty, now the problem would have to be dealt with by other means: hence surely, the doubts of the cynics.

Arbogastes attempted to continue as *magister militum* at Trier as the appointee of Theodosius, but the latter must have had his suspicions, too, for reaction to events in Constantinople had been generally hostile, although Theodosius must have realised that the death of his brother-in-law would give his elder son and co-emperor a clear run at power when the time came.

There was a cleavage between the two courts, exacerbated by Arbogastes' paganism in the face of the increasing tempo of the imposition of orthodoxy on Theodosius's part. The Frankish *generalissimo* decided to take matters into his own hands. Arbogastes realised that as a barbarian he could never rule on his own account, and the hostile reaction to events in the west at Constantinople also brought him to the conclusion that he needed an emperor of his own choice through whom he could exercise power. In August, therefore, he selected a man of senatorial rank, the *magister scrinii* (head of the civil service) Eugenius, to assume the role. His place of origin is unknown, but he had originally been a teacher of rhetoric, had risen high enough to become a *vir clarissimus* by 385 under Valentinian II and Magnus Maximus, and had reached his final bureaucratic post in 390.[3] There remains always the possibility that he had gained advancement under Maximus himself (he could even have been a Gaul, Briton or a Spaniard), but had perhaps not been sufficiently eminent to attract repercussions in the late summer of 388.

On elevation on 22 August 392, Eugenius received the tribunician and proconsular power, presumably from the senate itself, and served an immediate suffect consulship, recognized in the west but not in the east. Apart from his being middle-aged, nothing more is known about him, except that he had a wife (presumably never recognized as Augusta) and children. They were spared at his demise, mainly through the intercession of the tireless St Ambrose. The new emperor adopted a policy of toleration towards paganism and as the creature of an Arian *generalissimo*, a blind eye was turned there, too (which Ambrose might well have baulked at). The temples were all re-opened, making him popular with the majority of the senatorial aristocracy, who were mainly still pagan, all of which hardened Theodosius against the old cults, again suppressed with vigour after he had regained control of the west. Eugenius twice sought recognition from Theodosius, and indeed so proclaimed himself according to his coin issues, although, unlike Maximus, no form of recognition appears to have followed.[4]

Again, history seemingly repeated itself; Theodosius made no immediate effort to crush Eugenius for almost two years, although he elevated his younger son, Honorius to the rank of Augustus on 10 January 393 in a partial response. Arbogastes had been at first assiduous in attempting to reconcile Theodosius to the situation, but the controlling Praetorian Prefect of the East, Rufinus, blocked his messages from reaching the emperor. Once again, uncannily, it was Theodosius's empress who believed that her half-brother had been killed and like her mother before her, entreated the emperor to intervene. Eventually, the emperor gathered together a substantial expeditionary force and once again advanced as rapidly as possible through the Balkans. The two armies met in battle on the river Frigidus ('The Cold') in today's western Slovenia, not so very far from Aquileia, and a furious battle was fought over 5 and 6 September 394.[5] To Theodosius, the whole episode must have felt like a recurring nightmare, albeit one of his own making. Eugenius and Arbogastes both escaped the carnage, only for the former to be swiftly captured and summarily executed at the feet of the victorious emperor on the 6th. Arbogastes was hunted down and killed the following day. As with the battle of Mursa against Magnentius, it was extremely hard-fought and bloody, with a high casualty rate on both sides, so much so that it caused an acute manpower shortage in the imperial armies just when strong forces were going to be desperately needed. As with Maximus, it took Theodosius many months to prepare to move, once again, to eradicate this treacherous western marshal and his puppet.

Considering Theodosius's familial ties with the north-western dioceses, one might wonder why he never once visited Trier and the Rhine frontier throughout his reign; his neglect of Gaul, the frontier, Britain and Spain was, as these events so dramatically illuminated, the Achilles heel of his rule, and this neglect, having been perceived as a contributary cause of Maximus's elevation, was so again with Eugenius, and was be to once more in the near future under his younger son.

A peaceful island

We hear little of Britain for almost a decade following Maximus's downfall, a decade in which Arbogastes, in the renewed absence of Theodosius, had elevated Eugenius to the purple, as a result of which both died in 394. They were followed by Theodosius less than a year later. Yet to appreciate the elements of the story of Magnus Maximus which we shall encounter in Part II, as the story of Maximus mutates into British legend, some account needs to be given of the aftermath of his fall in Britain and northern Europe.

The fall of Eugenius, followed by the death just over four months later of Theodosius himself on 17 January 395, left another power vacuum, in which the entire empire was divided between his sons, two youths aged eighteen (Arcadius in the East) and eleven (Honorius in the West) under the guidance of military strongmen. In the case of the West, it was the half-Vandal *magister militum* Flavius Stilicho.[6] Stilicho was a man of ability and energy. He was also canny enough to marry into the dynasty he served, his wife Serena being the daughter of Honorius, the younger brother of Theodosius and his wife Maria. Nor did he stop there, for the alliance was further strengthened by the marshal's daughter Maria later marrying the emperor Honorius himself.[7]

While it has been suggested that Arbogastes, on Eugenius's behalf, took troops from Britain when they knew there was to be a fight to the death with Theodosius in 394, there is some evidence that having defeated Arbogastes and following Theodosius' death Stilicho was obliged to turn his attention to Britain in any case, in order to sort out some kind of disturbance there, quite possibly one set off by the perception that in fighting Theodosius, the western administration's attentions were damagingly engaged elsewhere. This may, in reality, have involved only the replacement of withdrawn units, rather than punitive action, for the evidence comes from another panegyric and is likely to have been exaggerated in order to enhance the qualities of the subject – Stilicho. Nor does the archaeology have much to say in this regard. Much of what has been attributed to Stilicho has been here adjudged as more likely attributable to Maximus. Yet Stilicho (or his Praetorian Prefect of Gaul) is thought to have withdrawn from the diocese a legion, presumably (unless the word legion is just a loose term for a large unit of soldiers) the VIth *Victrix*, which fails to appear in the British diocesan establishment in the slightly later *Notitia Dignitatum*; this perhaps to help defend Italy against the Goths. The panegyric to Stilicho early in 400 on his second consulship, delivered by the Egyptian senator and poet Claudius Claudianus, is surely the usual hyperbole:

> Next Britain, clothed in [the skin of] a Caledonian beast, her cheeks tattooed, her sky-blue cloak, rivalling Ocean's tide, trailing to her feet: Stilicho protected me too, perishing at the hands of the neighbouring peoples when the Scot aroused all Hibernia and the sea foamed with hostile oarsmen. The effect of his measures was that I did not need to fear Scottish spears, or tremble at the Pict, or watch on all coasts for the Saxon who would come with the dangerous winds.[8]

This passage gives the *impression* of the suppression of an incursion of Picts and 'all Hibernia', but does not actually say so at all, only that the general 'protected' Britain: some kind of re-ordering and possibly strengthening seems to be indicated. The withdrawn legion, and the one remaining (the XXth), would by this date number only about twelve hundred men, compared with the 5,500 or so of earlier times. They had been employed as frontier troops throughout most of the fourth century. Whatever Stilicho did in the late 390s, the force with which he defeated the marauding Visigothic leader Alaric at the battle of Pollentia in 402 also allegedly included 'a legion stationed among the far-off Britons, which reins in the fierce Scot and scans the strange pattern upon the dying Pict'[9] – presumably, the withdrawn VIth.

Stilicho is now believed to have been the man who created the permanent post of *Comes Britanniarum,* a position which previous authors have been tempted to ascribe to Magnus Maximus on his appointment to Britain.[10]

This left the diocese with a *vicarius* and military affairs in the hands of three senior commanders, for in addition to Stilicho's new *comes* there remained the *dux Britanniarum* and the *comes littoris Saxonici*. In 392, therefore, Eugenius seems to have had British support. British soldiers may either have been killed in action at the Battle of the Frigidus when Theodosius defeated Eugenius or were absorbed into Theodosius's army. If so, they probably did not return to Britain either. The foundation of a British field army under Stilicho's *comes Britanniarum* was probably a consequence of this gap in insular manpower, which the appointment helped to remedy. Indeed, there is nothing in the panegyric to suggest Stilicho himself even went to Britain. The first *comes Britanniarum* was probably his appointee, just as the elder Theodosius had been in 367 and Magnus Maximus himself in 379. Whether he subsequently withdrew this field army – 402 has been suggested as a likely date – is by no means established.[11] Subsequent events, however, clearly establish that there were still regular units stationed in Britain.

Crisis and a third Gallic empire

Stilicho's dispositions in the 390s may not have added to or made much difference to the arrangements left in place by Maximus; the references are too hazy and unspecific. Any minor action affecting the diocese of Britain would have been fuel enough for the panegyricist seeking flattering material. Thus, it might be reasonable to say that from Maximus's visit to Britain in 384 until a few years into the fifth century, Britain was mainly peaceful, despite the apparent withdrawal of a 'legion' by the Vandal *magister militum*.

Yet, in the autumn of 406, all this seems to have changed. The reduction of troops on the Rhine frontier by Stilicho to aid his campaign against the Goths in the south-east, and a demand from him to the authorities in Britain to contribute detachments to reinforce his planned efforts against the Eastern imperial government, seem to have led to the acclamation in Britain of one Marcus. Here we seem to see the same pattern of events which led to the elevation of Maximus and Eugenius. Birley wrote that it was reasonable to suppose that this man was one of the three senior Roman commanders in Britain: the *Comes Britanniarum* (C-in-C of the British provinces), the *Comes Litoris Saxonici* (Count of the Saxon Shore) or the *Dux Britanniarum* (GOC northern Britain) and points out that Sheppard Frere considered that he was in fact holder of the first of these positions.[12] The sources for Marcus are slender; Sozomen wrote: 'For first the soldiers in Britain, having mutinied, named Marcus *tyrannus*, and after him Gratianus, having deposed Marcus; but ... he too was murdered by them after no more than four months had gone by.'[13]

Polemius Silvius has a much more garbled comment about contemporary usurpations: 'Honorius, under whom Gratianus and Constantinus, and

Attalus twice, Maximus and Servatus, Marcus, Magnus and Maximus, Jovinus, Sebastianus, and Victor were usurpers.'[14] Zosimus, meanwhile, gets the order of events confused:

> In the time before this, when Arcadius and Probus were holding their consular office [406], the Vandals, joining forces with the Suebi and Alani, crossing these places [the Alpine passes], having caused harm to the transalpine peoples and carried out much slaughter, became objects of fear to the armies in the Britains also, and compelled them, in case the invaders might turn against them too, to hold a rushed election of *tyranni*, I mean Marcus and Gratianus.[15]

There were three British usurpers then, starting with the most ephemeral, Marcus and Gratianus, who were followed by the much more notable Constantine III. To arrive at the exact temporal sequence of events, we have to work back from a generally accepted fact: that the Emperor Honorius learned that the third of the trio had arrived in Gaul early in March 407.[16] From this we may reasonably deduce that he was elevated to the purple the previous month or a little before, say, January or February 407. Sozomen tells us that Gratian, his predecessor, reigned 'no more than' four months, putting his elevation at September or October 406. There is no indication when Marcus was made emperor, therefore, but the presumption is that his time in the sun was brief, which seems likely. Had he remained in the saddle for more than a month or so, he would surely have caught the attention of a chronicler or even have issued coins (although Gratian lasted four months without apparently doing so).[17] If this chronology can be accepted, the catalyst for the rebellion in Britain must have been the defeat of the barbarian general Radagaisus at Faesulae (Fiesole) in spring 406 and the unsettling and chaotic arrival of his defeated army in Gaul that summer, making summer 406 the likely time of Marcus's elevation. One ancient source says of the third of this sequence of three imperial claimants, 'They appear to have chosen Constantine thinking that, as he had this name, he would firmly master the imperial power, since it was for a reason such as this that they appear to have chosen the others for usurpation as well.'[18]

This statement almost sounds like a modern conspiracy theory but might suggest that the first usurper's name reminded them of Marcus Aurelius, an emperor well remembered as a doughty defeater of barbarian attacks. This seems unlikely, and perhaps influenced by the nomenclature of his supplanters; somehow, it is difficult to envisage the officers of the time being so naïve as to credit such a notion. It is probably better explained as the musings of a chronicler, short of firm information, over-thinking the episode. In any case, Marcus's name was most likely a *cognomen* rather than a *praenomen*, as was more usual in this period.[19] If any coins were minted in London, they have failed to emerge. For all the prestige Marcus may have borne on his elevation, it clearly evaporated fairly quickly. He was soon deposed, killed and, in the immediate aftermath, the soldiers, having made their choice of a suitable successor, 'led Gratianus into their midst and placing the purple robe and crown on him escorted him as their emperor'.[20]

One has to doubt, too, whether Gratian was chosen on the strength of the name of the late emperor, who was hardly held in particularly high esteem, in death as in life. Although for all his faults, had not Gratian's generals defeated and virtually annihilated a mass of German tribesmen who had similarly crossed the Rhine in 378? This second claimant to imperial power is described by Orosius as *municeps eiusdem insulae* (a civilian leader or citizen of that same island).[21] From this we might reasonably suppose that he was of Roman-British stock and perhaps held sway in London, although it has also been suggested that the use of *municeps* is merely a formula for saying that he was a native of Britain, rather than a senior official in the diocese or one of the provinces *en poste*.[22] As we have absolutely no other information, it may be that, as with other instances of 'regime change' – Allectus springs to mind – he may have been appointed to a senior post by Marcus, perhaps as a *comes* or a fiscal bureaucrat like the *comes sacrarum largitionum*, from which dizzy eminence he may have been encouraged, like Allectus, to replace his benefactor.

So the ancient authors tell us of these *tyranni*, or usurpers. The second was probably home-grown, rather than the usual cosmopolitan military man serving *en poste*. That being so, perhaps the third recipient of the soldiers' enthusiasm might also have been British, especially as his name and that of one of his chief lieutenants, Gerontius, both occur associated in later British sources, a consideration to be set aside until part II, where an unreliable reference suggests that Constantine's wife was of grand Gallic extraction, too. British or not, that Constantine was chosen because of his name is generally accepted, although it is difficult to credit that the officers and cadres responsible for his elevation would seriously have believed in the magic of a name in this way. What they surely required would have been someone who looked like getting the job done. Yet Britain did have some resonance where the great Constantine is concerned and the fact that the usurper's sons were called Constans and Julianus does suggest that rather than undertaking a vicarious re-naming of them in 407, he had felt, as a father, some empathy with Constantine the Great from having had his name bestowed upon him and had accordingly and perfectly reasonably named his sons after two of the great emperor's family at birth.[23] He assumed a *praenomen* and *gentilicium* as part of his imperial style – Flavius Claudius – to burnish his image.

The single source claiming that Constantine was said to have been *infima militia* ('of the meanest soldiery') does not seem at all credible.[24]

His entire subsequent career suggests that he was probably an experienced officer, which would strengthen the case for his having engineered his own acclamation as imperial claimant. He may have *begun* his career in the ranks, leaving aside quasi-legendary suggestions that his wife was a noble Gaul, which suggests otherwise. Senior officers who had risen from the ranks were relatively common, for the empire was reasonably fluid socially, at least in its upper echelons. Either way, by the time of his elevation, he was probably fairly senior in the island from well before the crisis in some significant military capacity, and was perhaps the beneficiary of promotion, perhaps to *comes Britanniarum* by Marcus as his replacement. Orosius is the only source to allege low birth – the other sources make no comment on his origins. Procopius (who wrote over a century later) calls Constantine 'a not undistinguished man'.[25]

Marcus then, deposed and killed 'because he did not agree with the soldiers' character', presumably failed to fulfil military expectations – how, is unclear; Gratian, likewise. These upheavals in Britain were caused, we suppose, by the reduction of the Rhine garrison and the arrival of Vandals and Sueves, formerly under the command of Radagaisus, running amok in Gaul and, as the British garrison seems to have thought, threatening the diocese. That threat expanded most dramatically on 31 December 406, on which day the freezing of the Rhine provided an opportunity for those Germanic tribes settled on the east side of that river to grab the opportunity to cross en masse into the diocese of Gaul and link up with the marauders already there. Whether this was an opportunity for which they had planned, or sheer opportunism, or whether indeed the leaders of the various peoples consciously colluded, is not really known. The effectiveness of it would seem though, with hindsight, to betoken some kind of co-ordination in the event of the river freezing, a phenomenon to which both sides were no doubt used. Nevertheless, it seems to have caught the military commanders at Colonia Agrippinensium (Cologne) and Trier completely unawares and before long the Franks, Burgundians and Alans had broken out of the frontier zone and were beginning to rampage across the Gallic provinces.

The aim of these peoples was, like the Visigothic leader Alaric's, to settle within the empire, for they were being impelled by the Huns and others crowding from the east, which meant that the numbers involved were huge, even if the fighting strength of each separate barbarian nation was limited. The situation closely resembled the incursion of 256, and the reach of the penetration – right down to the Gates of Hercules – was similar. In 256, Gallienus had been able to deal with it to a large extent, but in the medium term the turmoil, insecurity and discontent it bred had the same result as in Britain a century and a half later. In 259 Postumus had been acclaimed and the first Gallic Empire was born, lasting some 14 years. Likewise, in 407 the central government of Honorius – in reality, Stilicho – had its hands full elsewhere, and was not in a position to intervene immediately. The reaction, therefore, was similar but events moved faster, much faster.

The impetus behind the elevation of the third usurper originating from Britain, Constantine III, may have been in response to this threat.[26] The fact was that with barbarians overwhelming the border provinces of the two Germanies and Belgica, there was every chance that Britain would indeed be cut off, or threatened by barbarian incursions by sea from the mouth of the Rhine. As Britain was to a large extent economically dependent on the export of vast quantities of grain and meat (as *annona*) to feed the Rhine garrison, the prospect of the collapse of this trade would have been extremely worrying as it would have threatened widespread interests on the island.[27] Furthermore, potential commanders (or usurpers[28]) amongst the senior officers on the Rhine may have been discredited, overwhelmed or killed in the incursion, leaving their British colleagues as the only viable alternatives to lead a clean-up.

It is a measure of the assimilation of Britain within the empire that the prospect of insular independence was the last thing anyone appears to have desired or expected, Carausius notwithstanding. If this was so, then the response of Gratian might well have been to make an appeal to the Praetorian Prefect of Gaul, or to Stilicho, for advice or support. When such was not forthcoming, the garrison probably panicked, justifiably feeling far more under threat than six months before, especially with a civilian at the helm. The reasoning may have been that a military man was urgently required. In these circumstances, one would not have been impelled to raise an emperor up merely on the resonance of his name; a commander of proven competence was wanted and as the record unequivocally shows, that man was Constantine III. Therefore Gratian, after a reign of little more than four months, paid for his efforts with his life.[29] No wonder that St Jerome, eight years later was able to write:'*Britannia, fertilis provincia tyrannorum*' (Britain, a province fertile in usurpers).[30] Add in subsequent events, and one can see what he meant.

Having been acclaimed, Constantine and his advisers probably felt that the best way of keeping the diocese safe was to take the initiative and fight the fire at source, or as close the source as could be reached. He crossed the Channel without delay, presumably supported by the *comes Britanniarum*'s field army acting as his *comitatus*, with the laudable intention of rectifying the situation. If the frontier settlement in Britain postulated above as having been accomplished by Maximus still held, he presumably felt that his back was well protected. A quick success would therefore be perceived as having kept the British provinces safe. But quick success eluded Constantine. For roughly four years the north-western dioceses were governed by him and his elder son, followed by a series of much more ephemeral emperors who desperately tried to stem the chaos while at the same time having to cope with rivals. There was a general lack of co-ordinated action, resulting in disagreements and fissiparous tendencies in the body politic. And while it could be argued that both Carausius and Magnus Maximus founded Gallic empires in the mode of Postumus, in reality the former's never included the whole of Gaul, despite the wide dissemination of his coinage, let alone Spain and the Rhineland, while Maximus's *imperium* was not one in the end content to remain lodged within the north-west. In 407, the impression given is that these fire-fighting imperial claimants were content by and large to remain within the north-west provinces, where they had their hands very full.

The new British-proclaimed emperor must have been born not later than 360, in view of the fact that he had a mature elder son. He was apparently a monk and it has been suggested that he may have been a follower of the rule of St Martin, then still very highly regarded.[31] If so, it would seem likely that Constantine's family were anything but lowly as Orosius alleged, for Gallic abbeys like Lérins and Martin's foundation at Tours were packed with upper class young men.[32] However, Gregory of Tours (quoting Renatus Profuturus Frigeridus), tells us that the elder son, Constans was married with children by 410, three years later, which fact may cut across the entire story that he had taken the tonsure – unless he had relinquished his celibate life some time before his father's elevation.[33] Constantine himself may even, therefore, have cut his teeth as a tribune under Magnus Maximus in Britain and in Gaul, afterwards serving in a variety of theatres in the wider empire. Although the sources imply that Constantine completely divested the diocese of troops, it seems likely (supported by archaeology) that, as with Magnus Maximus, he left at least the frontier settlement in place – so Hadrian's Wall, Wales, the south-west and probably the Saxon Shore forts remained manned if, on a reduced basis using locally recruited militias.[34]

Once on mainland Europe, Constantine's dispositions included the appointment of joint *magistri militum*, Justinianus and the Frankish Nebiogastes (one cannot imagine either serving willingly under a former common soldier). Justinianus is just possibly to be identified with the *praepositus* in charge of a North Sea signal tower under Maximus; that he was related to a future Bishop of Tours of the same name is even more likely. If this connection was to be accepted, then it may strengthen the possibility that Constantine's elder son *had* been a monk at Tours, if only for a time.[35] Constantine appointed them on his acclamation, sending them across the Channel in advance to take command of what remained of the Gallic army, the main western army directed by Stilicho being then enmeshed with efforts to placate the Goth, Alaric.[36] In the event, they had to deal not only with the barbarians roaming around northern and western Gaul but attempts by Honorius to neutralise this upstart on his northern flank. A letter of St Jerome confirms that Constantine successfully stabilised the Rhine frontier and contained the Vandals and others until at least mid-409, although it seems that the intruders had definitely broken out by that year's end.[37] Had the government of the western emperor Honorius in Ravenna realised that Constantine's presence was more likely to help stem the barbarian incursion than hinder it and had ignored him, or recognised him immediately, more might have been achieved. Instead, within a few months, Honorius's general Sarus had defeated and killed Justinianus and later dispatched Nebiogastes too, after tricking him into a parley, instead of allowing them to battle the barbarians.[38]

We are even less well informed about the underpinning of Constantine's régime than Postumus's a century and a half before: did he call a council or senate of Gallic, British and Hispanic grandees? Did he nominate consuls and so forth? The course of events probably suggests that some kind of assembly of the great and good was constituted, but no consuls have ever been identified except for that of Constantine himself; it may be that he merely ruled advised by an enlarged *consilium,* or even something like the *senatus* set up by Hispano-Roman grandees in Cantabria in the later sixth century.[39] In 409, the third consulship of eastern emperor Theodosius II was not recognised, and Constantine himself held his first *in lieu.* He certainly made changes within the church in Gaul, too, by appointing at least two bishops, both with links to Tours and thus to St Martin.[40] No doubt alongside having a delegation of leading men from Britain to join his *consilium,* he must have kept the British diocese's administrators, military commanders and provincial governors in office, or replaced them with appointees of his own. If we accept that Magnus Maximus used local leaders to administer and command local levies in the west, north-west and north, that system continued to function successfully – thus far.

Meanwhile, towards the end of 407, Constantine's unfortunate general Justinian had been replaced by another Frank, Edobichus, and Nebiogastes by a man said to have been a Briton, Gerontius, both much more competent and probably fellow officers of Constantine.[41] Gerontius was possibly a close relative of a previous military man of that name, a *comes* of Magnentius, perhaps *comes rei militaris,* exiled to Arelate (Arles) in 353.[42] Gerontius could have been born in Britain to merit the description of Briton, rather than having been British by descent. We know that his wife was called Nunechia, suggesting to Mathiesen that she was probably related to another family of Gallic aristocrats, the Nunechii (or Nonnichii) of Portus Namnetum (Nantes).[43]

Interestingly (and quite probably serendipitously), in 353, the praetorian prefect of Gaul, Nunechius, also serving the usurper Magnentius, led a delegation to Constantius II to negotiate a settlement between the two emperors. He would almost certainly have served in tandem with the elder Gerontius, and both were probably former comrades-in-arms of

Magnentius.[44] This interconnectedness amongst the élite of the empire can be firmly established from numerous much better attested examples and suggests that Constantine's *consilium* may have included members of a closely-knit group with strong Gallic connections.

The two new appointees soon forced Sarus to lift the siege of Valentia (Valence), which he had invested after disposing of Nebiogastes, and drove him back into Italy. Most accounts of what transpired give a highly confused picture, and as such probably represent the situation on the ground fairly accurately. The barbarian hordes seem to have ravaged westwards rather than southwards, leaving Constantine to move south to secure those parts of Gaul untouched by the chaos, finally fixing his capital at Arles. That he lasted as long as he did implies that he did a fairly competent job in the circumstances; one could hardly imagine a former common soldier taking on such responsibilities so convincingly. He was only really challenged when the going became very rough. He must have also undertaken some stabilisation of the Rhine frontier, which, although more notional than actual after 407, still seems to have been manned to some extent by formally settled German *foederati* (federate troops), strengthened from 413 on the upper Rhine by Burgundians.[45] With regular units thereafter absent, the requirement for British-sourced *annona* on the Rhine had thereby evaporated, with knock-on effects being felt amongst the Romano-British civilian elite, not to mention their estate staff and support services.

Having secured Gaul as well as he could, in 408 Constantine elevated his elder son Constans to the rank of Caesar, by this time surely long divested of his tonsure and married.[46] The change from the cloister to the profession of arms clearly posed him no difficult moral questions. Constantine then sent him, with Gerontius as his *comes*, into Spain to settle matters there. He swiftly put down all resistance and then garrisoned the Pyrenean passes to prevent the barbarian tribes, by this time in western Gaul, from entering Spain. Constans returned to Gaul, leaving Gerontius in charge. This period of stability, combined with a period of extreme weakness and peril on the part of the official western government in Ravenna after the fall of Stilicho, caused Constantine to send one of his leading supporters, Jovius, to the imperial court at Ravenna to seek recognition as co-emperor.[47]

The weakness of his position led Honorius grudgingly to recognise Constantine, sending him an imperial robe and agreeing to serve with him as joint consul for 409. This arrangement was made easier to conclude as Constantine's foray into Spain had yielded valuable hostages in the shape of two kinsmen of Honorius, Theodosiolus and Didymus, seized from their estates by Gerontius as bargaining chips.[48] That some coin issues were minted at Constantinople confirms the extent of Constantine's recognition.

Annus Horribilis: 409

It was in 409, probably in the summer, that things began to unravel. Constans returned to Spain in company with another *magister militum*, Justus – conceivably a son of the unfortunate Justinianus – to relieve Gerontius.[49] The entire thing somehow went horribly wrong; Gerontius took grave offence and having won the support of his troops began plotting against Constantine by colluding with the barbarians, whom the latter had finally managed to settle in Gaul. The outcome was that he enrolled a large number of them into his forces in Spain, which was the thin end of the wedge to force the gates of disaster. From that year, the Pyrenean border became porous. These events were read at Arles, understandably, as an act of rebellion. But worse was to come. Gerontius – an 'experienced soldier and stern disciplinarian' – decided to secede from Constantine's empire and at Tarraco (Tarragoña) raised his *domesticus* (second in command) Maximus to the purple, probably in June. Maximus is said by Olympiodorus to have been Gerontius's son, but by others a 'dependant'; either is perfectly plausible.[50]

Worse was to come. With Constantine in Gaul dealing with the barbarian incursion, the Saxons (or conceivably other groupings of Germanic people from outside the empire), alert to potential weaknesses in Britain, were keen to exploit the situation and in 409 mounted a damaging raid on the island. According to the Gallic *Chronicle of 452* 'The Britains were laid waste by an invasion of the Saxons.' Zosimus seems to be describing the same event when he says:

> Since Constantine did not offer any resistance, given that most of his forces were in Spain, the barbarians from across the Rhine attacked everywhere with all their might and made it necessary for the inhabitants of Britain and some of the nations among the Celts to revolt from Roman rule and live on their own, no longer obedient to Roman laws.
>
> The Britons therefore took up arms and, braving danger for their own independence, freed the cities from the barbarians threatening them; and all Armorica and the other provinces of the Gauls copied the Britons, and freed themselves in the same way, expelling their Roman governors and establishing their own rule as best they could.[51]

While there is no evidence for the expulsion of Constantine's officials from within the Gallic dioceses, and not a great deal relating to Armorica (Constantine probably was able to rectify the situation on the Continent reasonably quickly), in Britain things were very different. When Zosimus (probably reflecting Olympiodorus) speaks of the Britons as 'no longer obedient to Roman laws' he does not imply an outbreak of anarchy and brigandage, as some would like to believe. The act of 'freeing the cities' betokens strong leadership, and the passage refers to those laws emanating from the courts of Ravennas or Arles. In this context, it is generally thought that this crisis was the context of a document called the Rescript of Honorius, which also comes in a passage of Zosimus: 'But Honorius, having written a letter to the cities in Britain announcing that they should protect themselves...'[52]

This seems to make perfect sense juxtaposed with the statement in the previous extract, but as Birley points out, it is well out of context in Zosimus's text and syntactically irregular. The historian is writing of events in Italy, with Alaric moving about and poised to capture Rome, and the MS is sufficiently corrupt to be amended to read 'the cities in Bruttium [S. Italy]' not Britain.[53] Taking this rescript at face value (that is, as referring to Britain) has led some earlier authors to assume that there was a purge of Roman appointees (which probably, as Zosimus describes, did happen to many of those appointed by Constantine), that Britain was divided between a 'pro-Roman' party and a 'native' party and that control of the island devolved thereby onto the representatives of the regional capitals (*civitates*) of Britain and the *consilium* of the diocese, of which they were presumably members.[54] Yet it has always seemed inherently unlikely that a crisis in a well-administered polity beset by marauding barbarians could be resolutely and rapidly solved by a disparately composed assembly without some kind of strong leadership. Accepting that the rescript has little direct relevance to events in Britain clears the air a little. Nevertheless, at least one minor chronicle seems to confirm that under Honorius, Britain was lost to the empire, as does Procopius: 'And the island of Britain revolted, and the soldiers there chose Constantinus, a not undistinguished man, as emperor ... However, the Romans could no longer regain Britain, but it remained under usurpers [*tyrannos*] from that time.'[55]

Even the post-Roman British writer Gildas seems to record an echo of this:

> The Romans, therefore, declare to our country that they could not be troubled too frequently by arduous expeditions of that kind ... They urge the Britons, rather, to accustom themselves to arms, and fight bravely, so as to save with all their might their land, property, wives, children, and, what is greater than these, their liberty and life.[56]

While being confronted by a crisis not apparently of his own making in Gaul, which itself had offered the opportunity for further barbarian attacks, control of Britain slipped out of Constantine's grasp. It is tempting to see the disastrous rift between Constantine and Gerontius and somehow behind it. Instead of the 'revolt' of the insular administration being perhaps a cause of Geriontius's secession from the cause, is it possible that the two were more closely linked?[57] Perhaps a delegation sent to Constantine by his *vicarius* (diocesan governor) asked him for help but was rebuffed, leading Gerontius to demur by refusing further assistance. From the very confusing accounts, it would appear that some of the administration Constantine had left behind there, presumably the *vicarius*, provincial governors and perhaps some senior military commanders, were ousted by an anti-Constantinian *putsch* led by another imperial claimant whose name has not been preserved, acting in concert with Gerontius, but whose prestige was much enhanced by having achieved a decisive victory over these barbarians recorded as raiding Britain – for defeated they appear to have been. Procopius's use of the word *tyrannos* in this context means '(imperial) usurpers' and Drinkwater notes of local usurpers that whatever the circumstances of their acclamation, and the local reach of their régime, that they were invariably effectively Roman emperors, seeing themselves as part of the whole and not, like the Germanic invaders, rulers of distinct local polities.[58] Others, like E. A. Thomson, take Procopius at his word, as seems reasonable.[59] These post-Constantine III rulers in Britain were surely 'full-blooded Roman emperors', but shorn of any surviving known link to the court in Ravenna and hardly aware that the pre-409 status quo was never going to be restored, as the famous appeal to Aëtius of 466 clearly implies.

From these very scanty accounts little can be deduced, although legendary material, reviewed in Part II, might suggest a man called Eugenius with strong but enigmatic links to Maximus may have taken the initiative.[60] If precedent is anything to go by, this new usurper (*tyrannus*, the conventional Latin term to be preferred) would rule on his own for the time being and perhaps, like Tetricus, the last Gallic emperor in 273, negotiate a reunification once the troubles in Gaul were settled. After all, it would have occurred to nobody, bearing in mind the history of the previous century and a half, that the chaos would continue indefinitely. As it happened, the 'time being' turned out to be a trifle open-ended – direct control was never fully resumed over the British provinces.

Constantine's fall

Disasters in their British diocese aside, a fragile *modus vivendi* was created between Constantine and Maximus so that Gaul and Spain enjoyed an uneasy peace, although in 410, the régime of the Gallic emperor suffered yet another a set-back. Probably early in that year, one of Honorius's disloyal commanders, Allobichus – a Frank – encouraged the Gallic rulers to join him in an attempt to overthrow Honorius and take total control of the Western empire, then in any case in utter disarray, with Alaric the Visigoth rampaging around Italy with an army, attempting to be appointed Honorius's *magister militum.* In spring 410, Constantine made the same mistake as Magnus Maximus and crossed into Italy, leaving Constans behind to look after affairs in Gaul. It was presumably at this stage too that Constans was made co-emperor with his father. Constantine's younger son, Julianus, who was probably only in his early twenties, was made Caesar in Constans' place.[61] From coins, it would appear that both Constans and his father still considered themselves recognised co-rulers of the West with Honorius.

While Constantine was mobilizing however, Allobichus's plot had been uncovered and the disloyal Frank summarily executed. Confronted with this information, Constantine beat a hasty retreat, but his absence from Gaul had encouraged Gerontius and his pocket augustus Maximus to make an attempt to take control of Gaul himself. They had crossed the Pyrenees and besieged Vienne (Vienna) on the fall of which Constans was killed, an act which seems to have been seized upon centuries later by Geoffrey of Monmouth, who attributes the deed to Vortigern seeking to become ruler of Britain.[62]

Needless to say, troubles notwithstanding, these upheavals in Gaul provided the government in Ravenna with an opportunity to pull things round, and Allobichus's much more competent successor as *magister militum,* Constantius, was sent to attack Constantine's capital at Arelatum. As he approached in 411, the city was already being invested by Gerontius, who, on realising this new threat, raised the siege and retreated back to Spain. With things going wrong, Constantine's praetorian prefect, Decimius Rusticus, connived with a Gallic notable called Jovinus (a possible close kinsman of Jovius, whom we have already encountered), posted on the Rhine frontier to keep order there, to have the latter declared emperor in Constantine's place.[63] The latter's last hope was the arrival of reinforcements from the Rhine under the ever loyal Edobichus, but Constantius, anticipating this, made a lightning march up the Rhône valley and confronted the Frank, whose forces promptly handed him over and deserted to Jovinus.

Realising that the game was up, Constantine III put aside the purple, took holy orders from Bishop Heros, a *vir sanctus et beati Martini discipulus* ('an holy man and a disciple of the Blessed [St] Martin') whom he had made Bishop of Arles, a move which went down badly with Pope Zosimus.[64] He then negotiated a surrender with Constantius, including a safe conduct to Honorius's court at Ravenna for himself and his younger son, Julianus. On nearing Ravenna, however, the party was intercepted and the imperial claimant and his son executed on the spot.[65] Despite having received a bad press as being the catalyst for the abandonment by the empire of the diocese of Britain, Prosper of Aquitaine could write of him that he defended the frontiers of Gaul better than any emperor since Magnus Maximus. Zosimus wrote that until this crisis the Rhine frontier had been neglected since the time of Julian the Apostate (omitting Maximus's efforts, no doubt on the grounds of his usurpation, of which he clearly disapproved).[66]

Meanwhile, it would appear from the evidence that Gerontius, for all his opportunism a first-class commander, was making all the running in Spain, arranging treaties with the barbarians and settling them, having been instrumental in conspiring to de-throne Constantine III, besieging Vienne and killing Constans. Had the usurper Maximus been the prime mover in all this, he would without doubt have been killed when his army mutinied on the retreat from Arles in September 411 and turned on Gerontius. He, forewarned, killed his wife Nunechia and then himself, with his *comes* (and possible kinsman) Alanus, but Maximus seems to have survived, in some sources still as emperor, until some time in 412, before going to ground. Thereafter, he is said to have lived quietly on an estate in Spain (presumably Gallaecia) amongst the very Vandals the local grandees had accused Gerontius of introducing into their diocese.[67] The Gallic aristocrat Jovinus, who had appointed his younger brother Sebastianus as his co-emperor, did not last long either and by 413 Honorius's marshal Constantius had restored imperial control over the diocese (after a fashion) and revived the diocesan *concilium*, rather suggesting that this had been the body through which Constantine III had also legitimised his rule.[68]

Because Constantine, Gerontius and Maximus produce powerful echoes in the later British sources, it has been necessary to follow their fortunes, despite the apparent separation of their neo-Gallic empire from Britain after 409. Moreover, as Maximus was either the son of Gerontius, or a 'dependant', itself implying kinship, it is worth appending a footnote. In July 419, we find another Maximus appearing in Spain as a *tyrannus*. It is not absolutely certain that this is the same man as Gerontius's emperor, but the circumstantial evidence strongly supports it.[69] This time, he was empurpled by the ruler of the Vandals, Gunderic, whose people had been forcibly moved after a spat with the neighbouring Sueves, both peoples having been settled by Gerontius in Gallaecia. Gunderic's people were moved to Baetica, another Spanish province, and the Gothic auxiliaries who had policed the move withdrew west of the Pyrenees. Thus, in about July 419, Maximus was trotted out, restored and the *vicarius* of the diocese of Spain expelled. The *comes Hispaniarum* Asterius, fresh from dealing with the Sueves, seems also to have been able to deal with the claimant – before the appearance of the Western empire's *magister militum per Gallias* (C-in-C Gaul) Castinus, sent to straighten things out. Asterius took the ever-useful Gothic auxiliaries with him and fought a series of running battles, in which Maximus was captured, probably in February 421. Asterius was made a patrician as a reward.[70]

Castinus then took over. Initially successful, by refusing to compromise he later suffered a crushing defeat, which sealed the future of Roman Spain for ever and allowed the Vandals to settle where they had triumphed (hence modern Andalusia). And the Visigoths were not to be dislodged from the diocese until the irruption of the Moslems from Africa in 711.[71] Maximus was, however, sent back to Italy where he was slaughtered in the arena as part of the emperor's thirtieth anniversary games, 10 January 423; the Emperor Honorius died just seven months later – but in his bed.

The British-led fifth-century Gallic empire had started well enough in true Magnus Maximus fashion, but after 409 went rapidly downhill, and while Gaul later underwent at least a partial recovery under Valentinian III's *magister militum* Flavius Aëtius, Britain, even if one can accept that there was some kind of attempt to re-integrate the diocese into the empire from *c.* 413, was well and truly lost to external control.[72] Yet in the island itself, the penumbra of empire took a very long time to fade.

Apse of the baths at Arelatum, fourth century. (The late N. Ellis)

6

The Long Fifth Century

Britain alone: the first phase

The devastating raid by the various barbarian groupings upon Britain that occurred in 409 did much damage and convinced whatever powers there were in the diocese, perhaps encouraged by Gerontius, that the elevation of Constantine III had done little to increase security at home. As a result, the emperor's top echelon officials were apparently expelled as part of a diocesan *coup d'état*. This may not have been as sweeping a change as it might at first glance appear. Roman officials, of whatever rank, generally displayed a consistent competency in civil administration throughout the empire, and by no means all will have been changed as a result of the three imperial contenders of 406-407, let alone the upheaval of 409.[1] A good number would have been appointed before the troubles and many may well have survived 'at their desks'. One suspects that it was only Constantine's identifiable henchmen and appointees who were driven out; for example, some of the provincial governors, army commanders and palatine officials. Archaeology seems to offer some support for this. At Shadwell on the south bank of the Thames a new house of some quality had been built *c.* 380 on the site of a tower and a closed bath house. This the owners abandoned in a very formal and ritualistic manner some time in the first two decades of the fifth century, consigning all their household goods, ceramic and metal, to the well, along with other fragments of the building, as if closing up shop and withdrawing.[2] This certainly sounds like some high official leaving, knowing it was going to be for good.

Yet who would have organised the purge, especially as not all of Constantine's appointees were going to pack up meekly and return to the Continent? Those who stayed would have changed allegiance, but not all. This could not have been a clean break, which would have involved a certain amount of coercion. Bearing in mind that (in Zosimus's words) they 'took up arms and ... freed the cities from the Barbarians ... expelling their Roman governors', what may be adduced is the removal of a substantial part of the top layer of the administration only, by top-down *fiat*. A decisive and undisputed leader on the spot must have emerged fairly promptly to bring this about, capable of organising and leading so complex a process. There can be little doubt that this person would have been another usurper, a *tyrannus*. He will have emerged with the authority and status to set things in motion. Although we do not know his name, there is a candidate.[3]

That this was organised by the *civitates* themselves working through a diocesan *consilium* as has frequently been suggested seems inherently unlikely. So drastic a change in the face of turmoil was hardly going to be the work of a committee. Furthermore, the delegates from the beleaguered cities would have needed to travel safely during the chaos of a barbarian raid to somewhere (presumably London) in order to confer and to bestow authority – which in reality they had no power to do, bearing in mind that we have rejected the validity of the Rescript of Honorius. Salway considered that: 'Romano-British nobles do not seem to have been playing the same sort of part in the Imperial government and ... it is unlikely that Constantine III could draw on a similar pool of experience from amongst them.'[4]

But that, surely, is because we have so little information; one cannot help but feel that the insular elite would have been an essential part of these events. One collateral of the second part of this work is an attempt to show that this supposed local disconnect was probably much less pronounced than thought. Later in the fifth century, civil administration (and some military leadership, too) may well have devolved into the hands of local magnates, able to summon up reserves of manpower from their estates at periods when the empire's reach was wanting, in Italy and Gaul especially, and there is no reason to suppose that things were any different in other parts of the praetorian prefecture of the Gauls, Britain not excepted. It is by no means clear that the essential 'Roman' administrative structure of the diocese of Britain actually did collapse in the wake of the failure of Constantine III, and the analysis below of the legendary and other insular sources suggests that it lasted a considerable time – unlike the material way of life, which, with the collapse of the *annona*-driven trade across the North Sea and the failure by Ravenna and Constantine III to pay any British troops, sems to have gradually fallen apart, forcing a new *modus vivendi* to emerge over the course of the century.[5]

What seems more likely is that in the chaos, some senior commander, perhaps a *magister militum* appointed by Constantine III to keep order, distanced himself from the usurper and took control. Thereafter, he presumably would have gathered together the necessary available forces from the garrison (assuming that the *comitatenses* were long gone to the Continent) and systematically replaced his predecessor's appointees along with any others considered unhelpful to the cause of the survival of the diocese – a paler echo of Maximus's efforts in 383.[6] It is quite possible that whoever took control had little trouble in enlisting the active support of those initially most affected, those on the frontier zone and probably settled under indigenous Romano-British leaders (essentially analogous to the mostly Arab phylarchs from this period appointed on the eastern frontier of the empire). After order had been established, there would have been the task of clearing the barbarian incursion and putting right the devastation where possible. Whoever the new *tyrannus* was, he would have been invited by his peers and other persons of influence to remain in charge and run the administration for the foreseeable future for the security of the island.

As in such a role persons were conventionally then seen as having *imperium*, such a man would have been perceived as a *tyrannus* – in wider imperial terms, an usurper – by any outsider, although in Britain there would be no such implication.[7] The prestige of such a position meant the holder could deal with barbarians and other internal groups with sufficient diplomatic authority; this, after all, had been one of the drivers of sudden assumptions of imperial power since the chaotic mid-third century. Thus, the conclusion of the events recorded by Zosimus was the elevation of a new pretender to imperial power with a mandate to secure the insular *status quo*, in line with Procopius's statement from a century or so later, that Britain 'remained under usurpers from that time'.[8]

J. P. C. Kent argues that the *consilium* to which Gildas alludes originated in a 'senate' like that which Constantine III fashioned out of the Gallic diocesan *consilium*, and speculates, from allusions in a letter written by the bishop Fastidius to the 'Sicilian Briton' (who appeared to preside over an unidentified tribunal as 'consul') that the post-Constantine III polity of Britain instituted consulships (again, as in Gaul) and even that the ruler himself may have so styled himself. This idea is adduced from Nennius's description of Ambrosius Aurelianus's father, the passage representing 'an early tradition' according to Dr Morris, Kent considering that 'the idea of the consul as head of state in post-Roman Britain is not unthinkable.'[9] Against this, however, we should balance the statement of Sozomen, writing at the end of the 430s, that after the defeat of Constantine III, 'the whole province returned to its allegiance to Honorius, and has since been obedient to the rulers of his appointment.'[10]

He was speaking of Gaul, meaning, it is supposed, the praetorian prefecture, which included Britain. If the statement was literally true, a new *vicarius* would have been appointed and lesser office holders too, yet we hear nothing of them. This perhaps means with nothing much to report from Britain from lack of concrete information, Sozomen was indulging in a sweeping generalisation, but we cannot be sure. If Britain remained 'under usurpers,' no source anywhere near the date has anything concrete to say about British events during the decades after 409. Victorius of Aquitaine, writing in or around 457, says only that: '... it came to pass that after this war between the British and the Romans, when their generals were killed, and after the killing of the tyrant Maximus and the end of the Roman Empire in Britain, the Britons went in fear for 40 years.'[11]

Bede, writing in his magisterial *Historia Ecclesiastica Gentis Anglorum* ('Ecclesiastical History of the English People') completed in about 731, says of the period following 409 about the Picts and the Scots: 'On learning that they [the Romans] would not return [the barbarians] were quick to attack and occupied the north up to the wall.' This suggests that the reported raid of 409 was a northern one, but north-eastern-based Bede's information was hardly first-hand. Bede does, though, add that the Wall was indeed garrisoned, despite Constantine III's alleged withdrawal of troops, although garrisoned by troops who (eventually) buckled under the pressure and let the marauders through (unless they by-passed it by sea). They may have been locally recruited militiamen, rather than seasoned troops. This was followed by much devastation, but eventually the intruders were driven back and calm and prosperity returned.[12]

Again, there is no mention of who carried out this surely considerable effort of restitution. The *Historia Brittonum* ('History of the Britons'), compiled around a century after Bede, includes within it a separate account of British history but largely confined to the south-east, which is inserted into the main narrative in separate parts in an attempt to match the chronology. This is known as the *Kentish Chronicle*. From internal evidence it seems that the *urtext* cannot have been written later than the sixth century. It differs from the Kentish entries in the *Anglo-Saxon Chronicle*, which covers the same time scale and apparent events, establishing their mutual independence.[13] It adds, closely aping Victorius of Aquitaine: 'It came to pass that after ... the killing of the *tyrannus* Maximus and the end of the Roman Empire in Britain, the British went in fear for forty years ... Vortigern (*Guorthigirnus*) ruled in Britain.'

Two 'kings'

This timescale, strictly interpreted, takes us to 428, and it provides us with a name, Vortigern, (*Vurtigernus* to Bede, *Wyrtgeorn* in the *Anglo-Saxon Chronicle*) for the ruler of Britain in that year.[14] The name Vortigern is unfortunately one beset with uncertainty: in the *Prosopography of the Later Roman Empire* (PLRE) it is entered hedged about with caveats, but the entry quotes from a passage later than Bede, from *Historia Brittonum* (828) stating that Vortigern, from 425, *tenuit imperium in Britannia*. This actually means 'holding power in Britain' rather than 'reigning' which would have been more appropriate had he been perceived as a king, which he is invariably called in later sources. Furthermore, *imperium* clearly implies someone perceived as an emperor in the traditional Roman sense. D. N. Dumville, the most critical commentator on insular sources, avers that, despite the doubts of PLRE, 'Vortigern's legend was known in both England and Wales at a very early date,' which suggests that the use of the term 'legend' might seem over-cautious. In either case, the sources do not actually say Vortigern *assumed* power in that year; he might have been around beforehand.[15]

If the dating of the *Kentish Chronicle* is correct (by no means guaranteed), then it provides us with the earliest mention of Vortigern's name, after Bede; it also appears in the main text of the *Historia Brittonum* and only then in the *Anglo-Saxon Chronicle*, of which Higham has commented 'The historicity of this late 9th-century account is so doubtful that it is best set aside as a source for the [5th and] 6th century.'[16] But we cannot afford to dismiss everything in these sources, concerning which J. P. C. Kent has written:

> I concede that a detailed discussion of what snippet from Gildas or Nennius [*Historia Britonum*] may be accepted and which rejected is an improbable exercise ... I will give my opinion that there must be a little wheat amongst the chaff. Since it is palpable that not everything they say is wrong, there must be underlying sources not all known to us, written or oral, however lacking in merit.[17]

Vortigern surely has to be accepted as having some basis in historical fact. Yet there is certainly no evidence for Vortigern as far back as 409, and precious little for anyone else, bar the semi-legendary Owein, whose possible candidacy for the role of post-409 *tyrannus* is canvassed in detail below. The *Kentish Chronicle* adds that: 'Vortigern ruled in Britain, and during his rule in Britain he was under pressure, from fear of the Picts and Scots, and of a Roman invasion, and, not least, from dread of Ambrosius.'[18]

Clearly, when the *Kentish Chronicle* was first set down, it was still believed that central authority might still be restored. If such a prospect had made Vortigern jumpy, then it may have been because he had seized control of the diocese from a predecessor whose legitimacy had been tacitly acknowledged, even in Ravenna.

This also introduces another name, Ambrosius. Gildas, who wrote in lowland Britain in the early sixth century and whose post-409 facts are generally accorded some credibility (despite writing what was a polemic railing against the moral shortcomings of his fellow Britons), fails to mention Vortigern by name, but does mention a person called Ambrosius Aurelianus. The failure to mention Vortigern is compensated for in that he refers to someone having full authority over Britain at this time whom he calls *superbo tyranno* ('the proud usurper'), which is taken as a play on the name Vortigern, derived from British terms meaning roughly the same thing.

Thus, Gildas is taken as a source for Vortigern, but a source which lacks full authority by not actually naming him. Later on, Gildas refers to him more sympathetically as *infausto tyranno* ('unfortunate usurper').[19]

A recent dissenting voice has been that of Guy Halsall who has proposed that Gildas is actually referring to Magnus Maximus as the *suberbo tyranno* and that he, not Vortigern, was the one to introduce Saxon federates, who later on seem to have gone ape all over the landscape.[20] The fact that these federates must have lain quiescent for five decades is somehow unconvincing. It would seem more likely that a revolt of the *foederati* of the early fifth century, caused by their not having received their *annonae* (payments in kind) on time, is a situation that might well have occurred before 428.

As regards the accession of Vortigern, we have only Welsh Triad 51, written down a millennium after the event (but from much older, probably oral, sources) which tells us that Vortigern 'caused the death of' the younger son of someone called Constantine the Blessed (whose possible origins will be examined in Chapter 10) and 'deceitfully took the crown' Whether this person was Vortigern's predecessor, however, is doubtful; it surely refers to Constans, the elder son of Constantine III, as was suggested in the previous chapter. If there is any truth in this, it might suggest that Vortigern must, in 411, have been a senior member of the entourage of Gerontius in Gaul. Vortigern also, however, exiled Ambrosius (as British *Emrys Wletic*) to Armorica, hence his reported apprehension concerning him. This tradition is actually different from that in Geoffrey of Monmouth's *Historia Regum Britanniae* (*HRB*) and thus may also pre-date the latter's 1130s *floruit*, thereby gaining a modest tincture of added credibility as a source of arcane historical memory.[21] Nevertheless, this sequence of apparent usurpation seems to confirm Gildas, who wrote: 'Kings were appointed ... and soon after slain ... by those who had anointed them.'[22]

This Ambrosius is distinct from the Ambrosius whom Gildas names, in a somewhat later context, as the man who defeats the Saxons over a lengthy campaign after years of yet more chaos. He provides this later Ambrosius with a *cognomen*, too: Aurelianus. Yet if Vortigern, in around 428, was in dread of an Ambrosius (whom he had exiled), it cannot be the same man mentioned by Gildas, who must have been active in the closing two decades of the fifth century. So there were two 'Ambrosii'. Gildas does, however, help by giving Ambrosius a background:

viro modesto, qui solus forte romanae gentis tantae tempestatis collisione occisis in eadem parentibus purpura nimirum indutis superfuerat...
He was a man of unassuming character, who alone of the Roman people, happened to survive in the shock of such a storm, in which his parents, people undoubtedly clad in the purple, had been killed...[23]

Note that the British of the fifth century are here clearly referred to as 'the Roman people'. The key phrase, that his parents 'undoubtedly wore the purple' seems quite unequivocal: his father must have been one of the men 'holding *imperium*', the *tyranni*, under the rule of whom Britain had been governed after 409. It also chimes with the reference to the consulate in *Historia Brittonum*.[24] It is just possible, therefore, that the Ambrosius of whom Vortigern was in dread was Ambrosius Aurelianus's father.[25] Ambrosius makes another appearance in the less trustworthy *Historia Brittonum*, which is much later than Gildas:

> *Et a regno Guorthigirni usque ad discordiam Guitolini et Ambrosii anni sunt XII quod est Guoloppum, id est Catguoloph.*
>
> From the reign of Vortigern up to the dispute of Vitolinus and Ambrosius are twelve years, which is Wallop, that is the battle of Wallop.[26]

This source then reiterates that Vortigern 'held *imperium*' (= imperial power) in the consulship of the emperors Theodosius (II) and Valentinian (III), which was 425. The reference to Vortigern, after apparently moving the story on to Vitalinus (the more correct Latin spelling) without explanation, unequivocally suggests that Vortigern was indeed a title, as used retrospectively amongst British speakers for instance, but that Vitalinus was in fact the ruler's true, Roman, name. The relatively late sources' use of the name Vortigern rather than Vitalinus seems to indicate a substitution of a Romano-British name with a British language epithet (such as were borne by the majority of post-Roman figures in later British writings) by which, in his notoriety, he was later known, the Roman name being largely forgotten over the interval. In time, Vortigern acquired a further epithet, *gwrtheneu* ('the thin').[27]

The extract fails to tell us who came out best at the battle of Wallop (presumably the place of that name in Hampshire), which is regrettable. If *c.* 425 represents a year early on in Vortigern's reign, then the date of 436 would fit with any postulated Ambrosius *père*. If Ambrosius Aurelianus was 50 or so in 490, say, then the father would be the obvious candidate for the opponent of Vitalinus. We might also believe that he prevailed on that occasion, if we may take as truth the death of this first Ambrosius and his wife in the Saxon uprising, which appears to have occurred around 442 or a year or two later. In much later British legendary history however, Ambrosius emerges as the final agent of Vortigern's destruction, but on the Monmouth/Herefordshire borders: 'Aurelius [*sic*] King of the Britons burnt the fortress of Genor in Ercing [*oppidum Genorem in Ergyn*] on the river Wye by Mount Cloart, and Vortigern in the castle [there].'[28]

This reference is one of our only remotely convincing clues regarding the demise of Vortigern, which perhaps followed the Battle of Wallop; another related account (but much more fanciful) occurs in the British life of St Germanus included in the *Historia Brittonum*; whatever his fate, it may have befallen him in or shortly after 436. This source also calls Ambrosius 'Aurelius', which seems to be a conflation with the more familiar Ambrosius Aurelianus, or alternatively a genuine authentic nugget of contemporary information surviving through eight centuries of chaotic transmission. But as will emerge below, the *gentilicium* Aurelius came to have some traction in post-Roman Britain. It looks like these disparate and confusing sources are allowing a crude narrative to emerge wherein the *tyrannus* raised after the events of 409 was succeeded by Ambrosius, who was exiled around 425 by Vortigern/Vitalinus and restored as a result of a battle in *c.* 436, only to be killed in a Saxon revolt around 442/443.

That Vitalinus may well be the same man as Vortigern is strengthened by a genealogy of the *tyrannus* in *Historia Brittonum*, where he is recorded as the son of Guital (= Vital[is]), grandson of Guitolin (= Vitalinus/Vitalianus), 'one of the sons of Gloiu', the other sons being Bonus (= ?Bonosus), Paul (= Paulus) and Mauron (= ?Magnus/Maurus).[29] We may confidently eliminate Gloiu, who in one place is identified as Gloyw Gwalltir (in Welsh, *Wallt Hir* = 'Long Hair'), son of Paul, as a name coined to represent the place from which either Paul or Guitolin came, and which over the passage of transmission a copyist, lacking the knowledge that it represented Glevum (Gloucester), interpolated it into the genealogy as a person; a frequent occurrence in later British genealogies.[30]

Kate Pretty considers that the (native) British population was relatively stable and that after the end of the period of direct imperial control, people switched their allegiance to the old hereditary ruling dynasties whose status had been recognised throughout the Roman period, but which had been, perhaps advisedly, downplayed during that era.[31] The evidence for this, however, would appear slim, except probably amongst the least Romanised parts of the diocese, where what seem to be native dynasties do re-appear, as we have seen, and probably with the connivance of Maximus, many claiming ancestry going back to legendary Iron Age figures, too. But in lowland Britain, long Romanised after more than 350 years, there can be no doubt that assimilation, as elsewhere in the empire, had been fairly thorough, merging the scions of any ruling houses into the wider imperial élite; one only has to note the descendants of Hellenistic kings and Athenian archons gracing the second century senate.[32] Hence, as with Vortigern's alleged pedigree, his antecedents all bear acceptable Roman names. This, if accepted, might well suggest that the *tyrannus*'s great grandfather (or more recent ancestor) had been a senior official hailing from the *colonia* of Glevum (Gloucester).

Interestingly, one Viteli[nu]s is even alleged to have been [arch]bishop of London in around 409, but he is of even shakier authenticity, only being named by Jocelyn of Furness as late as 1170, a source possibly informed by

Geoffrey of Monmouth, with whom we are on even more equivocal ground. Were the source more reliable and, bearing in mind that the celibacy of the clergy was a millennium away from imposition, this person could be seen as Vortigern/Vitalinus's father.[33] Even the uncle, Bonus, has resonance for the period in which he must have lived, for Ausonius had written a very laboured satirical poem about a critical Briton called Silvius Bonus in the 370s, using the name as a vehicle to ridicule Britons generally.[34] The dating of Ausonius works is much debated; this particular one is usually dated (vaguely) to between 368 and 379; it would have more resonance, here perhaps, were it established that it was written after Maximus had assumed power![35]

Yet, Gloucester connections notwithstanding, bearing in mind the physical mobility of the official classes under the empire, we also find a Vitalis was *praefectus annonae* (senior official in charge of supplies) in the west in 403, possibly to be identified with a senator of that name who had been Symmachus's correspondent seven years before. Such a post could easily have been a British one, bearing in mind the colossal quantity of supplies which crossed the North Sea throughout the fourth century from Britain to the army units guarding the German limes. It may be possible to expand on his career, too, for a Flavius Vitalis a little earlier appeared as a *vir clarissimus* (thus of senatorial rank), a *notarius* and *protector*, featuring on an inscription at Mutina (Modena) in Italy with his wife, Bruttia Aureliana, the latter bearing a name with some resonance when we come to consider Vortigern's more legendary connections in Chapter 8.[36] This man could easily have moved to Britannia Prima (in which Glevum lay) before 406 to take up a similar post, having fathered Vitalinus/Vortigern, whose Roman name is a typically late variation of that of his putative father, a common familial connection at the time, as the genealogy of the emperor Constantine I makes clear. Alternatively, he might have retired there, to a place perhaps with family connections, having been *praefectus*, which was a senior appointment and had perhaps seen it as the pinnacle of his career prior to retirement. If Jocelyn of Furness was providing us with authentic information, Vitalis might have relinquished an official career, as did Ambrose, Germanus and later, Sidonius Apollinaris, to be ordained, and as an aristocrat to be made a bishop. The family could even have come from Gloucester in the first place, despite the inscription at Mutina, where the connection could have been his wife's. The discovery in the early 1970s of an early fifth-century secondary burial in a Roman funerary building in Gloucester of a man who was 'more Briton than Roman' suggests that such speculation lies well within the bounds of possibility.[37]

Vitalis's earlier position as *praefectus annonae,* if true, would find an ironic echo in his possible son's supposed negotiations, recorded in the *Kentish Chronicle*, with a group of Germanic *foederati* – three or four years after Vortigern/Vitalinus is said to have come to power – to settle them in

Thanet provided with *annona*, in return for campaigning against the Picts and Scots, then again apparently giving trouble. We learn that these Saxons (but possibly in reality Franks) demanded their *annona* in a treaty struck according to this typically Roman stratagem to settle barbarians in return for service, Gildas actually uses the terms *annona, epimenia* and *hospes* (the latter for the settlers themselves) – significantly, formulaic Roman terminology for settling *foederati* in this sort of context.[38]

Whatever the historicity of this treaty of *c.* 428/429 (or 425), it was with British hindsight seen as the one act that allowed the 'Saxons' a foothold in Britain that they later exploited to the lasting disadvantage of the Romano-British administration and population as a whole, a fact for which later tradition never forgave Vortigern. A dispassionate eye might indeed take the view that much of the early Anglo-Saxon settlement of Britain was brought about under treaty, negotiated through whoever controlled the diocese after 409. The intermingling of high-status Romano-British, migrant Germanic and western British remains in the extensive early to mid-fifth-century cemeteries at Mucking, Essex, points emphatically to a generally peaceful and mutually beneficial co-existence here, and is reflected elsewhere, too, thanks to the application of stable isotopes as determinants of peoples' personal origin, not to mention ancient DNA.[39] There are, strangely, few associations with Vortigern outside the Celtic west, and the negative British references suggest that his policies as a ruler probably managed to alienate the western and northern frontier regions (areas suggested above as having been placed under indigenous military control by reforms attributable to Maximus) rather more than elsewhere, where people were more used to this sort of arrangement.

Thus, with heavy reliance on sources which are all to some extent unsatisfactory, we can only tentatively postulate that the collapse of Roman authority in 409 resulted in a further Marcus, or Gratian or other potential usurper of imperial power, who organised resistance to an attack by Saxons (or Picts and Scots – the sources are not wholly agreed). This was managed successfully and whoever brought this feat off seems to have stabilised the diocese, for neither in contemporary sources nor in legendary (or British) ones do we hear a word to the contrary. As we shall see, this may have been the work of a Eugenius/Owein, for it is surely too early to identify whoever it was with Vortigern himself. Nevertheless, by 424/425 Vortigern/Vitalinus had assumed power (*imperium*) at the expense of one Ambrosius. How far Vortigern's authority ran is utterly unclear, for we might suspect that if Magnus Maximus had struck an arrangement to allow local (tribal) leaders to assume control over the northern and western frontiers, then their allegiance may have been less to be relied on, although they would surely have followed the lead of whoever was perceived as the holder of diocese-wide *imperium,* as their predecessors no doubt acknowledged the hegemony of Maximus. No words to the contrary from the sources reach us at this stage.[40]

Then, in 436 or thereabouts, Vitalinus/Vortigern appears to have been worsted in a civil conflict by Ambrosius, who presumably took over (or resumed) *imperium* as *tyrannus* in his place, assuming the purple robe and other insignia as Gildas testifies and was killed in a Saxon revolt in the mid-440s. That the two represented pro-and anti-Roman parties, as has not infrequently been canvassed, seems pure speculation.[41] Some writers have suggested a political dichotomy between a faction in Britain 'loyal' to the empire and keen to get Britain back within its structure, and another faction of 'independents', for none of which is there convincing evidence. The belief that Vortigern settled his Saxon *foederati* in Thanet to protect the shore fort and port against a Roman attempt to re-occupy the island also seems highly dubious, despite the claim in *Historia Brittonum* that Vortigern was driven by fear of a Roman assault (*Romanico impetu*). If the statement is true, then he might, as a *tyrannus*, have looked nervously over his shoulder across the Channel if he could recall the *reconquista* of Constantius Chlorus or that of Theodosius the elder, unless of course, Ambrosius in his ambitions really did enjoy the support of the Praetorian Prefect of Gaul and his military commander.[42]

There were other obvious points of entry to Britain from Gaul, like Dubris (Dover), Anderida (Pevensey) or Portus Adurni (Portchester); Thanet was merely convenient as a peninsula (the better for containment). Rutupiae (Richborough), on the mainland side of the Wantsum channel at its southern end would seem an excellent place from which to police such unpredictable allies. It was also the closest point to the Germanic-dominated lands around the Low Countries and the mouths of the Rhine. It may be that by being settled there, they were well positioned to defend London as well. Their burial sites in the southern approaches to the capital certainly suggest this. The eventual loss of Kent by further treaty, apparently as a result of a mutiny, is made the more plausible by such a strategic deployment. The clear boundary between migrant communities and indigenous populations identified either side of the Medway seems instructive in the context of these developments.[43] Yet civil conflict amongst usurpers had never previously required an ideological impetus. More likely, the one had perceived in the other serious failings in his handling of affairs and supported by a sufficiently plentiful number of like-minded supporters had decided to bring matters to a head. Yet up until that time, the general perception was one of relative peace and stability.

St Germanus

Into this prolonged period of relative tranquillity, we do have a brief window on affairs in Britain thanks to the visit of St Germanus, Bishop of

Autissiodorum (Auxerre). In 429, the well-connected saint, a former Roman official, later appointed a *dux* (senior military commander) in Gaul, was sent to Britain to combat an outbreak of the Pelagian heresy.[44] This was a dispute over the nature of divine grace, which had originally been propounded in Rome by Pelagius, a charismatic Briton, and was promoted in the aftermath of the severing of Britain from imperial control by the bishop Fastidius, the probable author of *De Vita Christiana*.[45] The work in some ways defined the philosophy underpinning the political challenges being faced in the western empire Now, two decades on, Pelagius's beliefs were being proclaimed openly by another British bishop, bearing the good Gallic name of Agricola. If we only knew what symbolism was adopted by the Pelagians in their art, funerary arrangements or generally to distinguish themselves from orthodox Christianity, we might know a great deal more about the numbers involved and other aspects now lost to us.[46] There is some dispute over whether Germanus was sent by the pope or by the Gallic bishops in synod, but this does not really affect the information about his visit, written not long after his death by Constantius, who had known his companion on the visit, Lupus, Bishop of Tricassium (Troyes) and whose account enjoys a level of credence later hagiographers could never attain.[47]

Although Constantius admits to doubts about his recollection of events in the saint's life, and much ink has been spilt over its detailed reliability, it would seem invidious to reject the main elements. The two bishops seem to have had absolutely no trouble in moving about Britain, drawing considerable crowds in the process, rather underlining, by implication, the existence of a continuing stable Roman administrative framework, including a functioning church. Had society broken down, it would have been mentioned. In due course, a debate was staged in front of a large crowd, presumably in London, towards the end of which Germanus healed the sick child of an official, following which miracle the argument appeared to have been won for a general return to orthodoxy. The official was described by Constantius as a *tribunus,* which would imply a fairly high-ranking soldier, but many commentators have argued that this was merely a terminological inexactitude on Constantius's part and that he was probably a decurion. Others have suggested, more plausibly, that he might more likely have been a *tribunus et notarius* (senior civil servant).[48]

Such confusion does not seem very likely however, for Constantius, writing in the mid-fifth century, would have been perfectly well aware of the terminology of rank and status, while enjoying the oversight of Lupus. If the man was a senior civil servant, that would be reasonable if they were in London, as assumed. If Britain was, as seems highly likely, under a *tyrannus* – a person of imperial standing – then either a senior officer or a high-ranking bureaucrat would seem perfectly plausible.[49] Later British traditions that Germanus and Lupus had divided Britain up into dioceses and appointed St Dubricius archbishop of Southern Britain can safely be discounted; Constantius would undoubtedly have mentioned it.

After this, the two bishops proceeded to Verulamium to see the shrine of St Alban. At least that is the implication, for although they are recorded as having gone to a particular place to see the shrine of a martyr, neither place nor martyr are named in the text and it is only after Germanus was visited by St Alban in a dream that we can identify the martyr and the locale.[50] On the return journey (to London presumably), Germanus broke a leg, which detained him for some time. This was fortuitous as it turned out, for news arrived that the Picts and Scots had joined forces with the Saxons to initiate another serious raid on Britain. This seems an unlikely combination. Just as Hengist's men were described as Saxons when they may well have been Franks, the terminology was surely a generalisation from the start. The *vita* suggests that with Germanus' leg now being better, the bishops turned towards the sound of gunfire (as it were). After a journey, they encountered a British force engaged upon countering the depredations of the intruders, but who were in a tight corner, faced by superior numbers and forced to retreat to a fortified camp where they were pinned down with little hope of reinforcements. Ex-officer Germanus answered a plea for help, hurried to the scene and – never one to miss an opportunity – trading on the raised morale the arrival of his entourage had brought celebrated Easter in a makeshift shrine, after which he baptised a large number of the soldiers. It was the convention of the church at this period only to baptise at Easter and only after much preparation, which the troops the saint baptised on this occasion did not undergo. It does underline the fact that a hundred and twenty or so years after the Edict of Milan, by no means all Britons were as yet Christian. It was quite possible that some of the men were barbarian recruits, of course, and thus pagan in any case; others were probably rural inhabitants, branded as *pagenses,* presumably through their continuing adherence to the old gods; others may have been men whose route to baptism had already begun, or merely backsliders.[51]

At this point reconnaissance established that the enemy force was advancing, so Germanus volunteered his services to help them defeat what were apparently vastly superior numbers; presumably the unit's regular commander – a shadowy later tradition calls him Gerontius – was happy to relinquish so daunting a responsibility.[52] Germanus was, after all, a former general, he had possibly been *dux Tractus Armoricani et Nervicani,* a military post relevant to his home region attested in the *Notitia Dignitatum,* and was now appointed *dux proelii* (temporary commander) of the British force. Having undertaken his own reconnaissance, he took full advantage of the terrain – a 'valley enclosed by steep mountains' – organising an ambush (by concealing his forces and getting them to shout 'Alleluia!' at the critical moment on a given signal) thus routing the enemy, apparently bloodlessly!

'Thus this most wealthy island, with the defeat of both its spiritual and its human foes, was rendered secure in every way.'[53] One can but hope that Vitalinus was grateful!

This tale has much to tell us about Britain in 429-430. It is, for a start, described as 'most wealthy', which does not sound like either decline or the result of instability, and although archaeological evidence is unequivocal for a decline, it is rapidly becoming clear from recent discoveries that the decline was more gradual and should be dated later than simply the last issue of deposited coins. It also may reflect Gallic impressions of Britain at the time Constantius was writing, around 480. The wealth must be seen as a tribute to the unwritten effectiveness of the continuing central administration of the diocese, even then.

From the account, Britain also seems to have been served by armed forces little changed from a generation before. The fact that the battle took place in mountainous country tells us that the writ of Vortigern must then have run throughout much of the old diocese, as the legendary sources attest, for the incident must have taken place in the north, the Peak or Wales, to have been a place enclosed by mountains with rocky slopes steep enough to promote an echo; a long-standing suggestion that this took place in the Chilterns does not seem to wash. A convincing case has been made that it was in the valley of the Dee near Llangollen, which certainly fits the description, and is not so far from the important centre of Viroconium (Wroxeter) at the north-western termination of Watling Street. We might envisage the British regrouping in a former Iron Age fort, many of which, as we know from archaeology, were re-commissioned during the post-Roman period.[54] It may also be that the wicked (and entirely legendary) king Benlli, whom St Germanus is alleged to have fought in the alternative, *Historia Brittonum*, version of his *vita*, represents a much later record of a real Scots (that is Irish) leader, and one who may have been involved in this particular confrontation to boot.[55]

If the Vale of Llangollen really was the site, then such a fort can be identified in Dinas Brân, re-used yet again by the Princes of Powis in the medieval period.[56] One reason that this locality has been suggested is the remarkable concentration of churches dedicated to Germanus (modern Welsh, Garmon) in the area and across wider Powis.[57] One might be tempted to envisage the largely locally recruited (and newly baptised) troops involved returning home on demobilisation and inspiring the foundation of churches in their hero's memory.

It would, however, seem that Germanus's military achievement was more lasting than his spiritual one. Some years after the two bishops' return to Gaul, a further outbreak of Pelagianism was reported and the Gallic bishops urged Germanus to make a return visit and endeavour once again to eradicate the heresy. It is also possible that the Roman authorities in Gaul wanted an experienced view of the situation in Britain but bearing in mind the attested interaction across the Channel, one doubts if such intelligence was particularly hard to come by in any case. The date of this second visit is unknown, it must have been late 430s or early 440s, for the saint died at some date between 442 and 448. From Constantius's account of it, another bishop, Severus of Trier, accompanied him this time, and the voyage was so smooth that they arrived, presumably at Richborough or Dover, before the local people knew they were coming.[58]

The two clerics seem to have made short work of the leading heresiarchs, having them rounded up and brought back to the Continent with them to be dealt with. This achievement was boosted by a miracle, in which Germanus healed the withered leg of the son of *regionis illius primus* ('a leading man of the country'), Elafius. He was accompanied by 'the whole province' so one might be tempted to conclude that this 'leading man' of the province was presumably the governor/*consularis* of it (presumably the former province of Maxima Caesariensis), rather than the entirety of Britain, *regio* suggesting rather an area of the whole, from which we may reasonably infer that the late Roman administrative structure was then still more or less intact.[59] The crowds testify to the pulling power of the two bishops, presaging the late Billy Graham by fifteen hundred years. Elafius is a perfectly normal Roman name of the period; indeed, Sidonius Apollinaris, the letter-writing Gallic ex-consul and bishop, had a friend of that name, of senatorial rank, attested in 469 and after 485, when he was a senior official of the Gothic kingdom. Bearing in mind the enduring cross-Channel links throughout most of the fifth century, it is by no means impossible that they were kinsmen.[60]

In British tradition, other stories adhered to the life of this saint. They are inserted into the *Historia Brittonum* but cited as being from a British *Liber Beati Germani* ('Life of the Blessed Germanus') which by implication must be earlier than *Historia Brittonum* and would seem to be a life quite independent of that written by Constantius. Here, Germanus is supposed to have taught and ordained the Breton-born St Illtud and also to have taught Saint Patrick (Patricius), both perfectly reasonable assertions given the late date and parlous chronology of most saints' lives of the period, although the latter's crowded *Vita* gives precious little room for such an encounter.[61] This independent version, although burdened with material which has to be viewed as fantastical, does tell us that Germanus preached to Vortigern (presumably on the first visit), which might suggest that the ruler had become an adherent of Pelagius and Agricola too, a fact that might fit the context and explain why he ended up disliked and fighting Ambrosius, possibly just at (or just before) the time that Germanus made his second visit. A story that Germanus brought about 'régime change' in Powis by a miracle seems to be chronologically unlikely, despite the suggestion above that Germanus was militarily active in that area. (The origins of Powis will be explored in part II.)[62] Nevertheless Germanus's impact on Britain must have been considerable, with seven dedications in Wales, three in the west country, two in Yorkshire and one in Cleveland, Lincolnshire, Norfolk and Essex, not to mention in the Isle of Man; though some were later than the early medieval period.[63]

Britain alone: second phase

Professor Charles-Edwards, commenting on the *Historia Brittonum's* account of Vortigern, remarked that 'it seems to provide an unprovable but convincing sequence of events. Also the story of Vortigern opposing Ambrosius may reflect a dimly remembered reality.'[64] The outline of these dimly remembered events includes the story already touched upon that Vortigern concluded a treaty with the Saxons whom he had recruited, presumably from the Continent, so that in return for serving under his colours against the Picts and Scots (and in all probability other Irish too) they would be settled in Thanet (*in orientalis parte insulae*, according to Gildas), this in around 428 or 429. They were led, we are told by later sources, by a chieftain called Hengist, whose name is as ubiquitous amongst these sources, as is that of Vortigern, but neither are contemporaneously attested (*pace* Gildas), as we have seen. As we have also seen, this method of bolstering one's armed forces was perfectly normal late Roman policy and worked reasonably well all over the empire for many decades.

No doubt Hengist held office as Vortigern's *magister militum*, as had a number of barbarian leaders on the other side of the Channel at this time, nominally at least under the western emperor, as Kent has convincingly suggested.[65] That the term 'Saxon' as used by chroniclers seems to contain an element of imprecision (or generalisation) is reinforced by finds from Germanic cemeteries in Kent and Sussex, which resemble material from Frankish cemeteries on the near continent and might suggest Hengist and his men were indeed Franks.[66] As such, it would appear that between them, Vortigern and the 'Saxon' federates (no doubt aided by the polities between the walls) managed to neutralise the Picts, with the resulting period of peace seemingly lasting a considerable time.[67] Such arrangements only failed to work when the incomers got too strong or numerous, as gradually happened on mainland Europe.

As in Gaul, so in Britain, Vortigern's *foederati*, in Oliver Twist mode (though with more clout), eventually demanded increased *annonae* to meet the demands of expanding numbers, which, being denied (presumably for financial or logistical reasons and no doubt exacerbated by the climate anomaly of those years), caused the treaty to be abrogated.[68] The Saxons thereupon rebelled, supposedly wrecked much of Britain (more probably the south and east only), but were eventually brought to heel by British counter-measures. In the end, the Romano-British succeeded in pushing the Saxons back to those eastern parts of Britain where archaeology tells us they were at that time becoming settled, although who actually led the counter-attack, no one knows. Doubtless, the Saxons agreed to a further written treaty, being rewarded with an element of political control over much more of Britain than previously. Throughout all this, there must have been Britons living in areas under Saxon domination and after the restoration of the *status quo ante*, Saxons living under British rule; one suspects that a slow fusion between the various groups had begun.[69] The climate-induced plague mentioned by Hydatius *sub anno* 443 may well have coincided with all this, and may therefore have accounted for the sharp decline of towns and probably for a shortage of produce, which in turn would have led to shortfalls or failure in the delivery of the Saxons' *annona* and hence could well have been the underlying reason for the Saxon Revolt itself.[70]

There is contemporary attestation for this revolt by the Saxon federates, for the Gallic Chronicler of 452 wrote under the year 442 (possibly to be revised to 440/441 but surely three years or so too early): 'The Britains, having been up to this time afflicted by various disasters and vicissitudes, were brought under the control of the Saxons.'[71]

This information was surely well attested, bearing in mind the cross-Channel contacts which continued in the fifth century. Furthermore, the chronicler may well have been in touch with the British-born St Faustus, Bishop of Alebaece Reiorum (Riez), a former Abbot of Lérins (which itself occurs in the *Chronicle*). He was yet another friend of Sidonius Apollinaris, who was related by marriage to both Faustus and Avitus, formerly *Magister Equitum* in Gaul and briefly emperor following Petronius Maximus in 455-456. Sidonius admired the writings of Faustus, who is known to have received books from Britain through a priest by the name of Riocatus whom Sidonius also encountered.[72] This sort of link establishes the veracity of the chronicler's information and would be much strengthened were we able to plunge more confidently into the unreliable reaches of Vortigern's family history, cited previously. While the *Historia Brittonum* presents us with his family and posterity, these are to some extent repeated in later compilations, like the genealogy in the Jesus College MS 20.[73]

This tells us that a Faustus was a fourth son of Vortigern. Another son was Pascent/Pasgen (Pascentius) who had two sons, one of whom was called Riagath (Riocatus). Were these details of hoary enough vintage (of which we can never really be sure), we might reasonably suggest that both Faustus and the Riocatus known to Sidonius were one and the same as Vortigern's son and grandson, which would provide a greatly enhanced link between Britain to southern Gaul, through which information could have flowed. Whatever the link, it would be entirely reasonable to suppose that the Saxon revolt, as we may refer to it, temporarily cut the maritime south of Britain off from the

Continent, hence the *Chronicle of 452* entry. It would seem likely at this time that actual rather than nominal control of parts of East Anglia was probably lost and briefly, considerably more. Worse, Ambrosius appears to have lost his life in the upheaval. The devastating effect of it may be explicable in terms of surprise, possible climatic upheavals and unpreparedness of the British authorities.

Ambrosius Aurelianus

Things must have been desperate for, according to Gildas, 'the miserable remnants sent a letter again, this time to Agitius, a man of Roman power,' which read: 'To Agitius, thrice consul the groans of the Britons ... the barbarians push us back to the sea; the sea pushes us back to the barbarians; between these two kinds of death we are either drowned or slaughtered.'[74]

But they had no kind of help for these complaints. Gildas, being the only near-contemporary authority for the next phase, adds:

> A remnant ... that they should not be utterly destroyed, take up arms and challenge their victors to battle under Ambrosius Aurelianus. He was a man of unassuming character, who, alone of the Roman race chanced to survive in the shock of such a storm (as his parents, people undoubtedly clad in the purple, had been killed in it), whose offspring in our days have greatly degenerated from their ancestral nobility. To these men, by the Lord's favour, there came victory.[75]

This introduces Ambrosius Aurelianus, whom we have suggested may well have been the son of the Ambrosius who fought Vortigern/Vitalinus at the Battle of Wallop in around 436 and lost his life in the revolt. Gildas continues: 'From that time, the citizens were sometimes victorious, sometimes the enemy ... this continued up to the year of the siege of Badon Hill, and of almost the last great slaughter inflicted upon the rascally crew.'[76]

The dating of all this has proved a particularly thorny problem. Gildas seems to have compressed several decades into only a few years. The chaos caused by the Saxon Revolt need not have lasted more than a year or two. The appeal to Agitius (in reality probably conducted by a formal deputation) may have been seen as an element in the settlement by the British central authority in the aftermath, wherein Germanic settlers may well have been allocated large tracts by treaty – East Anglia and the middle Thames basin spring to mind – just as had Hengist's men in Thanet a few years before. To complicate matters, the appeal itself was 'corrected' by Bede to an appeal to Aëtius, who was indeed consul for the third time in 446 and remained as *magister utriusque militum* under Valentinian III until his murder in 454.[77]

Yet Bede was writing two centuries later, so on what authority did he correct Gildas? If the appeal *was* to Aëtius, it provides us with a neat time frame from his consulship in 446 to his demise in 454, but at this juncture, he had his hands full keeping Gaul under imperial control and later successfully taking on Attila the Hun, so his being unable to help would have come as no surprise. Yet things had changed rather from the accession of the emperor Severus III in 461. Control of northern Gaul and the Rhine border was being exercised by the *magister militum* and *comes* there, appointed in 456 by the emperor Avitus, namely Aegidius.

When the barbarian power broker Ricimer had the emperor Maiorianus murdered in late 461, he raised to the throne a puppet ruler, Severus, like Eugenius, a bureaucrat. A new appointee was sent out to replace the Gallic *magister militum*, but he was rebuffed, defeated and forced to return by Aegidius, who, needless to say, was another Gallo-Roman aristocrat, who had earlier in his career served under Aëtius himself. His self-appointment in 461 and subsequent success rather bears out the observation of Jill Harries concerning Gallic events at this period that 'the empire in the west was being run by a set of informal expedients, not by the rules.'[78]

This, therefore, could well be the Agitius to whom Gildas says the Romano-British authorities, under equally expediential control, had appealed to help, as under him, northern Gaul had been made fairly safe and settled from the mid-450s. If the appeal was in that decade rather the late 440s, then he still controlled the whole area, although after setting himself up as a *tyrannus* in 461, he was forced to cede control of Cologne and Trier to his Frankish allies.

After Severus III was proclaimed, Aegidius threatened to invade Italy, only being prevented by conflict with the Visigoths, whom he subsequently put down with aplomb. He was apparently distinguished both by his prowess and conduct.[79] He therefore ruled what appears to have been yet another breakaway Gallic empire, not dissimilar to that controlled by Constantine III, but of a considerably smaller area. He was noted for his courage, good character and faith. He died in autumn 465, although accounts vary as to how this came about, one version favouring poison and the other death in an ambush.[80] Nevertheless, he was succeeded almost seamlessly by his son, Syagrius. Professor Fanning has written, 'It would be extremely rash to suggest that Aegidius and Syagrius were in fact Roman emperors, but it is clear that Gregory of Tours and the *Liber Historiae Francorum* were using language that meant just that.'[81]

Their situation was then precisely analogous to that which seems to have pertained in Britain since 409. The Franks for their part acknowledged Aegidius as their overlord, referring to him as *rex* – king.[82]

The chief objection to the identification of Aegidius as the object of the Britons' entreaties is that he is not known to have held one consulship, let alone three. Yet when Postumus established his breakaway Gallic empire in 260, he had appointed his own consuls and, as we have seen, Constantine III may well have done likewise, and certainly appointed himself. Therefore, it is possible that from 461 until 465 Aegidius could have held three consulships within his own *imperium* quite unrecorded by posterity; it may even have been the style under which he ruled, which would fix the appeal firmly in 463. Indeed, his first consulship may have been a suffect (supplementary) one on the nomination of fellow Gallic aristocrat turned emperor Avitus or even Maiorianus, for the record of these appointments after the fourth century gets increasingly patchy.[83] There seems no reason, therefore, why the appeal should not have been made to Aegidius as Gildas's account suggests. One thing the appeal (to whomsoever) does tell us is that the British authorities still considered themselves at least nominally as part of the empire; otherwise, why should they have expected assistance from that quarter? As Professor Charles-Edwards writes,

> ... the appeal to Aëtius presupposes an allegiance on the part of Britain to an Empire of which he was then the principal military leader in the west. Only if Roman rule had been restored in north Gaul would such an appeal have made sense.[84]

This applies to Aëtius, but not to Aegidius, who certainly *was* in control of North Gaul. While Aegidius (or Aëtius) presumably did not come to the aid of the British administration, it does indicate that Gaul was a lot more settled, at least for a while, under both commanders. Aëtius had secured northern Gaul around 428, campaigning on the Rhine frontier once more, just at the time when Germanus was in Britain, a visit probably made less hazardous through the commander's securing the diocese from chaos. The Roman *magister militum*'s subsequent settlement of barbarians as federate troops in south-western Gaul from the 430s will have provided Vortigern with a template, too; in both, the barbarians eventually gained the upper hand, but not until decades of campaigning and negotiation had passed. At the time of his second consulship, Aëtius had his hands full, although the Rhine frontier was restored and the mint at Trier resumed issuing imperial coinage. Yet from the 440s until they were defeated in 451 and dispersed following Attila's death two years later, Aëtius was exclusively concerned with the Hunnic incursion. An appeal to him in 446, the British authorities would have known, would have produced precious little assistance. Also, with a *tyrannus* in charge in Britain, a task force from the imperial government was going to mean instant deposition – civil war, in short.

Later, Aëtius had been killed and chaos returned, a situation only rectified when Aegidius was appointed by the energetic emperor Maiorianus in 456. Thereafter, northern Gaul remained relatively settled and so continued until 486, when Aegidius's son, the *tyrannus* Syagrius, lost everything to the expansionist policies of his former ally, the Frankish leader Clovis. Yet was it not Syagrius's name that was inscribed on a batch of pewter ingots found in the Thames?[85]

The appeal, though, may be seen to have coincided with a considerable migration of Britons to Gaul and especially to Armorica, a part of the empire similarly positioned politically to Britain, having revolted in 409 and having apparently not been fully brought back under imperial control subsequently. The mystery there is that, although there can be little doubt that while the Saxon revolt or any of the other upheavals of the sort postulated above took place in southern and eastern Britain, the migrants seem to have come from the south-west. Archaeology (supported by legend) suggests that most mid-fifth century migration to Brittany from Britain came from Dumnonia, well away from the Germanic invaders of the era. This was a less Latinised area linguistically, hence the Bretons tended to speak British and not vulgar Latin or a romance derivative. One theory is that they were fleeing coastal raids made by Picts and the Irish *Scotti,* known to have marauded along the coasts of Wales and the south-west.[86] Somehow, that seems not to be the sole reason. Indeed, the spur to this important migration has yet to be agreed.

Considering that the appeal to Aëtius (or Aegidius) might have been a decade or so later than supposed, there would therefore be a less elongated timeframe from this point until the final victory of the Britons, which itself is the subject of much debate, due to Gildas referring to its dating rather coyly – or even cryptically. Gildas seems not to say specifically that Ambrosius Aurelianus actually led the British forces in these campaigns or even at the final victory over the Saxons, the Battle of Badon, but Michael Wood has carefully scrutinised all the surviving manuscripts of Gildas and especially the earliest (in the British Library), from which he has concluded that Ambrosius Aurelianus was indeed involved personally in the victory at Badon. We might also ask whether Britain was so overrun that Ambrosius Aurelianus was obliged to commence his fight-back from some stronghold within the federate-held frontier zones, which might explain the re-fortification of Cadbury Castle in Somerset, for instance. On the other hand, our perception of the disaster of the revolt may be too heavily influenced by Gildas's rhetoric, and that the Saxons' capabilities at this stage would have been constrained by their becoming over-extended. One can only feed an army by pillage for so long.

The location and date of Badon is much debated, but not wholly unresolved. A location on an eminence close to Bath is an attractive suggestion, supported by *Historia Brittonum*, which refers to Bath – *In quo balnea sunt Badonis quod est in regione Huich* ('where the baths of Badon are, in the country of the Hwicce).[87] Victory achieved, our rather shaky later sources suggest that Ambrosius Aurelianus went on to rebuild York and establish himself in London.[88] Parts of the heavily rebuilt Roman walls at York – notably the so-called Anglian Tower – to some extent support this view (the latter has been hard to date, but the early Anglian era is not necessarily the correct context). But the archaeological lacuna which is mid- to late fifth-century London does not.So much has been destroyed by subsequent re-buildings in the capital, however, wrecking the relevant strata, that this need not be seen as conclusive.[89]

One thing which does emerge from these confusing events is that Britain was still (or once again) under some kind of central control, a situation entirely consistent with the continental perception of the diocese being 'under usurpers'. That these people – presumably including Owein/ Eugenius, Vortigern/Vitalinus, Ambrosius and Aurelianus – enjoyed full control of most of lowland Britain (Saxon revolt notwithstanding) seems not in doubt. Whatever our *post facto* interpretation of the Anglo-Saxons and others 'taking over' vast amounts of lowland Britain, the likelihood is that following the turmoil of the 440, they were settled on land largely on borders between *civitates* probably depopulated by climatic perturbations or rural decline, through formal treaty or agreement. Interrogating the archaeology to confirm this is, however, complex, for it is now clear that the material culture of both groups was virtually indistinguishable in the majority of contexts in lowland Britain.[90] It is not until this shadowy central authority fades completely from view that the early Saxon kingdoms begin to emerge, some occupying similar boundaries to the old tribal *civitates*, and some indeed, as we shall see, with other enigmatic possible British roots, like Wessex, Lindsey and Mercia.

Life and money after 409

With Constantine III on the continent and running into choppy waters, we have seen Britain raided by Saxons (no mention of Picts and Scots on this occasion, but their participation may be confidently assumed) accompanied by much destruction. We have learnt that Constantine's appointees were thrown out but have no unchallengeable word from any source as to exactly what happened next, except that the island was ruled by tyrants. That these *tyranni* were home-grown magnates or senior officers by chance stationed in the diocese is partly supported by Gildas and Constantius, who use the term *regio* in lieu of *provincia* when referring to Britain's political geography. This implies that the term came into being in order to describe the vastly expanded estates undoubtedly built up by leading aristocratic families, possibly even in the wake of the post 409 'purge', which surely liberated some such estates from their legal proprietors or saw a substantial number of proprietors retiring to the Continent and either disposing of their estates or leaving them under the control of a nominee or bailiff.[91]

Similarly, of course, there must have been the question of imperial ones, previously run directly by the bureaucracy on the emperor's behalf. Members of such families, armed with the concomitantly expanded manpower reserves that came with the vast additional acreages, were consequently 'well on their way to usurping many of the prerogatives of empire.'[92] On the other hand, the loss of the demand for grain and meat from the voracious Rhine army and the ensuing loss of income must have reduced the notional or actual value of these estates considerably, although the demand for *annona* within the former diocese clearly remained. We have to assume that the cash still circulating would have paid for it at least at first; thereafter much barter and horse-trading must have been necessary to establish a stable economic basis for the surviving estates. Thus, we are thrown back on archaeological evidence and of other material, including numismatics.

One of the chief reasons that the money economy functioned reasonably well in the empire was that the army had to be paid and fed, and that required bullion coin. Silver and base metal issues were concomitantly necessary to provide change. Nevertheless, supply fluctuated. The use of silver as expressed in hoard finds went up in the period from 348 to 364 and rose to a maximum from 402 to 408, and in this period gold was hoarded, too. From the time of the so-called Barbarian Conspiracy there was a sharp increase in the supply of bullion coinage in Britain, which peaked in the period 394 to 402, whereas low-value coins are only apparent in hoards deposited from the mid-third century until the mid-fourth.[93]

By the later fourth century though, about three-quarters of a soldier's pay was in kind with the remainder in cash. Hence, cash still had to be minted either in the diocese in which the troops were stationed or shipped in from the nearest mint beyond. In Britain the London mint is not known to have been used after Maximus's time. This was the situation in the British diocese both in and after Magnus Maximus's reign. Fleming cites the conversion of the arena at Corinium (Cirencester, Gloucestershire) and the very late walling of Cunetio (by Mildenhall, Wilts.) – both of which could have been initiatives of Maximus's reign of only a decade or two before – as their preparation as collection depôts for produce to be moved forward as *annona*.[94] Yet coastal garrison *limitanei* in North Wales, Lancashire, Cumberland and the east coast of Yorkshire seem to have been paid at least partly in cash up until 402, judging by finds.[95] So with the field army at least absent after spring 407, the money supply, already five years in decline, would have plunged even further. Then, after 409, with Britain administratively and militarily cut off from the rest of the empire, the supply is thought to have been entirely discontinued.

Some recent commentators had asserted that this caused an immediate crash of the money economy and the collapse of the entire Romano-British way of life in less than a decade. Others, maybe intoxicated by the anti-colonial tropes of the modern era and perhaps impelled by an evangelical radicalism, support this view and conjure up pictures of valiant oppressed Britons forming groups of roaming *bacaudae* (outlaws and freed slaves), torching villas, plundering towns, throwing off the Roman yoke and reverting to a simpler way of life, something that can neither be inferred from a reading of Gildas – despite some apocalyptic purple passages – nor from any other source remotely near to the period; although roaming *bacaudae* are recorded from contemporary Armorica, albeit without the cataclysmic longer term results such theorising tends to imply.[96]

This does not seem to be what the evidence that we have demonstrates at all. True, the urban Roman way of life eventually *did* fall away, but it was a mutation forced by circumstances not of the Romano-Britons' choosing and was much more gradual and piecemeal that was once thought; after all, Viroconium, changed but still thriving, survived into the mid-seventh century. The currency, for instance, undoubtedly survived into the fifth century, but exactly how long is the pertinent question; there is evidence for a gold, silver and bronze currency functioning for a 'significant time' after 409.[97] It is one thing to determine a *terminus post quem* on the basis of the latest coin issue found in any one site, but this tends to lead to 'the great coin fallacy of assuming contemporary occupation by a similar coin range'.[98] Wear is a significant determinant, and in late fourth- or early fifth-century sites, coin wear, often considerable, is invariably present; the key is to determine from the wear approximately how long the coins were in circulation and at least a decade or more is thought to be a reliable yardstick. Furthermore, the clipping of late fourth- or early fifth-century silver *siliquae* to make home-grown copies was also rife. Currency use can thus be shown to have been extant in *c.* 409/410.

Clipping occurred in the fifth century, from 402 onwards, when the Milan mint stopped issuing *siliquae* as a result of the imperial court moving from thence to Ravenna.[99] Clipped *siliquae* found in the Pyrenees may be the legacy of the passage of British troops of Constantine III or those of Gerontius, brought with them from an immediate post-acclamation donative.[100] Clipping of *siliquae* always respected the image of the emperor and the silver was used to make exact copies of the coins, which is why we know they were intended to remain in currency.[101] When Kent adds that Theodosian issues 'show a marked recession from the north and west of Britain, the reason for which has not been established', he is underlining the fact that, as here proposed, Maximus had re-allocated control over these regions to native appointees as client fiefs with less need for coin.[102]

In Britain under Constantine III a smaller number of *siliquae* have been recorded of an issue of *c.* 407-408 bearing the reverse message VICTORIA AUGGGG (Victory of the [four] emperors) type, which represented an attempt to maintain a precious metal currency after the departure of the usurper himself. The hoard from Bishop Cannings (Wiltshire) contained one gold, 5,699 silver coins (many of them clipped) and 5,837 bronze, all datable to 364-402. The suggested date of deposition is after the end of the first decade of the fifth century and thus the coins must have been still valid and circulating. Kent cites three British hoards containing clipped *siliquae*, one including examples of the very rare URBS ROMA Trier issue of Honorius issued around 420, which he claims are the 'latest Roman coins to be found in an unequivocally Roman context'.[103] Evidence for a gold, silver and bronze currency that was circulating for a significant time after 410 is therefore strong. Coins of this date have been found on Hadrian's Wall and amongst the settlements nearby.[104]

After the approximate time of Constantine III's acclamation, less bronze turns up, but some issues from as late as about 430 do appear and the fact that Roman bronze from the eastern empire called *nummi* (debased of all silver content from the mid-fourth century) have been found in Britain, in issues up to the seventh century in date, suggest that there was still a need for a certain amount of small change, presumably generated by overseas trade. If the *only* coins found as late as this were of bullion quality (i.e. gold and silver) we might suppose that they were being traded as such, but the need for change suggests that some kinds of monetary transactions were being made from the 430s and even into the century following.[105]

Sam Moorhead supposes that currency may have been maintained certainly in the south-east, mainly on the evidence of the hoards discovered at Richborough and Patching (near Brighton, Sussex), the latter of mid-5th-century date, including a *solidus* of Severus III (reigned 461-465). Bland believes that this changes our view of the orthodoxy that coins ceased to enter Britain after the reign of Constantine III. Post-409 gold issues and even bronze are both apparent and, if the Patching assemblage in a straw in the wind, more may come to light. The alternative is that they were generated by small-scale trade or from well-heeled visitors from the Continent, which seems less persuasive.[106]

Viroconium has produced late bronze coinage as well as other post-Roman sites, supporting the continued circulation of coins even to some limited extent until the mid-seventh century, although this has been disputed.[107] Eastern empire coins seem to have been circulating in the south-west, in Gloucestershire, even to south-west Herefordshire (the legendary heartland of Vortigern) for even longer, undoubtedly through continuing strong trading links with the east; the last such coin found so far being a gold *solidus* of the emperor Phocas of 602.[108] There is a hint that gold coins may have been circulating even after that, albeit probably as bullion and not strictly as currency.

When Alfred the Great of Wessex allied himself with Coewulf II of Mercia against the Viking Great Army in 878, a coinage of silver *denarii* (pence) was struck showing on the reverse the two kings sitting, armed and sceptred within a square reserve with a winged victory (probably interpreted as an angel in 878) above them, a direct crib from Magnus Maximus's London mint 'two emperors' issue of *solidi* mentioned in Chapter 3. The implication is that there were still a good number of these around in the ninth century, which in turn prompts the speculation that whatever military settlement was made in 383/4 was perhaps lubricated by this issue.[109] That it might have formed the donative on Maximus's elevation seems less likely, as this, if really required in 383 and not in 380, would probably have been made in Trier-minted issues – unless the re-consideration of the chronology of the *Chronicle of 452* is right, in which case the *largitio* would have been made in Britain, when it would surely have been made in the AVG mintmark issues also set out in Chapter 3.

It has also been suggested that the end of Roman administration led to a reduction in demand for tax. The widespread conversion of arable land into pasture that characterizes the period is evidence of a shift away from high-density forms of agricultural production – required for the provision of *annona* – to those of lower intensity, with lower labour and capital costs, as well as being a response to climate change from the 440s and quite possibly from longer-term de-population. Without the demand of imperial taxation either in cash or in kind, fifth-century farmers retained a greater portion of their produce, and the élite was able to retain a greater portion of their slaves' and peasants' surpluses. Pastoral land use in the north continued uninterrupted from late Roman times until the early sixth century or even beyond, and many settlements saw continuing occupation well beyond the standing of mere squatters.[110] In both cases, though, tax would have been replaced by occasional levies in kind to support soldiers in the field, thanks to the military upheavals following the Saxon Revolt and at least until Badon.

Rural change

The general consensus seems to be that most villas proved economically unsustainable with the end of imperial demand for *annona*, although their estates may well have continued as physical and legal entities. Yet not all villas appear to have declined. Some villas, previously explained as being occupied by 'squatters', it now appears lost their élite domestic status and became estate hubs, with formal rooms adapted as corn dryers, storage, even manufacturing centres with probably just a bailiff dwelling in one part of the building.[111] Also, the change from cash payment to barter and *annona* seems to have brought a 'heightened importance of agriculture' to both town and country, although requiring the adaptation of existing buildings to cope with it.[112]

Other villas seem to have survived in use well after the beginning of the fifth century, for instance, a group of them in western Oxfordshire like

Barton Court and Shakenoak. That at Frocester (Gloucestershire) was extensively rebuilt *c.* 360 and remained in use, though to a diminished standard, throughout the fifth century and into the sixth, perhaps as an estate hub. This certainly accords with evidence from Cirencester and indeed most of Gloucestershire which, even on the shaky evidence of the *Anglo-Saxon Chronicle,* remained British-controlled until the third quarter of the seventh century, for doubt has been cast upon the finality of the apparent Saxon victory at Dyrham (Gloucestershire) in 577, or even whether it happened at all.[113] Another villa, at Lopen, Somerset, discovered in 2001, has a remarkably late mosaic floor.[114] More significant still is the discovery in late 2020 of a mosaic floor freshly added to the rebuilt room 28 of the opulent villa not far from the Fosse Way at Chedworth (Gloucestershire). This was made the more dramatic when a piece of bone found beneath the mosaic established without doubt that the works had been undertaken no earlier than 424 and quite possibly some time later. The workmanship may have left a little to be desired, but it suggests that other mosaics, in the north range especially, may be contemporary.

Also found on site over the years have been pieces of late Romano(-British) shelly ware (which may have lasted longer into the fifth century than previously assumed) including a near complete jar from Room 27, fragments of imported amphorae of fifth- and sixth-century date, and even some early Saxon ceramic pieces.[115] Without doubt it can be said that this villa was flourishing through the fifth and even well into the sixth century, perhaps even as a significant power base.[116]

In 2017 at Boxford, Berks., an exceptional late mosaic was uncovered at Mud Hole villa depicting Pelops and Bellerophon, which was fully excavated and recorded in 2019. Anthony Beeson has compared it with the fifth-century illuminations of the Vatican's British-originating *Virgilius Romanus* MS and the Bellerophon panel in the British Museum, also fifth century.[117] Beeson has, subsequent to the announcement of the late date of the Chedworth mosaic, suggested that the Boxford floor, too, is also possibly of fifth-century date.[118] It even names the villa's likely owners, Caepio and Fortunata, the inscription suggesting it was installed in their hunting lodge (for such the excavator considered it to have been) at the expense of Fortunata's parents, presumably as a wedding present. Fifth century or not, the historic patrician name Caepio is unique for the late empire; even Fortunata is rare for the period and neither are particularly British.[119]

Other villas in the general area seem to have continued, at least for a while, like those as Withington (the boundaries of which were thought by the late Professor Finberg to have survived as the parish boundary) and Turkdean, all notably extensive.[120] Many superior villas – the country houses of Roman Britain, with their hypocausted, well-proportioned rooms, mosaic floors and architectural embellishments – must have survived even if diagnostic finds are hard to identify. This evidence can no longer be explained as freakish or even exceptional. It may well be that late fourth-century archaeological data, based on declining pottery finds, late coin loss and so on, needs to be re-thought and substantially re-dated to the early fifth century; the time frames of some strata perhaps require temporal extension, too.[121]

Elsewhere we find villas sub-divided after the early fifth century for multiple occupation or adapted for use as forges, barns, industrial workshops and corn dryers. This is surely pragmatism in the face of changed circumstances, reduced incomes and general insecurity; it probably reflects the fact that some grandees of senatorial rank, although owning land in Britain, decided to become permanently non-resident, thanks to the incursions of barbarian raiders, and merely take whatever income in kind it was possible to realise, making their spacious seats redundant as centres of show, occasional resort and in which to receive *clientelae*: dependants, people under an obligation and tenants, as suggested by the Lundy, East Ogwell and Lanivet inscriptions (see chapter 10). What is apparent in many instances is the constructive re-use of redundant buildings, rather than evidence of barbarian takeover, widespread destruction (*pace* Gildas) or some kind of total collapse of Romano-British society.

The fact that much evidence is now to hand to establish continuity of estate and other boundaries from before the coming of the Romans to a time long afterwards and – as parish boundaries – even to the present, strengthens the case for continuity, whether or not the buildings themselves gradually became superfluous or an encumbrance. Parish boundaries now appear much earlier than once thought; several in Wiltshire seem to pre-date the Dark Age Wansdyke, which cuts across them. Ancient parish boundaries thus must therefore date back to at least *c* 550 or further, so that

> ... it is hard to see how such early boundaries were fixed if they do not relate in some way to the parcelling of land by Roman or earlier landholders. The legal processes however, which allowed ownership of such land to pass [undivided] from Roman to Saxon remains shrouded in mystery. We can perhaps then speculate that Roman boundaries were still visible or being observed, and were merely taken over wholesale in areas where there was ethnic change.[122]

Likewise, Wendy Davies, arguing from the evidence of the Llandaff Charters and other later material relating to south Wales, convincingly demonstrates that landed estates, in most cases quite large, being of thousands rather than low hundreds of acres in extent, continued into the fifth century and beyond. She remarks, too, on the use of Roman terminology in the earlier charters (use of words such as *ager* and *uncia*) for units of land, and the continuing complexity of property rights, which are discernible in the later donations made by local rulers, having to override long extant limitations on the disposal of land by sale, as was true elsewhere in the west in the late empire. One can trace some continuity of estate boundaries, although not one hundred per cent; the entire area's pattern of landholding underwent a very gradual change between the fifth and ninth centuries. She also notes the large amount of well-circulated late fourth-century coins which have been found in this area, even as far north as Hereford, and the allied fact that the cemetery at Venta Silurum (Caerwent, Mon.) continued in use well into the sixth century, too.[123] Roman settlement in early medieval Britain seems to have left a legal pattern of ownership which appeared to have survived even where full occupation did not. Plenty of Anglo-Saxon period charters, especially in the Cotswold area, record change, implying previous patterns of ownership, underpinned by much earlier charters.

In this context, Charles Thomas pointed out that St Patrick, on his return from captivity in Ireland in around 440 (via a sojourn in Gaul) was able to sell his father Calpurnius's estate, which he convincingly locates in the *territorium* of Luguvalium (Carlisle). Patrick seems to have had no trouble in finding a willing buyer, nor did his father's career as a decurion seem to have lost relevance a decade or two earlier, despite the dark chaos painted by Gildas. The province of Valentia, in which it seems to have lain, appears to have been a relatively safe place in his lifetime, despite his earlier abduction. Thomas proposes too that Germanus, on his second visit to Britain, may have encouraged Patrick to seek ordination.[124]

There was thus clearly no general dismemberment of existing property, possibly even in eastern England where Romano-British control was apparently lost or surrendered early on. Germanic incomers were not all members of war-bands intent on destroying the existing order:

> Most such men would want not a style of life to which they were accustomed but a Romanised existence and they might well in the world of late Roman Britain have been accepted as immigrants and develop[ed] a lifestyle fairly heavily indistinguishable from that of provincial Romano-Britons. Such men as were able to infiltrate thus would scarcely be the leaders of war bands … but craftsmen useful to society, mercenaries or recruitment material.[125]

Such craftsmen would have included those who collected Roman pot bases and turned them into moulds for the making of bronze saucer brooches: there's nothing new about recycling, or even up-cycling![126] Another mutation of the villa was to be adapted as monastic establishments, as is well attested on the Continent. The well-regarded monastic settlement of St Illtud was founded a few miles south-west of the late Roman fort at Cardiff by a Gallic or Breton monk, Iltutus – probably trained in the tradition of St Martin (and allegedly by St Germanus) – seemingly in a villa, the owner of which may have become the institution's first patron.[127]

Villas also became adapted as churches – house churches – and several examples have been identified in Britain, the earliest at Lullingstone, Kent. An interesting example occurs in Britannia Prima, nine miles south-east of Bath near Bradford on Avon. Here, a 15-foot-wide (4.6m) baptistry and font had been neatly inserted into a splendid mosaic floor in one of the finest rooms of the 'weirdo twin villa' (as described recently by Simon Esmonde Cleary) lying on a north-south ridge beneath the grounds of St Laurence's School. This impressive and puzzling dual structure was built, only partly on a fresh site, in the second quarter of the third century, and the baptistry was inserted competently in the (early) fifth, rather suggesting that it may have formed the basis for an adaptation into a similar role. William of Malmesbury informs us that Bradford on Avon was previously called *Wirtgernesburg* ('the defended settlement of Vortigern'), so one might be forgiven for wondering if this palatial ensemble had any connection with the family of its apparent eponym.[128]

The name Bradford first occurs in the ASC *sub anno* 652, where Cenwealh of Wessex fought a battle, presumably against the Britons, as ASC later records him defeating them further west at *Posentesburg* (Posbury, Devon) in 661. Assuming the name Bradford was then valid and not a retrospective coinage, this might suggest that there were two settlements: the villa complex then called *Wirtgernesburg*, and the town. The double villa might have been later part fortified, thus deserving its '–*burg*' suffix, as one finds in Gaul, as with Sidonius Apollinaris's *Burgus*.[129] The baptistry, however, strongly suggests modification later as a house-church, especially as the former field in which it lies was once called Church Ground.[130] As the modern settlement seems to have considerably post-dated the villa, William of Malmesbury's name may in fact have been that of the villa complex, which certainly survived well into the fifth century, and the religious focus may have migrated to Bradford itself once the latter had become established.

There are hints of others, similarly adapted. It was much more common in Europe.[131] Excavations around St Martin-in-the-Fields, London, in 2008 revealed an aristocratic sarcophagus burial datable to *c.* 390-430, accompanied by other Roman material including a late Roman tile kiln, which suggested that James Gibbs's magnificent church and its predecessors were also built on the site of a suburban villa. If so, it had probably been adapted to religious use in the fifth century.[132] In view of Maximus's links to St Martin and the influence of some of the saint's followers on Britain in the fifth century, the dedication of the present church may well represent continuity.

As Christianity continued to spread, there was also a rise in interest in the shrines of martyrs. We have seen how keen Germanus and Lupus were to see that at Verulamium dedicated to St Albanus; there was also a shrine (long lost) at Caerleon to SS. Aaron and Julian, and another, possibly in Kent, at Durolevum (Syndale, near Faversham) at Stone Chapel, perhaps to Crispin and Crispinian. Indeed, as Saints Crispin and Crispianus (patron saints of shoemakers and cobblers) martyred in 285 under the Emperor Diocletian, are said in one version of their legend to have been natives of Durolevum, here might have been their *martyrium*, or that of some other local saint, like the enigmatic St Sixtus, whose exploits perhaps attracted the legend of SS Crispin and Crispian from Gaul, but whose name is now lost to us. [133] In October 2021, during work on the HS2 railway beneath the church of St Mary, Stoke Mandeville, Buckinghamshire, a domestic mausoleum was revealed, complete with funerary busts, which appears to have been rebuilt for Christian use at about this period, probably explaining why a later church was superimposed upon it.

Although usually thought of as essentially an urban phenomenon in late Roman times, Christianity seems from the few examples quoted above also to have been moderately well established in the country, certainly amongst the élite. The survival of the British church beyond the dramatic events of the early 440s is certain, especially when one notes that it was a British synod that attempted to censure St Patrick in around 471. Professor Thomas thinks there was a single British bishop with metropolitan status in late fifth-century Britain and that he was based in York rather than in London. [134]

Urban change

The precipitous drop in the tax take removed only part of the *raison d'être* of the towns and cities, which is where taxes had been gathered, either in cash or kind, with net produce sold thereafter at market. The corps of tax farmers and related officials may well have continued to gather some kind of render under whatever authority followed 409, and the towns would seem still to have been a necessary adjunct of this process. Nevertheless, the Roman tax system, Professor Higham feels, probably survived for some time, initially at first highly bureaucratised, but evolving from a semi-monetary system into a tax-in-kind one, inevitably dominated by estate owners, later further developing into some kind of food rents, which kept the local warlords in the field and later the Anglo-Saxon ones, too. [135] Some officials, essentially redundant, may have left for the Continent after 409, hoping for preferment elsewhere. Whatever damage had been done in the raiding of that year cannot have helped, although the walls that surrounded a majority of urban centres, combined with the inability of most likely enemies to undertake a siege, would suggest that the countryside possibly bore the brunt of it, and that is likely to be true of the Saxon revolt thirty-three years later. Hydatius's plague outbreak in 443 may also have exacerbated the sharp decline of the towns in the mid-fifth century and of course affected the countryside as well. And as we have seen above, this may, in wrecking the harvest, have starved the federate troops of their *annona* and in consequence have been instrumental in provoking the Saxon Revolt. [136]

Yet even in the eastern parts of Britain, some continuity can be argued for in the fifth and sixth centuries, despite Gildas's jeremiad about abandoned cities. This might just as well derive from his observation of towns temporarily deserted during the upheavals he describes (exaggerated for histrionic reasons) and which had merely been sacked. Dr Alex Woolf has suggested that central control most likely survived for a long time from Western Dumnonia to the Wash and points east and south.[137] Evidence for continuing occupation of the larger towns and *civitas* capitals continues to strengthen, despite the dearth of archaeological evidence for repair and rebuilding. A loss of masonry skills may well be the explanation for the lack of stone buildings attributable to the post-Roman population, but this lack seems to have been compensated for by the probable use of buildings of timber sill construction, which leave few marks on the ground and fail to show in the archaeological record; excavations at provably post-Roman settlements such as Wroxeter seem to support this, as Dr Woolf has proposed.

'Dark earth' layers are also being seen not as a symptom of decline or desertion but of late Roman activity.[138] Viroconium continued into the seventh century, although considerably changed in almost every way over the two or more centuries of its post-Roman existence, yet still distinctly urban; Verulamium (St Albans, Hertfordshire), it can be demonstrated, despite some dispute, seems to have been thriving, relatively speaking, until the late fifth century if not beyond that, without doubt aided by its being the centre of a saint's cult, and enhanced by the derivative cult of unimaginatively named St Amphibalus, the Christian whose identity Alban took (by donning his cloak) prior to his martyrdom.[139] Lindum Coloniae (Lincoln) was re-paving its streets at the end of the fourth century and appears to have had a church in use (St Paul-in-the-Bail) in the century following, although another church there, suggestively dedicated to St Martin, may conceivably have had origins as early, and if so, presupposes a sufficient Christian population surviving to support both.[140]

Another city which appeared to survive 'in some style' as Salway puts it, was the capital of Britannia Prima, Corinium (Cirencester, Gloucestershire). Deva (Chester) supported a garrison until the time at least of Constantine III's bid for power; indeed, Deva, White suspects, may even have had its status raised to that of a *colonia* at some late period, although others have proposed that it became a *civitas* capital, presumably of the Ordovices of North Wales.[141] Eboracum (York), Luguvalium (Carlisle) and Aquae Sulis (Bath) also enjoyed an urban existence into the fifth century, although again, terribly changed: the formality of Roman urban life had vanished, prosperity had largely fled, but amidst what was left, people made do, lived and traded; some kind of urban life continued and more it would seem than merely a life within fortified places of refuge.[142] The same seems to be true for the *civitas* capitals: Durovernum Cantiacorum (Canterbury), Dorchester-on-

Thames, Venta Silurum (Caerwent), Calleva Atrebatum (Silchester) and Cataractonium (Catterick) all continued to be inhabited, although the evidence for Isca Dumnoniorum (Exeter) is slight, but for the implication of its continuing existence as a trading port in the sixth century thanks to the story in John the Almsgiver of activity which is almost certainly located there.[143]

In London, archaeological evidence has been remarkably equivocal for, as with many of the settlements mentioned above, sheer continuity has in all probability masked fragile evidence – or obliterated it. Yet the general picture is that some form of urban life seems to have continued recognisably very late into the fifth century. After all, a city which had been the diocesan capital and was populous enough to sustain Magnus Maximus's impressive new cathedral was hardly likely to vanish into desuetude overnight. The process was gradual and a deposit in the Thames by Battersea of eight silver ingots bearing Christian symbols and the name Syagrius, along with a (slightly disputed) amphora handle from the city of late fifth-century date, seem to show this. We have already encountered Syagrius, the late Roman *tyrannus* who headed an independent polity in northern Gaul from 465 until his death at the hands of the Franks in 486; given the dating of the ingots, the two Syagrii may be one and the same. This, in turn, might suggest a measure of cross-Channel control, as under Carausius, Maximus and Constantine III, rather than the reoccupation which Salway suggests could have been in the back of imperial minds for decades, but which would appear to have been consistently unrealisable in such turbulent times. Could this bullion have been an inducement to whatever authority was in control of lowland Britain – one has to postulate Ambrosius Aurelianus – to make common cause with the only surviving imperial authority in Gaul, between 465 and 486? It could even have been a payment on behalf of the emperor Anthemius as an inducement for the expeditionary force of Riothamus, which fought for the authorities in Gaul against the Goths – or was it merely evidence of trade?[144]

Some small towns also survived into the fifth century too, with varying success. At Morbium (Piercebridge, Durham) Roman life continued with repair of buildings, especially the baths where the drains were renewed, and olive oil in amphorae can be dated to after 450. Sub-Roman life as lived continuously since the mid-fifth century probably ended some time in the seventh century when a new ecclesiastical centre nearby came into being.[145] Likewise, life seems to have continued at Vinovia (Binchester, Co. Durham), at Derventio (Little Chester, Derby) but not apparently at Durobrivae (Water Newton, Cambs.) or Ariconium (Weston-under-Penyard, Herefordshire), although the latter did produce some late fourth- and early fifth-century low-value coinage minted under Arcadius, and gave its name to the early British polity, Ercing, today surviving as the Rural Deanery of Archenfield, south-west Herefordshire.[146]

And somewhere betwixt town and country, Professor Charles-Edwards assures us, 'a top quality education [was] still available in later fifth century Britain to enable the élite to help govern in some facsimile of Roman government.'[147]

Survival of practical skills, or at least those associated with urban contexts, can be argued for. The earliest surviving Saxon stone buildings, although crude by continental standards, can reasonably be described as Romanesque, and argue for some kind of survival of building techniques. Just because we are short of authentic standing post-Roman/British stone buildings, does not mean there were none in the first place, as has been argued above concerning the so-called 'Anglian Tower' in York, after all, the *principia* there was 'standing and in good repair' until the ninth century.[148] The early seventh-century interment of a skilled *agrimensor* (surveyor) amidst the remarkably grid-plan-like setting of early Bernician Yeavering (otherwise Ad Gefrin, Northumberland) with his *groma* – the Roman instrument used for laying out settlements or centuriations at precise right angles – along with a possible sighting pole, suggests a continuation of this skill.[149] Indeed, this important settlement could have begun as a British one, for the excavator noted that he 'could find little trace of Ida and his immediate descendants' there and that 'one au pair girl would have made and broken all the Anglo-Saxon pottery in Bernicia during the reign of Edwin' – that is c. 616-633.[150] Possibly this man equipped with surveying skills may have been taken over from a British predecessor by the conquering Saxon warlord Aethelfrith and his skills put to use in a way (the grid-plan) previously foreign to the Germanic settlers in Britain; the additional sophistication may have been counted on as a mark of status for the intrusive warlord.

To suppose that skills in surveying and building had to be re-imported by Roman priests following St Augustine's mission to Kent a decade or two before is surely a lazy assumption, just as the long-discarded notion that the Latin elements in Welsh were similarly re-imported into Britain by 'missionaries from the Continent'. That these skills represent near invisible but once tangible elements of continuity seems inescapable; and that Latin was spoken for very many generations in lowland Britain is now regarded as certain.

Military matters

There was activity at many Roman military sites in the fifth century, especially in the north and some of this has been noted already. In late Roman Britain, *limitanei* (border levies) policing and defending the frontiers, and *comitatenses*, as an active campaigning force, represented different types of warfare. *Comitatenses* were commanded by *comites*, *limitanei* by *duces*. The late fourth-century army was generally larger but units were generally smaller; as we have seen, the legion had shrunk from a nominal 5,500 to around a thousand, while cohorts had gone from 500 to between two and three hundred, probably mutating, as the unity of Britain began to fragment, into the 300 men who comprised a typical sub-Roman British war-band, essentially the local ruler's *comitatus* – the *teulu* of the later British warlords. Barbarians are estimated to have comprised at least a quarter of the establishment of *comitatenses* from the early fifth century but a much smaller proportion amongst the less élite frontier forces.[151] The most obvious weakness for post-Roman Britain was a lack of control of the seas surrounding Britain. The abolition of the *Classis Britannica* in the mid third century and the coming of the Saxon Shore forts saw a decline in naval capability, leaving Britain particularly exposed to maritime assault.[152]

At Vindolanda on the Wall, new baths and a church were built in late fourth century, consolidated in use into the 5th century and perhaps beyond. The church in 2020 yielded a crushed 6th-century lead alloy or pewter chalice covered in various Christian symbols, extending the active occupation of the site probably into the seventh century.[153] Earlier finds there include a nearby stone inscription naming an élite individual from the early sixth century called Brigomaglos, a British name. Having a carved stone inscription might well mark him out as perhaps *dux* or a local commander of the garrison, under one of the *Gŵr y Gogledd* (Men of the North) then striving to keep their former Roman province free from aggressive Germanic expansion and safe from Pictish incursions.[154] The Wall itself contains inscriptions relating to repairs undertaken by civilian groups from *civitates* including Dumnonii, which one assumes to have been those allies in western Scotland rather than groups all the way from the West Country.[155]

In Wales, archaeological evidence points to a post-Roman occupation on a number of sites; one is Segontium (Caernarvon, Gwynedd) the heyday of which was discussed more fully earlier. Excavation suggests that it was quite probably an ordered Post-Roman centre of government as Nash-Williams suggested seventy years ago.[156] Sir Mortimer Wheeler's 1923 excavation included the late fourth-century clearing of a Mithraeum at Segontium by fire, which he took to denote the attested fanaticism displayed by zealous fourth-century Christians, well acquainted with the nature of the building: he noted its proximity to the Christian church of St Peblig (in British tradition, a [grand]son of Magnus Maximus) which may well have been founded to replace the destroyed temple. Certainly, Segontium was a place with a post-Roman Christian focus.[157]

The chief military document surviving from late Roman times is the empire-wide inventory of all military installations then in use in both the eastern and western halves of the Roman state. The *Notitia Dignitatum* ('Register of Dignities') seems to have been compiled as an administrative and bureaucratic handbook some time in the decade and a half after the empire was finally divided between east and west, the latter section's entries having come down to us as an even later, perhaps *c.* 420s, revision. This final division of east and west was never intended to be permanent, but took place on the death of the Emperor Theodosius I in 395, and the precise dating of the document is still under some dispute.[158] However, as it includes Britain, generally accepted as lost to imperial control around 409, it is generally presumed to have been compiled before then, or at least at a time when the central administration considered that control over Britain would be re-asserted as a matter of course. Bearing in mind the chaos which affected the north-western dioceses of the empire 407-413, the compilation of the document must have been undertaken *c.* 400-407 or 413-425, the latter date being a generally agreed latest possible time and which may well have been an up-dating rather than a compilation made *ab initio*.

Notitia Dignitatum allows us some idea of the military establishment of the British diocese in the period 400/425 if only notionally, but strangely, it is missing some obvious insular elements. There are no recorded *foederati* or other barbarian units listed in Britain itself and nothing at all for Wales and the north-west, although, as we have just seen, a number of military sites are known to have been occupied.[159] The most obvious reason for this has to be the suggestion, already made, that British and Irish-led groupings were left in control of these areas under treaty late in the fourth century and were set up as virtual client states with Roman oversight and with a bullion inducement, a policy here attributed to Maximus.

Collins and Breeze, on the other hand, speculate that there must have been a late fourth-century military command in west Britain, perhaps under a *comes tractus maritime per Britannias* following the hints in Ammianus Marcellinus concerning the Barbarian Conspiracy of 367. Overall, it is estimated that there must have been between 12,000 and 30,000 soldiers in Britain *c.* 400.[160] The *Notitia* does mention the Saxon Shore forts, or at least some of them; they are attested by the document at Brancaster (Norfolk), Burgh Castle (Suffolk), Bradwell (Essex), in Kent, Reculver, Richborough and Dover, Lympne and Pevensey in Sussex and Portchester in Hampshire. Four, possibly six, are omitted: Caister-on-Sea (Norfolk), Walton-by-Felixstowe (Suffolk) – possibly also Dunwich in that county, but now too hopelessly eroded away for us to be sure – Bitterne in Hampshire, Cardiff (Glamorganshire) and Lancaster.[161]

All the purely Roman activity in the forts that have been excavated seems to fizzle out in the first decade of the fifth century, save for vestiges at Portchester and Richborough. The latter had always been the primary crossing point to the Continent and probably remained so, for the withdrawal of the imperial army and administration did not stop civilians, merchants and churchmen from crossing the Channel, as St Germanus' visits demonstrate. After all, it must not be forgotten that the average non-servile Roman citizen was a fairly cosmopolitan fellow, and that no such thing as a national border then existed. Richborough, like Portchester, may have retained at least a quasi-military function, as both feature as the *foci* of strife in the unreliable (at this period) *Anglo-Saxon Chronicle* and similarly well *post facto* British sources.

The status of Christianity has already been noted to some extent above in relation to country estates and towns. The one last post-Roman facet of these so-called Saxon Shore forts which deserves mention is that several (possibly more, were we better informed by our sources) were the sites of late Roman, post-Roman or early Saxon churches, at first mainly monastically serviced minsters, set up by missionaries either from Romano-British or Celtic areas of the British Isles, like St Cedd at Bradwell, or from Rome itself, like St Felix at Walton (or Dunwich) and Irish St Fursey at Burgh in Norfolk. Churches of very early foundation are also known from Portchester, adjacent to Pevensey and Lympne, probably within Dover and at Reculver. These all require further investigation.

The *Atlas of Roman Britain* names six such churches on the Saxon shore and another fifteen in former Roman forts elsewhere in the British Isles. Several have thus been identified, and the forts acted as the secure bases from which missionary priests were sent out to evangelise and convert the heathen Saxon population of the area, the British survivors being then still distinct, having been at least nominally Christian since Constantine's Edict of Milan in 313. It has also been suggested that their position in the forts, in the few cases where one can be sure, close to the headquarters building, enabled the priests to use the still reasonably serviceable adjacent bath-houses as baptistries, for a separate baptistry was long a *sine qua non* of early minster churches, certainly on the Continent.

Suggestions that Christianity was in decline during the fifth and sixth centuries are now thought wide of the mark. Dr Henig has made the case that congregations were actually growing during this period, not declining, and that 'to be a Christian was to be seen as the same thing as being Roman.'[162] Yet with the successful evangelisation later of the incoming Anglian settlers, grave goods dry up and British and Anglo-Saxon burials begin to be indistinguishable. Belts and brooches seem to take on well-nigh indistinguishable forms and were doubtless worn by both, making the interpretation of the likely cultural make-up of those populating areas like the upper Thames valley highly speculative as between Briton and Anglian.[163] Furthermore, when one looks at the trappings of Anglo-Saxon kingship apparent in the seventh century, like the Staffordshire hoard and those interred with King Raedwald of East Anglia at Sutton Hoo, we find a typical late antique ruler 'who perhaps saw himself as under the authority of the emperor in Constantinople'.[164]

Maximus's Legacy?

The non-appearance in the *Notitia* of Wales and contiguous regions may be because Magnus Maximus secured the area between the Hadrian and Antonine Walls, the north-west, Wales and perhaps even the south-west frontiers using settled federates under their indigenous leaders, removing them from direct imperial oversight, as suggested briefly above. The late Leslie Alcock was not alone in suggesting something along these lines. If in 367-368, in the wake of mopping up after the Barbarian Conspiracy, Count Theodosius replaced the *areani* with a treaty-based federation of tribal leaders north of the Wall, then Maximus in Britain after his victory over the Picts and Scots may have put this sort of arrangement on a much more formal footing, extending it to Wales and even Cornwall. Salway adds that the occurrence of Maximus's name in Welsh genealogies 'suggests he may have been responsible for establishing loyal men in posts of authority in Wales that later became hereditary'.[165] Knight, too, reminds us that 'The process whereby military titles could become hereditary can be seen in the exchanges documented by Avitus of Vienne [near the end of the fifth century] where the Burgundian Sigismund is pestering [emperor] Anastasius for titles.'[166]

But why should historians suppose this? Because so many of the semi-legendary British pedigrees of princes begin with his name or have close associations with him, specifically those of Cumbria, Dumnonia, western lowland Scotland, Isle of Man, Cumbria, Powis and the Midlands, along with much of Wales. These pedigrees, when they begin with a prominent figure like Maximus, represent a conflation of the founder of the dynasty with a powerful person who was remembered as a patron or perceived enabler. They represent a morsel of embedded veracity from which some believe it is possible to build up a picture of Britain under Maximus and in the decades between his time and the ending of Roman rule around 409. On this reckoning, it is conceivable that he also might have set up the British tribe of the *Novantes* in Galloway, in view of the fact that much later British pedigrees of their rulers derive their descent also from *Dunawt* (Donatus) 'son of' Maximus.[167]

Following on from this apparent attempt to keep the British north of Hadrian's Wall and south of the Forth-Clyde line on-side, it has also been tentatively suggested that Maximus was the most likely person to have set up the Votadini, who occupied the site of Edinburgh (later *Caer Eiddin*), the Lothians and to the south towards the Wall, as a client state. This time, the reasoning is based on the ruling family's Roman names at the head of their pedigree (starting with *Maxim guletic qui occidit Gratianum regem Romanorum* – 'Prince Maximus who killed Gratian King of the Romans') presumably representing people living in the later fourth century. In this, Maximus is given a son with a remarkably familiar name, bearing in mind the connections suggested in Chapter 3: *Anthun* (Antonius).

What was Maximus's policy in settling various people in southern Scotland? Was it to secure co-operation against the enigmatic Attacotti? One might go further and speculate whether it was Maximus himself who had raised three infantry regiments from the Attacotti mentioned in the *Notitia Dignitatum*, the *Honoriani Atecotti Seniores*, the *Honoriani Atecotti Juniores* and the *Atecotti Juniores Gallicani*.[168] Indeed, one might justifiably see the stability of Britain between Maximus's trouncing of the Picts and Scots in the early 380s and the mission, apparently sent by Stilicho, to subdue some sort of unrest in 396/398 (if the panegyricist Claudian is to be believed), as a tribute to the effectiveness of Maximus's organization of the provinces under his control.[169]

Maximus seems to have settled British federate dynasties in lowland Scotland, the western littoral, in Wales and perhaps in the south-west, under treaty and with a measure of freedom of action, maybe under prefectural supervision. In Wales, one encounters suggestive traces of the period, like the Roman-style enclosure built at New Pieces, near Welshpool (Montgomeryshire/Powis.) in the late fourth century, which might represent the efforts of a local dynast setting himself up under this new dispensation. Not all settlements were necessarily of local Britons either, for Irish appear in west Wales (see Chapter 8) and Frisians appear to have been settled in southern Scotland, for example near Dumfries, the name of which seems to translate as 'the fort of the Frisians'.[170] Such a mention of Frisians also contains echoes of Procopius's unexpected remark, written in the sixth century, that there were 'three very populous nations [in Britain], the Angles, Frisians and Britons, so numerous are they that every year great numbers with their wives and children migrate to the Franks.'[171]

Even the conventional model for the 'Saxon' settlement of England has been questioned; there is a growing consensus that the evidence from isotopic analysis, and ancient and modern DNA is inconsistent with what one might expect from models of large-scale invasion or conquest and displacement. These and isotopes from dental enamel strongly suggest assimilation, and the continuity of boundaries is most instructive in this context. Even the material culture may have been misunderstood. The whole process, enigmatic as it is, is becoming to be seen more as evolution rather than imposition.[172] Yet there is also evidence of a substantial clutch of post-Roman polities at the edge of the former diocese which do not fit this pattern at all. Some have strong legendary links to Magnus Maximus. Maximus, in the words of Miles Russell,

> ... may therefore have been remembered as the man who reorganised the political structure of British tribes, permitting a greater degree of autonomy in these areas where the official Roman garrison had been denuded. That too would perhaps have made him seem like the prime mover or progenitor in certain post-Roman households.[173]

Others in the north seem to have been ruled by men claiming descent, not from Maximus, but from entirely unknown people bearing Roman names. It may be that here we are looking at another phenomenon: Roman commanders staying and setting themselves up as dynasts in the absence of any superior power to replace them. Is this perhaps something that would not have taken place under Maximus, but after 409? Coel Hen (Chapter 9) may fall into this category. Nevertheless, Maximus's involvement cannot be ruled out, for Coel may have been of sufficient standing or sufficiently memorable to have become attached to a dynasty deriving from a loyal late fourth-century commander put in place by Maximus. While we might suppose that we are not primarily concerned with this dynasty, the Coelings, it nevertheless transpires in the British sources that there are connections to Maximus in one way of another.

We now enter the turbid waters of insular and other post-Roman sources to examine why on earth Maximus looms so large in subsequent British writing, in the legend-suffused histories and romances.

Seventh-century chapel of St Cedd built within the walls of the Saxon Shore fort of Othona (Bradwell, Essex) and out of its materials. (Carole Craven)

Valle Crucis, the Pillar of Eliseg *c.* 825. (M. Craven)

Clockwise from top left: Saxon Shore fort Garrianum (Burgh Castle, Burgh-by-Yarmouth), 11 July 2017 from the east. [M. Craven]

Aureus of Carinus with legend: Imp[erator] C[aesar] M. Aur[elius] Carinus Aug[ustus]

Derby Museum's aureus of Carausius, with Concordia Militum (the agreement of the soldiers) reverse. The legend reads: Imp[erator] Carausius Aug[ustus] Rouen mint.

Carausius and the two Augusti, the legend reading: Carausius et Fratres Sui (Carausius and his Brothers).

Aureus of Allectus. The legend reads: Imp[erator] C[aesar] Alle/ctus P[ius] F[elix] Aug[ustus].

Above left: Electrotype copy of the medallion celebrating Constantius's entry into London, 296. The legend reads R/edditor Lvcis/Aeterna/e (the return of eternal light) 'Lon' indicates that these are the gates of the city, and PTR is the mint mark for Trier. It is part of the Beaurains (Arras) treasure found in 1922. [British Museum]

Above right: Follis of Constantius I's first wife Helena from the reign of her son; legend: Fl[avia] Helena Augusta.

The Saxon shore fort of Anderida (Pevensey), 8 October 2017, west gate from within the walls. [M. Craven]

Above left: A truly barbaric bare-headed portrait of Magnentius on a bronze nummus. The legend reads: D[ominus] N[oster] Magnen/tius P[ius] F[elix] Aug[ustus].

Above right: Portrait of Decentius as Caesar from a bronze AE3 coin; the legend reads: D[ominus] N[oster] Decentius Nob[ilissimus] Caes[ar].

Above left: 'Fallen horseman' type bronze coin of Carausius II. The obverse legend reads: Domino/Con[s]tan[ti]o.

Above right: Julian the Apostate, as seen on a gold solidus, with diadem. The legend reads: Fl[avius] Cl[audius] Iulia/nus P[ater] P[atriae] Aug[ustus].

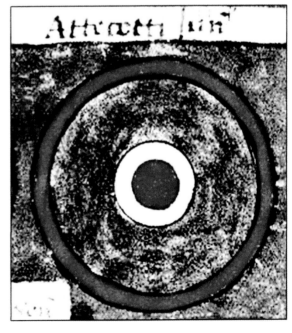

Above: Valentinian I on the obverse of a contemporary solidus. The legend reads: D[ominus] N[oster] Valentini/anus P[ius] F[elix] Aug[ustus].

Above right: A fragment of London's Roman walls with a (much rebuilt) bastion. The arch is later. [M. Milligan]

Right: Shield depiction of the [Honoriani] Attecotti Juniores from the Notitia Dignitatum V. 7. [Oxford, Bodleian Library]

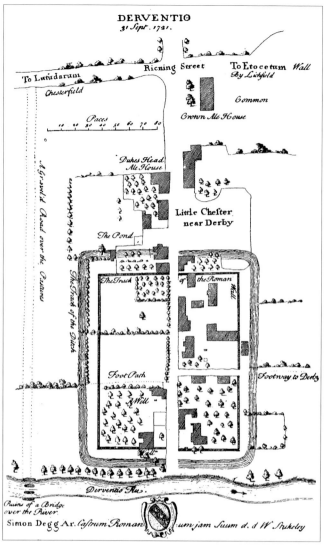

DERVENTIO
31 Sept. 1721.

To Lutudarum
Chesterfield

Ricning Street

To Etocetum Wall
By Lichfield

Common

Crown Ale House

Paces
10 20 30 40 50 60 70 80

Dukes Head
Ale House

The Pond

Little Chester
near Derby

The Truck

of the Roman

Wall

Foot Path

Footway to Derby

A Well

Wall

A gravel'd Road over the Pastures

The Track of the Ditch

Derventio flu.

Ruins of a Bridge
over the River.

Simon Degg Ar. Castrum Roman...um jam Suum d. d W. Stukeley

Left: Derventio (Little Chester, Derby): a Roman small town fortified by the fourth century with a wall. Bastions (not shown) were added in the later fourth century; from a map drawn by William Stukeley FSA, 1721. East at the top. [M. Craven]

Below: Magnus Maximus, profile portrait on a gold solidus from the Milan mint, *c.* 387. The legend reads: D[ominus] N[oster] Mag[nus] Ma/ximus P[ius] F[elix] Aug[ustus].

Below left: Silver siliqua of Gratian. The legend reads: Imp[erator] C[aesar] Gratia/nus P[ius] F[elix] Aug[ustus] [M. Craven]

Part of the rampart of Caerhun fort. [R. Johnson]

Caer Gybi. [The late R. Withington]

Segontium, remains of fourth-century bath house. [The late R. Withington]

Segontium, the south-west remains of the walls of Hen Waliau, Caernarfon, nearly 5 feet (1.5 metres), 2018. The facing stones have, as so often, been robbed for building materials. [A. Martin]

Top left: Late fourth-century polygonal tower in the Museum Gardens at York. The lower courses are Roman, the upper courses post-Roman and Medieval. [Leila Craven]

Middle left: Trier, prior to World War Two bomb damage; from a postcard postmarked 1920. [The late P. J. R. Withington]

Below left: Reliquary head of St Martin of Tours now in the Louvre. [The late June Craven]

Below: Mosaic portrait of St Ambrose in the Cathedral of Milan. [M. Craven]

Top right: Salonica; fourth-century façade of church of St Demetrius. [A. Zorin/ Wikimedia Commons]

Middle right: Roman Siscia; some structural remains visible today. [Andres Rus/ Wikimedia Commons]

Below right: Nave of the Cathedral of Sta Maria Assunta, Aquileia, showing superb fourth-century mosaic floor laid for bishop Theodorus, and contemporary Corinthian columns. [M. Craven]

Below: Emperor Petronius Maximus (reigned 455) depicted on a gold solidus; legend: D[ominus] N[oster] Petronius Ma/ximus P[ius] F[elix] Aug[ustus].

Above: Faesulae; remains of the Roman Baths, May 2017. [Wikimedia Commons]

Left: Colonia Agrippinensium; one of four surviving third-century wall bastions (top rebuilt) in modern Cologne – clearly not of much use in 407! [John Bradley]

Below left: Portrait of Constantine III on a gold solidus; the legend reads: D[OMINUS] N[OSTER] CONSTAN/TINUS P[IUS] F[ELIX] AUG[USTUS]. The reverse legend, VICTORIA AUGGGG, dates it to the time following Honorius's brief recognition of the Emperor, the repetition of the last letter indicating four reigning augusti: Constantine III, his son Constans II, Honorius and Theodosius II, thus 409/410. Constantinople mint.

Top right: St Germanus depicted in Victorian stained glass.

Middle right: Dinas Brân with its thirteenth-century Welsh castle superimposed on a reused Iron Age fort and commanding a valley 'enclosed by steep mountains'. [Clwyd-Powys Archaeological Trust 88-mc2-0014]

Below right: Relief portrait, thought to be of Flavius Aëtius, on a sarcophagus.

Below: The so-called 'Anglian tower' added to the Roman walls of York. This is post-Roman work, but not necessarily Anglian. [Leila Craven]

Top left: Clipped siliqua of Emperor Arcadius (above), minted at Milan [Private collection]; and of the 408 issue of Constantine III (below), reverse VICTORIA AVGGGG, minted at Lugdunum (Lyon). [Bamfords Ltd.]

Middle left: Durolevum (Syndale, Faversham, Kent) Stone Chapel looking west. [M. Craven]

Bottom left: Notitia Dignitatum: diploma of the *comes Litoris Saxonici* (Count of the Saxon Shore), showing the forts in commission at the time of issue. [Oxford, Bodleian Library]

Below: Tomb of the Venerable Bede in the cathedral at Durham. [Private collection]

Top right: Voteporix stone, CIIC 358.

Above right: The partly exposed remaining portion of the Roman amphitheatre at Carmarthen not built over. [Coflein]

Right: Tara, Co. Meath, Ireland, site of the so-called Banqueting Hall (more probably a ceremonial avenue leading to the summit). [Wikimedia Commons, B. R. Holden]

Below: Balline Hoard. Left: a carefully graded piece cut from a late Roman silver lanx (charger) decorated with a hunting scene; right: a specific weight silver ingot, complete with Roman officina mark: ex offi[cina] Isatis. [National Museum of Ireland]

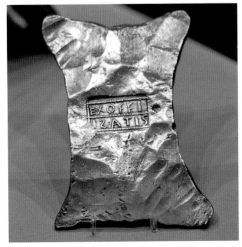

The Rock of Cashel (topped by later buildings) photographed in 2008. [Giorgio Galeotti]

Above right: The south gate of the recommissioned fort at Y Gaer (Breconshire) in 2008. [Private collection]

Above left: Viroconium (Wroxeter, Salop.): remains of baths, 2018. [R. S. I. Smith]

Left: The Dark Age citadel of Arx Decantorum (Deganwy Castle) in 2018. [S. Parry]

Antonine Wall, by Rough Castle,
Bonnybridge, Falkirk, Scotland.
[R. I. Smith]

Carlisle, the Irish Gate, from
a stone lithograph published
in 1835; it was one of the
Roman gates through the city's
defensive wall, much rebuilt and
subsequently demolished.

The Rock of Dumbarton
seen from the south. Almost
all pre-Medieval traces have
vanished.

Calstock, Cornwall; outline of the
Roman fort excavated from 2011.
[C. Smart]

Top left: The Newchurch stone (left) and the St Breock stone (right, showing two faces), from Thomas (1994) 243.

Top right: Lanivet, Cornwall, church: Annici fil[ ] stone, second quarter of the sixth century, originally found near the porch. [T. M. Glaser]

Above left: Portus Adurni (Portchester, Hants.): walls seen from the south-west with the harbour behind, July 2018. [Gavin Barrett]

Déols, St Etienne, late Roman stone sarcophagus, the bas-relief showing one of the local Gallo-Roman aristocrats enjoying the chase. [Private collection]

The Saxon Shore fort at Anderida (Pevensey, Sussex), from the south, October 2017. [M. Craven]

Castle Dore, Cornwall, from the west, 2018. [Private collection]

Canterbury: church of St Martin, south wall, showing Roman bricks, partly in situ, partly reused. [M. Craven]

The reliquary of Cynegils (Ceingair) of Wessex in the cathedral at Winchester.

Top left: Letocetum (Wall, Staffs.) by Watling Street; part of the excavated remains in 2004, Miss Cornelia Craven providing scale. It lies strategically beside Watling Street and seems to have passed from proto-Powis to Mercia in the third quarter of the seventh century. [Carole Craven]

Middle left: The Repton stone, now in Derby Museum. [M. Craven]

Bottom left: St Wystan, Repton; the crypt, a former eighth-century mausoleum, photographed 8 August 2019. [M. Craven]

Below right: Part of the early fifth-century hacksilber hoard from Traprain Law, East Lothian, the territory of the Votadini/Gododdin. Possibly part of a subsidy paid to ensure the continuing loyalty of the Votadini. [Royal Museum of Scotland]

Bottom right: Chedworth villa: part of the fifth-century mosaic floor. [National Trust]

PART II

The Conundrum of British Maximus

'A fearful and wondrous thing, we know, is the Welsh pedigree'

J. Horace Round, 1903

Alleged sarcophagus of Gildas in the chapel of St Gildas, Carnoët,
north-west Brittany. (Private collection)

7

'Are These Men Real?'
The Sources

While Part I attempted to set down what we do know with reasonable certainty about Magnus Maximus, the intriguing aspect of him as an historical figure is that he also enjoys a *doppelgänger* in British early history and Welsh legend, and any overlap between the attested Maximus and the Maximus of early medieval genealogies, historiography and romance is not at first glance at all apparent. Taken as a whole, the evidence set out below seems to suggest that in the late antique and early medieval period, Maximus held a special place within the material, especially in the genealogies. Here, for instance, there are no doubts about his wife's name, nor about his wider family, not hinted at in the contemporary Roman texts. Although only a solitary one of the various British sources endows him with his attested son, Victor, the remainder provide a whole tribe of other sons who could, taken at face value, amount to as many as seven. Closer analysis enables them to be reduced to a more credible four, but the contrast is still arresting. Had they really been Maximus's offspring, one might have imagined the *magister militum* Arbogastes being instructed by Theodosius to embark on an island-wide campaign to liquidate them, as threats to his post-388 settlement. There appear also to have been at least two legendary daughters, one attested in one of the earliest of the post-Roman sources, Sevira/Severa, married to the *tyrannus* Gwrtheyrn/Vortigern/Vitalinus who, in any other context than Britain, cut loose from Imperial control, would have been labelled a standard usurper. Indeed, as we have seen, Vortigern's position is almost exactly analogous to that of Aegidius and of Syagrius in Gaul, with the only difference that for the latter we have a more reliable account in sources like Gregory of Tours.

Arthur apart, Maximus comes across as one of the most important figures in the entire British post-Roman tradition, appearing in genealogies, the Welsh Triads and the *Mabinogion* as well as in largely unsupported historical accounts like the *Historia Brittonum,* not to mention essentially fantastic accounts like that of Geoffrey of Monmouth. Indeed, Maximus's standing seems to become raised with the passage of the centuries. We have to assume that an oral tradition of tales about Maximus took shape not so very long after his demise and certainly before the end of Roman rule, divergent from the admonitory rhetoric of Gildas and the imprecations of Pacatus. If British levies were involved in his acclamation, they might well have been a factor in this, especially if some ended up, as tradition indicates, in Gaul. Others, of course, will have returned.

Whether the tales about him became conflated with stories brought back to Britain by troops serving under Gerontius's appointee, the other Maximus, served to muddy the waters still further. Echoes of previous emperors Maximian and Maxentius may have played their part, too, especially as Maximus's name is often rendered, especially in later sources, as 'Macsen' or 'Maxsen' (Maxentius) instead of 'Maxim' (Maximus)[1] There may have been at the period of initial tale telling echoes of the period when Britain was under the rule of Magnentius, the retribution following whose reign by Constantius II being particularly harsh, thereby perhaps casting more favourable light on this usurper than he might otherwise have deserved, especially as his other name was also Magnus. In insular sources, Maximus's name as Maxen/Macsen/Maxim is most frequently qualified with *Wletic/Guletic*, usually taken to mean 'prince' but which is thought to have carried a more specific meaning originally. Rachel Bromwich has suggested that it meant 'a leader of local or native militia' and not someone bearing a Roman command, a contention that has been challenged but which remains generally accepted.[2] The simpler explanation that it just meant 'prince' is problematical because that term had synonyms in British and still has in Welsh, like *tywysog* and *arglwydd*. Nevertheless, prince rings truest as an appropriate term for the British Maximus.

This material is discussed in a separate section in this work because of its unreliable (or unverifiable) nature and generally late date. It does enable a broader critical picture to be built up about Maximus, but because of the nature of the sources, it is one that has to be viewed with caution. Yet it seems to be a worthwhile undertaking because some of the insights that emerge seem sufficiently convincing and are therefore worth airing for others to develop or refute, particularly the consistent appearance of his name as the progenitor of ruling dynasties in the north and west of Britain. As regards these sources, though, it is essential to remember that all were written down well after the events they describe, in most cases much later, and are thus sensibly recognised as being to a large extent legendary. On their reliability, John Koch writes: 'The degree of accuracy to be ascribed to them remains highly uncertain, a fact underlined by their internal inconsistencies. Nevertheless, the etymology of some of the names takes the date that some were first written down back much further, in some cases into the seventh century.'[3]

King-lists frequently begin immediately after the collapse of Roman rule, thus that event, as it gradually became perceived, was regarded as having immense significance. Gradually, developing external threats led to the creation of separate polities, originally at the fringes of the diocese and later elsewhere, in the fifth and sixth century especially.[4] Although the rulers of these polities are generally referred to as kings, an attempt has been made to avoid this term as being unlikely to have been deployed in the immediate post-Roman era. That their heirs and descendants later became seen as kings and in time so recognised is, however, undeniable.

The traditional view is that these king-lists, which seem later to have mutated into connected genealogies, probably represent successions of individuals to power rather than fixed father-to-son sequences. It is generally accepted that they were at first transmitted orally as stories around the domestic hearth or by bards praising rulers, but that a much greater degree of literacy was enjoyed in 'Dark Age' Britain has recently become much more widely accepted, and the longer survival of Latin-based culture consequently acknowledged.[5] Gildas makes it clear that characters such as Maelgwyn Gwynedd enjoyed a good education and basked in panegyrics about themselves, quite possibly Latin ones.[6] Concerning ancient British poetry, John Koch suspects that a literary continuum of the British/Welsh vernacular might have begun significantly earlier than AD 550.[7] When it comes to genealogies, however, he adds that he only considers them reliable for the seventh century and thereafter.[8] We also have to take into account inscriptions on stone. Concerning these, Professor Charles Thomas remarks:

> To the question 'are all these men supposed to have been real people of an actual historical past?' – the obvious response is, 'why not?' There is little reason to doubt that, though we have it from MSS of the twelfth and later centuries, such details were fixed in writing in both Wales and Ireland long before the Norman period. In this respect the Demetian rulers show up well...[9]

Other genealogical material is embedded in hagiographies (saints' lives) and seem to originate in the inscription of the deceased saint's family on the painted diptych read by the celebrant during mass and have been transmitted from thence to the *vitae*, most of which were written later, often very much later, again partly from oral transmission. If so, this might suggest that the familial information in the *vitae* is likely to be more reliable than the sometimes fanciful exploits of the saint's life. But unlike Welsh/British genealogies, Breton ones were not written down until the twelfth century.[10]

One matter which excites curiosity is the complete lack of surviving authentic documents from this post-Roman era from Britain, either concerning the Saxons or the Britons. Comparing this with a similar situation in Visigothic Spain before their Arian rulers converted to Catholicism, Barnwell suggests that it was because the Germanic invaders prior to *c.* 600 were pagan so official documents from before that era were considered as worthless and discarded by the Britons at the time and retrospectively by the Saxons after their conversion was complete, *c.* 655.[11] If some form of central authority continued throughout the fifth century in Britain, records would have been kept, given continuing literacy, but as the eventual collapse of lowland authority may have been drastic, such records may have been entirely lost or destroyed, leaving only oral accounts to filter out to the surviving British *civitates* and polities in the frontier regions. This may explain why figures such as Ambrosius/Emrys, Eugenius/Owein and indeed Arthur float around in the legendary material but appear in hardly any of the genealogies: the collapse of the centre may have destroyed much of the real knowledge of them. This may also explain the lingering penumbra of lost sources frequently referenced, from Geoffrey of Monmouth to recent scholarship.

Given this disastrous lacuna, the procedure must therefore be to look at the post-Roman sources which mention Maximus and assess their antiquity and reliability. Some of the later sources clearly draw upon earlier ones which we have to hand, as Bede, who quotes from Gildas, but others may be quoting from sources lost to us, as indeed, Geoffrey of Monmouth avers. These lost sources may still be far from being contemporary with Maximus, but others, for all we know, could well be reasonably close to the period. Transmission is not clear. Some may quote from lost documents or other written sources, destroyed in upheavals, while others (not to mention many 'lost' documents themselves) may depend on oral tradition. This tradition is widely thought to be in the form of epic tales related ceremonially by bards but also, as we have seen, perhaps from funerary mass diptychs. Much written material was destroyed during the dissolution of the monasteries from 1536; some material was rescued, literally from the flames, some copied prior to the event by early antiquaries. But not much was rescued or copied, and in the more remote houses, older material relevant to post-Roman Britain must have vanished forever.

Peter Wiseman tackles the problem of transmission of historical facts about early Roman history through times of non-literary culture in *Unwritten Rome*.[12] He asks:

> What can we know about the communal memory of a pre-literary society, when our evidence comes from much later literary texts whose authors … had little or no understanding of it? … 'Oral tradition' does not 'hand down the memory of events'; it elaborates, recycles, omits, invents, creates a succession of stories for a succession of audiences with ever-changing priorities.[13]

This might well apply to British post-Roman culture, too, but not so absolutely. H. J. T. Wood, more optimistically, wrote over a century ago that in view King Hywell Dda ('the Good') of Deheubarth specifying in his law code that degrees of kinship needed to be known to the thirteenth degree,

The ancient laws of Wales [i.e. as codified by Hywell] necessitated the keeping of official records of pedigrees; the bards were entrusted with the keeping of them; we have a continuous series of collections of pedigrees dating from very early times. Is it likely that, with authentic material at hand, most pedigrees should be inventions?[14]

In the context of Maximus's British 'offspring' as founders of later polities, J. F. Matthews writes:

The entire complex skein of ancient genealogies is customarily either written off as too unreliable and written down too late to be of the slightest value, or is merely ignored. Yet it would seem entirely wrong to take the latter course. Some of the legendary material is indeed eminently reasonable, could we but confirm it from other sources, yet the impression being given almost of a closely related coterie of what appear to be serving senior Roman staff officers, just like the kin of Valentinian I and Valens, but other elements appear as clearly fantastic.[15]

The earliest genealogical collections in the Welsh canon (which in reality is a British canon, for much material from parts of Britain lost much earlier on to the Saxons, was assimilated through British exiles to Wales) dates to the mid-tenth century, but the historical credibility of some of the pedigrees contained within them has been shown to reach back into the sixth century. For the Britons, legitimisation was conveyed through Rome.[16] This material is largely preserved in Welsh (and occasionally Breton) but began as British with some even originating from a Latin source.

One distinguished scholar took a topographical approach, drawing attention to the location and distribution of the dedications to members of the family of *Macsen Wletig* like Peibio (as set out in various places below) on memorial stones. They are concentrated in the south-west and north-west of Wales but with evidence of an extension eastwards. We also find evidence of a *Macsen Wletig* cult in Monmouthshire and south-west Herefordshire (Ercyng), areas which are today completely bare of surviving early Christian inscribed stones. In Britain, this emperor cast a very long shadow. Another anomaly is that much of the material concerns the north of Britain but is densely intermixed with British/Welsh and Dumnonian material. Most of this has without doubt come about from the collapse of most British polities in the North from the mid-seventh century (bar a reduced Alclud/Strathclyde, which lasted until the mid-eleventh century) after which many of the élite from those parts must have re-located to Wales, Ireland and the West Country, strengthened by others in the wake of the merging of the ruling lines of Man and Gwynedd. We shall also see that place names play their enigmatic part, but rather than try to corral those in this chapter, they will be referred to as they crop up in the more regionally based chapters that follow. The extracts below (in which Maximus's name appears in bold) are arranged in date order as generally accepted, although in view of Koch's remarks noted above, some may be of earlier origin.

The evidence of Gildas, writing *c.* 515/520:

At length also, as thickets of tyrants were growing up and bursting forth soon into an immense forest, the island retained the Roman name, but not the morals and law; nay rather, casting forth a shoot of its own planting, it sends out **Maximus** to the two Gauls, accompanied by a great crowd of followers, with an emperor's ensigns in addition, which he never worthily bore, nor legitimately, but as one elected after the manner of a tyrant and amid a turbulent soldiery. This man, through cunning art rather than by valour, first attaches to his guilty rule certain neighbouring countries or provinces against the Roman power, by nets of perjury and falsehood. He then extends one wing to Spain, the other to Italy, fixing the throne of his iniquitous empire at Trier, and raged with such madness against his lords that he drove two legitimate emperors, the one from Rome, the other from a most pious life. Though fortified by hazardous deeds of so dangerous a character, it was not long ere he lost his accursed head at Aquileia: he who had in a way cut off the crowned heads of the empire of the whole world.

After this, Britain is robbed of all her armed soldiery, of her military supplies, of her rulers, cruel though they were, and of her vigorous youth, who followed the footsteps of the above-mentioned usurper and never returned. Completely ignorant of the practice of war, she is, for the first time, open to be trampled upon by two foreign tribes of extreme cruelty, the Scots from the north-west, the Picts from the north; and for many years continues stunned and groaning.[17]

This is more or less accurate, and the space accorded to it by Gildas (who was clearly of a mind with Pacatus on the subject of Maximus) might suggest he was influenced by Sulpicius Severus's account of St Martin's interactions with Maximus. The additional information it carries consists of the allegation that Maximus stripped the diocese completely of its armed forces, an allegation which in Part I was suggested to be only part of the truth, but which is a persistent element of the story. The fact that some of the forces Maximus took with him to the Continent never returned, however, re-appears in the legendary sources as a *leitmotiv* of Maximus's rule, especially in respect of demobilised Britons settling in Armorica, and may be seen as not wholly without foundation when one considers the diaspora of clearly British units like the *Seguntienses* and others – unless their transfer, was, as we have seen, possibly brought about outside the 380s.

John of Nikiou, writing *c.* 685

And, during the stay of the Emperor Theodosius in Asia there arose an usurper named **Maximus**, of British descent.[18]

There can be no doubt of the Emperor's Spanish antecedents, but it is possible that this much later reference to his British descent perhaps refers to that of his anonymous empress or even to his possible period as a *tyrannus* in Britain only from 380 to 383.

Bede, *Historia Ecclesiastica Gentis Anglorum*, completed 731:

At this juncture, however, **Maximus,** an able and energetic man, well suited to be emperor had not ambition led him to break his oath of allegiance, was elected Emperor by the army in Britain almost against his will, and he crossed into Gaul at its head. Here he treacherously killed the Emperor Gratian, who had been dumbfounded at his sudden attack, and was attempting to escape into Italy. His brother, the Emperor Valentinian was driven out of Italy, and took refuge in the east, where Theodosius received him with fatherly affection. Within a short time, however, he regained the Empire and trapping the tyrant Maximus in Aquileia, he captured him and put him to death.[19]

Bede's use of the phrase 'an able and energetic man' suggests that he had read Sulpicius Severus, whereas the remainder of the excerpt seems to be a paraphrase of Zosimus; unusually for Bede, the reliance on Gildas is minimal in this passage; there is no mention of removing troops.

Historia Brittonum (HB), British Library, Harleian MS 3859, 26f. written 829:

[26] The sixth emperor to reign in Britain was **Maximus.** From his time the consuls began and they were never again called Caesars. In his time too, the powers and miracles of Saint Martin flowered and Martin spoke with Maximus.

[27] The seventh emperor to reign in Britain was **Maximianus.** He went forth from Britain with all the troops of the British and killed Gratian, the king of the Romans and held the empire of all Europe. He refused to send the soldiers who had gone forth with him back to Britain, to their wives and children and lands, but gave them many districts from the lake on the top of Mount Jove to the city called Quentovic as far as the Western Mass, that is the western ridge.

For all the Armorican British, who are overseas, went forth there with the tyrant Maximus on his campaign and since they were unwilling to return, they destroyed the western parts of Gaul to the ground and did not leave alive those who piss against the wall. They married their wives and daughters and cut out their tongues lest their descendants should learn their mothers' tongue. That is why we call them in our language *Letewicion*, that is, half dumb, because their speech is muddled. They are the Armorican British and they never came back even to the present day.

That is why Britain has been occupied by foreigners and its citizens driven out until God shall give them help ... the ninth (emperor to rule in Britain) was Constantius. He reigned 16 years in Britain and in the sixteenth year of his reign he died in Britain.

[29] ... Gratian ruled 6 years with his brother Valentinian and the bishop Ambrose of Milan was famous for Catholic teaching. Valentinian reigned eight years with Theodosius ... While Gratian ruled throughout the world, **Maximus** was made emperor in Britain by a mutiny. He soon crossed to Gaul and overcame Gratian who was betrayed at Paris by his commander-in-chief Merobaudes and fled and was taken at Lyon and killed. **Maximus** made his son Victor his colleague ... After a long lapse of time, he was stopped by the consuls Valentinian and Theodosius at the third milestone from Aquileia, deprived of his Royal raiment and sentenced to execution. His son Victor was killed in Gaul in the same year by Count Arbogast.[20]

J. K. Knight suspects that some of this material was drawn from the lost British *vita* of St Germanus, which was touched on in the previous chapter.[21] It is riddled with inaccuracies, although it does mention Maximus's relationship with St Martin. Unfortunately, he is entered as two separate people, for in chapter 27 he becomes Maximian, Diocletian's western colleague, although the author is still writing about Magnus Maximus, referring to his murder of Gratian, but introduces immediately thereafter the alleged settlement of Armorica by his troops, although mention of Quentovic (which was not in Armorica but Normandy) anticipates the port's foundation by a century. There follows a lengthy piece about Armorica which is entirely unsubstantiated elsewhere and ends with a reference to Constantine the Great (as 'Constantius') whom he has *following* Maximus as emperor. In chapter 29, however, we seem to have another source again and revert to the correct Maximus, complete with a mention of his son Victor and of the British emperor's death at the 'third milestone from Aquileia' suggesting that this section derived from Orosius, possibly via Prosper of Aquitaine, written in the mid-fifth century.[22] Use of 'consul' *in lieu* of 'emperor' seems to carry echoes of the Sicilian Briton alluded to in the previous chapter, pointing to the possible style adopted by the British rulers who followed Constantine III.

Pillar of Eliseg, Valle Crucis, Llangollen.
Inscription (lines 1-3, 20-26), carved before 854:

CONCENN FILIUS CATTELL CATELL
FILIUS BROCHMAIL BROCHMAIL FILIUS
ELISEG ELISEG FILIUS GUOILLAUC
[*long portion omitted*]

[...] AIL **MAXIMUS** BRITANNIAE
[*CONCE*]NN PASCEN[*T*] MAU[*N*] ANNAN
[+] BRITU A[*U*]T[*E*]M FILIUS GUARTHI
GIRN] QUE[*M*] BENED[*IXIT*] GERMANUS QUE[*M*]
[*QU*]E REPERIT ET SE[*V*]IRA FILIA MAXIMI
RE]GIS QUI OCCIDIT REGEM ROMANO...

Cyngen son of Cadell, Cadell
son of Brochfael, Brochfael son
of Elise, Elise son of Gwylog...
Maximus of Britain
[Cynge]n Pasgen *maun annan*
Brydw, however, son of Gwerth
eyrn was the one whom Germanus blessed and
whom Sevira bore to him, the daughter of **Maximus**
[the ki]ng who killed the king of the Romans...

The inscription and *HB* are roughly contemporary (Cyngen died at Rome in 854) and it traces the ruling family of Powis from Vortigern via Sevira (a late Roman spelling of Severa) the daughter of Maximus.[23] In mentioning that Maximus 'killed the King of the Romans' we are seeing an echo of *Historia Brittonum*, 27, otherwise the information is an addition to what has arisen so far.

British Library Harleian MS 3859, genealogies –
2. The genealogy of the dynasty of Dyfed (Demetia):
Ouein map [son of] Elen merc [daughter of] Ioumarc map Himeyt m Tancoslt merc Ouein m Margetiut m Teudos m Regin m Catgocaun m Cathen m Clothen m Nougoy m Arthur m Petr m Cincar m Guortepir m Aircol m Triphun m Clotri m Gloitguin m Nimet m Dimet m *Maxim guletic* m Protec m Protector m Ebiud m Eliud m Stater m Pincr Miser m Constans map Constantini et Helen Luicdauc que de Britannia exiuit as crucem Christi querendam usque ad Ierusalem etc.[24]

A tenth-century collection in an MS of *c.* 1100 but written 829/830 [25] or *c.* 954.[26] The genealogies invariably start with the figure contemporaneous with the date the account was written down and run backwards in time to the earliest 'ancestor'.

Here we have a correctly named Maximus (*maxim guletic* = Lord/Prince Maximus) as son of someone called Protector (a Roman title of a sort) whose entry is a double ('Protec map Protector') and a descendant apparently, via three completely unfamiliar names, of Constans II. Maximus's son is Dimet, which is the name of the *civitas*, Demetia, of which Nimet may be another (mutated) double. His great-grandson (omitting two further British names) is really another Roman military title, Triphun (*tribunus*/tribune) whose son Aircol (Agricola) is father of Guortipir, who is generally believed to be the same as the Vortiporius *Demetarum tyranne* ('usurper/tyrant of Demetia') inveighed against by Gildas as a 'worthless son of a good king' – the latter presumably Aircol/Agricola.[27] The ultimate ancestor is Constantine the Great (here 'Constans') and his mother St Helena, discoverer of the True Cross. The filiations are British, but comments, as in the last line or so, are Latin.

4: The genealogy of the rulers of Ynys Manaw (Isle of Man):
Iudgal m Tutagal m Anaraut m Mermin m Anthec m Tutagual m Run m Neithon m Senill m Dinacat m Tutagual m Eidniuet m **Anthun m Maxim** guletic qui occidit Gratianum regem Romanorum.

Here we encounter again *Historia Brittonum's* point regarding Maximus that he 'killed the King of the Romans', but it omits any fanciful ancestry for him. His son here is called Anthun (Antonius), an interesting echo of the suggested family connections of Maximus set out in Chapter 3. Thereafter, the names are all British but, as with the previous extract, the comment is in Latin. The descent closely resembles that of St Llawddog in *Buchedd Llawddog* ('the book of Llawddog', i.e., his *vita*, life) written in the late sixteenth century.[28] The dynasty, much later on, allied itself with the heiress of Gwynedd, to which kingdom they succeeded and thereby acquired another, separate, alleged descent from Maximus.

The genealogy of the rulers of Powis:
22. [S]elim map Cinan map Brocmayl map Cincen map Maucann map Pascent map Cattegirn map Cadell Ddyrnllug.
23. [H]esselis map Gurhaiernn map Elbodgu map Cinnin map Millo map Camuir map Brittu map Cattegirn map Catell.
24. [S]elim map Iouab map Guitgen map Bodug map Carantmail map Cerennior map Ermic map Ecrin.
27. Cincen map Catel map Brocmayl map Elizet map Guilauc map Eli [?Beli] map Eliud map Brocmayl map Cinan map Maucant map Pascent map Cattegir[n] map Catel map Selemiaun.

The Pillar of Eliseg notwithstanding, none of these mention Vortigern (and through his wife, Maximus), although Vortigern's alleged sons Pascent, Britu and Cattegirn all appear. These genealogies descend from brothers Pascent and Brittu, here said to have been sons of Cattegirn son of Catell. However, elsewhere we find both of them as sons of Vortigern (with the implied descent from Severa daughter of Maximus) instead of Catell. In numbers 22 and 24, Selim is the Selyf ('f' mutates from 'm' in Welsh = Solomon) who was killed at the Battle of Chester in 613/5; he was succeeded by his brother Elise/Eiludd map Gwylog/Gwyfog, as on the Pillar of Eliseg, above.

It is only on the pillar that the dynasty's connection with Maximus (and even Vortigern) are clearly apparent, in Brittu son of Vortigern and Sevira, 'blessed by Germanus'. The inscription on the Pillar of Eliseg was the official view of the dynasty in the ninth century, of people we assume to be his descendants. The Vortigern origin here is of course incompatible with the origin from Vortigern's rival Cadell Ddyrnllug ('gleaming hilt'), supposed in legend to be of servile birth, in numbers 22 and 23 above. Possibly the dynasty of the Cadellings ('the progeny of Cadell') in Powis were displaced or became extinct in the senior male line by Vortigern's successors who had previously ruled in Buellt and Gwerthrynion (western subdivisions of Powis). Powis again crops up in a genealogy in the Jesus College Oxford, MS 20, recorded 'before 1200' (but at an unknown date) although the copies we have were written c. 1350/1400 (see below).

BL Harleian MS 3859.67, Annales Cambriae [AC], the St David's Annals:
516 The Battle of Badon in which Arthur carried the cross of our Lord Jesus Christ for three days and three nights on his shoulders and the Britons were the victors.
537 The Battle of Camlann in which Arthur and Medraut fell and there was plague in Britain and Ireland.
547 A great death in which Maelgwyn king of Gwynedd died.
580 Gwrgi and Peredur sons of Elifert died.
595 The death of King Dunod son of Pabo (also given as the year of the mission of St Augustine).

Perhaps first written down in the 780s or 809/829, continued to 954 and further transcribed c. 1100,[29] the *Annales* appear to be in three parts: 450-613 selected material, mainly from the *Chronicle of Ireland*, 614-777 selections from a North British source, and 777-975 selections done at St David's. The relevance or otherwise of these entries will emerge later.

Anglo-Saxon Chronicle (ASC), compiled *c.* 885:
AD 381. This year **Maximus the Caesar** came to the empire. He was born in the land of Britain, whence he passed over into Gaul. He there slew the emperor Gratian; and drove his brother, whose name was Valentinian, from his country. The same Valentinian afterwards collected an army and slew Maximus; whereby he gained the empire. About this time arose the error of Pelagius over the world.

Here we appear to be moving away from the accepted canon. Like John of Nikiou, the *Chronicle* has Maximus born in Britain, and if we could trust the dates given in the ASC (which are much disputed), Maximus's elevation is closer in date to that calculated from the *Gallic Chronicle*. It also endows him with the rank of Caesar from before his acclamation, which is new. Thereafter, Valentinian II is conflated with Theodosius.

Vita of Ca[ra]doc of Llancarfan, written *c.* 1100:
Maximianus itaque genuit Ouguein. Ouguein genuit Nor. Nor genuit Solor. Solor genuit Gliuguis. Gliuguis genuit Gundleium. Gundleius genuit beatissimum Cadocum...[30]

After a long diversion through a list of Roman Emperors from Octavian (Augustus) to Maximus (here, again presented as 'Maximian,' son of Constantius II), typically set out as a succession from father to son, we get the above. Note the appearance of Maximus's alleged son Owein/Eugenius, a name we have suggested as a possible insular successor to Constantine III. The same source, chapter 46, adds the saint's mother's pedigree from Coel Hen via the kings of Gwent and this is followed by another descent from Cunedda, alleged founder of the dynasty of Gwynedd.

Vita of St Gurthiern, Breton *c.* twelfth century (claimed sixth-century source) in translation:
Gurthiern, of noble birth, and the praiseworthy service, which a certain faithful layman, named Juthael, the son of Aidan, delivered, not for earthly treasure but for heavenly. Accordingly, Gurthiern was the son of Bonus, who was the son of Glou the son of Abros the son of Dos the son of Jacob the son of Genethauc the son of Jugdual the son of Beli the son of Outham the Elder, the son of **Maximian** the son of Constant[i]us the son of Constantine the son of Helen who was thought to have held the Cross of Christ. This is the genealogy of Gurthiern on his mother's side: Thus, Gurthiern was son of Dinoi, the daughter of King Lidinin who was the king of all the Britons, Beli and Kenan were two brothers, the sons of Outham the Elder. Kenan himself held the kingship when the British came to Rome. They held power in Laeticia (Brittany) ... Beli was the son of Anne who was said to be the cousin of Mary who bore the Christ.

This pedigree of a Breton saint takes his ancestry back to 'Maximian' (the real Maximian this time) via 'Outham the elder'. The latter name is that of Maximus's alleged legendary father-in-law, Eudaf Hen (Octavius), possibly confused with Owein, his son in *Vita Cadoci*. The saint's father and grandfather bear names which evoke the pedigree in *Historia Brittonum* of Vortigern, from whose name/epithet that of the saint derives, which rather dents any claim it may have for authority.

De Situ Brecheniauc ('Concerning Brychan') written *c.* 1200 from an
original 'at least as old as the eleventh century'[31]
Arthur m Uthur m Kusthenin m Kynvawr m Tutwal m Morvawr m Eudaf
m Kadwr m Kynan m Karadoc m Bran m Llyr.

Section 14 includes the three wives of King Brychan. In a note, P. C. Bartrum
adds that the three wives have been made out of one and, citing BL Harleian
MS 2414 fo. 68v, he mentions the marriage of a daughter of a Roman emperor
to a prince of Cornwall, possibly referring to a daughter of Maximus, but see
Chapter 10. He adds that 'it is remarkable that such a marriage is actually
recorded' and names the daughter as Gratian(a), a daughter of Maximus
who married Tudwal ap Morfawr.[32] This Tudwal is identified in Mostyn MS
117 (written *c.* 1290 from an earlier source) section 5, quoted above.

This rather suggests that the compiler had been working from Geoffrey
of Monmouth's *Historia Regum Britanniae* (*HRB*), as he quotes Arthur and
Uther, who appear there, Uther uniquely with the latter's supposed father
Constantine (of Cornwall) who is recorded as the grandson of Tutwal.[33]
There is no mention of Tutwal's wife, but we learn that he was grandson of
Eudaf Hen, himself great-grandson of Karadauc map Bran – in other words
P. Ostorius Scapula's protagonist during the conquest of Britain after 41AD,
Caractacus. 'Llyr' is identifiable with *Leir* (King) Lear, taking us, at a gallop,
into pre-history.[34] Thus Geoffrey of Monmouth has muddied the waters
completely, although in *his* narrative, Tutwal seems to have passed him by.

Jesus College MS 20 (source before 1200, copies 1350/1400) –
4: The collected ancestors of St Cadoc:
Cattawc m Gwynlliw m Gliws m Filur m Nor mab Owein m **Maxen**

This contains a group of related descents mentioning Maximus. Cadoc's
descent in the male line is given above.

Owein son of **Maximus** by Keindrech daughter of Reiden, son of Eledi son
of Mordu son of Meirchawn son of Kasswallawn son of Beli Mawr son of
Anna.

Maximus's descent from Constantine the Great is given, who is shown as
married to Elen Luedyawc (Helen) instead of being his mother, founder
of the True Cross. The manuscript shows 'no sign of influence of *HRB*'
according to Bartrum.[35] This is exemplified by the fact that Maximus's
wife in later legend, [H]elen Leudyawc/Llydawc ('Helen of the Hosts') is
identifiable as Constantine's mother but moved to become his wife. Instead,
it endows Maximus with a British wife, but one royally descended from
Cassivellaunus, the British king who fought Julius Caesar in 55 and 54 BC.[36]

It also again endows the son, Owein (Eugenius) with some genealogical resonance, if he is the man we have tentatively identified with the otherwise anonymous successor of Constantine III in Britain.

Glywysing (South Wales):
[10] … Peredur m Cado m Gereint m Erbin;
[11] Gereint m Erbin m [Custennin m] Kynvawr m Tutwal m Gwrawr m Gadeon m Cynan m Eudaf Hen…

This is a version of the pedigree of Tutwal, alleged son-in-law of Maximus. Here the compiler has inserted Custennin/Constantine from parallel sources. This version also looks uncontaminated by Geoffrey of Monmouth's genealogical manipulations, as the Uther is replaced by Erbin (Urbinus), but Gadeon, Cynan and Eudaf Hen all appear in the *Dream of Macsen Wledig* (below) representing an apparently parallel tradition but one bearing no more apparent authenticity when it comes to having preserved likely nuggets of real history. Peredur's immediate forebears would appear to be Dumnonian, cf. Chapter 10.

18 Powis:
Rodri Mawr map Nest merch Cadell Pywys … map Brochmael map Elise map Coleddag map Beli [map Selyf] map Cynan Garwyn map Brochfael map [Cyngen] map Manogen map Pasgen map Cadell Ddyrnllug map Cadegyrn [Categirn] map Gwyrtheyrn.

This, the pedigree of Nest, mother of Rhodri Mawr, King of Gwynedd, tries to square the circle by making Cadell Ddyrnllug the son of Vortigern's son Categirn, but the result is to add a generation. Elise is of course the Eliseg who erected the pillar at Valle Crucis. Note the presence of Gwyrtheyrn/Vortigern, son-in-law of Maximus according to Eliseg, but absent in the Harleian MS 3859 version.

19 Gwynedd/Man:
Rodri Mawr m Meruyn m Guriat m Elidyr m Celenion merch Tutwal (Tuclith) m Anarawd gwalchcrwn m Meruyn mawr m Kyuyn m Anllech m Tutwawl m Run m Neidaon m Senlith Hael … m. Dingat m Tutwawl m Edneuet m Dunawt m **Maxen wledic**…

Here we have the (edited) descent of Rhodri Mawr from Celenion, daughter of Tutwal of the Isle of Man (as Harleian MS 3859.4 above) but calling Maximus's son not Antonius but Dunawt (Donatus). Edneuet was a ruler on the south bank of the Forth (Manau Goddodin/Votadini); the Manx rulers seem to have been an offshoot of his line.

Bonedd y Saint ('**Lineage of the Saints**') *c.* 1275, was a list of British saints, some acknowledged as having been first written down somewhat earlier than 1275.[37]

18 Votadini:

... Dyngat m Nud Hael m Senyllt m Kedic m Dyuynyeual (Dyfnwal/ Domnall) Hen m Ydnyuet m **Maxen wletic** a Thenoi verch Lewdwn Lluydawc o Dinas Eidyn yn y Gogled eu Mam.

Here we find a descent of the rulers of the Votadini (Manau Goddodin) again and their descendant Dyngat, cognate with that above, but Antonius/ Donatus has been left out and the son Ednyvet (Ydnyuet) has been attached to Maximus. It also introduces the father of Maximus's wife of later tradition, Helen Lluydawc. Nud Hael may possibly be identifiable with the Nudus of the Yarrowkirk stone (Chapter 9).

63 St Peblic:

Peblic Sant yn y Caer Aruon [Caernarfon] m **Maxen wledic** amherawdyr Ruuein ac Helen verch Eudaf y uam.

('St Peblic of the fortification of Arfon, son of the lord Maximus Roman Emperor and Helen daughter of Eydaf.')

Bartrum MSS C & F.

Pebic [*sic*] ac Owain Vinddu m **Maxen wledic** brenhin y Bryttanieid ac amerodr Ruvein ac Elen verch Eudaf ap Karadawc.

MS E

... Evdaf Hen vrenin Prydain (Eudaf Hen, 'King of Britain')'

MS H

... Eudaf Hen brenin Ynys Brydain ('Eudaf Hen, King of the Island of Britain').[38]

This firmly fixes St Peblic in the former Roman settlement of Caernarfon, claims him as a son of Maximus and St Helena, but derives, it would seem, from the *urtext* of the *Dream*. An alternative version of the genealogy occurs in Bartrum's MSS C & F:

Again, much of this is distilled from *The Dream* or its earlier source, however, Peblic (Publicius) is given as Maximus's son in the first version but in the second his grandson by his son, attested elsewhere (eg. Jesus College MS20.4 above), Owain Vinddu/Finddu (Eugenius 'Black Lips'). St Peblic was the alleged founder of the church that bears his name, Llanbeblig, close to Segontium (see Chapter 6), alleged place of Maximus's elevation to the purple. Late Roman material had been found beneath the church, including corn drying kilns and post-Roman mortuary enclosures.[39] In this second version Maximus's wife is included along with her father, Eudaf Hen' king of the Island of Britain.' Another genealogy in *Achau'r Saint* ('Pedigrees of the Saints'), a compilation written down from much earlier material as recently as 1527, we get simply '*Peblic vab* **Maxen Wledig**' ('Publicius son of [Prince] Maximus') as in the first extract above.[40]

76 St Kyngar:
MS F version
    [Kyngar a] Iestin a Selva[n] y Mhennmon a Llys. a Chyngar yn Llangevni meibion Geraint m Erbin m. Kwysdenin Gornev m Kynvawr m Tudwal, m Gwr[m]wr m Kadiawn m Kynan m Euda[f] hir, y gwr a vv dwysawc ymlayn Lymru pann ayth gida **Maxen wledic**...
    MS G & K versions
    'Kyngar a Iestin a Cattw [Gadwy] a Selyf meibion Geraint ap Erbin ap Custenin Gornev ap Kynvar ap Tudwal ap Kurmwr (nev Morvawr o henw arall) ap Caden ap Kynan ap Evdaf as Caradoc ap Bran ap Llyr llediaith.

Here we have a largely Dumnonian ascendancy to Kynan m[ap] Eudaf Hir [*Hir* in error for *Hen* = old] Maximus's legendary brother-in-law, in other words, Conan Meriadoc, the second version merely elaborating Conan's ancestry. This again is rooted in the sources of *The Dream of Macsen Wledig*.

Bonedd Gwyr y Gogledd ('**Lineage of the Men of the North**') **written down** *c.* **1280:** 11 Gauran m Aedan Vradawc m Dyuynwal Hen m Idnyuet m **Maxen wledic** amherawdyr Ruuein

This is the lineage of a largely forgotten figure, enjoying the same descent from Maximus as the dynasty of Man, above. Aed[d]an is really an Irish name; perhaps Dyuynwal Hen had an Irish wife. As we shall see in the next chapter, this is by no means unlikely.

Achau Brenhinoedd a Thywysogion Cymru ('**Pedigrees of the Kings and Princes of Wales**') *c.* 1180/1240) –
6 (k) **Gruffudd ap Cynan:**

    ... Elise map Kyllan/Kynllo map Beli map Eiludd [map Selyf] map Cynan Garwyn map Brochfael map Cyngen map Cadell Ddyrnllug map Pasgen map Britu/Brydw map Rhuddfedel map Cyndern map Gwrtheyrn.

Cf. (above) Harleian MS 3859, 22/23/27 & Jesus College MS 20, 18. Here, again, we have a (somewhat garbled) descent of the House of Powis. Elise (Eliseg), Pasgen and Britu all appear on the Pillar of Eliseg, but the latter are here great-grandsons of Vortigern and thus implicit great-great-grandsons of Maximus (who again is not mentioned), Rhuddfael and Cyndern making an errant appearance in between. The following pedigree, 6(l), takes us instead back through the dynasty of Man to Maximus via Ednyfet, as *Bonedd y Sant* 18 (above).

18 Dyfed [a]:
Iwein ap elen ferch Llywarch ap Hyfeidd ap Tangwystyl ferch Ewein ap Maredudd ap Tewdos [as Rhain] ap Kadwgon ap Kathen [Kynddelw] ap Nowy ap Arthur ap Pedr ap Kyngar ap Gwerthefyr ap Erbin ap Aergul Llawir ap Tryffin ap Ewein Vreisg ap Kyndeyrn Vendigeit ap Ewein ap Kyngar ap Ewein ap Gwledyr ap Amweryd ap Kustennin ap **Maxen wledig.**

This is another version of the genealogy of the House of Demetia (Dyfed), but with Nimet and Dimet elided and Maximus gaining a new son called Kustennin (Constantine), who may in fact represent Constantine III (but cf. Chapter 10).[41] Note 'Arthur son of Pedr' (Peter), the naming of whom has occasionally been held up as evidence of the existence of the rather more illustrious but infinitely more elusive Arthur.

Breudwyt Macsen Wledig ('The Dream of Macsen Wletic') in *The Mabinogion*:[42]
The *Mabinogion* is collection of tales, mostly ancient, written down *c.* 1350/1400 but much seems to date back earlier (by the language and orthography used), some to *c.* 1050-1120, just pre-dating Geoffrey of Monmouth and some, like *The Dream* itself, a little later.[43] Yet the tale seems to tell how two ruling families came together.[44] For convenience, a précis is given here.

Macsen/Maximus is depicted as a reigning emperor based in Rome. He has a dream while taking a snooze during a hunting trip. The *breudwyt* (dream) is really more like 'astral travel', an occult construct in which one leaves one's sleeping body and floats freely seeing what is afoot round and about and, in some cases, willing the direction of travel. Thus, Maximus leaves Rome, travels over the Alps and down a wide river, perhaps the Rhine, and across the Channel. Thereafter, he crosses Britain until he arrives over Snowdonia. Crossing the mountains, he reaches another wide estuary whereon there is a fortress of unparalleled beauty. He enters the hall of the fortress, described rather like a major *praetorium* or basilica, but with the most lavish décor imaginable. In this room are four people: two boys, playing chess, an elderly man enthroned and a beautiful girl, lavishly attired. Needless to say, on leaning forward to embrace this vision of loveliness, the dream ends, and the sounds of the chase obtrude.

The story turns more formulaïc at this point, for the emperor becomes completely love-lorn and, after numerous attempts, identifies the locale encountered in his 'astral' journey and sends messengers to beg for the lady's hand in marriage, but the lady, Helen Luyddog (Elen Llwydawg, or Helen of the Hosts), quite rightly demands that he comes in person to plight his troth.

This Maximus decides to do, but on landing in Britain is obliged to defeat the King of Britain, Beli ap Manogan and his sons (who really belong in British pre-history), which he duly does, driving them into the sea.

Is this a shadowy reflection of the real Maximus's defeat of the Picts and Scots? Alternatively, it may be a way of legitimising Roman hegemony in Britain without demonising it, much like the later Saxon occupations, as a large number of the British dynasties of which genealogies survive claim an ascendancy of one sort or another (albeit hopelessly lacking in sufficient generations) to Beli Mawr (Beli the Great). However, in the British pedigrees it emerges that Helen is descended from the ancient ruling dynasty in any case, so that her subsequent alliance with Maximus can be seen as legitimising in a British context as well.[45]

But we are getting ahead of ourselves. The emperor at last arrives, meets the old man who turns out to be Eudaf Hen and the two lads, brothers Cynan and Gadeon, not forgetting the lady, their sister Helen. Having met, they fall in love in the material rather than the ethereal world and he is post-coitally obliged to stump up for a marriage portion. This is to be the whole island of Britain and three adjacent islands for her father, to be held under her as empress (a piece of feudal terminology creeping in), and three forts are to be built, at Caer Seint, Caerllion and Caerfyrddin (Caernarfon, Caerleon and Carmarthen).

There arises then a sort of Roman civil war, containing obvious echoes of the clashes between not only Constantius and Carausius but also those between Constantine and Maxentius, in which Maximus loses control of the City of Rome. Macsen responds by assembling an army of fierce Britons and appoints Helen's brothers as commanders. They successfully recapture the city after a very long siege, but the brothers have to be enticed with the right to conquer any part of the world they might wish in return for allowing Maximus and Helen to take their rightful places in the city. In the end, Cynan and his men settle in Brittany and turn out to be the reason why the Armoricans thenceforth spoke British and not Latin, this being brutally achieved by removing the tongues of the native women, the tale being an attempt to explain the Bretons' name for themselves, *Llydaw* ('half-silent').[46]

It is generally held that all this was written *after* Geoffrey of Monmouth, but the essential elements could just as easily have preceded him, acquiring later elements, like the feudal expression 'held under' and the obvious associations with the early career of king Llewellyn ap Iorwerth (Llewellyn the Great), in later recensions, for the two works seem to embody parallel traditions. The bare bones of the story could originally have been put together between the *Historia Brittonum* and Geoffrey's *Historia Regum Britanniae*. The *Dream* is also a romantic tale and has a firm place in literature and particularly that of Wales, as the distilled essence of all preceding British literature by the time it was written down.

Nevertheless, the late John Morris grants it the accolade of being 'among the best told tales in the early prose of any land'. As was tentatively suggested above, Morris also agrees that Maximus's wife 'may indeed have been British'.[47] He further remarked that 'The story used a description of Roman Segontium by someone who had seen its buildings and its furniture before time wore them and who knew something of his remoter ancestors' ornament and dress,' adding that the building of the three forts and the creation of the north to south road in Wales, the Sarn Elen, also described therein, must derive from an early sixth century account.[48]

Geoffrey of Monmouth, *Historia Regum Britanniae* (History of the Kings of Britain) *c.* 1135/1139 [49]

Geoffrey's work is generally accorded a place in the canon of British literature, the more so because it encompasses some of the Arthurian material, which can only dimly be discerned in preceding literature. It is the *urtext* of most subsequent literature of this type. Geoffrey, of course, intended it to be taken as history and assures his readers that it was based on a translation of 'an ancient book in the British language that told in orderly fashion the deeds of all the kings of Britain … given to me by Walter, Archdeacon of Oxford'.

As was observed in the previous chapter, it is *possible* that such an account could have survived up to this point, bearing in mind the lack of record surviving from the post-Roman period of insular central control. Yet no source between Geoffrey's time and the destruction of ancient records brought about by the Dissolution contains any suggestion of Geoffrey's source, ensuring that it has to be regarded with considerable circumspection, despite Dr Russell's identification of an unknown version of the Roman conquest buried, in mutilated form, in the text (see below). The narrative embodies much that has been quoted above, and other material of unknown provenance besides. A quotation of the first section sets the tone, while the remainder of his account of Maximus follows in *précis*.

Worn out with eld and desirous of making provision for his people at his death, he [Octavius, Eydaf Hen] inquired of his counsellors which of his family they would most gladly raise to be king after that he himself were departed. For he had but one single daughter, and was without heir male unto whom he might hand down the rule of the country. Some, accordingly, proposed that he should give his daughter to wife along with the kingdom unto some Roman noble, so as that thereby they should enjoy the firmer peace. But others gave their voice that Conan Meriadoc, his nephew, should be declared heir to the throne of the kingdom, and that his daughter should be given in marriage with dowry of gold and silver unto the prince of some other kingdom. While that they were debating these matters amongst themselves, in came Caradoc, Duke of Cornwall, and gave it as his counsel that they should invite Maximian the Senator and give him the King's daughter and the kingdom, that so they might enjoy perpetual peace. For his father was a Welsh Briton, he being the son of Leoline, uncle of Constantine...[50] By his mother and by birth, howbeit, he was Roman, and by blood was he of royal pedigree on both sides. Caradoc held therefore that this marriage did promise an abiding peace, for that he knew **Maximian** [i.e. Maximus], being at once of the family of the Emperors and also by origin a Briton, would have good right to the kingdom of Britain. But when the Duke of Cornwall had thus delivered his counsel, Conan, the King's nephew, waxed indignant, for his one endeavour was to make a snatch at the kingdom for himself and, aiming at this end only, stuck not to run counter to the whole court beside. But Caradoc, being in nowise minded to change his purpose, sent his son Maurice to Rome to sound **Maximian** on the matter. Maurice himself was a big man and a comely, as well as of great prowess and hardiment, and if any would gainsay aught that he laid down, he would prove the same in arms in single combat. When, therefore, he appeared in presence of **Maximian**, he was received in becoming wise, and honoured above the knights that were his fellows. At that time was there a mighty quarrel toward betwixt **Maximian** himself and the two Emperors Gratian and his brother Valentinian, for that he had been denied in the matter of one third part of the empire which he had demanded. When Maurice, therefore, saw that **Maximian** was being put upon by the twain Emperors, he spake unto him in these words:

'What cause hast thou, **Maximian,** to be afeard of Gratian, when the way lieth open unto thee to snatch the empire from him? Come with me into the island of Britain and thou shalt wear the crown of the kingdom. For King Octavius is sore borne down by eld and lethargy and desireth nought better than to find some man such as thyself unto whom he may give his kingdom and his daughter. For heir male hath he none, and counsel hath he sought of his barons unto whom he should give his daughter to wife, with the kingdom for dower. And, for that his barons would fain give obedient answer unto his address, his high court hath made resolve that the kingdom and the damsel should be granted unto thee, and unto me have they given commission that I should notify thee of the matter. If, therefore, thou wilt come with me into Britain, thou shalt achieve this adventure; the plenty of gold and silver that is in Britain shall be thine, and the multitude of hardy men of war that dwell therein. Thus, wilt thou be enough strong to return unto Rome, and, after that thou hast driven forth these Emperors, then mayst thou enjoy the empire thereof thyself. For even thus did Constantine thy kinsman before thee, and many another of our kings that hath ere now raised him unto the empire.'[51]

Thereafter Maximus (as Maximian) arrives in Britain with a large retinue and is accepted by all but Conan, who is eventually persuaded by Caradoc of Cornwall and his son Maurice to accept the situation. He weds Helena, daughter of Coel of Colchester (what happened to Coel Hen?), further annoying

Conan, who goes to Scotland and plots to overthrow Maximus. After several armed encounters they are again reconciled. Five years later, Maximus invades the Continent and, having achieved much success, grants Conan a kingdom there. Conan conquers and settles Brittany and allies himself with Dionotus of Cornwall (Caradoc's brother) to settle more Britons in Armorica and also desires Ursula, Dionotus' daughter. But things go awry, and Guanius and Melga, 'dukes' of the Huns and Picts, ravage Britain, but Maximus appoints Gratian the Burgess (the first appearance of the hapless usurper Gratian since Zosimus) to deal with them, which he does. Meanwhile, Maximus is killed in Rome by the friends of (emperor) Gratian and the continental Britons are scattered. Gratian the Burgess then takes over in Britain.[52]

One can see here the tattered shreds of the history with which we became familiar in Part I, intermingling with new material: elements of Gildas and from *Historia Brittonum*, while introducing characters like Conan, Coel and Octavius imported from the hagiographies and genealogies, and others, like the dynasty of Cornwall – Caradoc, Maurice and Dionotus – the later pair unknown elsewhere, although bearing perfectly good Roman names. As Miles Russell observes, 'There are no significant sections of text which supply archaeological and historical detail in sufficient quantity to show that they can only have come from sources earlier than Geoffrey of Monmouth.'

Nevertheless, elements in Geoffrey 'indeed appear to derive from older sources', like names in his account of the Roman invasion of Britain, which we now know appear on Iron Age coin issues.[53] Gratian hunting out the Huns and Picts, too, may be a conflation with Gratian I or even the reflection of a separate tradition about an event in the brief reign of the British-acclaimed Gratian II. Furthermore, the invasion of Britain by Guanius/Wanius, a Hun and Melga, a Pict, maybe a remote echo of the events of the Barbarian Conspiracy of 367, just as Maximus's invasion of Britain in the *Dream of Macsen Wletic* may echo the Roman *comes*' successful fight against the Picts and Scots fifteen or so years later. One important matter is that the elements of the story in Geoffrey are too divergent from those found in the *Dream of Macsen Wletic*, from which it would appear that an independent tradition must have preceded both and informed both.[54] The conclusion from this plethora of sources is that the positive memory of Maximus lived on, just as Carausius's memory seems to have done in Wales and the North, reinforced by the homonymous fourth-century coin-issuing *tyrannus* and the evidence of the Penmachno stone.[55]

If Maximus's wife was indeed British, then when he came to devolve power in his absence, he may well have appointed relations as local commanders and administrators and that after 407/409, they 'went native'. Constantine III (if also British, which is by no means certain, as discussed in Chapter 6) may perhaps have done something similar. The problem is that we hear no detailed mention of Maximus's wife until the *Dream of Macsen Wletic* and in Geoffrey of Monmouth. The earliest pedigrees that include

Elen Lluydawc are in *Bonedd y Sant*, written down after both. All earlier ones fail to mention her when mentioning Maximus, as in the *Vita St Cadoci* in Jesus College MS, where the Helen of the later tradition assumes the identity of Constantine's mother St Helena, which might indeed be a plausible inspiration behind the subsequent name of Maximus's wife.[56] However, the same pedigree still supplies him with a British wife, and one of impeccable princely descent, albeit lacking (in the pedigree as given) sufficient named ancestors to carry her ancestry safely back to Julius Caesar's time.[57]

This is why commentators dismiss Helen of the Hosts as merely a double for St Helena. Yet, if we remember that in reality, the emperor spent a couple of years in Britain in 367-369, when he was probably around 30, and thus at a most suitable age to be married, his alliance with a distinguished British resident is not inherently unlikely and, the name of the Augusta Helena was by then sufficiently revered as to have inspired the nomenclature of countless infant females. Even if we cannot accept this, he is still endowed elsewhere with a British wife, in Keindrech/Ceindrech ap Rhydion whose name re-appears amongst the descendants of several British dynasties, like that of Brycheiniog.[58]

Trioedd Ynys Prydein 35(R):

... and the second [host] went with Elen of the Hosts and **Maxen Wledig** to Llychlyn and they never returned to this Island.

Bromwich points out that Llychlyn really refers to Scandinavia, but clearly Llydaw (Brittany) was intended, and looks like a post-Galfridian re-working of the Triad which originally started with first element 'Elen of the hosts and Cynan her brother' (no mention of Maximus).[59]

Trioedd Ynys Prydein Appendix II:

Uradauc mab Dyvnywaul Hen mab Idnyvet mab **Macsen Wledic** Amheraudyr Ruuein.

This genealogy is that of the descendants of Coroticus (Ceredic Wletic) of Alclud, where Maxen Wletic has replaced the correct name of Ceretic Wletic.[60]

Trioedd Ynys Prydein from Iolo Morgannwg's collection 17 (translated):

There were three monarchs by the verdict of the Isle of Britain. The first was Caswallawn the son of Lludd, son of Beli, son of Mynogan; the second was Caradog, son of Bran, son of Llyr Llediaith; and the third was Owain the son of **Maximus**. That is, sovereignty was conferred upon them by the verdict of the country and the nation, when they were not elders.

If genuine, this endows Owein with regal status and repeats his relationship to Maximus.

Trioedd Ynys Prydein from Iolo Morgannwg's collection 41:

The three supreme servants of the Isle of Britain: Caradog, the son of Bran, the son of Llyr Llediath; Cawrdav, the son of Caradog with the Brawny Arm; and Owain, the son of **Macsen Wledig**. They were so called because all the men of the Isle of Britain, from the prince to the peasant, became their followers at the need of the country, on account of the invasions and tyranny of the foe. And wherever these three marched to war, there was not a man on the Isle of Britain but who would join their armies and would not stay at home. And these three were the sons of bards.

In the later eighteenth century Edward Williams, writing under the *nom-de-plume* of Iolo Morgannwg, compiled a collection of Triads, which he claimed were derived from manuscripts in his possession and other, mainly oral, sources. While many replicated those in the earliest collections edited by Bromwich (although with elaborations) others were not. They were published first in 1807. In the later nineteenth century Sir John Morris-Jones wrote that he believed Iolo was a talented forger and no more, however, Griffith John Williams, a scholar working between the wars, studied his output in depth in order to discover how much was attributable to Iolo's sources and how much was embellishment. He ended up by feeling able to dismiss some material, but by no means all. Recent research has proceeded along the same lines. Thus, on the basis that these extra Triads *might* owe their origin to a genuine early tradition, it would seem right to include them, if only with added caution in taking them at face value.

In using the material in the genealogies, the rule of thumb, unless otherwise indicated, has been to assume that out-and-out Roman names other than that of Maximus himself in the earlier parts of the pedigrees almost certainly represent a first ancestor, even when British ancestors precede them going back further (often much further). On all the evidence and past analyses, these additions have invariably been judged fictitious or vicarious additions. Yet when one reviews the wealth of legendary and other related material about Maximus, we do seem to find ourselves faced with a sort of unseemly scramble amongst the British to claim a relationship with him, long before he appears as a much more rounded, romanticised and rather different figure in the *Dream* and in Geoffrey of Monmouth than as the army-stealing usurper of Gildas and earlier sources. In the former, he appears almost as a flawless super-hero rather than the tarnished usurper of the panegyric.

Having reviewed the sources in which Maximus appears in the first millennium after his life and death, we now examine what we know, or think we know, about those post-Roman polities the rulers of which made so strong a claim upon him; and also about two figures, both identified as 'old', whose presence in the sources (and many not quoted above) seems ubiquitous and who seem inextricably allied to the Maximus of romance: Eudaf and Coel.

8

Maximus as Founding Father

It emerged from Chapter 7 that Maximus was seen as the founding father
of several post-Roman polities, all clustered around the extremities of the
diocese of the Britains, the areas which we have postulated Maximus might
well have placed on a sound long-term footing during his rule. Although
there seem to be a bewildering number – Powis, Dumnonia, Demetia, the Isle
of Man, Gwynedd and at least one beyond or straddling Hadrian's Wall –
some of them in fact are merely sub-branches of the same dynasties and the
total actually comes down to just three: Demetia, Powis, and the North. It is
necessary, too, to say something of Brittany, allegedly founded as a result of
Maximus's time on the Continent and, according to legend, by his brother-
in-law, the elusive Conan Meriadoc (see Chapter 10).

Demetia

The earliest source, Harleian MS 3859, produced a pedigree of the dynasty
of Demetia, today called Dyfed, from the Welsh mutation of the Roman
name ('m' to 'f' and 't' to 'd'). This included Maximus's name and it would
be gratifying to know quite why this anomalous-looking insertion into the
succession of rulers came about. The most obvious assumption must be that
he caused the dynasty to be founded. This has to be understood in the light
of the fact that south-west Wales is full of evidence that it had been settled by
Irish in the late Roman period, despite the apparent continuing civic functions
at the *civitas* capital, Moridunum (Carmarthen).[1] This genealogy is reinforced
by an Irish document called *The Expulsion of the Déisi*, of which the oldest
copy can be dated to the twelfth century.[2] Written in Irish, it tells us that

> Eochaid son of Artchorp went over the sea with his descendants into the
> territory of Demed and it is there that his sons and grandsons died. And from
> them is the race of Crimthann over there, of which is Tualodor son of Rigin

son of Catacuind son of Caittienn son of Clotenn son of Naee son of Artuir son of Retheoir son of Congair son of Gartbuir son of Alchoil son of Trestin son of Aeda Brosc, son of Corath, son of Eochaid Allmuir son of Arttchuirp.[3]

The *Historia Brittonum* is in no doubt about Irish settlement in Wales, dramatically supported by this early and unexpected tale. The inference that this Irish group, settled in Demetia, derived from the much later British pedigree set out in the previous chapter.[4] There, Maximus is given a grandson called 'Protector' – *Maxim Guletic map Protec map Protector*.[5]

Although Alchoil above (Agricola) and Triphun (*tribunus*/tribune) are Roman (a name and a rank), it is possible they were conferred in Ireland pre-migration, for Professor Thomas reminds us of Cn. Julius Agricola's sheltering of the renegade Irish prince in the 80s, and the rank of *tribunus* could conceivably have been a usage imported into Ireland.[6] The ancestors of Brychan, ruler of Brycheiniog (from which Brecknock/Breconshire) as given in *Cognatio Brychan* appear to have been an offshoot as well, to which strands Thomas adds names from inscribed stones at Castell Dwyran, Llandysilio and Nevern (all in Carmarthenshire/Dyfed), which he links together to create something of a dynasty (see *stemma* 2).[7] A final, rather later genealogy of the rulers of Demetia tells us that Tryffin (Tribunus) was a descendant of Amweryd son of Kustennin (Constantine) son of Maxen.[8] This Constantine is a new son for Maximus, and the pedigree is too late and garbled for any real reliance to be placed upon it. Yet it does reinforce this Demetian link with Maximus, apparent in the Harleian pedigree.

Dating all this presents problems. An approximate date for *Triphun* may be possible through a carved stone from Crickhowell (Brecon) which reads:

TURPILLI [H]IC IACIT PVVERI TRIBUNI DUNOCATI[9]

Where Dunocatus is the father of Turpili[o] and was in the service of (or close kin to) Tribunus/Triphun of Demetia, assuming that the Tribunus is the same man as the Demetian ruler, which seems highly likely.[10] This man's son, Alchoil/Agricola, Thomas suspects, *fl* 480/500s and may have been the first Christian ruler of Demetia ('king' would be premature at this date). We know from an entry in the (admittedly problematical) Llandaff Charters that as 'Aircol son of Trifun, King of Demetia', he bore the epithet *lauhir* (Welsh *Llawhir*) which means 'long hand' or 'open handed', taken to indicate generosity.[11] When it comes to the son of Alchoil/Agricola, Gartbuir, we have a better-known person in that he would seem to be one and the same as Vot[e]por[ix], who appears on a late fifth- or early sixth-century memorial stone from Castell Dwyran (Carmarthenshire/Dyfed – a minuscule parish containing an unexcavated rectangular earthwork) which reads:

MEMORIA VOTEPORIGIS PROTICTORIS[12]

With an Irish Ogham script (a series of parallel lines carved either side of one edge of the stone representing Latin letters) echoing this and transliterating as VOTECORIGAS, it was found at Narberth, Pembrokeshire, not far from the place called Liscastell, which the Llandaff charter describes as the place where Aircol Llawhir held court, *llys-* in the (mutated) place name being the Welsh prefix for a princely court. Voteporigis is the genitive, thus 'the memorial of Voteporix'. The Ogham consolidates the belief that this line of rulers (who may not have been a father to son succession at all, but merely a succession of rulers, probably from within the same family) had Irish connections if not origins. The rank, *protector* (allowing for mutation from the correct Latin) is a perfectly reasonable one for a late Roman federate barbarian leader and has parallels elsewhere in the empire at this period.

Most historians have conflated Voteporix with the Vortiporius attacked by Gildas writing *c.* 530:

> Why also art thou, Vortipor, tyrant of the Demetae, foolishly stubborn? Like the leopard art thou, in manners and wickedness of various colour, though thy head is now becoming grey, upon a throne full of guile, and from top to bottom defiled by various murders and adulteries, thou worthless son of a good king.[13]

The problem with assuming these two to be one and the same is that their names' first syllables are different, with different British meanings, and secondly, that if Vortiporius was living, a man 'becoming grey' *c.* 530, then Aed Brosc cannot have been in his prime much before 450, whereas the migration of this tribe from Ireland is generally reckoned to have occurred considerably earlier, if only because it is hard to see anyone in the former diocese of Britain having the ability to organise Irish settlers as federated troops (*foederati*) as late as the mid-fifth century, by which time the unfortunate consequences of Vortigern's doing the same thing in Kent might well have been only too apparent. Philip Rance particularly comes down in favour of the Déisi being Attacotti and that their recruitment into the Roman Army was post-368 and their settlement 'small-scale and familial' and probably initiated under Magnus Maximus.[14] Yet, as we shall see in looking at fifth-century Irish links, such may not be as unlikely as it might appear. Charles-Edwards is sure that Voteporix and Vortiporius (530s) are not to be conflated but were probably two men belonging to the same dynasty, in which case, Vortiporius does not show up in the regnal list, although that should not surprise us unduly; he may, after all, be hiding in full sight masked by another name, bearing in mind that Vorteporius could be interpreted, like Vortigern, as a style or title.

The dynasty's interest in stressing links with their *romanitas* and the Roman past in the names and titles of its members would much be less likely to occur if the move from Ireland was as late as the mid-fifth century.[15] Charles-Edwards also suggests, as does Thomas, that the move from Ireland was probably very late in the fourth century, whereas the pedigree in Harleian MS 3859.2 specifically associates the group with Magnus Maximus, barely a generation earlier. Leslie Alcock even postulated that an Irishman (name unknown) was appointed *tribunus* (hence Triphun) of a Roman army unit (of Attacotti?) perhaps called the *Numerus Dessorum* (Déisian Regiment) or similar and brought over to Britain to strengthen the *comitatus*. He also speculated that Maximus might have taken one of Irish King Eochaid's sons as a bodyguard (loosely masking an effective piece of hostage-taking against good behaviour), thus gaining the style of 'protector' in the court, and that he eventually returned to his people as a *tribunus*.[16] Thereafter, one assumes that the style of *tribunus* mutated into a name and that *protector,* as used on the Narberth stone, became perhaps the ruling style of the family in Demetia, the term 'king' being resorted to when much of this early history (quite possibly transmitted in garbled form) was being finally written down by twelfth-century monks, who may well have had trouble understanding such non-standard titulature.

This proposition that Vortiporius and Voteporix were separate people does enable us to explain the great trouble the dynast had trying to hang on to the association with Magnus Maximus. Another method of calculating the antiquity of the dynasty and the period of its founding is to calculate back from a known date. In Ouein map Margetuit (Owain ap Maredydd, King of Deheubarth) we have a supposed descendant who died in 811, exactly fifteen years after his father. Most attempts to calculate back in 25, 30, or 33-year generations have come to nought, mainly because we have no idea if these people really succeeded father to son and whether some may have had long (or short) reigns, which is perfectly plausible, or have included a succession of brothers.[17] Yet the existence of Maximus as father of Dimet (Demetia) as a pillar of the Harleian version of this family's ascendancy cannot be too lightly discarded; our Maximus may indeed have been behind this settlement of Irish people.

That this migration was peaceful and therefore planned and managed is notable. It was possibly done for modest settlement in Demetia as *foederati* or *laeti* in exchange for contributing to the raising of the four regiments of Attacotti as *auxilia palatina* noted in the *Notitia Dignitatum*. This seems confirmed by the lack of overt Roman coastal defensive infrastructure around south-west Wales west of Cardiff, unlike those in the northern part and indeed the west coast of Britain north of Chester to the Wall (Lancaster excepted), unless Pembroke castle over-lies a substantial fort, as has been recently proposed.[18] That the transition was peaceful is surely confirmed by the fact that the incomers took over a probably somewhat depopulated Demetian *civitas* intact. In short, we seem to see in the settlement of Demetia from Ireland a situation analogous to that undertaken on the southern African *limes* by Theodosius the elder, in which Maximus may well have been involved, with the clan chief as phylarch, instead of the imposition of a Roman-appointed *praefectus*.

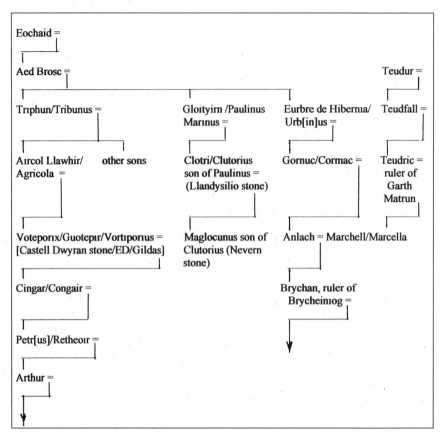

Stemma 2. The Dynasty of Demetia.

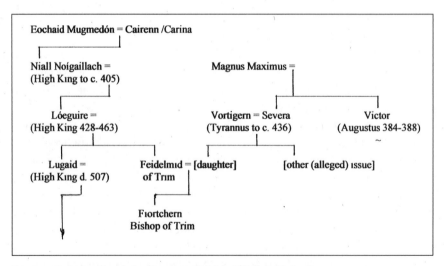

Stemma 3. Ireland and the Romano-British: Niall & Foirtchern.

Irish connections

Rance has pointed out that the settlement of the Déisi must have been officially sanctioned, so if we accept that Magnus Maximus was highly likely to have been responsible for their move, we need to consider whether he was in contact with the Irish when in Britain, or even later. After all, if one undertakes to transplant a whole people from Ireland, intelligence must have been obtained – and top-quality intelligence, too. Or did Maximus make a *de jure* recognition of a *de facto* event?[19] If not the latter, did Maximus bring about some kind of diplomatic *détente* between the Déisi/Attacotti and the Roman administration in order to secure tranquillity for at least one of Britain's borderlands after his suppression of the Picts and Scots (the latter were, after all, Irish, too), made more probable if he was planning to withdraw fighting units to the Continent and needed to fill the resulting manpower vacuum?[20]

It is possible to discern other connections, familial and commercial, across the Irish Sea, apart from the innumerable raiders like the Scotti – a confederation led by the Laigin of greater Leinster – as well as the Attacotti.[21] Another grouping, possibly also an element of the Attacotti, was the *Filii Liethan* mentioned in *Historia Brittonum* as having also settled in Demetia, seemingly to the northern side of the Pembrokeshire promontory.[22] This grouping is identified by Rance as the *Uí Liathán* from East Cork, where they had been neighbours of the Déisi, and were also a tributary grouping, thus justifying the term Attacotti. There is evidence in Irish sources that they settled (or were settled) in Cornwall, too, but whether on their own initiative and unopposed is beyond recovery.[23] When St Palladius was sent to Ireland, his charge was to minister to and expand an existing Christian community, presumably settlers and traders from Britain, in the general area of southern Leinster; Ireland was closer to Roman Britain than is often realised.[24]

Links went deeper than raiders and saints. Although later than the move of the Déisi, Scotnoë, daughter of an unnamed 'king of the Britons' married Prince Feidelmid of Trim, son of that Lóeguire, who was High King of Ireland 428-463 and was himself son of the first High King, Niall Noígiallach ('of the Nine Hostages'), a man who claimed to have harassed Roman Britain on a grand scale.[25] A child of the union was Foirtchern, which is a straight transliteration of Vortigern, from which we may reasonably adduce the name of the bride's father. The match was one of equals and high-level, probably involving some diplomatic trade-off. Foirtchern himself was converted to Christianity by the British missionary Lommán, supposed nephew and disciple of St Patrick, perhaps at the insistence of his mother. Foirtchern later became Bishop of Trim (Co. Meath), and an Ogham inscribed stone (transliterating as VORTIGURN) from Knockboy, Co. Waterford may relate to him.[26] Ogham inscriptions on both sides of the Irish Sea at this period attest to considerable interaction between Britain and Ireland.[27]

Morris also pointed out that the semi-legendary king Tigernach of Airgiailla (by his estimation also mid-fifth century) had sons called Fortchernn and Catchernn, the latter being an Irish rendering of Cattegeyrn (Categirn), the name also born by one of Vortigern's supposed sons in the Harleian Powis pedigrees. The Airgiailla's fortress is supposed to have been the hillfort at Clogher, a place where some Roman finds have emerged. [28] One can hardly believe that the British *tyrannus* had yet another marriageable daughter and can only assume that far from being the figure of later Welsh hatred, Vortigern must have enjoyed no small reputation in both Britain and Ireland (if only briefly) to inspire the nomenclature of a pair of minor princes in Ireland, kinship notwithstanding.

A similar connection may be surmised from the name of the mother of the notorious late Roman-period Irish High King and raider Niall, Foirtchern's grandfather; she was called Cairenn, which equates to the Roman name Carina.[29] She married Eochaid Mugmedón, whose epithet means 'slave ruler', which might imply that he, too plundered Roman Britain, returning with captives. Was Carina an upper-class victim of such a raid, or a diplomatic pawn in some lost treaty negotiation between the *vicarius* and the impudent raider? The *Annals of Innisfallen* date his death to before 382, the *Chronicon Scotorum* to 411, but the later *Annals of the Four Masters* dates his reign to 379-405.[30] If we may accept the Irish annals and genealogies, then Niall must have been a contemporary of Magnus Maximus, and Carina of the *comes* Theodosius, meaning that she might have been an abductee of the Barbarian Conspiracy or a diplomatic consequence of it, in which case Maximus, as a young officer, might even have become familiar with whatever Irish links were forged then or in the aftermath.

Of course, from this there is a link to Vortigern, Feidelmid being the great-grandson of Carina. As we shall see when looking at Powis, the inscription on the Pillar of Eliseg tells us (four hundred years after the event) that Vortigern was married to Maximus's daughter Severa. Were we able to discover who Carina was, a link might even reveal itself to Maximus or to Theodosius, explaining their success in settling the fallout from the incursions in Britain of the Irish (Scotti/Attacotti) and Picts in both 367 and prior to 383.

An oddity relating to Ireland occurs in the British genealogies. St David, alleged to have been a descendant of Cunedda (on whom see Chapter 9), is said in one source to have had a sister called Magna, a name, incidentally, which recurs frequently amongst the impossibly grand descendants of Maximus's putative but anonymous Roman daughter, who is thought to have married into the senatorial aristocracy (see Chapter 4). Now this Magna is said to have married Irish prince Eisen of Artraige and had a son Setna/Setnae. He had brothers Mogobba and Moeltioc, although whether they were half-siblings of Setna or full blood is unclear.[31] Setnae was a largely legendary Irish prince, figuring in the pre-history of the Kingdom of Leinster and said to have been father of Mes Delmánn, described in an ancient poem which praises him as a mighty *tribunus* [*sic*] and ruler of the Domnainn.[32]

Elsewhere, these poems tell of Leinster raids on Britain, Scotland and the Orkneys, and even battles with Roman legions. The Laigin, the founding tribe of Leinster, is embodied in early traditions which see them allied with the Domnainn (cf. the place names Irrus Domnann, Co. Mayo and Inbe Domnann, Co. Dublin), a group which Byrne points out 'can hardly be dissociated from their British namesakes, the Dumnonii of Devon and of south-west Scotland'.[33] Does Magna, whose name might even suggest yet another daughter of Vortigern and Severa (were we able to accept the possibility of this alliance in the first place) represent another diplomatic transaction, supporting an alliance across the Irish Sea? The date, if authentic, would be mid-fifth century or a little later, and would have involved a different grouping to that into which Vortigern's other alleged daughter seems to have married. If true, it would suggest that these continuing ties between the leaders of the beleaguered Romano-Britons and Irish princes were not exceptional. As the enigmatic emergence of Gwynedd demonstrates (Chapter 9), there seems to have been Irish settlement in north Wales, too.

Thus, if we were to postulate that Maximus was responsible for transplanting the Déisi to south-west Wales around 380/383, which is, as we have seen, perfectly feasible within the constraints of the meagre evidence, we have to wonder how it came about. We also saw, in Chapter 2, that *Incursantes Pictos et Scottos Maximus tyrannus strenue superavit* ('Maximus the tyrant achieved an admirable victory over the invading Picts and Scots') and we have noted that many of the more legendary sources accuse him of stripping Britain of its defences. Yet he would not necessarily have withdrawn troops to the Continent after his accession without having planned for the consequences. This, of course, carries the implication that he was planning his coup for some time before it happened, and that he wanted to arrive at an innovative solution (in a British context), creating either loyal federated groups (their loyalty no doubt guaranteed by hostages, as Alcock suggested, backed by a bullion subvention) to replace permanent garrisons of *limitanei*, henceforth re-classified and re-trained as regular units, or putting trusted men into frontier areas with unusually enhanced powers.

While this might have been fairly straightforward in the North, in south-west Wales, an area easily reached from south-east Ireland, raiding had clearly been a problem; witness the necessity for a large late Roman fort at Cardiff. There was also depopulation, either through economic or natural decline, perhaps exacerbating the very raiding Maximus was keen to neutralise. The evidence for a decline in population is certainly apparent, as excavations over many years at the *civitas* capital Carmarthen have shown.[34] Yet the long-held though essentially unlikely belief that the peninsula west of the town was beyond the reach of imperial administration has been more recently rendered obsolete by the identification and partial excavation of a well-constructed road running nearly due west from Carmarthen in the direction of Milford Haven, a natural harbour, the utility of which in connection with communications and trade with Ireland the Romans would have been unlikely to have overlooked.[35]

How, therefore, did Maximus (if Maximus it was) come to select the Déisi as a likely group to recruit to settle in Demetia with uncultivated land available? Charles Thomas sets out the evidence and background in exemplary fashion, suggesting a late fourth-century date.[36] The belief is that this group, believed to have been a sept of the Uí Liathán (the 'sons' of Liethan), were then occupying south-west Ireland, partly in the kingdom of Munster, west of Waterford. The Déisi themselves are thought to have originally had their territory between the rivers Suir and Blackwater and to have been expelled after some internecine strife, as the later story of their move across the Irish Sea (dating originally from around 750) suggests. The expulsion saga tells us that the group was driven from Tara and wandered through Leinster before settling just west of Waterford.

The tales of Irish proto-High King Tuathal Techmar provide literary evidence for Roman incursions into Ireland, for he is claimed to have gone to Britain and regained his throne at Tara with Roman help, a tale that finds an instructive echo in Agricola in 81, who contemplated an invasion of Ireland to reinstate his exiled Irish prince, a point also made by Juvenal.[37] Indeed, limited quantities of Roman material found in the relevant area connected with Tuathal rather confirm this, along with more such material found at the promontory fort at Drumanagh, north of Dublin in 1995. As the *Annals of the Four Masters*, in which this tale appears, was assembled from ancient material only in around 1636, its reliability is doubted, especially for so early a period, and the material that the compiler saw is thought to have been destroyed in the conflagration of the Irish Revolt of 1641 and its subsequent suppression, putting it beyond assessment. Yet this king's name finds an echo in Tudwal/Tutagual, a king of Galloway, a grandson of Anthun/Dunawt and another alleged 'son' of Maximus. whom we shall encounter in the next chapter, and whom St Ninian (another disciple of St Martin) cured of blindness.[38]

Furthermore, Roman material dating from the second/third centuries has been excavated from the Rath of the Synods at Tara, also pointing to continuing links.[39] Richard Warner has shown that it is possible to infer substantial intrusions into the south-east of Ireland beginning in the first century, reinforced by Ptolemy, whose *Geography* recorded tribal names identical to those of Gaul and Britain, some of these peoples having a strong tradition of origins in Britain, not to mention the appearance of British (Brythonic) and Latin loan-words in their literature and amongst their toponyms. We have already seen that the Dumnonii seem to have left clear traces in Ireland in between their having been recorded both in Scotland and the west country. Cashel (a place name deriving from the Latin *castellum*) has produced a late Roman brooch, while later Roman material has been unearthed at Tara and further north at Clogher (Co. Tyrone), both of which places 'later became capitals of new ascendancies whose ancient origin-tales derived them, with their armies, from Britain'.[40] Irish academic orthodoxy has short-sightedly tended to dismiss such claims as unpatriotic.

That Irishmen were serving in the Roman army in the fourth century seems to be supported by the Balline (Co. Limerick) hoard, the *hacksilber* (cut-up plate) and ingots from which seem to represent the close equivalent of the *largitio* made by the emperor Julian in 361: five *solidi* and a pound of silver. Rance notes *en passant* that 'it looks more like payment than booty.'[41] If this is true, and the material is not the result of raiding but of participation; there were Irishmen in the Roman army of the mid-fourth century and Irishmen fighting them in turn. As today, so seventeen hundred years ago – links across St George's Channel were a deal closer than some like to believe.

Vittorio di Martino goes further and makes a case for the penetration of Ireland by a fourth-century Roman punitive expedition, making its way from the coast to Cashel, from landfall probably near the present Waterford or, from the fourth-century Roman finds in the area, from close to Cork.[42] The low intensity of finds rather suggests a lack of armed encounters (which would have resulted in a concentration of material) implying that if such an expedition had been mounted, it would more likely have been a diplomatic one enhanced by a show of strength. Di Martino suggests that this could have been undertaken in 364-367 under the *comes* Nectaridus (hence, 'cut off' during the Barbarian Conspiracy), but while the fact of such a punitive expedition (as di Martino calls it) is not completely unlikely, the timing seems unconvincing. Considering the (admittedly fragile) dating of the first high kings, strengthened by the date of St Foirtchern, an expedition in the wake of the barbarian incursions suppressed by Maximus would make a great deal more sense. Furthermore, the location would have put the emperor in the right area to have made the acquaintance of Aed Brosc/Eochaid.

If, then or later, it had come to his attention that this group was wandering through what is today part of Co. Limerick as exiles, what could be more logical than to offer them the chance of settling as *foederati* in south-west Wales, in return for acting as a permanent defence for that area and contributing some men to the imperial army? While this rests on some speculation and the pressing of evidence, the postulation does carry a certain cohesion and links the re-organisation of Wales strongly to Maximus, which previously was no more than a persuasive assumption made by a number of authors.

While the Déisi may be understood as having been installed in Demetia as federate troops, they integrated fairly seamlessly, no doubt aided three generations down the line by the gradual decay of civic life in Carmarthen and filled a political vacuum in so doing. Yet while lines of communication must have continued, with diocesan headquarters in London and with whatever *tyrannus* and his *consilium* that followed, there was also slowly developing a gradual schism between the two as central authority waned, which is why Gildas was able to write about Vortiporius as a 'king' and not as *dux* or *protector*; that is also how he perceived the border chieftains in the 530s – '*reges habet Britannia sed tyrannos*' – [43] although he calls Vortiporius a *tyrannus* and his father a *bono regis*, a 'good king'; the terminology was becoming elastic.[44]

The foundation of Brycheiniog

With the foregoing in mind, we seem to find, as time went by, the *civitas* of the Demetae mutating into a kingdom and then expanding slowly as its dynasty acquired more territory. An example is modern Breconshire, where the dynasty's kinsman Brychan had been installed. This seems to have arisen via an inheritance, and Thomas considers the core of the main source, *De Situ Brecheniauc* ('Concerning Brycheiniog') although written down in Brecon *c.* 1100/1125 was a good sub-Roman text composed locally about 580.[45] We learn that the Demetian prince Anlach, Brychan's father, married Marchell (Marcella), daughter of a powerful family settled at a place called Garth Madron, which appears to have formed the original centre of Brychan's kingdom and, as Anlach was Demetian, the new polity may be viewed as an extension of the original transplanted Irish settlement, which, we have suggested, was initiated by Maximus.[46]

This nucleus, Garth Madron, from which the later principality of Brycheiniog appears to have grown, was possessed, we are informed by our sources (suggested by Thomas as being provably early), by a succession of people with British names – supposedly four generations (or successions) all beginning with a 't' including one pair doubled up to fill an obvious gap in a copyist's understanding – but starting with a person called Annhun (Antonius) but with a couple of generations missing.

The related but later document called *Cognatio Brychan* ('the kin of Brychan') calls this Annhun *Annun rex Graecorum* ('Antonius, king of the Greeks'), concerning which Thomas, pointing out the similarity of 'Graecorum' (rendered *Groegwyr* in British) to 'Gregor[ius]' as written in the manuscripts, suggests that this ancestor was in fact called Antonius Gregorius.[47] In other pedigrees he also appears as *Annun Ddu* (Antonius the Black), suggesting someone called Antonius Gregorius *Niger*.[48] Epithet apart, such a person is indeed recorded in fourth-century Roman history as a *vir spectabilis* and *praes* (governor) of the Thebaïd, in Egypt.[49] Thomas, passing on a suggestion from a colleague, daringly suggests that this person could easily have served a term later in his career as *praeses* of the Roman province of Britannia Prima (which included Wales) based at the provincial capital, Corinium (Cirencester) and have acquired a local estate perhaps by marriage and settled there.[50] The alternative supposition which comes to mind is that we have here Antonius, Maximus's 'son' in several of the pedigrees, but in the genealogies invariably relating to the *Gwr y Gogledd*, 'the men of the North' (see Chapter 9). The geography is against this, as is the nature of the reference to the name: specifically, the addition of Gregorius and *Ddu*.

The name of the estate, Garth Madron, seems to support this sort of background. *Garth* is a spur of land or a parcel of land with a defined border. One might differ from Thomas's Celticising interpretation of the name Madron (Matrona, a well-attested Celtic deity) and propose instead a Latin proprietorial personal name, though of similar derivation: Matronus or Matronianus. This is perfectly feasible as the name of a Romano-British estate owner of the fourth century.[51]

It is also worthy of note that Vortimer, in British sources a son of Vortigern, had a daughter, Modrun (Matrona) again attested elsewhere at the time as a Roman name. Strangely, the only source for her, *Bonedd y Saint*, names her mother as an Annun/Anhun (Antonia) and her husband as Ynyr (Honorius) of Gwent.[52] Her fame, as regards dedications and place names, was once clearly widespread, suggesting that as a saint, she flourished at a time before the fragmentation of the united polity rooted in the former Roman diocese. It is possible that Garth Madron, perhaps once called in Latin *Matroniacum* or similar, took its name either from her of from a forebear of her mother before acquisition by Antonius.

Garth Madron, indeed, would appear to have occupied the wide vale north and east of Brecon, including the vale of the river Llynfi and Talgarth (note the 'garth' element again; it is a reputed site of King Brychan's court). It encompassed Llangorse (where King Brychan's posterity later built an impressive Crannog, sacked in 913 by Aethelfflaed of Mercia), part of the upper Usk valley, and territory west to Y Gaer, a Roman fort reoccupied in the later fourth century – possibly under Maximus (see Chapter 3) – and still occupied much later, too, itself close to Y Fenny (a colloquial Welsh name for Abergavenny, Roman Gobannium).[53] Y Gaer is a place named in the saga *De Situ Brycheiniog*, as a stop on the journey taken by Marchel to find a husband in Demetia. It is important, too, not to forget that Roman culture persisted, even in Wales, well into the fifth century – St Patrick and Gildas both considered themselves *cives*, Roman citizens. St Paul[in]us (see Chapter 10) was patron saint here, too.[54] Recently, the existence of a Roman Road has been identified by Mark Merrony running much further west into Demetia than had been previously appreciated, despite having been hinted at by Edward Lhwyd in 1698 and so marked on the first edition one-inch Ordnance Survey. It appears running west from near Crymych (Pembs.) well into the Preseli Hills and was perhaps intended to serve a silver mine. It confirms the extent of Romanisation in south-west Wales.[55] Even in remote Aberhydfer, near Trecastle, to the west of Brecon, a well-to-do citizen could be buried around 425/450 under a stone bearing the inscription:

[LV]CIUS [FILI]US [T]AUR[I]ANUS [HIC IACIT]
('Here lies Lucius son of Taurianus')

Here are two names as Roman as one could expect anywhere, despite an ogham inscription added later to 'Taricorus', who may or may not have been a kinsman 'gone native'.[56] Furthermore, a gold Roman *armilla* described by Giraldus Cambrensis in the twelfth century as being then at Brecon may also be linked to this interesting dynasty, which, as Professor Thomas points out, 'may have set up their own polity amid the Brecon uplands' and one quite probably rooted in an hereditary Romano-British estate.[57] Certainly, Lucius son of Taurianus suggests that the Romanisation of south Wales was more thorough than often credited and had seen little diminution in the fifth century, if this example of élite nomenclature is any measure.

We have seen the evolution of Demetia from a late fourth-century transfer of a tightly knit group of landless Irish clansmen into under-populated Demetia, tasked, in return for such a benison, with defending the south-west of Wales (then part of Britannia Prima) from raids by their fellow Irishmen (whom they would have had no reason to love). We can presume that they were supported by existing (and re-commissioned) military infrastructure in such sites as Cardiff shore fort (and any signal stations which once may have supplemented it), walled Carmarthen and various forts inland, like Cicucium (Y Gaer) and Bwlch (Breconshire). Hence, no formal appearance of Roman detachments in Wales in the *Notitia Dignitatum*. We have also observed Demetian expansion into a separate kingdom, founded by the same dynastic group, completing its transition from a Romano-British *latifundium* (large, landed estate) into a strategic self-perpetuating polity.[58]

Powis

While there were clearly more small princely states in early medieval Wales than we can name, we can be sure of the more important ones. To the north of Brycheiniog lay a neighbouring polity that also boasted of links to Maximus, Powis; although it had allied or occasionally component parts, Buellt, Elfael, Gwrtheyrnion, Maelienydd and Rhwng Gwy a Hafren.[59] The connection with Maximus occurs, as the extract in the previous chapter illustrates, on the well-known pillar of

Eliseg. The relevant passage read (in the seventeenth century, for today it can no longer be deciphered) '...Brydw (Britu), however, son of Gwertheyrn (Vortigern) was the one whom Germanus blessed and whom Sevira bore to him, the daughter of Maximus the king who killed the king of the Romans.'

The problem here is that the later genealogies of Powis singularly fail to go back either to Vortigern or Maximus. As Knight points out, the pillar's inscription, intended for formal recitation at assemblies, makes no claim for Eliseg to a *descent* from Maximus as far as we can see – acknowledging the script loss – but merely associates Britu son of Vortigern and Severa with the dynasty.[60] In Harleian MS 3859 there appears to be, as Bromwich has pointed out, 'a deliberate attempt to suppress a tradition that the Powis line descends from Vortigern' and that both it and *Historia Brittonum* (written within rival kingdom Gwynedd and thus with an axe to grind) are unfavourable to Vortigern, whereas the later Jesus College MS 20 backs up the version of the Pillar. Hence the Harleian version presents us, working back from Selyf (Solomon), King of Powis killed at the Battle of Chester in 616: 'Selim son of Cynan son of Brochmael son of Cyngen son of Maucann son of Pascent son of Cattegirn son of Catell Dunlarc (*dyrnllug*).'[61]

The presence of Pascent seems anomalous, as he does occur in the earlier *Historia Brittonum* as a son of Vortigern. Worse, pedigrees of the House of Powis are wonderfully inconsistent, with alleged sons of Vortigern cropping up one or two generations out of place, as above, with Pascent placed as a son of Cattegirn, although both are supposedly *sons* of Vortigern in other sources. Furthermore, as in many of these genealogies, collateral and heiress lines tended to get incorporated into the main lineal descent. Hence, Vortigern is recorded as having sons called Guorthemir (Vortimer), Categirn (Cattegirn), Pascent and, by another woman (recorded, elsewhere – surely fictitiously – as his own daughter, by Ronwen/Rowena, the daughter of Hengist), Faustus, later Bishop of Riez, whom we met in Chapter 6, not to mention Scotnoë. Another element of this anti-Vortigern emphasis is the striking paucity of references to him in the Triads.[62]

Bishop Asser, writing in 893, linked a people called the Gewissei with Wessex, thus associating Vortigern (who was, in Geoffrey of Monmouth, allegedly 'of the Gewissei') with Gloucester and the area of southern Powis. One sub-division of Powis was *Rhwng Gwy a Hafren* ('Between Wye and Severn') in which lay the commote (a Welsh division of land analogous to the English hundred) of *Gwrtheyrnion*, literally, 'Vortigernianum'; a similar name emerges much later, Anglianised, as *Wirtgernesburg*, equated by William of Malmesbury with Bradford-on-Avon (Wiltshire).[63] Looking at the majority of the genealogies, the first ruler of the polity we later learn of as Powis was Catell Dyrnllug, not Vortigern. We encountered the latter in Chapter 6 as a *tyrannus* with overlordship of the former Roman diocese but noted that later sources have him as a descendant of a Gloucester family.

If, therefore, this family *had* held a large Roman estate to the north of the city of Glevum, this could have remained in the family, been expanded in the uncertain times of the fifth century to have become a petty kingdom – as did Garth Madrun – the main dynasty of which perhaps later married the heiress of the original dynasty of Powis (or vice-versa). If true, this would have been rehearsed in the missing part of the ninth-century inscription on the Pillar of Eliseg. This polity, it may deduced, was *Rhwng Gwy a Hafren/Gwrtheyrnion* which, according to the genealogies, mutated (through marriage or conquest) into the slightly larger cantref of *Buellt*, just north of Brycheiniog, hence modern Builth (Co. Brecknock, now Powys).

An expanding polity

Confusingly, the name Powis is not recorded before about 825, and it is widely assumed that it originally comprised the *territorium* of Viroconium, the *civitas* of the Cornovii. It has been suggested that once formal troops had been withdrawn from Deva (Chester) that city became part of this expanding polity, which is also thought to have included the small towns of Magnis (Kenchester, Herefordshire) and Letocetum (Wall, Staffordshire) to the east.[64] The name Powis seem to have evolved from the inhabitants of a *pagus,* the rural district of the expanded *civitas*, the inhabitants of which would be called *pagenses* (countrymen) which mutated into British Powis (and English 'pagan'). Previously, the tribal name attached to the region similarly mutated from Cornovii to *Cernyw/Kernew*, long misinterpreted as an early name for the Cornish, and over whom King Cynan Garwyn had been victorious at some stage prior to his death in 616.[65]

Morris makes the valid point that the first rulers of *Cernyw*, Catellus and Bruttius – alleged sons of Vortigern – bear 'ordinary Roman family names, appropriate to the landed families of the *civitates*'.[66] In the wider Roman context, we find Bruttia Aureliana, a late fourth-century Roman matron boasting impeccable connections. In her we discover a concatenation of names with echoes of Vortigern, Maximus and Ambrosius, for she married one Flavius Vitalis, and was granddaughter of Antonius Marcellinus, consul in 341. We saw in Chapter 3 that Maximus was the brother of a Marcellinus and probably the cousin of an Antonius Maximinus, while in Chapter 6, that Vortigern was probably to be identified with Vitalinus (or, perfectly reasonably, Vitalis), a name also used by his supposed forebears.[67]

What is more, an unlocated object of Gildas's imprecations was Aurelius Caninus, often thought to have been a degenerate descendant of Ambrosius Aurelianus. He is noted by Leslie Alcock as a possible ruler of south Powis/Lower Severn – *Rhwng Gwy a Hafren /Gwrtheyrnion*.[68] In contrast, however, *Historia Brittonum* states that Ambrosius gave south Powys to Pascent son of Vortigern, about which Alcock is more doubtful.[69] Ambrosius, whom the British called *Emrys Wletic*, has also in the past attracted speculation about continental links as much as Maximus and Vortigern, including a proposed kinship with Bishop Ambrosius of Milan, St Ambrose. Aurelius Caninus has also been proposed by other commentators as a ruler either in Dumnonia or in Gwent; all this is speculative. Nevertheless, it is still thought that the Aureli[an]i might have made up a wide-ranging Romano-British noble family, continental connections or not, with the possibly Demetian aristocrat St Paul Aurelian thrown in as kin, too (see Chapter 10).[70]

The marriage of Severa to one of the founders of the dynasty of the Cornovii, whose son Bruttius/Britu is attested by the Pillar of Eliseg, introduces a new association: St Germanus. The dynasty is referred to as the Cadelling, from Cadell Dyrnllug, in lists of rulers, compiled under the influence of the House of Gwynedd (which eventually defeated and absorbed Powis). It is attested that that Cadell was raised to primacy from slavery, a serious slur in the eyes of contemporaries. Yet the *Historia Brittonum* has Cadell 'blessed by Germanus', which, combined with the reference on the pillar, suggests that Britu and Cadell were probably one and the same, bearing a Romanised version of both names.[71] In Germanus's destruction of a giant in *Historia Brittonum* we may perhaps see a garbled retelling of the fate of a non-Christian pretender to power in Viroconium – assuming that is where the tale is set. Koch, however, sees Cadell's dynasty as having arisen originally at Magnis, the name of which appears to have mutated into *Magan* and thence evolved into the Saxon sub-kingdom of the *Magonsaete*.[72]

As a focus, Wroxeter was still inhabited to the middle of the fifth century, survived to be considerably rebuilt *c.* 560 as the seat of a substantial ruler and so continued until a non-violent Mercian takeover occurred in the later seventh century, probably by 685, when it was perhaps ceded as part of a diplomatic *quid pro quo*.[73] The continued importance of the city and its wider *territorium* is reflected in the anomalous Lichfield/Hereford diocesan boundary at nearby Cound (Salop.).[74]

Koch sees the Cadelling ultimately eclipsing the rival dynasty of Powis (descended from Maximus), to which belonged Cynddylan, subject of a surviving early British lament (*marwnad*). He fought the Mercians at *Luitcoed* (Letocetum/Wall, Staffs.) in the 640s with Morfael, whom Koch proposes might be identifiable with Merewalh, King of the *Magonsaete*, a British prince mediatised by King Penda of Mercia, and Davies suggests that he represented a lost dynasty of the West Midlands, central Marches and east Wales, replaced by Penda.[75]

Prior to erecting their column in the Vale of Llangollen, the Cadelling dynasty survived a crushing defeat in 616 outside Chester at the hands of Aethelfrith of Northumbria, the battle site being at the Roman settlement at Heronbridge, Cheshire, where a mass grave or charnel of damaged male skeletons was unearthed and has been dated to this period. The battle is described in another ancient British poem, the *Trawsganu Kynan Garwyn map Brochfael* ('the satire on Cynan Garwyn son of Brochmael').[76] Although Aethelfrith was the victor, he withdrew having suffered heavy losses (including the death of an allied British king, called Cetula according to the Irish *Annals of Tigernach*, but probably to be identified with the northern British ruler in the Carlisle area, *Catguallaun Liu* (Cadwallon) and Powis bounced back.[77] As regards Chester itself, the city was the site of a church synod in about 601, and the presence of the large retinues likely to have accompanied the visiting bishops and clerics imply that, like Viroconium, the city was in some way still functioning. Indeed, the baths are thought to have endured into this era in use; the former *principia* may have done so, too.[78]

Not only was the early dynasty of Powis in control of Viroconium and Chester, but possibly (as we have seen) through control of *Rhwng Gwy a Hafren/Gwerthrynion*, also of Gloucester. Koch sees the dynasty also having a power base at Cirencester, too. Cynan II son of Brochmael grandson of Cynan I had a power base in Herefordshire and south Shropshire, and this possibly extended further south into the *civitas* of the Dobunni through control of Cirencester. These potentates are not called king or prince in the earliest sources but were probably recognised even in their own time as *duces* or even *tyranni*.

Cynan II was ancestor of the kings on the pillar of Eliseg and of Cynan II's elder son Selyf Sarffgadau ('Solomon Battle-Serpent'), who lost his life at Chester in 616.[79] Control of Cirencester and Gloucester was not necessarily lost permanently as a result of the Battle of Dyrham, recorded in the *Anglo-Saxon Chronicle* for 577. This record is no better than that in the *Historia Brittonum*. What reads as a victory – Cuthwin and Ceawlin (Kings of Wessex and probably of British descent, see Chapter 11) 'fought with the Britons' and 'slew three kings, Conmail, Condidan and Farinmail…and took from them three cities, Gloucester, Bath and Cirencester' – sounds pretty punishing for the British. Yet even the battle itself has been called into question and these 'victories' did not always result in settlement.

Seven years later, Wessex Kings Ceawlin and Cutha fought another battle against the British of the same area, in which Cutha was killed in action, but although they still took booty from another three towns, they 'retreated to their own people'. The likelihood is that Dyrham did *not* divide the Britons of Dumnonia from those of the rest of Britain, Powis and Wales, as so often claimed, merely that three cities and surrounding country were looted before the raiders returned to their core territory. Quite what there was worth looting in these towns by this date is moot. The three kings – British spellings would have been Cynfelyn, Cynddylan and Ffernfael – probably represent an alliance; the latter reigned in south Wales (Gwent) at this approximate period, but the identification of the other two remains problematic, for Cynddylan would be too early to be identifiable with his namesake, subject of the seventh-century *marwnad*.[80]

In due course, Powis lost much of its eastern and southern territory not to Wessex, but to Penda of Mercia, probably by treaty; in 750, it lost a good deal more of what remained when Mercia, no longer an ally against the Northumbrians, invaded and penetrated across Powis as far as the Gwynedd citadel of the Decanti (*Arx Decantorum*, the Vadre at Deganwy, Caerns./ Gwynedd), which they destroyed. However, chaos broke out in Mercia on the death of King Aethelbald in 757, the perpetrator of this devastation. Eliseg regained Powis by reconquest thereafter, which Charles-Edwards considers was probably the import of the lost wording in the middle of the king's pillar.

As we have seen though, there is no proof that this section included a stated link between Eliseg and Magnus Maximus, although this is considered by most to have been likely. Probably, at some stage, the dynasty of Buellt and Gwerthrynion had merged with that of Powis, as suggested earlier, allowing the latter to claim the bloodline by *ymgyfathrathu* (mutual inter-lineage), especially as the Powis dynasty was the more dominant.[81]

This was surely something to celebrate, and Concenn/Cyngen was keen to emulate the Roman forebears the inscription celebrates in displaying a kind of victory column, copied from the Roman manner complete with swags below the (lost) capital.[82] The dynasty is not claiming descent from Maximus as a ruler who may have put them in place as the Demetian ruling house, but it is celebrating descent from the élite of a late-Roman *civitas* and indeed of the wider diocese. The claim was to a descent from Maximus via Vortigern, two major players, it would appear, in the saga of late Roman Britain.

Vortigern's family (again)

Temporarily setting aside our doubts about the reliability of the information furnished by the pillar, we can say that Sevira/Severa would have to have been born before 383, say, in 380. This would make her marriageable from *c*. 395. She could therefore have married *Gwrtheyrn Gwrtheneu* (Vortigern the Thin/Vitalinus Gracilis) in around 400, which would fit in with the birth of Faustus of Riez, too (his dates are usually assumed to be *c*. 405/410 to 490/495), one of their alleged sons, and a man upon the reality of whose existence we can actually rely. Unfortunately, the other legendary sources, which affiliate him to Vortigern, make him the son of the *tyrannus* and Ronwenn, Germanic leader Hengist's entirely legendary daughter, whom he would have married (if we can accept the story at all) *c*. 429, making Faustus impossibly young. As a son of Severa, Cadell/Britu, the future founder of the dynasty of the Cornovii (or at least that of *Gwerntyrion* and *Buellt*), could thus have been born *c*. 402/410.

Stemma 4 attempts to make sense of the conflicting later British sources. It seems impossible to escape the conclusion that Britu/Bruttius and Cadell

Dyrnllug/Catellus must have been one and the same person. Pasgen's (Pascentius's) name is also late Roman.[83] In the genealogies, the latter appears as Vortigern's son, as his great-grandson (as son of Cadell and grandson of Cattegirn) and thrice as a son of Britu.[84] Jesus College MS 20 gives descendants of Cyndeyrn/Cattegirn, but his son is given as Cadell and *grandson* as Britu, and is therefore ignored as a gross and late conflation.[85] Likewise, genealogy 18 does the same, except that Pascent is substituted for Britu as the son of Cadell, and another source lists the sons of Vortigern as descendants of each other and can be similarly discounted as hopeless confusion.[86]

The *Historia Brittonum's* account of the ancestors of Vortigern/Vitali[nu]s set out in Chapter 6 included the suggestion that his father might conceivably be identifiable with Flavius Vitalis, the former imperial *praefectus annonae* who married Bruttia Aureliana, albeit with reservations. Bruttia's ancestry is remarkably well attested, however, and includes yet another Antonius, described on an inscription as of *illustris familiae*.[87] Of Vortigern's issue, Vortimer appears in the *Historia Brittonum* and Geoffrey of Monmouth, and in *Bonedd y Saint* where his apparent only child St Modrun (Matron[ian]a, see above) is husband of Ynyr (Honorius) of Gwent, supposed ancestor of the ruling dynasty there, which produced a late sixth-century ruler also called Ynyr. Vortimer's wife (or perhaps mistress, she is described as a 'handmaiden') is called Anhun (Antonia), a name redolent of links to the Maximus of history, not to mention the dynasty of Garth Madrun.[88]

With regard to Ronwe[i]nn, Charles-Edwards remarks that the story given in the Kentish Chronicle in the *Historia Brittonum* 'seems to provide an unprovable but convincing sequence of events'.[89] Miles Russell goes further: 'Vortigern and the Rowena/Ronwe[i]n incident may represent a legal transfer of territory by *foedus* (treaty).' But he dismisses Vortigern's subsequent marriage to his own daughter by Ronwe[i]n (thus committing both incest and bigamy) as a hopeless confusion with a story probably linked to Gildas's condemnation of Vorteporius, whose activities were alleged by him as having been far more along those lines.[90]

Hengist is first named by Bede, thus preceding *Historia Brittonum*, and thereafter is picked up by the *Anglo-Saxon Chronicle*.[91] The Irish connection has been discussed above, as to some extent have the legendary connections of Faustus, allegedly son of Vortigern. He is recorded as having been baptised by St Germanus, but as we have observed, this son of Vortigern so blessed is recorded as Britu/Bruttius on the Pillar of Eliseg.[92] Yet Faustus was born, plausibly enough, *c.* 402/410. He was highly educated (in Britain, confirming that such education was then still available) and elected Bishop of Riez after a stay at the renowned monastery of Lérins, in 461 or 462. When Riez fell to the Visigothic king Euric in 477, he was promptly exiled by the Arian Goths. He returned in 485 but died shortly afterwards. Thus, Faustus must have had Severa (or someone else, entirely unrecorded) as his mother if he was Vortigern's son. St Germanus might well have blessed him when he moved to Gaul; his blessing of Cadell/Britu would have occurred in the latter's young adulthood in 429, not to mention an implied blessing of Cattegirn too, his name invariably also coupled with the epithet *fendigaid* ('the blessed') and, like Vortimer, killed in action against the Saxons in Kent, presumably in their father's lifetime.[93] As for the supposedly sinful origin of Faustus, Charles-Edwards has pointed out that Sidonius Apollinaris refers to Faustus's mother as 'hallowed', which is hard to square with bigamy and incest, quite apart from the chronological problems involved. Had Faustus's mother indeed been the daughter of the Frankish/Saxon *magister militum*, the incident of Germanus blessing him would have to date to the Gallic saint's second visit in the 440s, by which time the real Faustus was probably forty-odd and ensconced in piety at Lérins.[94]

The alleged daughter of Vortigern, Scotnoë, who seems to have married the Irish prince Fedelmid, is discussed above in the context of the settlement of Demetia. Pasgen/Pascentius, according to one genealogy, married a daughter of Owein, the alleged 'son' of Maximus and possible successor of Constantine III (see Chapter 9).[95] Pawl Mawr (Paullus Magnus) has been included in *stemma* 4 not because we know anything of him, but because, unless it is an epithet, he also bears Magnus Maximus's name (like several presumed descendants in the wider empire) as well as Paul, favoured in Vortigern/Vitalinus's ancestry, if *Historia Brittonum* is to be believed. The genealogies make Paul father of Tegau Eurfron ('golden-breast') who marries a particularly elusive character, Caradoc Vreichvras ('strongarm').[96]

In spite of everything, it is Vortigern who seems to have been the lynchpin of the dynasty of Powis, despite the vitriol poured upon him by the author of the *Historia Brittonum* and, by implication, Gildas, for allowing the 'Saxons' to be settled in Kent as federates and their subsequent exploitation of that situation when the *annona* dried up, possibly something beyond anyone's control. The descendants were apparently oblivious to this 'baggage' and sufficiently proud to retain him embedded in the canon of their ancestral tables, complete with the emphatic connection with Magnus Maximus.[97]

While the creation of Powis and its antecedents as a separate entity from the central control of the diocese of the Britains was probably a relatively late occurrence, unlike the transplantation of the Déisi, it would nevertheless appear that the disasters which subsequently befell central authority under Vortigern were not seen in the same light on the fissiparous edges of the polity as those writing nearer the centre, like Gildas. Whatever the circumstances of Vortigern's fall and subsequent demise, a dynasty believed to have been directly descended from him survived in the former province of Britannia Prima, possibly even set up through his dispensation in the second quarter

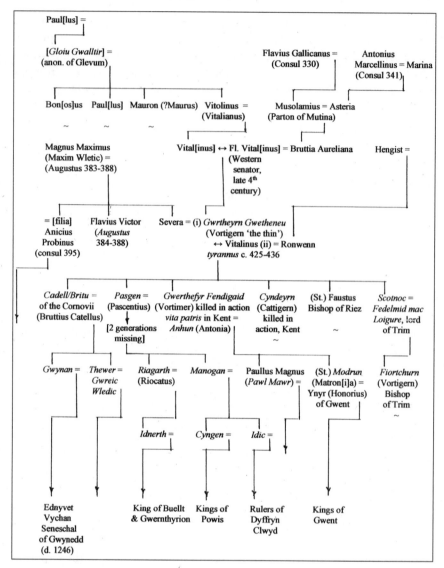

Stemma 4. Vortigern's family.

of the fifth century, or through the dispensation of one of his successors, in acknowledgement that the sins of the father do not necessarily have to be visited upon the children.

If the southern Cornovian polity did reach as far south as Gloucester, the creation of the dynasty may have been a reflection of a familial power-base held in the area by Vortigern, his family or wider connections, long before he became the next *tyrannus* but one after Constantine III. There may be an echo of a family of similar territorial reach in the Aurelius Ursicinus named on items included in the Hoxne Hoard, where one can detect links to the hoards at Mildenhall and Water Newton, implying holdings extending over an impressive tract of central eastern England.[98]

Gwent

Gwent in south-east Wales took its name from Venta Silurum/Caerwent, a Roman walled town which seems to have remained occupied long after the departure of Roman government; burials are recorded there up until the ninth century.[99] It also boasts a connection with Magnus Maximus, but the most understated link in the sources. The inclusion of south-east Wales as a polity with connections to Maximus rests on his connection with Vortigern, as expressed through the inscription on the Pillar of Eliseg and the somewhat oblique reference to St Modrun in *Bonedd y Saint*: Ynyr is said to have married St Modrun (Matrona) daughter of Vortimer and Annun (Antonia), himself son of Vortigern.[100] The link is essentially the same as that of Powis, insofar as it existed at all.

Ynyr (Honorius) himself seems a perfectly plausible candidate for someone married into Vortigern's posterity. If he had been born prior to 423, then his name would be readily explicable as one worthy of bestowal upon a leading citizen of Venta Silurum. Modrun was probably born *c.* 430, to allow sufficient generations from Sevira, assumed to have been born around 380. Unfortunately, the connection with the subsequent line of the kings of Gwent, which picks up with Iddon son of a later Ynyr (who lived in the mid-sixth century) and moves to the apparently unrelated Meurig (Mauricius) son of Teudrig (Theodericus), ancestors of the remaining rulers of Gwent/Glewyssing, is opaque.[101] Nevertheless, both their names seem to maintain the tradition of the dynasty in naming sons after current emperors, for Wendy Davies suggests Meurig must have been born *c.* 600, just when the unfortunate Eastern Emperor Mauricius was still reigning, while the name of his father (which is alleged to have a Celtic origin, too) surely reflects that of the Ostrogothic king in Italy, Theoderic (491-526).

It must not be forgotten that these people still saw themselves as somehow part of the fragmenting empire of Rome, despite the best efforts of some historians to rather see them as anti-imperialist native British 'freedom fighters'. The family of a citizen of north Wales (whose name time has, sadly, eroded from his gravestone) recorded the interment as having occurred 'in the time of the Emperor Justinus twenty-five years after his (last) consulship'. Justin II (567-579) was a ruler 'largely popular and recognised in the west' (and remembered through the bestowal of the name Iestyn amongst the British from about this time) through his religious rapprochement with Rome and at that time 'there was a sense of belonging to a far-flung and loose-knit community of citizens of which he was head.'[102] Although the hagiographies of the leading saints of Gwent as we have them were written down for inclusion in the *Liber Landavensis* not much before 1130, their genealogies, however untrustworthy, are peppered with Roman nomenclature. The name of Oudoceus, bishop there in the sixth century, is a corruption of the British version of Eudoxius, just as the name of Ergyng's early saint, Dubricius, is a re-translation of Dyfrig. Dubricius appears to have been important, but too little is known about him, bar numerous church dedications and mentions in the much later *Liber Landavensis*. Doble makes the point that he was 'one of the chief figures in the creation of Christian Wales…Ariconium/Ergyng may have been the source of the Welsh Christian movement of the fifth and sixth centuries…Welsh Christianity came from Romano-British sources.' [103] The name of Oudoceus's paternal grandfather was Eussyllt, the British rendition of the late Roman name Auxilius/Auxiliaris.[104] Even St Illtud's Armorican mother, Rieingulid would appear to be a direct translation of Regina Pudica ('modest queen'/'gentle maiden').[105]

Although Demetia, Brycheiniog, Powis and Gwent had rather different origins, all in one way or another can be seen to have had a connection with Maximus in later British tradition. The first pair it is suggested were ruled by exiled Irish leaders put in place by Maximus and whose name was subsequently attached to their written ancestry; the others, emerging rather later, were ruled in one case by an alleged direct descendant of Maximus via the Pillar's link of a daughter with Vortigern and the other by a man who had married the 'proud tyrant's' granddaughter: notional genealogical connections with Vortigern. The way in which these polities originated also appears deeply embedded in a continuing *Romanitas* that the upheavals of Constantine III and the Saxon revolt seem to have done less to diminish than is usually believed. When looking at the remaining connections with Maximus, similar patterns emerge, but nearer the diocesan periphery.

9

The Men of the North

The 'sons' of Maximus

There are seven genealogies or king-lists in Chapter 7 which relate to rulers of parts of Britain in the north, and taken at face value, they seem to provide Maximus with another four sons, three with Roman names and one with a British one. They are set out in *stemma 5* in approximate accepted order of antiquity, oldest first, reading left to right.

Harleian MS 3859.4 (the ancestry of the Kings of Man and eventually, by inheritance, of Gwynedd), gives our emperor a son called Anthun (Antonius), a name which, as we have seen, repeatedly crops up in connection with him both in contemporary imperial sources and in British ones. Some caution is needed, however, as Antonius was a common Roman name, although less so as the fourth century wore on. The grandson is called Ednyvet, who is succeeded by Tudwal (a name we met in an Irish context in the previous chapter) and then Dingad.[1] Precisely the same sequence is apparent in Jesus College MS 20.19, also the ancestors of the Kings of Man, except that Anthun/Antonius is replaced by Dunawt/Dunod (Donatus). The suspicion is that we have here, as with Pasgen/Pascentius and Britu/Bruttius in Powis, the same person who originally bore both names; Antonius Donatus seems entirely plausible for a Roman of the late fourth or early fifth century.[2] Likewise, in other genealogies, Maximus is equipped with a son bearing the entirely British name of Ednyvet, father of Dyfnwal Hen.[3] Dyfnwal also bears the epithet *hael* (generous, Latin Liberalis) and two of his sons may have been commemorated in the inscribed stone from Yarrowkirk (Co. Selkirk):

HIC MEMORIA PERPETUA IN LOCO
INSIGNISIMI PRINCIPES NUDI DUMNOGENI:
HIC IACENT IN TUMULO DUO FILII LIBERALIS

('Here, an everlasting memorial, in (this) place,
lie the most famous princes, Nudus and Dumnogenus
in the tomb, the two sons of Liberalis.')

Although the stone is probably early sixth century, it may nevertheless be
a retrospective commemoration of these men, descendants of Ednyvet, one
of the 'sons' of Maximus. The names in British are Nudd and Dyfnwal,
and, as Bromwich has suggested, Liberalis bore the British epithet *hael*,
one borne by several descendants of Ednyvet, which may denote an
hereditary family name.[4] If we were to assume that the alleged sons of
the emperor were in fact his appointees, as in Demetia, it may be that
Ednyvet's Roman name was Liberalis and that he acquired his translated
British name when appointed. In other genealogies Nudd's father is given
as Senyllt (or better, as in more than one MS, Seisyll, Cecilius) and his
great-grandfather was Dyfnwal Hen (Dumnogenus 'the old' – hence
perhaps Senilis), so an unrecorded brother of the same name is highly
probable. Other descendants bearing the epithet *liberalis* (i.e. *hael*) include
Rhydderch and Mordaf.

Dyfnwal, Latinised as Dumnogenus, means 'born of the Dumnonii', in this
case the Dumnonii of the area south and south-west of the Antonine wall,
the polity of Alclud. The rendering on the stone of the name Nudd in a Latin
form might well be taken to emphasise the family's Roman origin, although
most authorities aver that the name derives from the Celtic god Nodens, or
the Irish equivalent, Nuadu. This is probably preferable to a Latin derivation
because after the late Republican *praefectus classis* P. Rutilius Nudus and
the triumviral ex-praetor, C. Nunnuleius Nudus, the Latin name is hard to
come by under the empire. Liberalis however, is attested in the early fifth
century, having rather fallen out of favour amongst the élite from the third
century. Nudus may also be the Nud Hael of *Bonedd y Saint 18* (quoted in
Chapter 7).[5]

As Ednyvet also appears twice as the grandson of Maximus in the earliest
of these sources, Harleian MS 3859, and in the later Jesus College MS, is
seems reasonable to suppose that Ednyvet was the successor or son of the
conflated Antonius Donatus. Interestingly, a late Triad names one Gwythir
ap Greidol as seventh in descent from Maximus (via Ednyvet and Dyfnwal),
the name being a British rendering of the Latin name of Magnus Maximus's
son Victor. His appearance in the Triad is because he is said there to have
been father of Gwenhwyfar (Guinevere), 'second great queen of Arthur'.[6]
Arthurian glosses aside, having thus accounted for three surplus 'sons' of
Maximus, we are left with just Antonius Donatus and Owain (Eugenius),
although there is a pedigree of St Peblig that makes the Caernarfon saint
also a son of Maximus rather than a grandson, although it would seem more
plausible to prefer Peiblic as a grandson and to acknowledge Owein, known

from a Triad as 'One of the three chief officers of the Island of Britain' as his father.[7] Owein son of Maximus is also recorded as the ancestor of St Cadoc.[8] Peiblic's Roman name may have been a consequence of education or a religious novitiate on the Continent; bearing more than one name was quite normal for these people, although the hypochoristic would appear to be the one that tended to survive.

Having made these adjustments, it becomes clear that the sons of Maximus, Antonius Donatus and Eugenius, bore Roman names, although in the third generation only Peblig (Publicius) bore one, Ednyvet may have borne one, while the others, Dyfnwal and Nor, were very definitely British. Of Owein, an uncanonical Triad says:

> ... all men of the Island of Britain from prince to peasant, became ... followers at the need of the country on account of the invasions and tyranny of the foe ... and whenever [he] marched to war there was not a man on the Island of Britain but who would join their armies and would not stay at home.[9]

Other later Triads claim that he was the unanimously agreed ruler of Britain and inform us that he 'resumed sovereignty from the Roman emperor'.[10] One might, were we able to overcome the hurdle that is Iolo Morgannwg and track such claims back to a time *before* Geoffrey of Monmouth, be able to identify Owein Finddu/Eugenius as the missing *tyrannus*, a possible *dux Britanniarum* stationed in the north and untainted by links to Constantine III, who perhaps seized power in 409 and was ultimately succeeded by Ambrosius, who was then, it seems, deposed by Vortigern. It cannot be coincidence that the name Owein thereafter quickly begins to appear and gain traction in the genealogies of the men of the north and further afield, but is never attributed to forebears living before this era in the genealogies. His link with Maximus may have been an appointment in the north, conceivably renewed subsequently, which might explain how he became attached to him genealogically. With the surviving garrisons at his back and whatever was left of the *comitatenses* he may have been able – even if called out of retirement as a safe pair of hands – to have united with the Roman-appointed tribal groupings of Valentia, to drive back the Picts and Scots and stabilise the diocese in 409.

His descendant, Gliuguis/Glywys is, however, called Cernyw (*Cornubiensis*) suggesting Cornwall, but at the date he is supposed to have lived it is anachronistic, and one should either discard the link or associate him more securely with Powis, but how this line might fit in there is hard to comprehend. Such epithets tended to become attached to names much later on and cannot be relied upon. Subsequent legendary associations, fuelled by the *Mabinogion*, associate Owein with south Wales/Glewissing, probably through importation from the imploding north, or perhaps a separate tradition which lingered from the eclipse of the central control of the diocese after the time of Ambrosius.[11] That Owein began as an appointed commander in the north therefore seems highly likely; that he was Vortigern's predecessor as *tyrannus* in Britain seems a perfectly plausible proposition.

Ednyvet's son, Dyfnwal Hen, appears as the ancestor of a second dynasty ruling Alt Clud/Dumbarton, or Strathclyde as it became. A previous line seems to end with Coroticus, whom St Patrick admonished in a famous letter, and the succession of kings resumes with Dyfnwal probably married to the daughter or sister of Coroticus, thus father of Neithon and grandfather of Beli, living 627.[12] If we proceed upon the premise that Antonius Donatus may well also have been established in the north in the 380s, there would appear to be three generations missing in the list of Kings of Alclud, assuming the date of 627 for Beli is reliable. It may be, nevertheless, that Dyfnwal Hen became king of Alclud after the rascally Coroticus – about whose own parentage we shall have more to say later – perhaps through marrying into the dynasty or even by conquest.

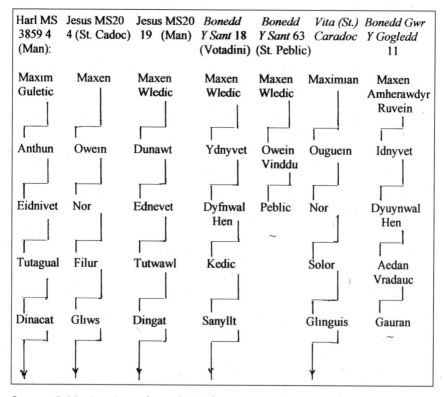

Stemma 5. Maximus's northern 'descendants'.

Liber Hymnorum	**Poem attributed to Flann Mainistrech**	*Lebor Breec*
Maxim =	Maximus =	Maxim =
Leo =	Leo =	Leo =
Ota =	Moiric =	Otta =
Muric =	Opric =	Muric =
Opic	Ota	Opici

Stemma 6. Maximus's 'Irish' son.

The northern frontier

We have seen in the previous chapter that the Irish Déisi were settled in Demetia as federates probably in the time of Maximus's rule; the chronologies fit reasonably well and the legendary material supplies much unprovable detail, none of which really jars. Therefore, it should be possible to look at the northern frontier and see whether the names in the genealogies there stem from some similar sort of permanent military settlement in the territory between Hadrian's and the Antonine Walls. Although the Antonine Wall had long ago passed into desuetude, the more southerly barrier had undergone various modifications in the late Roman period or a fraction later, including the narrowing or blocking of ways through, enabling control of movement to be tightened, suggesting the 'rise of a late and sub-Roman military elite'.[13] After all, Maximus had subdued a serious raid by the Picts and Scots (and no doubt the Attacotti, also from Ireland). As we have already seen, he may have recruited some numbers of Attacotti, for three units of them appear in the *Notitia Dignitatum*, two with names suggesting that they were raised after the birth of the future emperor Honorius in 384, perhaps by Maximus after his recognition by Theodosius as a complimentary gesture.[14]

We have also noted the creation of the elusive fifth British province of Valentia, which seems now to be agreed as straddling Hadrian's Wall, and surely extending to include the entire area bounded by that briefly manned under Antoninus Pius connecting the estuaries of Clyde and Forth to the north. This arrangement seems to have replaced the 'defence in depth' wherein 1,500 men were stationed north of the wall in this area, spread over five forts, being the 'outer tripwire' of the scheme as propounded by J. C. Mann.[15] But far from being abandoned by Rome after 367, as Mann suggests, it would seem more likely that the so-called 'sons' of Maximus were part of the solution, and that accumulations of wealth as represented by the Traprian Law treasure constituted part of the inducements involved in moving to a new dispensation under Maximus in the 380s.[16] In this tract, today lowland Scotland, there were the Dumnonii, Selgovae, the Votadini and the Novantae. The former, of course may well have been connected with the Irish Domnánn which we encountered in the previous chapter, and Dumbarton Rock was the focus of the community, around which the later Kingdom of Alclud grew up. The late Professor Leslie Alcock certainly thought that Maximus established the dynasty of Galloway (Novantae) and later that of Man.[17]

Three Irish sources supply yet another son of Maximus, unanimously named as Leo, again a perfectly reasonable Roman name.[18] He is presumed to have been ruler of the territory of the Novantae, in British sources named as Anthun/Dunawt, but the latter's posterity bears no correlation whatsoever with Leo's. The latter's son and grandson, albeit reversed in one version, seem named in a straightforwardly Roman manner, too. Thus, Leo is endowed with a son or grandson called Muric/Moiric (Mauricius) and a son or grandson called Ot[t]a/Opic[i] which in the following generation get changed round. While Mauricius is also Roman, Ota seems not, unless Opici is a copyist's error for Opili, in which case the rather grand late western Roman name was originally intended; certainly there are no obvious British equivalents for Ot[t]a/Opici.[19] It has, though, been suggested that this is really the Kentish ruler Ochta, (supposed grandson of Hengist) whose position in the Kentish king-list varies with his father Oisc just as Ot[t]a/Opici does with Moiric/Muric, and who the *Historia Brittonum* claims left soldiering north Britain to succeed his father.[20] Quite what he was doing in north Britain is never made clear – conceivably serving as a *condottiere* with the local British or Roman leaders.

The earliest date for the *Liber Hymnorum* appears to be late eleventh century, so we may be looking at another line completely here, although fitting them in seems impossible bar 'somewhere in the north'. It partly confirms a connection between Maximus and Ireland (albeit somewhat tenuous from its lack of specifics) but who is to say that it does not represent the sponsorship by the emperor of a grouping actually settled on the west side of the Irish Sea, included in the complex web of mini-client states, perhaps to guarantee the policing of a too-permeable south-eastern Irish littoral?

Because the lists set out above all commence with the name of Maximus, it is reasonable to suggest that each so-called son was probably a local leader or more plausibly (bearing in mind the North African example) a *praefectus* set up in his time. If it was Maximus's intention to stabilise the northern frontier, there was here no need to import an Irish tribe: there were British peoples inhabiting the region who had been interacting with the empire for over three centuries; this may have been to strengthen an underpopulated region. Also, with the continual raiding by the Picts, based further north in eastern and upland Scotland (and their Irish allies), these people may well have been only too pleased to come to an arrangement of mutual protection with Maximus. Higham suggests that the creation of the province of Britannia Secunda had allowed the re-organisation of the tribes near and beyond the wall, which structure then became 'ossified ... and probably survived into the 480s in some recognisable form', drawing attention to Gildas' use of the Roman technical term *rectores* to describe the provincial administrators of his time. John Koch, though, avers that the *comes* Theodosius 'relinquished all control over the area north of the wall, leaving secure allies in place and troublemakers sealed off', which implies that he would have left British warlords in a position to exercise control over the northernmost *civitates*. This itself eventually bred internecine strife 'into which eventually the Anglo-Saxon invaders took a hand and eventually imposed themselves entirely'.[21]

It may well be, as suggested in Part I, that the *comes* Theodosius did indeed re-organise matters in the north, and that it was he who created Valentia as a wall-straddling or intramural extra province, but it would seem much more likely, given the subsequent scramble to associate ancestors with Maximus, that it was under Maximus that some troop withdrawals were made from the frontier zones and other arrangements that better suited the local notables were consequently put in place along the lines suggested above, as with south-west Wales.

It may be, too, that the northern tribes had co-operated with remarkable success with Maximus in the early 380s in evicting the Picts south of the Antonine wall. Assuming, in consequence, the emperor had built up a good and trustworthy relationship with them, he might have realised that in future he would safely be able to devolve power to them, accompanied by some official style and standing, as we see elsewhere in the western empire being bestowed upon various German and Frankish leaders. Thus it is proposed that he may well have made each tribal group in the north into a quasi-*civitas*. One might ask if Dumbarton, the epicentre of Alclud, was given such a status, for instance, not to mention Dumfries; the latter certainly features as such in the *Historia Brittonum*. He could have either imposed a resident *praefectus* or *dux* to direct defensive strategies and punitive expeditions, or merely designated whoever was perceived as the locally pre-eminent citizen as a *dux*, or *protector* or even *rector*, endorsing such an appointment with a military title and insignia carrying tangible prestige.

There were four main groupings between the Walls, the Selgovae, the Novantae, the Votadini and the Damnonii. Straddling Hadrian's Wall were the Carvetii, their *civitas* at Luguvalium (Carlisle), arguably the provincial capital, but their *territorium* perhaps extended to Dumfries. The other major grouping south of the Wall were the Brigantes, by this date thought to have been sub-divided with *Bryneich* (Bernicia) in the north-east, marching with the Votadini/Manau Goddodin to their north, and stretching south to Catterick and Bamburgh.[22] Bryneich may well be a developed British form of Brigantica and the name of the otherwise unknown Brigomaglos interred at Vindolanda would appear to be a similar derivative therefrom; perhaps he was a leader of the pre-Saxon polity of Bryneich.

The *civitas* of this group was probably Cataractonium (Catterick), although Coriosopitum (Corbridge) has been suggested.[23] The southern portion of Brigantian territory lay south of Bernicia: British *Dewyr* (Deira) with the *civitas* at Isurium Brigantum (Aldborough, Yorkshire). Alcock considered that Maximus had established one dynasty in Galloway (the territory of the Novantae), which seems to have had no obvious *civitas*, but note *Pen Ryoned*, in the first of the Triads, thought by Bromwich to have been Ptolemy's *Rerigonion*, situated at the head of Loch Ryan (his *Abravannus*), Galloway.[24] From this power-base the dynasty of Anthun/Dunawt would have been ideally placed for a cadet branch to have become settled later as rulers of Man, either in competition or arrangement with the Irish, who themselves also had a considerable presence on that island. Indeed, one of Dyfnwal's descendants may have married an heiress of one of his Irish predecessors on Man, securing his position, and the dynasty remained there until Gwriad of Man married Etthil/Ethellt – the daughter of Cynan [of] Dindaethwy, 'King of the Britons' who died in 816 – and heiress of Gwynedd. Gwriad's name appears upon a carved cross at Maughold, Isle of Man, the design of which carries Norse overtones.[25]

Another name on the succession list is Gavran son of Aed[d]an. Aedan's name is Irish, on which basis we could speculate that Dyfnwal Hen's wife might have been an Ulster princess. Gavran himself is only mentioned in the Welsh Triads as the leader of a notably faithful war-band, but who all disappeared without trace ('went to sea for their lord' in one MS). A later Triad alleges that they 'went in search of the Green Islands of the floods and were never heard of after'.[26] The father, Aedan 'The Wily', appears in a Triad, too, as instigator of the 'third unrestrained ravaging', coming to the court of Rhydderch Hael ('the Generous') at Alclud, leaving 'neither food nor drink nor beast alive.'[27] Although very late, this Triad was probably distilled from a much earlier tradition and geographically places the dynasty in the right place to attack Alclud, confirming their base on Galloway.

A final point of interest about the seven king-lists (or ten, including the Irish ones) is that a variant gives Antonius (*sic*) a son, Aeddan, whose son, Prydein (Brittan[i]us) was ancestor of another line which, via several characters of dubious authenticity, ends as part of the ancestry of the House of Gwynedd.[28] In this, Antonius is equipped with ancestors quite divorced from Maximus: Antonius [son of] Seirioel/Seisil [son of] Gorwst/Gwrwst and thence through various Roman emperors back to the Holy Family and Adam, as was common with these later compilations. It is impossible to know whether or not this embodies any real ancient information, but Antonius's father and grandfather's names may a degree of authenticity, uncomplicated by a spurious filiation to Maximus.

The father's name Latinises as Caecilius, a name which has already cropped up in relation to Nudd on the Yarrowkirk stone. As a Roman name it enjoyed more resonance in the republic than under the empire, but it was even so by no means extinct, and it possibly identifies him as part of the ruling élite far more securely than connecting him with Maximus. Yet interestingly, Ammianus Marcellinus tells us of a Caecilius, an official in the entourage of Romanus, *comes* of Africa, from 364 to 373. Romanus treated the inhabitants of the province abominably, including a native prince; this unwise policy caused the revolt which led to the declaration of Firmus as emperor in 372. In Chapter 2, we saw how Magnus Maximus and the younger Theodosius arrived in Africa under the command of the latter's father, the *comes* Theodosius, to put down this very revolt and dethrone the *tyrannus*. Caecilius, who Ammianus's narrative suggests must have known Maximus, was falsely accused of conniving with Romanus but appealed to the emperor, obtained a hearing and was acquitted.[29] The possibility of his then going on to Britain, like Antonius Gregorius Niger (postulated in Chapter 8), as a senior bureaucrat, cannot be ruled out and if he had a son in the army, he might have made an ideal choice as a nominee for an important appointment between the Walls.

Seisil's father's name, Gwrwst, may be intrusive British or mangled Roman. Confusingly, Geoffrey of Monmouth retrospectively Latinised it as Gurgintius/Gurgustius. The entire situation in the north is complicated by other dynasties descending from men bearing obviously Roman names, but *not* claiming descent from Maximus. Is it possible to adduce more about the settlement of the north made in the later fourth century from what we know of these people, too, even when derived from sources so late?

Cunedda

The first grouping to consider is the intramural Votadini, which occupied much of the eastern part of Britain from Hadrian's Wall to the Forth, which was called Manau Goddodin and which appears to have had its *civitas* (if such is the correct term here) at Caer Eidin/Edinburgh. They had probably absorbed the Selgovae of the central lowlands at some stage, for we hear no post-imperial mentions of them. The genealogy/king-list of the Votadini is of interest for its succession of three Roman names, although it, too, is taken back to St Anna via half the Roman emperors in most accounts. It also includes an ancestor called Dumn ('deep'), which evokes the Dumnonii of Alclud and might point to a strong connection there, otherwise lost. The main character in the genealogy is Cunedda, accepted for a millennium and a half as the progenitor of the kings of north Wales (Gwynedd). John Koch, in his analysis of the ancient British poem *Marwnad Cunedda* ('Lament for Cunedda'), has established securely that Cunedda/Cunedag is not in any way to be associated with Gwynedd, and accepts, on excellent grounds, that the poem is 'an archaic source ... not a composition of Gwynedd of the sixth century but a north British, pre-Old Welsh one'.

The *marwnad* laments an inter-British civil war and looks forward to a return to the *status quo* – the secure borders of late Roman Britain. Cunedda in the poem has neither named sons nor a named successor, nor is he seen as a King but as a *pennadur* (chief).[30] The immediate lineage is: Cunedda [son of] Aetern [son of] Patern Pesrut [son of] Tacit [son of] Cein.[31] Some genealogies insert an extra two generations of British names between Tacit and Cein, but while it one might assume that these genealogies reflect local British nobles suddenly adopting Roman nomenclature around 300, this would seem inherently unlikely. As John Koch muses, 'Are we asking too much of the genealogists of early medieval Wales to have made up credible names for men whom we can estimate to have lived in Roman times?'[32]

One suspects that what we actually have is a short genealogy of a Roman or Romano-Briton with the usual Latin names and some resplendent British ancestry grafted on, in this case, back to St Anna (or Adam), as convention saw fit. Cunedda himself bears a British name, and probably his mother was a northern Briton, keen to see her son bear a name that reflected *her* ancestry. The situation is analogous to that of the family of Gregory of Tours a century later, whose maternal great uncle Gundulfus (*dux* in Gaul 581-683) bore a Germanic name, despite being the son of an upper-crust Roman from northern Italy called Florentinus.[33] Cunedda's great-grandfather was probably called Tegid (Tacitus), of which there are plentiful examples in the third to fourth centuries, including the short-lived emperor. The inscription of a late Roman ring found in Votadinian territory (Midlothian) naming a Tullia Tacita might even relate to this character.[34] Patern/Padarn (Paternus, Welsh *Padarn*) 'a mid-fourth-century military man' in Bromwich's words, bore a name very common in the period, while the name Aetern is attested only by the senator Aeternalis, in Africa in 396.[35]

Amongst those named Paternus in the fourth century is Lucretius Paternus, an unlocated *vicarius* or provincial governor in 329; had he served in Britain, he would have been ideally placed to be identified with Cunedda's grandfather.[36] In fact, Cunedda's grandfather is certainly taken for a Roman commander of some sort, especially as his epithet was *pesrud* meaning 'of the red cloak', a known accoutrement of Roman officers of the period.

Cunedda's *floruit* has to lie within the timescale of 383/490, but the impression given in the *marwnad* is that there is no higher power than the *civitates* (no *tyranni* on the horizon), neither coin nor bullion but plenty of Mediterranean trade, wine and oil being mentioned. Furthermore, all attacks seem to be seaborne, typical of the Picts seeking to by-pass the inter-wall tribes and indeed the Wall itself.[37] Towns are referred to as not yet ruined and despoiled, as with Gildas before the Saxon revolt: there are *cives* and *civitates*.[38] The suggestion by Koch that there is 'no higher power' revealed in the poem does not, one suspects, mean quite that, for if the events of the poem rook place between the Walls, and Cunedda was the heir or inheritor of a commander placed there, perhaps by Magnus Maximus, whoever then held sway in London might well have seemed too remote to intrude on their world.

Indeed, the strife recounted appears to be between the followers of two separate Roman era commanders whom the *tyrannus* in the south may well have confirmed in their positions and trusted to deal with the Picts and Scots, who had become, as we have seen, accustomed to raiding Britain from the sea (hence the Yorkshire and north-east coast signal stations and the Welsh and Lancastrian forts and signal stations). All of which appears to have been Cunedda's main concern. Eventually, Cunedda met his end at the hands of a rival faction as a result of internecine strife, the *gûr Bryneich* ('men of Bernicia'), who are seen as Britons and certainly not at this stage English. This strife may have had its origins in the gradual Christianisation of the area, probably originating through St Ninian's Whithorn (Galloway); not every polity between the Walls was Christian until at least the mid-fifth century, and the Picts remained pagan for much longer.[39]

Koch has established that the kings of North Wales/Gwynedd were entirely unrelated to Cunedda, and that he was grafted onto existing pedigrees retrospectively when the annals and poems of the Men of the North were transmitted to Wales towards the end of the seventh century, when their hegenomy either side of the Wall was largely shattered by Saxon expansion. Thus, he was attached to genealogies in a similar way to Maximus. The *Historia Brittonum* is the first source to re-locate Cunedda and tells us that he drove out numerous Irish intrusive settlements in Wales 'with his sons' and that he came from the north, from Manaw Gododdin, 146 years before the reign of Maelgwyn of Gwynedd (whose *atavus* – descendant in the fifth generation – he allegedly was), who died 547.[40] The agent for this transmission of information may have been the northern prince Sawyl Penisel (Samuel 'Hang-head'), son of the alliterative but obscure ruler of York, Pabo Post Prydein (Paul[lus] 'Pillar of Britain'), exiled with his father to Powis in the very early seventh century.[41] Koch, on the other hand, suggests that the *marwnadd* Cunedda lament came to Wales through the recapture of the north by the Britons in around 632/3, led by Maelgwyn's descendant Cadwallon, and that the story got attached to a separate tale about the expulsion of the Irish from North Wales, actually achieved by the quite unrelated warlord, Einion, who features in the later sources as the senior of Cunedda's alleged sons.[42]

This disconnect is worth examining, as it is possible to some extent to adduce a later fourth-century settlement in North Wales, as in Demetia and the North, although what part Maximus might have had in it is impossible to say, for his name is nowhere attached to the accounts we have. Gwynedd had originally been the *civitas* of the Ordovices (a name preserved in a post-Roman inscription from Cardiganshire) but the designation seems to have changed quite suddenly to Gwynedd/Venedotia, and another stone has also been found recording a 'citizen of Venados'.[43] Charles-Edwards postulates an early fifth-century takeover of the area by the *Brega*, an eastern central Irish tribe, who were presumably amongst those driven out from north Wales by Einion Gyrth (Ennianus/Annianus – Gyrth, 'the Stricken'), quite possibly another late Roman appointee; might his efforts have been related to the campaign led impromptu by St Germanus in 429? In the Welsh sources Einion has eight brothers, some of whom bear toponyms and are said to have been Cunedda's sons (see below).[44] Thereafter, it is suggested that a change in the balance of power in south-eastern Ireland *c.* 500 (the conquest of Leinster by the *Uí Néill*) saw the expelled *Brega* replaced by the *Feni*, which grouping seems to have eclipsed the remnants of the former in north Wales, and finally ended Irish raiding through settlement as federates. Even the name Gwynedd it seems, actually derives from the Irish *Feni*.[45] It is worth noting also that

> ... during the fifth century, it might still have been possible to defend what had been Roman Britain as a whole with a carefully planned strategy ... but interests founded in this period subsequently became fragmented and localized. In the sixth century they could not continue or even understand the former scale of operations.[46]

This, of course, could equally be true of the later fourth century. Thus, the 'sons' of Cunedda may have been a group of Romano-British officers charged with helping to expel the Irish and thereafter to consolidate designated areas, bearing in mind there was no proper *civitas* between Chester and Carmarthen – although Ann Dornier has argued that the missing *civitas* capital of the Ordovices was in fact Chester.[47] Therefore only a quasi-military structure could have filled the vacuum once the Irish had been neutralised, a process that could have taken some time in the event, as witness St Germanus aiding the commander Gerontius in his struggle with intrusive Irish aided by Saxons, possibly in the Llangollen region, as described in Chapter 6.

Of course, as Koch argues, both versions could be true: Cunedda *might* have been tasked with coming from the Wall to sort out the occupation of the coasts of Wales and *might* have installed a lieutenant, Einion, to finish the job, who in his turn settled various officers in various liberated parts to secure them, which would at least account for the presence of Cunedda in the mythology of Gwynedd.[48] In this connection, the poem *Moliant Cadwallon* ('Eulogy of Cadwallon'), composed to the memory of the most successful ruler of Gwynedd (described at the time as 'King of the Britons', suggesting that central authority had long vanished but that the concept remained extant) who, with Penda of Mercia's help, briefly secured the northern British kingdoms, is thought to have been equally as ancient as *Marwant Cunedda*. Yet it makes no mention at all of Cunedda who, by later reckoning, had founded his dynasty. It does, however, inform us that it was Einion who 'drove the heathen into the sea', all of which seems reasonably conclusive.

When these events occurred, though, is harder to fathom. The *Historia Brittonum*'s figure of 146 years before Maelgwyn Gwynedd would give us 410 if calculated from his death in around 547 (from the effects of Justinian's plague, a pandemic exacerbated by the dramatic climate anomaly then being experienced, driven by two cataclysmic volcanic events), but well within the compass of Maximus's reign if Maelgwyn acceded to power twenty years or more *before,* as seems equally possible.[49] Likewise, Bromwich argues that it is sensible to calibrate the 146 from the *fall* of Maximus (which she suggests the context supports) giving a start date for Maelgwyn of 534. Maelgwyn was certainly around to be admonished by Gildas, in the 530s.[50]

The 'sons' of Cunedda were Tybion, Osfail, Rhufon, Dunod, Ceredig, Einion Yrth, Dogfail and Etern. Some early accounts omit Tybion and insert his son Meirion as the eldest son, but most name Meirion as the son of Tybion.[51] Of these, several have Roman names: Tybion according to our earliest source died before his father in Manau Gododdin, and he may be a genuine son of Cunedda, in view of his predeceasing his father who, as we have seen, was apparently without an heir. Yet the name is quite possibly a Celticisation of Tiberianus.[52] Interestingly, one late fourth-century Tiberianus was noted holding an unknown but senior position in an unidentified province at some stage prior to 385. While this could have been Africa (through a secondary association) it could easily have been within Magnus Maximus's part of the west.[53] Tybion's son was Meirion (Mari[ni]anus), who divided up the realm of Gwynedd with his uncles according to Harleian MS 3859, endowing Meirionydd, a former north Welsh county, with his name.[54] Osfael (Ishmael) seems hardly a British name but credible enough at a time when Christianity and the vulgate Bible were only beginning to exert an influence over the wilder reaches of the island.

Rhufon/Rumon/Run (Romanus) was given Rhufoniog (southern Denbighshire) as his portion, while Dunod (Donatus) received Dunoding (the most part of the Lleyn Peninsular west of the Dwyryd).[55] Ceredig (as in Caradoc/Caractacus) received Ceredigion, later marked by the County of Cardigan/Ceredigion, but Afloeg/Abloyc/Abalach's name seems suspiciously Irish and he is not credited with a territory in the grand share-out overseen by Meirion.[56] If he *was* Irish, then his presence amongst the 'sons' of Cunedda may suggest the recruitment and settlement of a group of Irish, not part of those expelled by Einion and may represent a phenomenon similar to that encountered in Demetia: the mediatisation of an allied group as part of an overall strategy, here presumably the *Feni*, mentioned above. Einion/Annianus seems on disparate and circumstantial evidence to have been the one who oversaw all this, Meirion's alleged role notwithstanding. The final pair, Dogfail and Etern (Aeternus/Aeternalis) also get included in the territorial share-out, Dogfail giving his name to a commote – subdivision of the *cantref* – covering the middle Clwyd valley, and Etern apparently named after his alleged grandfather (taken to be a later embellishment) ending up with Rhôs, the northern coastal strip of the later county of Denbigh.

The settlement of north Wales could easily have been the work of Maximus and executed at his behest by Einion. This may explain the re-fortification of Segontium as a focus for this regional military administration and possibly, too, for post-Roman Christianity in the area. Other re-fortified Roman forts, probably abandoned under Maximus's far-reaching re-organisation of the frontier zones, may have acted as bases for some of the lesser commanders – the 'brothers' we have noted above. Thus, in Pen Llystyn, Brynkir (Anglesey) two stones commemorating one Icorix were found, the larger reading ICORI[X] FILIUS POTENTI/NI (Icorix son of Potentinus). The Welsh place name element *llys* is cognate to a seat of princely power, or court.[57] The father's name is a good Roman one so one might conceivably be looking at a Roman lieutenant of one of Einion's appointees or his descendant. Sidonius Apollinaris had a friend of this name in the later fifth century, thus a contemporary, as the inscriptions are datable to the early sixth century.[58]

Laing suggests on similar grounds that Tomen-y-Mur fort at Maentwrog (Meirionydd) may have had a similar post-Roman role, especially as another sub-Roman stone (albeit bearing an archaic Roman *Dis Manibus* formula) was found nearby commemorating one Barectus Caranteius, the latter element a typical Roman *gentilicium*.[59] The fact that Maelgwyn of Gwynedd later gave the re-used Anglesey fort at Caer Gybi (which we have suggested as part of Maximus's western defences) to St Cybi (hence its name) seems to point in the same direction.[60] Laing sees these re-used forts as the bases for the post-Roman campaign to clear and secure northern Wales, instigated by capable appointed officers whose successors founded dynasties. He suggests that they also formed nodal points for the spread and consolidation of Christianity in the area.[61]

In the same way, the Votadini of Manau Goddodin seem to have been under the control of a Roman commander, from whom Cunedda, a second-generation leader of this grouping who, whether he was recruited to continue the fight against the Irish in north Wales or not (but probably wasn't), most certainly clashed with the other British commanders to his south. According to the northern British pedigrees, the Votadini were, after the demise of Cunedda, ruled by elements drawn from this more southerly grouping, for we find Cynfelyn ap Arthwys, apparently ruling there later in the fifth century. Cynfelyn's name is analogous to Cunobelinus, and while perhaps a surviving traditional name, may well have been drawn deliberately from lost British accounts of the efforts of the Britons to see off Julius Caesar, as postulated by Miles Russell in his analysis of elements of the story embodied in Geoffrey of Monmouth's account, but not found in any other sources.[62] This man's father Arthwys Mawr, is recorded as 'son of Mor' in the genealogies, although the name Mor is inauthentic and intended as an archaic version of *mawr* ('great'); it is to be attached to Arthwys, thus Arthrwys the Great, who is sometimes trotted out as a northern prototype for the more elusive but more famous Arthur, the name Arthwys Latinising as Artorius. More to the point for our purposes, Arthrwys (as 'Mor') was the grandson of a man called Coel Hen, who is even more ubiquitous as an ancestral hero than Maximus amongst the dynasties of the north.

Coel Hen

Who, therefore, was Coel Hen, and does he fit into the pattern suggested by the 'sons' of Maximus, Cunedda's antecedents, Einion and others? The most pertinent and indeed inconvenient fact is that he only appears in genealogies; no poem or other tradition about him is preserved.[63] Any attempt to assign a date to him by counting back generations from descendants whose dates are known tends to end with placing Coel firmly in the second quarter of the fifth century. His name appears to be Roman, strongly suggesting Coelius.[64] In some sources he also bears a toponym and two British epithets. The toponym was 'of Aeron' (central Ayrshire) suggesting that he had some sway over the lands ruled by the Novantae or even Alclud, territories of 'descendants' of Maximus.[65]

Coel's epithets are never recorded simultaneously; there are *hen* (= 'old') and *godebog* (= Latinised as Votepacus, meaning, once again, 'protector'), the latter being strongly reminiscent of the title born by Voteporix of Demetia. This is complicated by the fact that *godebog* is sometimes given as his father's name, in which case the similarities to the Demetian genealogy are even more striking: 'son of Protector'. The question is, does the rank *protector* hide a name, and if so, was it Roman or British? In other sources, his father's name is British, Tegfan, and the next two generations are also British and alliterative, before we reach another Roman name, *Urban map*

Grat, 'Urbanus son of Gratianus'.[66] Finally his epithet *hen* recurs several times amongst his numerous posterity and, like *hael* amongst the descendants of Dyfnwal 'son' of Maximus, might well have been a quasi-hereditary name, perhaps continued from Coel, whose Roman name might have been a translation, as for example Coelius Priscus or Coelius Senecio.[67]

It is tempting to try and unpick all this by supposing that Gratianus was named after the boy emperor (proclaimed Augustus in 367) and that Urbanus was therefore born approximately in Maximus's reign, reaching adulthood in the first decade of the fifth century. Thus, a son of the latter could be Coel Hen, who might well have been given the style *protector*. One suspects that the three alliterative British names in the pedigree may well be those of Coel's maternal line interpolated by a later copyist; that is, if we might reasonably surmise that he married a British woman. The place most associated with his dynasty, known as the Coelings (ironically, rather a Germanic way of describing them, as with the Cadellings of Powis), is York, Yorkshire and the north-east. It may be that he was appointed by Vortigern or Ambrosius to the post known in the previous era as the *dux Britanniarum*, which is thought to have been based at York. We can speculate that he might have been appointed as a successor as *dux* to Owein/Eugenius who, we have suggested, might have held this appointment as the gift of Maximus before seizing power in 409 after crushing an incursion. Such a situation would explain the ubiquity of his progeny as power-brokers in this general area.[68] In the chaos of the Saxon revolt, he could have remained *en poste* and by successfully consolidating his hold of the area established a viable polity, paying only lip service to central authority.

Coel, who has come down to us as Old King Cole of the nursery rhyme, is alleged in *Bonedd Y Sant* to have married [H]elen, the self-same lady whom the *Mabinogion* attaches to Magnus Maximus; elsewhere she is Gwreic, daughter of Gadeon, son of Eudaf Hen.[69] This just goes to show the chaos into which the appearance of both the *Dream of Maxen Wledig* and the *Historia Regum Britanniae* (*HRB*) managed to throw these characters, for the *HRB*, also for the first time, associated Coel with Colchester and has him a contemporary of Carausius and Constantine.[70] Another source calls Coel's wife Stradweul/[Y]stradwal.[71] This would suggest she was the daughter of either a native leader stationed, as part of the late- or post-Roman settlement on Hadrian's Wall, or a later Roman appointee 'gone native' there – or even one on the Antonine Wall, which might suggest a lady of the house of Cunedda. Whoever she was, she must have brought him some political security in the former Valentia, for the name means nothing more than 'the wide land of the wall' which one might reasonably interpret as being the self-same province and the match, however much the name has been distorted, as a nugget of genuinely archaic information concerning the area at that time.

Coel is attributed with four children, the most prominent in terms of descendants and references in the texts being Ceneu. The name means 'whelp'

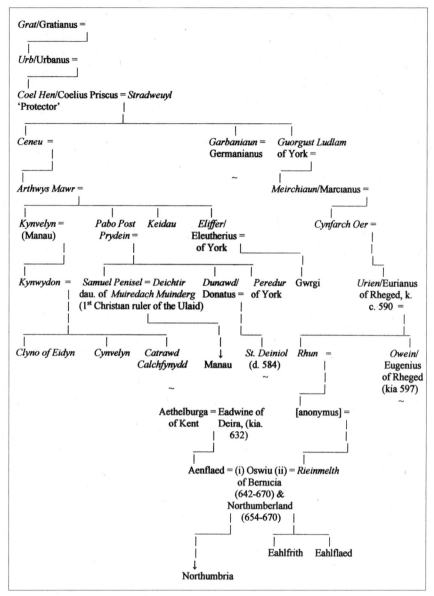

Stemma 7. The family of Coel Hen.

or 'dog', from which we might infer that instead of being the obviously British name it appears, it might have started out as Latin Canin[i]us. This name as a *cognomen* is rare in the élite of the Empire, but as a *nomen* can be detected amongst the ranks of the senate to the end of the third century at least, which prevents us from being certain. As we have postulated a British wife for Coel, a British name may well have been chosen, especially as the next son's name, Garbaniaun, is a clear British derivative from the Roman Germanianus, which may have been chosen in honour of St Germanus (of which it is an adjectival version) or may even be, as suggested by H. M. Chadwick, after Valentinian's praetorian prefect of Gaul from 364 to 379 under whom, inevitably, Maximus would have served, if only indirectly, when he was with Theodosius the elder.[72] Garbaniaun appears to have no recorded issue.

A third son of Ceneu, Guorgust/Gwrwst (another British name) appears as 'king' of York (and also an ancestor of St Cadoc), whose own son, Meirchiaun, was named after the emperor Marcianus (who acceded to the eastern throne in 450), which helps to fix the period, if it were not for the fact that Gwrwst Ludlam ('ragged') is also given as a son of Ceneu rather than of Coel and indeed was father of one Meirchiaun: it looks very much like a mix-up rather typical of the later genealogies: real people getting misplaced, or falling through holes in the vast fabric of time between the events and their final recording. As this latter Meirchiaun was the grandfather of the famous Urien of Rheged, whom we are able to date to an event in 573, this would better suit the chronology of the House of Coel, which would strongly suggest that Gwrwst should be regarded as a son of Coel and not of Ceneu; even then there would seem to be too many generations between Coel, if adult from *c.* 430 and Meirchiaun, possibly born *c.* 450/457. Remove the link between Grat and Meirchiaun and their imperial namesakes and the succession can be seen to fit and would allow Coel to have been flourishing under Constantine III.[73] Certainly, the names in their Latin forms all accord with the period and carry echoes of contemporary rulers and saints.

Urien of Rheged himself was the son of Cynfarch Oer ('the dismal') and was victor in a battle fought at *Armteria*, now Arthuret, just north of Carlisle.[74] The leader of the polity of which the centre was Carlisle (latterly the Roman *civitas* of the Carvetii and possibly the capital of Valentia), Gwenddolew ap Ceidau of 'Caer Gwenddoleu' (perhaps Carwinley, Cumberland) was killed in the action, having been attacked by a group of descendants of Coel: Gwrgi son of Ellifer (Eleutherius) and Peredur, son of Pabo, along with Rhydderch of Strathclyde and Urien. The result seems to have been the uniting of the territory of the Novantae, ruled by descendants of Maximus's alleged son Antonius/Donatus, with that of the Carvetii, including present Cumbria and probably much of Lancashire. The outcome of this internecine conflict may have had its roots in religion: we cannot be sure if all these descendants of putative Roman appointees were Christian; there may have been a crusading spirit abroad amongst the protagonists. The battle seems to have marked a turning point in the fortunes of the north, where areas of command, almost certainly grown into hereditary or quasi-hereditary fiefdoms, were thus united across the north under one grouping, of whom Urien seems to have emerged pre-eminent, a sort of ersatz *dux Britanniarum*.[75]

The name of Rhydderch of Strathclyde (pronounced 'rūtherk') became embedded in those of Carrutherstown and nearby Ruthwell in this very area.

From this point, Rheged seems to have included Galloway, the *territorium* of the Carvetii, henceforth including a much greater area, its limits marked by other place-name derivations: *Yr Echwyd* ('the land of the flowing waters' = the Lake District) and probably as far south as Rochdale (= British *Reced* + Norse *dalr*, 'valley', thus 'Valley of Rheged'),[76]) the river Rached (*Tra Merin Reget* = 'the Sea of Rheged', thus the Solway Firth into which this river flows), Dunragit ('the fort of Rheged' in western Dumfries and Galloway, the *Dun Reichet* of the *Calendar of Oengus*), not to mention The Raggat, a locality of Peel, Isle of Man. Luguvalium (Carlisle) retained its British name, *Caer Ligwalid*.[77] The existence of such derivations on Man and in Lancashire seems to support the notion that the ruling dynasty of Galloway did indeed control Man and presumably Lancashire after Arthuret. Urien was also referred to in the *Book of Taliesin* as the 'Lord of *Catraeth*' (Catterick) implying that his new polity stretched to the north-east, too. McCarthy estimated his dates as from around the 530s to *c.* 585/595.[78] The battle of Arthuret seems to have consolidated several polities in the north and can be seen as a strategic move to strengthen the entire area against the burgeoning Germanic advance from previously unexceptional enclaves on the eastern coast.

Owain, Urien's son and successor, was also prince of *Lawyfenydd* (= Lyvennet near Crosby Ravensworth, Cumberland, also, still the name of a river rising there, a tributary of the Eden), clearly a much larger *territorium* at this time, centred on the Penrith area. Note also Levenwood on the river Kent estuary and *Llwyfein* (= Levens, Lancashire).[79] Higham considers it the most northerly post-Roman kingdom towards the west of northern Britain, but which must also have included the Ribble Valley to Dentdale including the Domesday Book wapentake of Craven (at one time seemingly a separate British polity),[80] Cartmel and the western coastline north of the Mersey. 'The distribution of *ecles* place names per territorial hundred throughout most of south Lancashire implies that these tenth-century divisions were based on earlier territorial units which date back to before the English takeover.'[81]

As regards Carlisle itself, there are indications of remarkable urban longevity, as befits the probable capital of the northernmost province and a crucial strategic walled city. Emblematic of its longevity is St Cuthbert's visit to the city in the 670s with the Queen of Northumbria, to visit the monastery founded there by King Oswald in the 640s, where they were greeted by a reeve (*praepositus*) called Waga (perhaps a Briton called Gwygwr) who conducted him round the Roman walls (our only reference to them) and showed him a *fons* (fountain) 'marvellously wrought of Roman workmanship'.[82] McCarthy adds that, in the context of the re-use of the *principia* at Carlisle:

> The continued use of formerly key buildings ... might allow us to infer that this is an element in one archaeology of lordship. If so, it is lordship

in transition from a Roman command structure to one of sub-Roman leaders emerging as local chiefs or kings with military titles and authority derived from that of the late fourth century ... they were not yet kings nor princes but neither were they members of the Roman army linked to a wide-ranging command structure ... their authority was derived from the former prestige attached to the place ... and their dwellings may ... [have been] large and imposing.[83]

Presumably, some form of occupation of Carlisle continued under the kingdom of Strathclyde and until English domination was permanently established in the area in the eleventh century.

Rheged aside, Coel's extended 'family' also ultimately ruled southern Scotland, Manau Gododdin, Lothian, Carlisle to Lancashire, east to Catterick, York, Leeds and Elmet (a polity south of and including Leeds, the name of which has survived as a locality), evoking some comparison with the vast tract of northern Gaul ruled for two decades by Syagrius (see Chapter 6).[84] An attempt to cherry-pick enough from the better sources to produce a suggested *stemma* appears above. Whether fifth-century central British authority – Vortigern, Ambrosius or Aurelianus – ever had nominal or stronger control over these regions is quite unclear. Probably such a situation pertained initially, but with Kent and the east of England beginning to slip from British control, any overlordship was probably becoming increasingly hard to assert and thus nominal, as in contemporary Gaul.

Unfortunately, human nature seems to have allowed the gains achieved at Arthuret to slip, just when the descendants of Ida, Anglo-Saxon king of Bernicia (his polity initially a small enclave on the coast of an area then mostly still under British control) were beginning to cause the Britons trouble, notably his son Theod[e]ric Fflamddwyn ('flame-bearer') – note that his name is also found amongst the British dynasties (see Chapter 8, amongst the Kings of Gwent). Was he part-British by descent? This brought Urien to the east coast, and it was while investing the Saxons holed up at Lindisfarne, in alliance with Guallauc of Elmet, Rydderch Hen (a descendant of Antonius/ Donatus, a 'son' of Maximus) and Morcant, he was assassinated around 590 in a fit of jealousy by the latter.[85] Morcant was the great grandson of Dyfnwal Hen, also a grandson of Antonius/Donatus, but ancient tradition fails to tell us more of him after his dastardly act, which fatally weakened Rheged, despite the determinedly heroic efforts of his son Owein, whose brother, Rhun map Urien, is said to have baptised the Saxon king Eadwine in 626.[86]

It may be that the Coelings and those claiming descent from Maximus had coalesced into two rival groupings competing for control of the north. If so, it presented an unexpected opportunity to advance their sway to the expanding Saxon settlements on the east coast, which was exploited with gusto, for by this time, the British kingdoms of Bryneich and Dewyr (Bernicia and Deira) had been diminished both in size and potency by a series of strong Anglo-Saxon rulers, of whom Eadwine was one – indeed, his power encompassed both at that time, although the polity he created was still largely coastal.[87] Yet Bernicia and Deira were quickly given over to Saxon control in a relatively short time after this: as ever, internecine strife appears to have been the undoing of British alliances in this age.

Thereafter Rheged and the dominion of the Coelings began to contract, despite the almost triumphant *reconquista* of the Saxon north in the 630s by Penda of Mercia and Cadwallon of Gwynedd, until much of both was united by the marriage of Rienmelth, granddaughter and effectively heiress of Rhun of Rheged with King Oswiu of Bernicia. This enabled Oswiu's dynasty to absorb Rheged relatively bloodlessly, which act essentially forged the new combined kingdom of Northumbria. Peaceful assimilation seems highly probable, with British princes surviving within Northumbria for a time as *subreguli* (under-kings) and independently in Cumbria and north of Carlisle for much longer.[88] At the time of Oswiu's predecessor Eadwin's death at the hands of Penda and Cadwallon in 632, the latter was described as 'king of the Britons' (suggesting that central control was by this date long gone) and ruled a kingdom stretching east into the Peak district and which appears also to have encompassed Lancashire south of the Ribble. This is suggested by the naming of the Roman Shore fort at Lancaster as *Caer Gwerid* (reported by Camden in the later sixteenth century), from which is said to derive the present name for the surviving fragment of this large fort, the Wery Wall.[89]

Despite the ephemeral irruptions of Eadwine and Ecgfrith into Man in the 620s and 680s, Gwyrid ap Elifir (a 'descendant' of Maximus) was able to succeed as King of Man around 800. His son Merfyn Frych married the heiress of Gwynedd; the name Gwyrid in this context, if it bears any validity, suggesting that the dynasty of Man had managed to exercise some control over Lancashire after the collapse of Rheged and then the Coelings in the seventh century. This might far better explain why the ruler of a modest sized island in the Irish sea could have been deemed suitable to marry the heiress of the powerful House of Gwynedd, its rulers still styling themselves 'Kings of the Britons'. If he controlled a good portion of the mainland abutting Gwynedd (and presumably the sea to the west) he would have had sufficient standing to satisfy the most demanding of prospective fathers.

Owein, Urien's eldest son, allied himself in marriage with the Coeling ruler of the Lothian area and having won two battles against the Bernician Saxons under Theod[e]ric the Flame Bearer, perished fighting his father's nemesis, Morcant, around 595.[90] The Lothian kingdom was shortly afterwards seriously compromised or even extinguished by the Saxons of Bernicia under Aethelfrith at the Battle of Degsastan in 603, for although the defeated leader was Áedán the Irish king of Dál Riata to the north-west, who appears to have invaded Votadinian territory, his allies also suffered the consequences of the defeat. The Saxon victory left Aethelfrith in a position to extend his control over the entire area, which Oswald consolidated by suppressing Lothian completely following a siege of Caer Eidin (Edinburgh) in 641, with the Picts and Dál Riata having to pay him tribute as well.[91] They may, however, have regained their independence in 685 when Ecgfrith was killed fighting the Picts, for Bede says that 'one section of the Britons recovered their liberty which they have now enjoyed for forty-six years.'[92]

As we have seen, the remains of the polity of Rheged seems to have ended in the 640s with the marriage of Rieinmelth to Oswiu.[93] The British princes who remained as *subreguli* in some of the north-west territories of the Carlisle region were ultimately absorbed with the unexpectedly freed Votadinians into the greater kingdom of Alclud, by this time called Strathclyde.

Alclud

The polity called Alclud returns us to our line of enquiry, for although the later rulers of Alclud were seemingly at first descendants of Antonius/ Donatus, putative son of Maximus, and later still of Coel, the initial four whose names are known belonged to an earlier succession, beginning, once again, with two generations bearing Roman names, Cluim (Clemens) father of Cinhil (Quinctilius), followed by the more British Cynloyp/Cynllwyb, the supposed father of St Patrick's Coroticus.[94] The kingdom at this early stage also embraced much territory north of the Clyde, where was its stronghold of Dumbarton (from *Dinas Prydein*, Scottish Gaelic *Dùn Breatainn*, 'the fort of the Britons') which had originated as an iron age fort surmounting a 240-ft high volcanic plug now called the Rock of Dumbarton. Later, it appears to have developed into a Roman fort and associated harbour, presumably from the mid-second century. So far, its duration as such has not been ascertained on the ground.[95] As *Cair Brithon*, it was listed as one of the 28 towns in the *Historia Brittonum*, which list adds to the accepted canon of Romano-British cities or specifically *civitates*, although quite what the author meant by that term remains obscure. Although some in the list provided in the *Historia* seem rather too fanciful to accord much credibility, the list itself may dimly reflect a planned re-ordering of *civitates* and territories effected in or after 383. Some may indeed represent a Roman re-ordering of the fifth province by providing the intermural tribal groupings with all the trappings of official standing.[96]

In effect, the creation of Valentia (if we can accept that it did include this intermural tract) and the formalisation of its tribal structures that some entries in this list seem to imply, represent a considerable and undeniably bold expansion of the empire in Britain, and this in the last quarter of the fourth century, too. This, of course, seems to emerge from the legendary British sources as in all probability the result of a careful and radical re-ordering of the northernmost province by Magnus Maximus.

The chief stumbling block in teasing out some inkling of the timeframe in which these men flourished is that the dating of Patrick's life as revealed in his *Vitae* is not universally agreed. Morris suggests that the *Letter to Coroticus* was composed late, around 450 (Patrick died in 459) after the ruler of Alclud had been raiding north-eastern Ireland, probably in retaliation for Irish raids on his own coasts. By counting back generations and assuming that Coroticus had been in power for, say, a decade, then Cluim/Clemens would once again be a contemporary of Magnus Maximus, and therefore not impossibly another potential appointee of his, as we have suggested with Coel and Antonius/Donatus, although in this case, no claim was made in the only genealogy we have upon Maximus as progenitor. Instead, prior to Cluim, we find only three names, unknown in any other context: Cursalem, Fer and Confer, which are either highly distorted ancestral names (they appear unique) or, more likely, grafted on in mutated form from some half-remembered local tradition.

As an élite name, Clemens occurs twice in the fourth century, Quin[c]tilius four times and the related Quintillus twice, establishing their relative ubiquity, but it is difficult to see how Clemens could have been a senior Roman officer assigned to the peoples of the western Clyde with sufficient standing to establish a dynasty, or at least a succession.[97] The alternative is that like the dynasty of Demetia, the British princes of Alclud were much more Romanised than previously supposed; unless, like Aircol/Agricola of Demetia, Clemens's father had been a hostage or otherwise well embedded into Romano-British life generally to have wished to endow his son with a Roman name. He may even have served at a fairly elevated level in the imperial army. Much later, in 870, Dumbarton (as *Dun Bretan*) was captured by the Vikings and was never regained by its kings, who retreated to Govan south of the river. The name of the polity, as emerges with the death of King Arthal of the [North] Britons in 872, was henceforth Srath Clúade/Ystrad Glud. But recovery was quick, for the kingdom had expanded south as far as Penrith and west Cumbria by about 927.[98]

Owein II was father of Mael Coluin II (Malcolm), 'King of the Britons' who from 1054 was also King of the Scots, uniting much of the British kingdom with that of the Scots, with whose rulers the British dynasty had long been allied by marriage. In 1092, William II of England captured Cumbria, removing the last element of the Strathclyde kingdom south of Hadrian's Wall.[99] It was the last of the old northern British post-Roman polities (*Hen Ogledd*) to be absorbed by the English.

These northern entities seem to have been robust post-Roman mutations of an expansionist administrative structure put in place before 409 – here suggested as most likely by Magnus Maximus – but, instead of recruiting Irish to settle a sparsely populated frontier region as in Demetia under a phylarch-like figure, here it seems more likely a case of persuading the settled tribal groupings (and, south of Hadrian's Wall, *civitates*) to act as buffer states against the Picts and Scots as formally recognised units. They would be overseen by Roman *praefecti* (or similar) who in most cases were probably grafted onto later genealogies as founding fathers – indeed in some cases, possibly literally as founding fathers, once central appointments had dried up.[100] These groupings appear to have been fairly stable, too, for they all seem to have survived into the seventh century and in some cases beyond, occasional outbreaks of internecine strife notwithstanding. It was only after Cadwallon of Gwynedd was driven out of the north as a result of the Battle of Heavenfield in 634 and Penda of Mercia was killed at the battle of the Winwaed in 655 that these polities began to be picked off by the 'English', being either absorbed or eliminated.[101] There also seems to have been substantial continuity between them in the seventh century and their Anglo-Saxon successors, bearing in mind the second (or third) marriage of Oswiu, the fact that both Deira and Bernicia previously bore British names and, as here suggested, were indeed actually British polities. As P. S. Barnwell has said, 'That aspects of Roman administration could have continued into the British period is no longer a matter of great controversy.'

Barnwell argued for the likelihood of such continuity in Bernicia and Deira, as they passed from British to Saxon control and even for a similar situation in Wessex, a polity long recognised as having been founded by a leader bearing a British name – Cerdic – and having immediate successors also with (mutated) British names.[102]

10

South-west and Beyond

Dumnonia

Quite apart from the tribal name Dumnonii/Damnonii recurring in Ireland and in the area of south-west Scotland later occupied by the Kingdom of Alclud (see Chapters 8 and 9) there are two items that oblige us to turn our enquiry to the south-west. One is that the post-Roman rulers of what had been the tribal area of the Dumnonii (but part of Britannia Prima latterly) were uncommonly fond of the names Custennin (Constantine) and Gereint (Gerontius), which might incline those of a suspicious nature to note the fact that Constantine III had, as one of his lieutenants, one Gerontius (see Chapter 6). The other is that a genealogy in a Harleian MS, outside the canon of MS 3859, reads

> *Mam Eleri oedd Aurbost verch twysawg Kerniw. mam Aurbost oedd vech amherawdr Ryvain.*
> 'For Eleri married Aurbost daughter of the prince of Cornwall, who married the daughter of the Roman emperor.'[1]

Bartum, noting this, wrote 'This suggests a prince of Cornwall married the daughter of a Roman Emperor, presumably Maximus,' adding that 'it is remarkable that such a marriage is actually recorded ... that the wife of Tudwal ap Morfawr was Grantian[a] daughter of Maximus.'[2] The source is inevitably late, for the term *Kerniw* for Cornwall would be anachronistic at the period allegedly being described. *Cornubia*, its Latin equivalent, first occurs as a name in the Saxon bishop Aldhelm's writings around 700.[3] We have already encountered the term *Kernew* interpreted as representing the Cornovii rather than Cornwall, when looking at the ramifications of early Powis, centred on Viroconium Cornoviorum (Wroxeter), which has in the past tended to act as something of a distraction.[4]

John Morris considered some of the Cornovii must have been transferred to the far south-west of Britain to expel an incursion of Irish as part of the upheavals and make-do-and-mend settlement in Britain of the years 407/410. This receives some corroboration from the *Historia Brittonum*, where the settlement of Irish groupings is set out. Amongst them are 'the sons of Liethan', clearly the Uí Liathán of the area in the south-east and Cork, which, we are told in Cormac's *Glossary*, were settled, or attempted to settle, in Cornwall.[5] It may be, therefore, that a group of the Cornovii was detached in the later fourth century (perhaps by Maximus) or early fifth (perhaps by Constantine III or his insular successor), to counter this incursion, thus having the unintended consequence of creating a sub-division of Dumnonia called, as it turned out, Kerniw/Cornwall.[6] This is reinforced by the fact that, in Susan Pearce's words, 'All the traditions of the royal line of Dumnonia relate to early ancestors firmly rooted in Wales.' In this connection she cites the legendary characters Eudaf Hen, Conan Meriadoc, Helen and Gadeon as being associated in *The Dream of Maxen Wledig* with *Aber Seiont* (Caernarvon) and even citing Geoffrey of Monmouth's description of Eudaf as 'Duke of the Gewissei', suggesting south-eastern Wales and the marches, thus part of Powis, which connection brings us back to the possible origin of Cornwall.[7]

Charles Thomas emphasises the 'cultural poverty' of Dumnonia, in the pre-Roman period at least, which supposition is frequently repeated for the occupation period, drawing parallels with the Demetian peninsula west of Carmarthen. But just as a major Roman road was recently discovered running west from Carmarthen (implying a much further reach of *Romanitas* there), so another has much more recently been identified running 18½ miles (30 km) up the Tamar Valley with adjacent probable Roman sites, a suspected villa at Magor near Camborne and forts at Calstock and Restormel in Cornwall, which suggests an analogous situation in Dumnonia, at least in its more westerly parts.[8] We also know that tin was being worked extensively in Roman times and beyond, which required organisation, supervision and transport. That there was no Roman presence in Cornwall seems highly improbable; it is only that the vestiges of this presence are only now beginning to emerge.

We should perhaps put these speculations aside and accept that, lacking more direct evidence, Cornwall/Cornubia/Kerniw is a largely post-eighth century construct and in the mainly late sources the term really refers to a somewhat shrunken Dumnonia as then constituted. Thomas estimates that the east boundary of the *civitas Dumnoniorum* – thus of Dumnonia – was probably the north-south line marked by the rivers Parrett and Axe.[9] The Wessex Saxons, under Ine, a successor of their apparently British-descended kings, took the western part of the territory of the Durotriges, advanced into Dumnonia and defeated the last king, Gereint II – *Gerent W[e]ale cyning* ('Gereint, King of the Welsh') – as recorded in the *Anglo-Saxon Chronicle sub anno* 710/711, suggesting the victory at Posbury had hardly been decisive. By 722, Ine's successors had apparently reached the Tamar, leaving only modern Cornwall under British control.

That said, Dumnonia might have survived thereafter as a subservient kingdom (or a partially subservient one, as with the minor British polities in Northumbria) for it was not until 823/825 that the *Anglo-Saxon Chronicle* (by this date fairly reliable) mentions the men of Devon as being integrated with Wessex (in fighting the British of Cornwall), so full absorption may have occurred at any time over the century following Gereint's death. It may be ithat Gereint's successors constituted a client-kingdom, ruling as *subreguli* but being gradually pushed into Cornwall. In either case, from the first quarter of the eighth century, Cornwall had probably become a separate entity and remained so until around 872 or even into the tenth century.[10]

Dumnonia as a kingdom may only have developed out of Britannia Prima later in the fifth century, held back through lack of geographical unity, for the relief of the peninsula did not make control by one entity easy and Thomas believes it was probably at first a patchwork of emerging *subreguli* or warlords and indeed may have long remained so, with the king being chosen from amongst them. Alternatively, it may have owed its origin to Collins and Breeze's suggestion (see Chapter 3) that there may have been a late fourth-century military command in west Britain, perhaps under a *comes tractus maritime per Britannias* following the hints given by Ammianus Marcellinus, from which it eventually grew under a post-Roman official undertaking such a role.[11] In either case, fragmentation of the *civitas* and its later cohesion as a larger polity must surely have come about through the gradual loss of control by central authority.

Unfortunately, there are very few sources for reconstructing the political history of the kingdom.[12] This may explain why the genealogies that have survived seem to contain successions of names that are very hard to reconcile one with another. Ken Dark considered that western Dumnonian kingship at least might have arisen from a late Roman devolution of government and security to native hereditary rulers in the manner outlined in the previous two chapters.[13] The suggestion in the two Harleian manuscripts noted by Bartrum that a Roman emperor's daughter – supposedly Gratiana, 'daughter' of Magnus Maximus – married a Dumnonian grandee, gives this some added traction. One problem is that both sources were written down exceedingly late, although they are thought to have been copied from much earlier ones.

Spanning two seas

Professor Thomas ranks the kings of Dumnonia in three categories: historical (identifiable from other sources), like Aldhelm's Gereint; those that are semi-legendary, like Constantine *Gorneu* (*HRB's* 'Constantine of Cornwall') and those he considers entirely mythical: Teudar, Cador, Mark. He adds, following the precepts outlined in the preceding two chapters: 'Whether or not any of their native kings ... were truly descended directly or obliquely from fourth-century usurpers and generals is immaterial ... [but] from an early stage it became desirable to claim as much.'[14]

Not necessarily immaterial though, if we are trying to identify a definite pattern of peripheral areas being placed under the control of imperial appointees, even if it was not necessarily the doing of Magnus Maximus. We seem to be seeing this pattern emerging generally under his aegis; in Dumnonia, it may be a successor in a similar quandary emulating his example, despite a late source actually naming names. As Susan Pearce points out, some of the material in the genealogies resembles portions of the genealogical material relating to Gwent.[15] Indeed, the more one looks at Dumnonia, the more one can spot close relationships spanning both the Severn Estuary and the Channel and the three peninsulas of Demetia/Gwent, Dumnonia and Brittany. For instance, in the story of *Geraint and Enid* in *The Mabinogion* (not historical in any meaningful way), King Ynwyl, by implication a ruler of proto-Gwent or Morgannwg, appears with his court at the deserted Saxon Shore fort at Cardiff. The Geraint of the story is a semi-legendary fifth-century king of Dumnonia.

Thomas suggests that some families may have lived on both sides of the Severn Estuary, quoting the example of an inscribed stone from Newchurch, Carmarthenshire:

SEVERINI FILI SEVERI
('Severinus son of Severus')

There is another at St Breock, Cornwall:

VICAGNI FILI SEVER[I]
('Vicanius son of Severus')[16]

Both are considered to be early sixth century and contemporary, but of course the caveat has to be that Severus, even then, was perhaps a relatively common name, as with *Seferus ap [Cadwr ap] Cadwr Wenwyn*, in the genealogy of Gwerthrynion/Gwy a Hafren, of a probably slightly later date.[17]

There is evidence for a dual polity combining under one rule in the two peninsulas on either side of the Severn Estuary. The genealogy of Rhiwallon (Rigimalus/Ragmialus/Rivalus) associates him with that of Dumnonia and also of Morgannwg (south Wales between Gwent and Dyfed): *Riwal ap Cadovius ap Geraint ap Urbian*. Furthermore, the Breton *Vita* of St Leonor refers to him as 'Chief of the Britons on both sides of the sea' and suggests that he is to be identified with the Rigual who died around 558, according to the *Vita* of the Breton St Brioc, thus extending his putative *imperium* to all three peninsulas.[18] Giot *et al.* point out that although Rhiwallon's name is absent from most of these genealogies, the forebears all match.

His successor Conomorus seems to have been in the same position as a ruler until he later lost his control over Brittany. It is presumed that the regions of Brittany on the north coast, named Dumnonie and Cornouaille, acquired their names at this time, which implies the pushing back of the first use of the Latin name for Cornwall itself to a time two centuries before Aldhelm, unless, of course, these toponyms were applied retrospectively by the copyist.[19] There is further concordance in place names between the insular south-west and Brittany: not only Cornouaille and Dumnonie but also Trigg in Cornwall. This was previously rendered (in Latin) as *Trigorii*, and before that *Tricurius*, and in Brittany we find *Trefgor* (now Tréguier), all of which Charles-Edwards thinks came about in the sixth or seventh century, but not before.[20] An inscribed memorial stone from Rialton (Cornwall) reading F]ILLI TRIBUNI further inclines Professor Thomas to believe that it marked the burial place of a son of Triphun/Tribunus of Demetia, perhaps clerical, and thus a brother of his successor Aircol/Agricola, again suggesting close contacts and even an element of control across the Bristol Channel in the earlier sixth century.[21]

The late *Vita* of St Teilo (based on a ninth-century Breton source) also shows the closeness between the polities lying either side of the south-western approaches of the Channel. In it *Gerennius rex Cornubiensis regionis* (Gerontius, king of the region of the Cornubienses = Cornwall) lay dying and a stone sarcophagus was therefore sent to him, at the request of (St) Teilo, from Brittany. Gerennius was presumably based either at Gerrans, six miles south-west of Truro or perhaps Killa Gerran in Roseland.[22] This closeness is perhaps indicated by the epithet of King Gerennius's probable forebear, Gereint mab Erbin, as *llynghassawc* – 'seafarer'.[23] It is possible to view this close cross-channel co-operation as a continuation of that already flourishing in the days of St Germanus, Faustus and even Syagrius.

Furthermore, the activities of certain saints, like Samson and Paul Aurelian, seem to span the watery tracts and all three land masses. Preceding them was Illtud (Illtut[i]us), an Armorican who was allegedly recruited by Poulentius, a ruler in south Wales, to be his *magister militum* [sic].[24] Unfortunately, the only *vita* we have of him is in the *Book of Llandaff*, written contemporaneously with Geoffrey of Monmouth's *Historia Regum Britanniae*, so little of it can be trusted, although some information can be gleaned from the much earlier (*c.* 600) first *Vita* of St Samson.[25] This tells us that Illtud was a pupil of Germanus at Auxerre, was ordained by him and that he founded a monastic community based on the villa at Llantwit Major, the *Vita Illtuti*. Claims that he was a pupil of St Cadoc of Llancarfan seem unlikely, although Cadoc's hagiographer refers to Illtud as a former *dominus et tribunus*.[26] Illtud and St Samson may well have been acquainted, and St Samson, whose *vita* is much more reliable, was the son of a Demetian with a Roman name, Am[m]on[ius][27] who had married Anna from Gwent, and was a courtier of Aircol of Demetia (see Chapter 8). Having been instructed by Illtud and made a bishop, Samson moved through western Dumnonia preaching. The majority of the population there is not thought to have become Christian until the later fifth or early sixth centuries (thanks mainly to his efforts, presumably). From thence he proceeded to Brittany where he became Bishop of Dol. He was present at the Synod of Paris held some time between 556 and 567. Likewise, St Paul Aurelian, supposedly a relation of Samson and son of a *comes* called *Perphuis* (Porphyrius) based in the emergent polity of Glywissing, later Morgannwg, in central southern Wales. He, too, was a pupil of Illtud, and then of Samson, before also going once again via Dumnonia to Brittany.[28]

Here, as with Coel Hen, the direct connections are obscure. The link with a daughter (Gratiana) of a Roman emperor is our slender lead at this stage. This is a reference which disappears, not being really picked up in the genealogies until one reaches the enigmatic *Chronicle of the Kings of Britain* attributed to Tysilio, but thought by some to *precede* Geoffrey of Monmouth and indeed to have been the 'most ancient book in the British language', given to Geoffrey by Walter, Archdeacon of Oxford, from which he wrought his own work; a notion effectively dismissed by Bryn Roberts.[29] He, too, fails to name the emperor or his daughter, but the child is not Aurbost but Aemilia (or, in *HRB,* Ursula) and the father is Dunawt, King of Cornwall (Donatus).[30] She marries Conan Meridoc, alleged founder of Brittany in the time of Magnus Maximus and according to the *Dream of Maxen Wletic* the emperor's brother-in-law. The only element that stands out here is the name of Dunawt/Donatus, which is absent from any other genealogies relating to Dumnonia and, of course, is the same name as one of the alleged sons of Maximus, who we have suggested in Chapter 9 is Antonius, based securely in the north. Here, there might be a trace element of one of those earlier traditions Dr Russell so convincingly teases out of Geoffrey's text.[31]

If the extract from Harleian MSS 2414 and 1974 quoted above contain anything of value at all, then it is either in underpinning Geoffrey's piece of information, or it has more resonance, and that we should seek elsewhere for the Roman emperor and his daughter. If the MS 1974 is correct, then we have another direct connection with Maximus. The name Gratiana would be perfectly plausible for a daughter born between 367 and 380 assuming she took her name from the Emperor Gratian, whom Maximus only turned against after the latter year. Her husband Tudwal ap Morfawr certainly belongs in the genealogies pertaining to Dumnonia, as he is shown as the great- or great-great-grandfather of Gereint map Erbin, yet the relevant sources are all late and two are Arthurian, clearly deriving from Geoffrey of Monmouth.[32] It is thus necessary to approach the conundrum more open-mindedly.

One character seemingly absent from the British genealogies is Constantine III. Constantine, suggested by Dr Morris as being probably identifiable with

Custennin Fendigaid ('Blessed Constantine') may possibly have been a Briton, but this was implicitly rejected in Chapter 6 and we certainly cannot be sure; no source actually says so, although Constantine's name (albeit relatively common at the period) does recur in the ruling dynasty of Dumnonia.[33] The fact that he is absent from the genealogies – the identification with Custennin Fendigaid being unlikely, as this is usually taken to refer to Constantine the Great – suggests the usurper was almost certainly of non-insular origin. It is with the name Gereint (Gerontius) alternating with Custennin (Constantinus) in the genealogies, that a link is apparent, in that the *magister militum* Gerontius was conceivably a fairly close relation of Constantine himself (and probably also of non-insular origin), despite the possibility that they may have fallen out drastically in 409.[34] There is plenty of precedent for emperors employing close relations (and falling out with them often fatally) and Maximus certainly had close family at court.

We can tell for certain that Constantine had no living wife (or he would have named her Augusta and perhaps issued coins bearing her image), but two certain sons, one of whom, Constans II, was married as after the defeat of rebel forces in Spain in 408, he left his wife and household in Caesaraugusta (Zaragosa) while he returned to Arelate (Arles) where Constantine had his capital. One might assume that they were swiftly dispatched by Gerontius, but this does not necessarily have to have been the case; they could even have escaped to Britain or elsewhere.

A superfluity of Gereints

The usurper in Spain, Maximus (the fourth Roman emperor or claimant to power so named, almost all *tyranni*) is described as the '*domesticus* and dependent' (guard commander and close relative) of Gerontius and is sometimes thought of as his son, which may indeed have been the case. The only reason to doubt it is that if Gerontius was held responsible by the Roman population of Spain for allowing the barbarians in, then why would they have let his son live? The answer may lie in the gratitude of the Vandals, amongst whom Maximus seems to have lived for the eight years between his deposition in September 411 and his re-elevation to the purple a second time in July 419, when showing defiance to a Roman administration which his barbarian supporters felt had not dealt fairly with them. Sozomen, in his description of the deaths of Gerontius and Nunechia his wife, also refers to their close aide, Alanus, who died with them.[35] The passage rather reads as though he might be another close relation, perhaps her brother. If so, Alan[us] is an example of yet another name of some resonance found in the later Breton/Cornish annals, alongside those of Geraint and Custennin.

It is therefore entirely possible, though unproven, that in the attempt to sort out the chaos in Gaul which began in 406/7, these three players – Constantine,

Gerontius and Maximus – were all close kin and that from them or their family, somehow, the shadowy post-Roman rulers of Dumnonia and even of parts of Brittany descended from them.[36] That Constantine or Gerontius might have been a *praefectus*, earlier put in charge of overseeing the transfer of the Conrnovii to what became Cornwall is possible. Needless to say, the traditional British genealogies would have them descend from Eudaf Hen via Conan/Cynan Meriadoc, who was, in their eyes, a brother-in-law of Magnus Maximus, but none of these can be proved to pre-date Geoffrey of Monmouth.[37]

So it may be that the usurper and his entourage had started out as a group of senior officers serving in Britain before 406/407, possibly but not certainly, locally recruited. That a member of the next generation might have married a daughter of Magnus Maximus (or Maximus, the ephemeral emperor of 409-411, or even Constantine III) in that context might seem less unlikely than at first sight.

The dynastic nomenclature on display in these genealogies of Dumnonia might suggest that the daughter's husband was a son (perhaps the Tarraco usurper Maximus himself) of Gerontius, and that the genealogy retrospectively accords him membership of the dynasty of Dumnonia. The daughter of the match, Aurbost, married a man called Eleri son of Dingat son of Nud (all British names), but whose ancestry seems to take us back to one of the men commemorated on the Yarrowkirk stone.[38] If the *magister militum* Gerontius was therefore really an ancestor of the house of Dumnonia, then a brother for Aurbost must be supposed.

We then run up against the fact that there are two conflicting accounts of the dynasty in the genealogies, in that one Gereint (Gerontius) was son of Erbin (Urbanus) and grandson of Custennin Gorneu (Constantine 'of Cornwall') but the other tradition makes the same Erbin a son of Kynvawr (Cunobelinus).[39] While Custennin Gorneu seems to belong to nobody much in one tradition, in the other he is the son of Kynvawr. This Kynvawr, however, appears to be the great-grandson of Cynan/Conan (Meriadoc), supposed founder of the British settlements in Armorica, legendary brother-in-law to Magnus Maximus and son of another elusive character, Eudaf Hen, and thus entirely untrustworthy in this context.

To resolve this, or at least to suggest a resolution, a date is needed. The only one to hand is that of the demise of a Gereint in 501. This is reported in the *Anglo-Saxon Chronicle*:

> 501. This year Porta and his twin sons Beda and Mela came into Britain with two ships at a place called Portsmouth. They soon landed and slew on the spot a young Briton of very high rank.

As it stands, the very unreliability of the *Chronicle* apart, this tells us little. The name Porta looks entirely made up to suit the location, although one son bears a homonym of the eminent Northumbrian historian and cleric of the early eighth century. Nor did Portsmouth then exist, only the shore fort later called Portchester, both of which appear to derive their first syllables from the Roman name of the fort, Portus Adurni.[40] However, the entry is instructive if read with an ancient British poem, the *Marwnad Gereint* ('lament for Gereint'):

> In Llongborth, I saw the clash of swords
> Men in terror, bloody heads,
> Before Geraint the Great, his father's son
>
> In Llongborth I saw spurs,
> And men who did not flinch from spears
> Who drank their wine from glass that glinted...
>
> In Llongborth Geraint was slain,
> Heroes of the land of Dyfneint
> Before they were slain, they slew...[41]

The place is surely Portchester. The alternative, frequently put forward, that this was an encounter between Wessex and Gereint II in the early eighth century at Langport, Somerset. This fails to stand up both on chronological grounds and upon those concerning the place name, being Old English, *langa* (= 'long') + *port* (= 'market' or 'town') as opposed to Latin *longus* (= 'long') + *portus* (= 'harbour').[42] If, then, the *ASC* account of the 'young British man of very high rank' being killed can be taken as the same incident as that in which Gereint of Dumnonia died, then we might risk fixing 'young' Gereint's *floruit* as something like 475-501, although some commentators would have the *ASC* entry a decade earlier, in which case 465-491. It would also allow us to date Erbin as being born about 445/450 and Custennin around 420/425, comfortably making a supposed and unnamed son of Gerontius a contemporary of Constantine III's sons Constans II and the *caesar* Julianus. This Gereint may well have been the prototype for the Gereint in the much later romance *Gereint and Enid*.

He is also assumed by several authorities to have been the 'Gereint of the South' who figures in the early poem *Y Gododdin* about a group of Coelings with their war-bands taking part (to their fatal detriment) in what was probably an internecine battle for control of Catterick (*Catraeth*) in c. 590.[43] This would have been a somewhat later Gereint, possibly a cadet of the house of Dumnonia, occupying his time as a soldier of fortune and hence absent from surviving genealogies. One of these Gereints left his name incorporated in Cornish place names, as with Mark – unless it was the same man who received a sarcophagus from St Teilo.[44]

If we suppose that Custennin was a grandson of Gerontius, the time scale looks about right. However, a much more persistent tradition has it that

Custennin was a descendant in the fifth generation of Cynan Meriadoc son of Eudaf Hen, an arrangement that would make a descent from Gerontius impossible, the persistence of that name notwithstanding, but would make possible a link with Constantine III, if we accept that it was his daughter and not one of Maximus's who married *twysawg Kerniw* – a prince of Cornwall. Yet Kerniw might even in this context really refer to Powis, in which case we may be looking at a garbled echo of Sevira and Vortigern (as a 'prince' of proto-Powis).[45] So far, this theorising has not led us back to any potential appointee of Magnus Maximus, and the number of generations separating the unfortunate Gereint from the usurpation of Constantine III would preclude the Roman emperor's daughter being attributable to Maximus, who seems to be becoming over-endowed with daughters in any case.

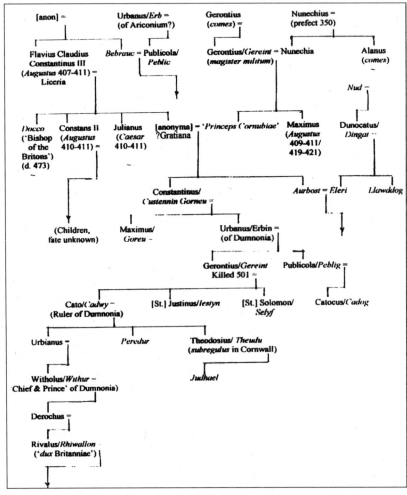

Stemma 8. Dumnonia: a possible reconstruction.

Eudaf Hen

It would be a help if we knew where Eudaf Hen fitted in. The earliest genealogies allow him quite comfortably to have been in mid-career in the mid-fourth century, so having a daughter of the right age to marry Magnus Maximus presents no problems of chronology. Unfortunately, in later genealogies, he becomes inexplicably enmeshed with Constantine the Great, Maximian and events of the early fourth century. Yet, even the earlier references turn up in collections which post-date the *HRB* and echo Geoffrey's text. This calls him 'Octavius Duke of the Gewissae' and King of Britain, in succession to Constantine the Great, whose daughter (nameless) marries Maximian (intended for Magnus Maximus). He is the son of Leolinus – an anachronistic Latinisation of the Welsh name Llewellyn – whose niece, Helen, is daughter of Coel son of Nud (the latter a Celtic god much venerated in Roman Britain as Nodens, best remembered as the dedicatee of a late Roman temple at Lydney in Gloucestershire), conceivably the man named on the Yarrowkirk stone.

Octavius also has a nephew, Conan Meriadoc, and has dealings with Caradoc, Duke of Cornwall and his son, Mauricius.[46] Jesus College MS20 has versions where Maximus marries the daughter of Eudaf, son of Constantine (the Great), repeated in *Bonedd y Saint,* and two in which Gereint son of Erbin is made a descendant of Eudaf Hen, while *Bonedd yr Arwyr* also mentions him four times, but two of these deal with Arthurian characters, which doesn't help, and all cases owe more to Geoffrey than we can be comfortable with.[47] Finally, in the *Dream of Maxen Wletic,* we have a full-blown array of these same characters, Eudaf son of Caradoc, his sons, Conan and Gadeon, along with Helena his daughter whom Maximus marries.

The only earlier mention of someone whose name is cognate with Eudaf appears in Breton sources. In the *Vita* of St Gurthiern, we find that the saint was a descendant of 'Outham Senis', and earlier, a similar descent in the *Vita* of St Goëznovius which, although only known from an early sixteenth-century copy, appears to go back to the very early eleventh century, certainly before *HRB*. This information is echoed in the *Cartulaire de Quimperlé,* which pre-dates Geoffrey of Monmouth by a decade or two as well.[48]

All of this does at least seem to endow Eudaf with a pre-Geoffrey existence, but one still linked with Conan/Cynan, bolstered by an unprovable belief that these characters lie deeply embedded in Breton foundation myth.

> Beli et Kenan duo fratres erant filii Outham Senis. Ipse Kenan tenuit principatum quando perrexeunt Britones ad Romam. Illic tenuerunt Laeticiam...[49]

Here, Beli is an interpolation drawn from British pre-Roman legend, and Outham Senis is widely thought to derive from 'Octavius the old', thus being identifiable with Eudaf Hen. If someone with the fairly mundane name of Octavius Senecio existed either in Constantine the Great's time or under Maximus, it might well have survived corroboratively, in some other source. If it was the name of a British citizen or administrator, it might not; nor can etymologists even be too sure that Outham really did mutate from Octavius.[50] When it comes to scrutiny of the genealogies of Dumnonia, it would seem prudent to discard the entire saga of Eudaf Hen and his kin.

Further continental links

Constantine III is not completely absent from our legendary sources though, for he appears in the *Vita* of St Docco with a wife, Luciria, and an additional son, St Docco, 'Bishop of the Britons', who, we are told, died in 473. He is normally given as son of a Sulien (Solomon), and it would be sensible to discard him in this context for he properly belongs in Gwent.[51] With regards to Luciria, her name opens up interesting possibilities, if it really does represent a nugget of reliable archaic information; we find the name (as Veria Liceria) as the wife of Ausonius, the Gallic courtier-poet's nephew Aemilius Magnus Arborius at precisely that time when Maximus was in Trier instigating changes; Arborius himself had been prefect of the City of Rome in 380.[52] Not only that, but Liceria's *nomen* appears in the mid-fifth century as that of a gallic grandee whose grandson (by the sister of prolific ecclesiastical letter-writer St Ennodius) Flavius Licerius Lupicinus was a man of senatorial rank living in the opening years of the sixth century.[53] When one bears in mind the involvement of high-ranking Gauls in the enterprise of Constantine III, a possible wife drawn from the self-same background looks perfectly reasonable and confirms the contention put forward in Chapter 6 that Constantine was no common soldier but a person of some status (now endowed with important Gallic connections), as were his two short-lived successors, Jovinus and Sebastianus. All of which would explain the relative success of his enterprise before Gerontius took a hand. And if his daughter *was* married to a son of Gerontius, it would even more readily explain the latter's elevation to *magister militum*. Suddenly, we are beginning to see Constantine III, like Maximus, acquiring a legendary presence and at the same time allowing us potential non-legendary insights into him. The only disappointing part, as always, is the fragility of the sources.

Yet if we imagine a son of Gerontius the *magister militum* as remaining in Britain, in a position of responsibility, marrying a daughter of Constantine III (not impossible, in view of the willingness of Gerontius to follow the usurper to the Continent, initially no doubt as a *comes*) and remaining *en poste* in the aftermath of 409 or of his father's death in 411 as *praeses* of Britannia Prima, then he and his progeny might well have ended up embedded in the south-west and wielding ever more influence as central authority weakened as the fifth century progressed. The suggested genealogical table makes these connections and shows how the people on the Dumnonian king-lists/ pedigrees might descend from such a union, complete with a surprising number of Roman names surviving amongst the well-attested revival of British ones. It is important to note that apart from the known sons of Constantine III and the wife of Gerontius, none of these relationships are any more than speculative, although all appear in one of other British genealogies in the relationships shown.[54]

In the case of the suggested fathers of Gerontius and his wife Nunechia however, these are certainly speculative connections added in the light of these being homonymous and chronologically possible. The name on a later, mid-sixth century Dumnonian inscribed stone from Cuby, Cornwall, to one Nonnita, buried with her two brothers, children of a man called Ercilingus, is cognate with Nunechia.[55] Morris also noted that a Gerontia living in the right part of the empire at the right period married a Gallo-Roman from Lutetia Parisiorum (Paris) and was the mother of St Genofra (Genevieve) a woman also blessed by the tireless St Germanus.[56] Furthermore, a Dumnonian woman of senatorial rank (*clarissima femina*) was buried at Salona (Dalmatia/ Croatia) in 425, suggesting little had changed from an imperial perspective.[57]

The first three generations in the table accord with those suggested above with additions: *Pebio/Peblic mab Erb* and his putative spouse.[58] Peibio/ Peblic seems to be a British mutation of the Roman Publicola/Poplicola, a *cognomen* of the patrician Roman house of the Valerii going back into the early Republic; another *cognomen* of the Valerii recurs on an inscribed stone from Lundy (a site of a fifth/sixth century monastic centre) to a probable priest, POTIT[I], in which context St Patrick memorably had a grandfather, also a priest, called Potitus, but the inscription is too late for them to be one and the same.[59] The use of the form 'Poplicola' is confirmed by an inscribed mid-sixth century stone from East Ogwell, Devon, reading CAOCI FILI POPLIC[60] The son's name would appear to have been Ca[d]oc, close to Cato/ Cadwy in the Dumnonian table, but perhaps not actually cognate.

Distinguished Roman names continued to be recorded in Dumnonia, even in the early to mid-sixth century, for at Lanivet (Cornwall) there was found a stone which reads ANNICV FIL[ ][61] This dates from the second quarter of the sixth century, and Thomas notes that the final letter of the name is an error by the carver of '- v' for '- ii', thus 'Annicii', so 'This is Roman Anicius.'[62] This perfectly reasonable suggestion by Thomas would make the person commemorated a scion of the most prominent of all late western Roman families, eminent in Rome itself into the sixth century and in the east and Gaul even longer.[63] If the suggestion made in Part I that a daughter of Maximus married into this family, then a number of the descendants would have been his kin. What a member of the *gens* might have been doing in western Dumnonia at this date is quite beyond recall, yet one has to remember that the high aristocracy of Rome held estates scattered far and wide across the empire.[64]

At the beginning of the fifth century for instance, the newlyweds St Melania and Pinianus, having decided to commit themselves to celibacy, divested themselves of vast estates in Britain and in six other provinces.[65] This is of interest in that St Melania was the daughter of a (Valerius) Poplicola, a senator of immense nobility but little distinction who died around 406 having held only the praetorship, an expensive but empty honour at the time. His uncle was (Valerius) Potitus, *vicarius* of Rome 379-380, and the family went back through one female line (allied with an adoption in the first century AD) to the Valerii Publicolae (which family also used the *cognomen* Potitus) of the very early republic. Could these connections explain the Potitus and Poplicola commemorated later in western Britain? If Melania's estates were situated in that region of Britain, the likelihood of kinsmen acting as local estate administrators bearing their names and continuing on the estate is likely, as suggested in the discussion of villa estates in Chapter 6. More interesting still is the fact that Melania's grandmother of the same name was herself a granddaughter of Antonius Marcellinus and thus first cousin to Bruttia Aureliana (see table, Chapter 8).[66]

Continuing consideration of the genealogical table above, we see that Liceria has already been noted, as has Docco from the same source. Goreu (= 'best', thus surely Latin 'Maximus') appears in Triad 52, and the descent from Custennin Gorneu to Gereint mab Erbin is from the Jesus College MS.[67] Cadwy is the hero of the *Dream of Rhonabwy* in *The Mabinogion* and Morris considers that his area of control had included the *territoria* of both the Dubunni and the Belgae (Dorset, Wiltshire, Hampshire and parts of Gloucestershire) as well as that of the Dumnonii, which seems a leap of faith, if convincing, given the death of his father at Longborth in 501; perhaps he was effectively governor of Britannia Prima by hereditary succession. His brothers appear in *Bonedd y Saint*.[68]

But there is a ghost at the feast: the Constantine, labelled by Gildas 'the tyrannical whelp of the unclean lioness of Dumnonia'. No-one of this name appears at the requisite period, the 530s, elsewhere. It is possible that he may also be the Constantine converted (to Christianity) in 589, although this could just as easily be another of the same name, and not even necessarily a Dumnonian.[69] Clearly it would appear from Gildas that his mother *was* Dumnonian. It may be that his father's *origo* lay elsewhere, yet his name certainly suggests that he belongs within this family grouping somewhere, presumably in the generation of Cadwy. It may be that he had more than one name, in typical late Roman upper-class fashion, and was consequently known to later traditions by a *cognomen*, the connection between the two having been lost.

The general profusion of contradictory names which occur in connection with Dumnonia give the impression that here perhaps was not a single united polity but a number of smaller, rather more fluid ones undergoing much change, rather as is apparent in Breton history at the same period. Thus thereafter, in the suggested *stemma*, the descent from Cadwy to Rhiwallon is drawn from a Breton source.[70] In the *Vita* of St Guenolé, Rhiwallon is Riwal '*dux* of Domnonia' (meaning Dumnonie in Brittany) and as Rigomalus, also appears as ruler of Cornouaille there too, in the earlier to mid-sixth century. In the *Vita* of St Leonor, he is described as 'Chief of the Britons on both sides of the sea', while in another piece of hagiography he appears as 'Rigual who settled in Dumnonie from Britain' around 520 and who died *c.* 558.[71]

Cunomorus/Mark

Rhiwallon appears to have been succeeded on both sides of the Channel by Cunomorus, who appears in the pages of Gregory of Tours, and who eventually lost his Breton possessions.[72] He has been identified with the King Mark of legend, mentioned by the hagiographer of St Paul Aurelian, who is said to have visited 'Marcus Quonomorus', ruler of Dumnonia, who lived at the Villa Banhedos. The *Vita* of St Pol-de-Léon (St Pol and St Paul being one and the same) says much the same, although Susan Pearce was unconvinced, unlike Morris and indeed Giot, who identified him with Gregory of Tours' Conomorus and considered his existence as being 'more than plausible' rather than 'largely legendary', agreeing that the name of Mark can be attached to him. He identifies Ruvarq, near Lanmeur in Brittany, as deriving from *Run Marc*, thus 'Marc's tumulus'.[73] The Jesus College MS identifies him with Kynverch mab Meirchiawn (Cunomorus son of Marcianus), who also had a son called March (Marcus), whom a Triad identifies as 'one of the three navigators of the Isle of Britain' meaning, by 'navigators' owners of boats, which would be an important requisite of anyone enjoying sovereignty on both sides of the Channel.[74] St Samson, having arrived in Brittany, also tangled with him during what appears to have been some kind of dynastic war, and Cunomorus was eventually driven out. We even find mention of Cunomorus acting as a *praefectus* of King Childebert of the Franks, in charge of conducting the crossing from Breton Dumnonie to insular Dumnonia of a bard who had been summoned to play at the Merovingian Court; another reference calls Cunomorus *iudex externus* ('visiting judge').[75] There have been suggestions that in the variant spellings of the name we are dealing with more than one person, a proposition dismissed by Charles-Edwards who considers him a 'Gallo-Roman outsider' living in the 540s and killed around 558.[76] Cunomorus has been fixed in Cornwall too, because of the well-known mid-sixth-century Castle Dore stone, which appears to read (according to consensus, there have been variant readings): HIC IACIT DRUSTANUS [FILI] CUNOMORI.[77]

The name of the person commemorated, Drustanus, is invariably linked to the story of Tristan and Isolde, which appears to have been known in some form in Brittany before the end of the first millennium, which is of great interest in itself but not strictly germane to the present enquiry. That Cunomorus/ Mark was located in Cornwall is doubted by most commentators, although toponyms of some antiquity bear his name in the county, as Carnmarth (= 'Mark's cairn') south of Redruth and Kilmarth (= 'Mark's house/retreat') near Fowey, but the actual antiquity of these is unclear. Another problem is that he does not seem to belong to the dynasty of Dumnonia, raising the suspicion that he should really be associated with southern Wales.[78] Furthermore, another Mark, *March ap Meirchiawn* appears to belong to the dynasty of Coel Hen, which would take him well out of the area, although the Welsh rendering of Cunomorus as Kynvarch is not that rare a name in the genealogies.

The Aurelian House

Mention of Paul Aurelian, who bore a perfectly respectable Roman name, despite the late period (and one never, it seems, transliterated into British) prompts one to look into his possible connections. These, predictably, take us away from Dumnonia and back to south Wales. It was clear from the analysis of the genealogical table (*stemma* 8 above), that there was an enduring legacy of Roman nomenclature in Dumnonia into the mid-sixth century, despite the tendency, seen elsewhere in Britain – especially in the north – for a swift reversion to the use of British names, often drawn or adapted from an heroic past, although quite how the names from that past were preserved through the centuries of Roman control is unclear. Perhaps the élite of the period had Roman authors, like Caesar, available (we know Roman authors were still read) and no doubt, *objets trouvés*, like pre-Roman coins bearing rulers' names.[79] There was an oral tradition of some sort, too, that had made it through almost four centuries, and it should not surprise us if a written source or annal managed to survive then but has since utterly vanished, no doubt consumed in the Saxon Revolt, destroyed by Mother Nature, or by the burning of monastic libraries and missed by collectors during the Dissolution of the Monasteries.

If Paul Aurelian bore a Roman name in the sixth century, what do we know of his antecedents, and could there be another connection to Maxim Wletic? There do seem to be a number of figures called Aurelius or (the adjectival form) Aurelianus, amongst whom Aurelius Caninus, the *catulus leonine* ('lion's whelp') lambasted by Gildas stands out, again in the second quarter of the sixth century.[80] However, we must – perhaps regretfully – temporarily set aside the speculative temptations offered by the late fourth-century matron Bruttia Aureliana and her husband Fl. Vitalinus as being possible parents of Vortigern, set out in Chapter 6. A 'lion's whelp' chimes with Gildas's Constantine, the 'whelp of a ... lioness' (obviously a favourite insult of Gildas) and one might wonder whether there might have been a fairly close relationship being hinted at by him (in one of his more opaque moments), such as that which earlier gave us *superbus tyrannus* instead of naming Vortigern directly as the object of his derision. Conventionally, it is considered that Aurelius Caninus (the *cognomen* may be a Latinisation of Conan/Cynan, both being cognate to 'whelp'/'dog') was a descendant of Ambrosius Aurelianus, whose posterity in his day, Gildas tells us, had 'greatly degenerated from their ancestral nobility'. As we have seen, the early first *Vita* of St Samson when relating the saint's visit to Cornwall, also says that he visited *Marcus quem alio nomine Quonomorum* ('Mark, who is also called Cunomorus').[81] M. Giot and his collaborators add that upon onomastic grounds it would be possible to identify Marcus Cunomorus (accepting that Cunomorus really could be identified with Mark) with Aurelius Caninus: 'The family relationship between St Paul Aurelian and Mark [Aurelius] Cunomorus can be suspected.'[82] Professor Thomas echoes this, but more cautiously: 'In late Roman Britannia Prima, the Aureliani made up a noble family, one with whom both the sub-Roman Ambrosius Aurelianus and Gildas's (unlocated) Aurelius Caninus were presumably connected.'[83]

This seems bold, especially as M. Giot and his colleagues would equip Cunomorus/Caninus with a Roman *tria nomina*, a formula which, although lingering on in North Africa into the seventh century, was largely rendered anachronistic by Caracalla's grant of universal citizenship, the *Constitutio Antoniniana* in 212.[84] Only a handful of very refined grandees in the fifth-century senate continued to use a *praenomen*. M. Giot and his colleagues even float the unlikely suggestion that these Aurelii, Cunomorus especially, were descendants of M. Aurelius Ma[*****] Carausius, the British-based usurper, in power from 285 to 293.[85] While Carausius's name recurs on the sixth-century stone found at Penmachno, in north Wales (see Chapter 1), such an audacious idea surely presses slender evidence to the limit.[86] Despite that, it still seems likely that the Aureliani did indeed 'make up a noble family' in post-Roman Britain, the more the matter is examined.

Meanwhile, to revert to Ambrosius Aurelianus, Pierre Fleuriot along with Miles Russell has suggested that he might well be identifiable with Riothamus, briefly discussed in Chapter 6, which has not met with universal agreement. Riothamus was quite probably brought in through a direct appeal to whoever was in control of Britain by Magnus Felix, the aristocratic new praetorian prefect of Gaul.[87] Chronicler of the Goths, Jordanes, tells us that Riothamus arrived with an army of 12,000 British men in 469 to fight Euric's Goths in Aquitania on behalf of the Emperor Anthemius, making landfall 'in the state of the Bituriges by way of the Ocean' – presumably having arrived at the mouth of the Loire from Britain rather than from Brittany. Gregory of Tours adds that as a result of the conflict the Britons were expelled from *Vicus Dolensis*, near Aviracum (Bourg-de-Déols) by the Goths and that many were killed there. Riothamus therefore, having lost 'a greater part of his army, fled with all the men he could gather, to the Burgundians', who were also fighting Euric in alliance with Anthemius.[88] Having fought some more, they then appear to have lingered in Gaul and caused trouble.

Three years later (around 472) these British detachments are found harassing established landowners in the area, causing Sidonius Apollinaris to write to Riothamus, whom he clearly knew, asking him to bring them under control.[89] Riothamus is referred to by Jordanes as 'king' but this may not necessarily have been his real status. Jordanes tends to call anyone in charge of an ethnically homogenous military group a king, as was the convention of his time when speaking of barbarians. Sidonius, on the other hand, addressed Riothamus as 'friend': no subservience here, nor mention of any title. The implication is that the recipient was perfectly literate to the same standard as the sender. Sidonius went on to state that he would write 'once more in my usual way', emphasising that they were by no means strangers, and his is a fairly warm letter, for he adds, after stating that he is about to pass on a gripe, that 'I do my best to recall the burdensome and delicate sense of honour that makes you so ready to blush at others' faults.'

Soft soap aside, Riothamus's status may have been akin to a *magister militum* or *dux*, acting on behalf of whatever authority in Britain underwrote his enterprise. At this date, he may well have been *sent* by Ambrosius Aurelianus (if he was in control of Britain by then), rather than being identified with Gildas's paragon himself. The alternative is that he was the *tyrannus* of Britain of the time who was invited to help the Roman authorities in Gaul, suggesting that the situation in Britain by this time was both stable and peaceful enough for an expeditionary force to be mounted safely. It surely inspired the continental enterprises of the legendary Arthur in *HRB*.

Some commentators then suggest that Riothamus and his men thereafter settled in Armorica, but this is by no means certain, nor that Riothamus was Breton.[90] He and his remaining men might well have taken service subsequent to their defeat with the newly installed breakaway ruler in the area, Syagrius (see Chapter 6) whose capital was Noviodunum (Soissons) in northern Gaul.[91] We know that British troops had made up part of the forces led by Syagrius at some stage, as after his fall in 486 some still on the loose were defeated by Clovis, king of the Franks in 490. They may have continued in Frankish service, too; there was a *Legio Britannica* stationed at Aurelianorum (Orléans) in around 530, if, that is, we trust the late Breton *Vita* of St Dalmas.[92] This supposition is reinforced by Procopius, writing in 539, who said that even in his time soldiers in Roman uniform, of recognisably Roman units and carrying Roman battle standards, were protecting Gaul on behalf of the Frankish kings there.[93] These units could easily have been the self-same that had once been part of the army of Syagrius. Presumably, the local Gallo-Romans were still pleased to be recruited into a familiar military environment to that enjoyed by their fathers and grandfathers. Some of Riothamus's men *may* have been Breton (or ended up there rather than return to Britain) and it is notable that coins of the emperors Julius Nepos (reigned in the West 474-480) and Zeno (reigned in the East 474-491 and nominally in the West as well from 480), the circulation of which is linked to Syagrius's régime, have been found at Castel Kerandroat, Plesidy, in Brittany.[94]

The fact that Riothamus's army was active within Sidonius's horizons suggests that the Britons were in the most part probably *not* from Armorica, otherwise their continued (and it appears somewhat tiresome) presence would not have been making itself felt in his area three years later, they would have retired to Brittany, easily accessed from Déols, once defeated. Russell,

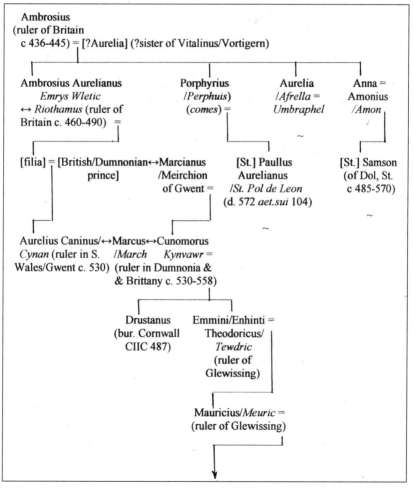

Stemma 9. The possible connections of Ambrosius Aurelianus.

with others, sees the expedition as being a contribution to the empire's efforts to bring stability to Gaul, organised and led through a central authority in Britain. He has suggested that the landing of the alleged Saxon leader Aelle in Sussex, recorded in the *Anglo-Saxon Chronicle* (*sub anno* 477, which would fit the postulation) and repeated by Bede, was actually Riothamus (as Ambrosius Aurelianus) and his army, arguing that the name Aelle, appearing nowhere else, was just the ninth-century chronicler's idea of making sense of a fragmentary and unreadable name of a leader who was in fact a Briton returning from Gaul and having on arrival to put down an insurrection amongst the Britons.[95] The subsequent sack of Anderida (Pevensey shore fort, Sussex) with its heavy casualties, Russell sees as internecine conflict on the part of the Britons masquerading, thanks to the misunderstandings and distortions of four centuries, as part of the Saxon *anschluss* in the south. He notes the *Chronicle*'s use of 'Britons' in this account in lieu of the usual perjorative 'Welsh' and draws parallels with the burning of Vortigern (by the earlier Ambrosius) in the castle of Genoreu recorded in *Historia Brittonum*.[96]

To return to St Paul Aurelian: his *vita* was composed by the Breton monk Wrnonoc around 884, in which we are told that the saint was the son of a *comes* in Demetia whom we have already encountered, called *Perphuis* (Porphyrius), also a good Roman name. Because the name means 'purple', it is reasonable to be taken as denoting a person with imperial connections. Ambrosius Aurelianus's father, according to Gildas, 'undoubtedly wore the purple', so we may have a possible sibling of Ambrosius Aurelianus.[97] For Porphyrius to have named his son Aurelianus would thus make perfect sense from the perspective of late Roman naming conventions. If we bear in mind the audacious suggestion that Vortigern's mother could have been the Roman matron, Bruttia Aureliana, and that the British ruler's great-grandfather and an uncle were both called Paulus, one might be forgiven for thinking that we are irresistibly being drawn to the conclusion that the house of the Aureliani was a reality and was really quite close kin to the family of Vortigern. For the Aurelian name to have passed down, one can only propose that Vortigern/Vitalinus had a sister married to Ambrosius the elder, which would certainly add piquancy to their alleged (but destructive) rivalry that appears to have culminated at the Battle of Wallop.

Porphyrius also had siblings, allegedly nine brothers (presumably adulatory hyperinflation), amongst whom were Notolius and Potolius (surely genealogical doublets, but later separate saints, the latter siring the Breton St Leonor[ius]), along with a sister Sitofolla (St Sidwell).[98] Paul Aurelian became a pupil of St Illtud, and spent time on Bardsey before moving across Dumnonia (specifically Cornwall) to Brittany – hence his supposed visit to Mark/Cunomorus, claimed as a kinsman. An alternative genealogy makes him younger son of Glywys, a *subregulus* of Demetia, made lord of Penychen (Glamorgan), linked by Giot *et al* with Paul Aurelian, but whom most consider a separate Celtic Saint, Paul[in]us. However, Glywys, in the *Vita* of S. Cadoc, Paul's nephew and heir, is given a descent from Maximus through Owein (Eugenius), who was suggested in the previous chapter as a possible early fifth-century (post-409) British *tyrannus*. While it is of interest to note another putative descendant of one of Maximus's appointees, it seems sensible to go along with other commentators and consider this Paul a different person.[99]

St Samson of Dol seems to have been closely related to St Paul Aurelian, too. The *Vita Prima Sancti Samsonis* was copied in the ninth century from a lost original written around 630 and from it we can work out that the saint was born *c.* 480/490, ordained 520/530, made a bishop *c.* 540/550 and was present at the Synod of Paris (held some time between 556 and 573), dying, like Paul Aurelian, at a very advanced age, in the 570s. His father Amon (A[m]monius), like Porphyrius, was also a Demetian *comes*, son of an unnamed courtier of Aircol or Triphun of Demetia (see Chapter 8). St Samson's father was married to Anna 'of Gwent' whose sister Afrella was wife of one Umbraphel, a name which sounds very much like a badly corrupted Roman one.[100] Now the British name Afrella is directly cognate with Aurelia, and it seems likely that they, too, were kin to Ambrosius Aurelianus, like Porphyrius.[101] The *vita* goes on to tell us that St Samson was a cousin (*consobrinus*) of Iudual Candidus, a Breton prince and son of none other than the Dumnonian-born Rhiwallon of Brittany.[102] Thus, this moderately reliable source provides the *gens Aurelia* with a base in Gwent, suggesting that Venta Silurum (Caerwent, Monmouthshire), or the territory round about, was closely associated with it. It may be that the continued expansion of the villa at Chedworth (see Chapter 6) was associated with them. However, if we are talking about the same dynasty that provided us with the two Ambrosii, then they may have had property much more widely scattered, perhaps in Gaul, which might explain the British authorities' willingness to risk a continental expedition against the Visigoths in the 460s (albeit probably in exchange for a subsidy, as suggested by the lost silver ingots in the Thames bearing Syagrius' name. These people were living at exactly the period of the Battle of Badon and this same expedition to Gaul. If there was a familial link to Vortigern/Vitalinus, then the two dynasties had their core territories in relatively close proximity.

Yet we do not know from where these Aurelii sprang. The British genealogies only mention Ambrosius (as *Emrys Wletic*), his family inextricably intermixed with the kinsfolk wished on him by Geoffrey of Monmouth. Only in the *Historia Brittonum* and in Gildas do we find Ambrosius Aurelianus, and even in the former, we find that he is becoming a figure of enchantment, emerging fatherless from a world of magical events. In some ways, this probably reflects the truth, in that he appears, miraculous events aside, as a 'fatherless boy' (because, as Gildas attests, the Saxons had killed his parents) and later he tells Vortigern, who comes across quite clearly as a pagan, that his father was 'one of the consuls of the Roman people', which is a garbled version of Gildas's account of Aurelianus.[103]

The fact that in this account the parents are dead (or at least the father), suggests this could reflect earlier knowledge that Vortigern outlived Ambrosius *père*, in which case, the suggestion that Ambrosius the elder prevailed over Vortigern at the battle at Wallop in 436/7 would need to be revisited. Yet the story here seems almost too fantastic to be relied upon. This lack of Emrys as a character embedded in the later genealogies only goes to emphasise the wide insular role he seems to have enjoyed, perhaps with an origin beyond the shores of Britain in the wider Roman world. Vortigern, whose family origins may have been similar, seems to have a strong presence in some genealogies but simply because his family had that link with the future kingdom of Powis via Maximus's daughter Sevira/Severa. And of course, he was reviled as the man who allowed the Saxons to settle and then run amok.

Ambrosius's same lack of surviving genealogical connections (or remotely reliable ones) goes for others proposed as amongst the hard-pressed *tyranni* who we have proposed strove to keep Britain on an even keel in the fifth century. Those such as Owein/Eugenius, the 'son' of Maximus and to some extent, Vortigern. Arthurians must accept the same for their hero, also completely absent from the pre-Galfridian genealogies. Ambrosius's lack of other connections has suggested to some that Ambrosius might have been a kinsman of Magnus Maximus's ecclesiastical adversary St Ambrose, although Guy Halsall goes further and suggests he may have been conflated with the bishop himself by Gildas and thereby have entered British historical tradition, emphasising that St Ambrose was also called Aurelius. For this assertion there is no attestation. The bishop was born the son of another Ambrosius, in 340 Praetorian Prefect of Gaul. The latter is unattested outside Paulinus the deacon's *vita* of Ambrose, which, however, is generally regarded as reliable – no hagiographer, Paulinus. It is not unusual to encounter Roman officials attested just once.

The alternative suggestion, that he was son of one Uranius, a provincial governor to whom the emperor sent a rescript in 339, is less convincing. Uranius was almost certainly an eastern official, and we are sure that Ambrosius was born in Trier, where his father was based. There is no evidence to preface the bishop's name with 'Aurelius', which is an error based on the eulogy he himself delivered at the funeral of his brother Uranius Satyrus, whose name clearly inspired the suggestion that the eastern official of that name was Ambrosius's father. He said, 'you were summoned home by the noble Symmachus, your parent (*parens*)...'[104] In this context *parens* does not imply a blood relationship, but friendship and patronage. Thus Q. Aurelius Symmachus, Ambrosius's eloquent and distinguished adversary in the dispute – partly carried on under Maximus's rule – about the removal of the pagan Altar of Victory from the senate house at Rome, was without doubt a friend and possibly, in terms of *clientelae*, a mentor. They were both born in the Gallic prefecture (Trier and Bordeaux respectively), Ambrose having been a provincial governor prior to elevation to his bishopric and may, of course, have been kin, but it is not certain.

In any case, both St Ambrosius's siblings, the senator Satyrus and Marcellina died without issue.[105] Although the Aurelii Symmachi can be traced as senators back until the time of Constantine, they are tolerably well recorded and any line of descent from them in Britain seems on the face of it unlikely, in contrast to the clutch of possible Valerii and Anicii in Dumnonia.[106]

That Ambrosius Aurelianus's *imperium* was widespread rather than localised, surely explains the use of his name not in British genealogies of the frontier parts of the island but as a leading element of a surprising number of settlements, localities and earthworks from the South Midlands to the Cotswolds and Wiltshire, which Morris suggested were places garrisoned against Anglo-Saxon attack by units raised by Aurelianus from his own estates and *clientelae* and, in late-Roman military style, bearing his names, such as *Ambrosiani*. Morris uses the example of the senator Ecdicius in Nemetum (Clermont) who did just that to help beat off a Visigothic attack in 471, just after the failed effort to do likewise by Riothamus.[107]

Ecdicius was a son of the emperor Avitus (455-457) and the brother-in-law of Sidonius Appollinaris, thus suggesting a strong cultural link with Riothamus at least, much strengthened if it is accepted that the latter was one and the same as Ambrosius Aurelianus in the first place.[108] Indeed, Ecdicius was a descendant of a late fourth-century Gallic grandee (who may have been mixed with Magnus Maximus's régime during his time in the sun) called Philagrius, a name that, corrupted, could easily have mutated to form the final syllable of Umbraphel – St Samson's uncle – better still had he borne the *nomen* Umbrius, well attested from the third century.[109] Place-name studies have long denied this association of Ambrosius with places like Ambrosden (Oxon.), Ambersham (Sussex) and Amesbury (Wilts.), most suggesting that the '*ambros-*' element is merely Old English for a bunting or a yellowhammer, or that it represents an unattested name.[110] Place name experts have been particularly slow in acknowledging that recent scholarship has left little doubt that the assimilation of Britain into a full-blown Saxon cultural social framework was more gradual than previously supposed, although Watts does at least admit the possibility of some at least of these names having a link with Ambrosius.[111]

Apart from in Kent and East Anglia, British culture was dominant until the mid-sixth century and was so a lot longer in the north and north-west. There seems little doubt as to Ambrosius Aurelianus's stature as one ruling the whole island, as had his predecessors, including his own father. Who might have preceded him in the immediate aftermath of the Saxon revolt and who followed him, before the gradual post-Gildasian break-up of the

British-ruled parts of Britain into fractious smaller polities, frittering away resources on internecine and dynastic strife, is something that can be left to the Arthurians. Through it all, at least until the years following Badon, with the internecine strife condemned by Gildas, the fundamental unity of Britain seems to have survived as a fragile perpetuation of the late-Roman state, semi-autonomous chunks of Germanic held parts notwithstanding.[112]

The British sources merely know Ambrosius as *Emrys Wletic* ('the lord Ambrosius'). Nowhere are his antecedents mentioned, except the post-Galfridian genealogies which make him son of Custennin Gorneu, *alias* Custennin Fedigaid (usually to be understood as Constantine the Great), yet such unlikely associations notwithstanding, his family, by the late fifth century (if these people are indeed his family) seems ubiquitous in the Dumnonian, Demetian and Gwentian spheres of influence. If Aurelius Caninus – equally elusive in the British sources and therefore possibly a successor as a *tyrannus* claiming hegemony over Britain rather than a regional eminence, like most of Gildas' targets – was really Ambrosius Aurelianus's descendant, as Gildas suggests (but fails to state directly), then the concentration of characters who appear to belong within this nexus in the estuarine south-west is explicable. Even the place where the *Historia Brittonum* claims the young Ambrosius was discovered by Vortigern's agents, Maes Ellefi ('Ellefi's field') 'in Glywysing' fits, in that the polity so-called was that which lay between Gwent and Demetia,[113] Note, too, that John Koch reminds us that Glywys, who was the eponym for this shadowy kingdom (and also largely absent from the British genealogies), derives from *Glevenses*, people from Glevum – the very place at which the *Historia Brittonum* places Vortigern/Vitalinus's ancestors.

The Armorican link

Much of Dumnonian history seems inextricably intertwined with that of Brittany, and its importance to this enquiry was in that very aspect, as the connection in the British sources was the foundation of Brittany by settled elements of Magnus Maximus's army, made up of British veterans and led by a *comes* called Conan, the brother-in-law of Maximus himself, and son of the enigmatic Eudaf Hen.

We can neither confirm the Breton foundation legend, nor can we pin Conan down in any sufficiently early source. The archaeology is against it too, with late Roman military accessories, for instance, straddling the Saxon shore, with some diagnostic items found in both Portchester and Oudenburg shore forts, with others following the late Roman army along the north-eastern continental *limes,* but precious little in Armorica.[114] As a result, we are obliged to fall back on the attested migration from Britain to Armorica of the mid-fifth century.[115]

Substantial movement seems to have taken place as a result, Gildas suggests, of the supposed revolt in Britain of the Saxon *foederati* brought in by Vortigern to help protect the island from raiding in the aftermath of the end of direct Roman rule.[116] The British rather than Latin language was prevalent in sixth-century Brittany because settlers there had come from less Romanised and less Latin-speaking parts of Roman Britain, the south-west and Wales, underlining the fact that they were probably originally recruited in Britain as troops, not refugees, perhaps as elements of Riothamus's army. Troops brought over in 383 would have been predominantly Latin speaking.[117] But if this migration, as is often averred, took place as a result of the Saxon revolt, then why were the exiles from part of Britain believed, on secure grounds, to have been unaffected by that upheaval? As we have seen, one theory is that they were fleeing coastal raids made by Picts and Irish *Scotti,* known to have marauded upon the coasts of Wales and the south-west. If that is so, then the transplanting of elements of the Cornovii to the south-west must have been singularly ineffective, despite the fact that the name stuck.[118]

Evidence for fifth-century migration to Armorica extends beyond archaeology. If the bishop Charito who attended the Council of Angers in 453 can be equated with Bishop Mansuetus 'of the Britons' who appeared at the Council of Tours eight years later (their names essentially mean the same thing, although this has been questioned), we have evidence of British ecclesiastical organisation in Brittany, unless Charito was from Britain itself.

Thus, with the developing history of Brittany converging with that of Dumnonia, and with the added ingredient of the Gwentian/Glevensian Aurelian family intermixed, to avoid looking at the problems thrown up by the three peninsulas and the two seas is unjustifiable. Yet, when all the evidence is reviewed, we can say nothing positive about the veracity of the Breton foundation legend, which depends so heavily on the story of Maximus as epitomised in the really very late *Dream of Maxen Wletic.* In part I, it was acknowledged that the emperor certainly had an empress, and that she could easily have been called Helen, but there is no contemporary evidence for it, let alone for her father and siblings. The presence in British legendary sources of St Helena, the attested wife of Constantius Chlorus (who campaigned in Britain and died there), in several different genealogical contexts, along with Helen of Troy and Helen 'of the Hosts' (who was associated with the Sarn Elen, the north-south road in Wales and who would appear to have been derived from an ancient deity) complicates the matter hugely. It explains the hybrid origin of Maximus's empress according to the *Dream.*[119] Yet Rachel Bromwich makes the interesting observation that the Welsh tale of Maximus, Helen and Conan, not older than the latter half of the twelfth century as it stands, is entirely uninfluenced by Geoffrey's account of Maximus's marriage, where again, we are not even vouchsafed the empress's name and there are no mentions of Segontium (Caernarfon) either, a place which looms so large in the *Dream*. She observes of Geoffrey: 'Though his account of her antecedents may in some respects preserve a trace of an older and more authentic tradition with respect to her identity, yet it is quite clear that he knew nothing of the Welsh figure of Elen Luyddog.'[120]

It would be rewarding to be able to identify this tradition for, without it, we still do not know for sure the name of the empress; one has however, the sneaking suspicion that she might well have been British.

The stole of St Paul Aurelian, preserved at the Cathedral, St Pol-de-Leon, Brittany. (Wikimedia Commons)

11

'Owein Son of Maxen' and Lowland Britain

Not only did Gereint 'of the South' fight at Catraeth in *c.* 603, but so did another character, Isag (Isaac[i]us), also 'from the regions of the South'.[1] Yet we have no idea exactly from whence he came, although Harleian MS 3859 gives us *Isaac map Ebiaun* (Einyawn/Einion) *map Mouric* as a descendant of Dunawt (Donatus), alleged son of Cunedda and one of the probable Roman appointees sent to strengthen the western littoral of north Wales; the descendants were rulers of Dunoding, the eponymous polity, later absorbed by Gwynedd, although north Wales, even in the context of Catraeth, seems hardly 'the south'.[2]

Lowland British polities

The existence of post-Roman polities away from the frontier zones is only hinted at in our sources. Yet it is likely that after the period of calm following Badon, central authority gradually began to break up, and even in lowland Britain some polities were formed. As by the second quarter of the sixth century German settlement (probably achieved by orderly means under British control at first) was fairly widespread in the lowland zone, these polities, although Romano-British in origin and related geographically to former tribal *civitates*, were quite probably mostly Germanic or at least soon taken over by Germanic leaders, either as a result of marriage alliance or by force. It is likely that the Anglo-Saxon kingdoms we later know as the Heptarchy had some kind of British origin. And, as has been suggested earlier, the process was quite separate from the vicissitudes of the British polities of the frontiers and would not have been conducive to record keeping, the preservation of annals or even of oral transmission, even if there had been a relatively smooth transition from British polity to a nascent Anglo-Saxon kingdom. The late antique habit of bureaucracy probably withered before the more direct administrative methods of a pagan Saxon warlord.

Hence records, legal documents and archives were lost, as well as any annals and genealogies, which survived in great numbers, probably orally transmitted at first, amongst the frontier peoples. There was unlikely to have been a bardic tradition amongst the élite of the Romanised lowlands, which is one of the reasons why those elusive heroes so dramatically brought to life by those such as Geoffrey of Monmouth have so little contemporary factual and genealogical underpinning.

The north, north-west, Wales and Dumnonia may have been previously designated frontier areas established by treaty, being those locations most vulnerable to barbarian penetration and raiding. There were probably no subdivisions of central control elsewhere, except perhaps as reflections of the old remaining four provinces, as Valentia fell within the re-ordered frontier. Maxima Caesariensis with its capital London, Britannia Prima (consisting of all or part of the south-west and non-frontier Wales), part at least of Britannia Secunda and Flavia Caesariensis (comprising approximately the Midlands) would have been under direct diocesan control, perhaps at first under governors. With parts of the lowlands gradually coming under Anglian, Saxon and Jutish occupation, quite possibly by treaty, this single polity may well have tended to splinter.

We need to find the beginnings of this process, noting any further light that might be shed on post-Roman Maximus, for a legendary son seems to have become inextricably linked with the immediate aftermath of the crisis of 409. Some threads need to be teased out. Mixed up with the relatively early stories of the loss of Thanet and later of Kent, we hear of Gwynangon, British 'king' of Kent being dispossessed because of Vortigern's policy of settling Germanic migrants there, seemingly as *feodorati*.[3] He was surely an appointed official, though, only a king to later Welsh chroniclers, who assumed a man with authority over a large tract of land must by regal. His name may be a mutated British form disguising a Roman one (the first element in Welsh means 'white'), and he represents a period of upheaval that Alcock saw as leading to the collapse of the *civitas* capital, Canterbury, weakening Christianity in the east and south-east; there would have been no remaining British Christian congregations to welcome St Augustine's mission in 597.[4]

This argument is to a certain extent undermined by considerable numbers of coins of Honorius recovered at Canterbury with significant wear. There is also the survival throughout of the name of the Iron Age Cantii as the name of the later county and as an element of that of the principal city, the existence of the church there dedicated to St Martin – thought to have been continuously in use from the late Roman period and still containing much re-used Roman material in its fabric – and the various *eccles* elements (from Latin, *ecclesia*, Welsh *eglwys* = church) in local place names.[5] The 'exceptionally large and important' villa at Eccles in Kent seems, significantly, to have been partly adapted as a house-church in its later phase, with an early Anglo-Saxon cemetery adjacent, although this is played down in the report of 2021, which notes a decline in the quality of the villa's use, and quite a few burials appear to be earlier than the Germanic cemetery.[6]

The Medway valley has an unusually large number of place names incorporating British elements, that of the villa being pre-eminent. Wickham, Chatham, Chattenden and Upnor are all cited in this context by Jillian Hawkins.[7] Even the Saxon-sounding Aylesford, alleged site of a famous fifth-century battle, seems to include a British *eccles* element, being recorded in 959 as *Æglesforda*. Hawkins sticks to other commentators' preference for a notional Germanic name, here Egil, but one might note Eagle Tor at Stanton-in-Peak, Derbyshire, marking an *eccles* name deriving from a very early church site, thus here one is much inclined to suspect *eccles* + old English *-forda*. Such names also appear in the territory of the South Saxons, too, as in the river Ecclesbourne and Eccleston Manor (Angmering),[8] as well as Ecchinswell (Hants.) from *Domesday Book* there, *Eccleswell* and a stream (a tributary of the Enborne) also called *Ecclesburna* in 931.[9] Furthermore, Canterbury is the only former *civitas* capital to have retained it tribal suffix rather than its Roman name and the evidence would suggest extensive British survival in Kent, the dominance of Frankish *magistri militum* notwithstanding.[10]

Bede reminds us that St Martin's Church Canterbury was a late Roman foundation where the Frankish Queen Bertha used to pray, prior to the arrival of St Augustine; he also tells us that the local cult of St Sixtus, an unattested British martyr (thus presumably a Sextus originally, rather than the Greek name), survived until it was suppressed, mainly out of confusion with Pope Sixtus II (martyred in 258), by St Augustine.[11] Substantial British Christian populations survived within the expanding Anglo-Saxon areas of the late sixth and early seventh centuries, but according to Bede, they did not attempt to evangelise their Saxon masters – surely they were in no position to do so; indeed there may still even have been a preponderance of pagans amongst them. We have no other information upon which to take a view one way or another.

Central lowland Britain

British continuity in the fifth and sixth centuries in eastern, southern and middle Britain is argued for by Ken Dark. In the early sixth century there seems to have been a long-enduring enclave of considerable extent around London, however much reduced. Maxima Caesariensis may have been the origin of this region, although, as the later factious tendencies began to take hold, the units which emerged in lowland Britain seem to have most closely followed the *territoria/pagi* of the *civitates*. Yet variations in burial and other practices, like settlement and pottery in the northern Thames basin (an area with a dearth of furnished burials and Saxon *grübenhauser*) would seem to add credence to the idea that this area may have formed a substantial Romano-British enclave long after the collapse of central authority, perhaps a fading penumbra of that authority. This seems underpinned by a distinct ethno-political identity possibly referred to in later British sources as Calchfynydd (= 'chalk hills').[12] Whether Calleva Atrebatum (Silchester, Hants.) was included in this area, we cannot be sure, but it has produced fifth-century glass and its *territorium* seems to be bounded by sub-Roman earthworks. And the well-known fifth-century Ogham-inscribed stone was found there in the well of insula LX in the early twentieth century.[13]

Verulamium (St Albans. Herts.) lay well within this enclave, even into the seventh century, as evidenced by the entry in the *Tribal Hideage* of *Cilternsaete* ('The people of the Chilterns'). St Albans was still developing in the early fifth century and, of course, we have seen how St Germanus headed there to see the shrine of a saint. Houses were still being built and rebuilt in the very late fourth century and mosaics patched; a hoard of 159 late fourth- or early fifth-century largely unworn *solidi* was discovered in 2012. Low level habitation began to assert itself, but the town was still occupied well after 450.[14] One house added an extension with a mosaic floor and hypocaust in the fifth century, just as the Chedworth villa did, but was thereafter demolished and replaced by a large stone hall measuring 111ft x 46ft (34 x 14m) to which a timber water pipe was added.[15] Water supply was maintained, as were the streets. A Christian cemetery 500 yards (457m) outside the city wall door of the Abbey (probably around the site of St Alban's grave), remained in use from the third to the sixth centuries. Roman buildings were extensively re-used and there were still people living in the Roman town according to Abbey's *Chronicle*, possibly even into the twelfth century, long after the foundation of the present (upper) town.

A late Roman basilica recently uncovered close to the present cathedral has been hailed as the 'oldest continuous site of Christian worship in Great Britain'. Certainly, in later legend, St Cadog, a descendant of Owein Finddu – possibly Britain's first diocese-wide ruler after 409, the saint being fifth in descent from Owein via Peblic's supposed brother Nor – was killed, presumably by Saxons, while building a church in *Calchfynydd* in around 580. As this means 'chalk hills', it has been supposed to have been in the Chilterns, but in truth could just as well have been in Wiltshire.[16] Possibly Verulamium, Britain's only formal Roman *municipium*, may be identifiable with the *Cair Muncip* in the list of twenty-eight cities in *Historia Brittonum*.[17] Cadog's church may be identifiable with the later Roman church of St Alban and traditions associated with it, according to Bede, implying a population which included a significant British element. A new monastery was established by King Offa of Mercia seventy years after Bede wrote.[18] At Dorchester-on-Thames (Oxon.), further west, late coinage was also abundant; official payments and provision of small change seem to have been maintained to a much greater extent than elsewhere, possibly to pay mercenaries.

As pointed out earlier, absolutely nothing appears to survive regarding the names of the people who dominated this or most other lowland British polities; unlike in the north and west, the descendants seem to have stayed put and thus ensured that historical material – proto-legendary, historical, genealogical or otherwise – was lost in the gradual Germanic takeover of lowland Britain. It did not survive to be integrated into the corpus of British material preserved in Welsh via British from the north and west. This explains why Owein, Emrys Wletic (Ambrose) and other apparently prominent figures fail to show up in later genealogies: this was their heartland, later utterly transformed and with memories and all records lost. We cannot connect any of these polities directly or indirectly with any settlement made by Maximus or his immediate successors in the diocese. Nevertheless, they are an important element in the narrative lying between the Maximus of history and the Maxim Wletic of British tradition.

While the *civitates* formed the more easily controlled local polities of lowland Britain, as central authority crumbled, they do seem to have been prone to subdivision, some prior to the lapse in imperial control, some later. The division of the *pagi* (wider areas of control) of the *civitates* shows this, for instance when the territory of the Durotiges was partitioned between Durnovaria (*Durngueir*, Dorchester, Dorset) and Lindinis (Ilchester, Somerset) in the late third century. That of the Corieltauvi, formerly centred upon Ratae Corieltauvorum (Leicester), seems also to have been split, Margidunum (Castle Hill, Bingham, Notts.) emerging as the *civitas* of the eastern part of the *pagus*.[19] While Saxon takeover of the *civitas* area of the Durotriges, if we are to believe the *Anglo-Saxon Chronicle*, took place in the mid-seventh century, Charles-Edwards has speculated that from the rarity of early furnished burials of the type common in the south-east, there could have been a mid-fifth-century Germanic over-running of the area, reversed by the British within a generation or so and only rolled back again later.

Professor Charles-Edwards also emphasises that there may have been a distinction between conquest and actual settlement whenever we see these 'milestone' dates in the *Anglo-Saxon Chronicle*. Thus, even if 658 *did* mark a Saxon advance over much of the *territorium* of the Durotrigian *civitas*, a British polity may well have survived in the area of Dorchester (as exemplified by a possible British monastic community at Poundbury) and south to Purbeck, a supposition strengthened by the Wareham (Dorset) British inscribed stones, a rarity in the south, midlands and east of Britain (but who knows how many others may lie concealed in the fabric of parish churches in England?). These four were discovered embedded in the fabric of the parish church during demolition of the Saxon nave in 1842.[20]

Davey suggests that the Durotrigian *civitates* 'were in a strong economic position' at the end of Roman rule and points to an agricultural surplus identifiable in the area, which would have enabled long-distance trade and exchange, thus bringing in luxury goods, like North African pottery, continental wine and oil. He suggests that the Durotrigian *civitas* was able to assume some regional authority following the likely breakdown of central control early in the sixth century, hence probably the re-occupation of Cadbury Castle, South Cadbury.[21] Further north, Bath Abbey was founded by the Saxon St Osric in 675 and while flooding, lack of maintenance and the removal by metal scavengers of iron and bronze clamps from the fabric had forced the closure and collapse of the baths themselves in the earlier fifth century, the remainder of the town appears to have continued in some form until at least 973 when King Edgar was crowned there.[22]

The puzzling origins of Wessex

This whole area of Britannia Prima, according to Higham, was divided by the treaty implied by Gildas, post-Saxon revolt, along a line Wales-West Midlands-Chester and south of the Severn, with a Saxon-controlled area in the upper Thames Valley, as supposedly attested by the presence of late Roman troops at Dorchester-on-Thames, although this rather flies in the face of the Gewissei being a British grouping in this locality. The cosmopolitan nature of the evidence from a wide variety of lowland burials indicates these groupings were not racially homogenous.[23] Later, this Germanic-dominated area must have included Wight (allegedly conquered by the picturesquely named Stuf and Whitgar), and later still the *territorium* of the Dobunni, centred upon Corinium (Cirencester), the very heart of Britannia Prima, and from the early eighth century, Dumnonia. In a battle of 626, the rampant Northumbrian ruler Eadwine defeated and presumably killed Cuichelm, a probable Wessex usurper, whose demise may (Higham thinks) have ushered in a completely new Wessex dynasty and for a while slowed the expansion of his polity. He suggests that it may be that the 626 conflict led to the *Cerdicingas*, as British *subreguli*, seizing power in Wessex in the chaos under Eadwine's protection and maintaining it thereafter, creating Wessex proper. This would explain the dual and unusually unsatisfactory Wessex origin myth and the diverse genealogies of its ruling house.[24]

While the origin of Wessex as it comes down to us through the distorting prism of the *Anglo-Saxon Chronicle* appears to have no relevance to the afterlife of Magnus Maximus, it presents an anomaly which might throw light on other origin legends concerning emergent polities in the diocese. Central to the story is this grouping called the Gewissei. They are mentioned by Bede and after that by Geoffrey of Monmouth (in the shape of Eudaf

Hen, Maximus's fictional father-in-law, styled as their 'Duke'), which might appear an unpropitious start.[25] What does it mean? Is the term cognate with Gwent, which derives from the Latin Venta Silurum? Russell wondered if Gewisse was cognate with 'allies', perhaps in the form of the proto-West Saxons. It is clearly not originally the same thing as Wessex, but the Welsh courtier Bishop Asser in the tenth century did equate the two and later, in Geoffrey of Monmouth, they certainly become so. More to the point, it seems to originate with a British term, which gains traction because the earliest dynasty of Wessex begins with a man carrying a thoroughgoing British name: Cerdic (Caractacus/Caradoc). That Cerdic is said in *ASC* to have led an *adventus* of Germanic settlers, when clearly a British leader, betrays the essential unreliability of *ASC* for the period and the spin it places on some events.[26] Cerdic's ancestry makes him son of Elesa son of Elsa (these two quite possibly a doublet) son of Gewis (the eponym) and thence back, via names doubtless grafted on later and more obviously Germanic, to Woden.[27] Several other British names occur amongst Cerdic's posterity:

Saxon name	(= British/Welsh equivalent)
Cynric	(= Cynwrig/Cunorix)
Ceawlin	(= Collen)
Cedda	(= Ceada/Siat)
Caedwalla	(= Cadwallon/Catguollaun)
Ceol[a]	(= Coel/Coelius)
Cynegils	(= ?Ceingair)
Cuthwine	(= Cathen)[28]
Cenwalh	(= Cynwal)

These names appear to be all of British rather than Teutonic derivation.[29] However, as Kirby shows, the early dynastic history was heavily sanitised by the later Wessex chroniclers and was clearly fragmented in the earlier phases of the kingdom's development, with discrete elements expanding from Dorchester-on-Thames (the Gewisse), Wiltshire and Winchester, almost certainly under different dynasties. It looks very much as if, with central authority in Britain weakening, a British-led war band was fighting to establish control of a large tract of southern England. The idea that Cerdic landed on the south coast in 495 (or 514) and succeeded to kingship in 519 is probably two decades too early and in any case likely a complete fiction.[30] Had the genealogy been concocted by chroniclers in, say, the ninth century, these generations would have been provided with Germanic names; so a much earlier king-list underlies them.[31]

Leslie Alcock, calculating back generationally from the fixed and certain date of the baptism by St Birinus of Cynegils in 634 (a date he saw as deriving from an Easter table and thus more reliable than most) gives *c.* 523 as the date of Cerdic and Cynric's 'landing' (rather than 495/514). Perhaps the battle of

Badon kept Cerdic and his allies stuck on the coastal strip for decades; perhaps Cerdic participated in it.[32] But then, if Cerdic was a Briton (and presumably a pagan one, as his successor Cynegils required baptism in 634), who were his supporters and on which side would he have fought at Badon in any case?

If Germanic migrants did settle in the late fifth and early sixth century along the central part of the south coast of Britain, then their appearance may have been linked to Syagrius and then Clovis in Gaul, who had both fought successfully against the Saxon enclaves on their northern coast and driven them away, quite probably across the Channel.[33] Thus the war-band of Cerdic may have comprised Saxon mercenaries.

This strong British thread in the supposed first dynasty of Wessex being as it appears, the concordance of a number of names on show with those in certain British genealogies can be overstated. Matthews, for example, asks if Cerdic is in fact Caradoc Vreichvras, the name of his descendant Ceawlin, a Christian, having prompted reference to St Collen, a supposed descendant of Caradoc Vreichvras in the fourth generation, just as Ceawlin was a descendant of Cerdic in the third generation. Yet Bartrum points out that the authentic tradition relating to the saint's ancestry in *Bonedd y Saint* has him son of Petrawn (Petronius) son of Coledauc son of Guynn (Coleddog ap Gwynn).[34] Generally, Caradoc Vreichvras is supposed to have been the progenitor of the dynasty of Morgannwg.[35] More likely, as Russell suggests, Cerdic might more closely equate with Geoffrey of Monmouth's egregious 'king' of all Britain, Keretic, whose misrule accelerated the final decline of Britain. He was a 'fomentor of civil discords' who used Saxon federates against an attack by the 'Affricani' from Hibernia (presumably Attacotti?), and was perhaps therefore the last of the post-Roman *tyranni*.[36]

Either way, the Cerdic claimed by the House of Wessex was most probably a British dynast of the Gewisse locked in a war of mutually assured destruction with his fellow Britons, while Saxons, perhaps in alliance with him, took the opportunity to expand from the coastal areas in the 530s under the leadership of his family. After a battle at Wodensbarrow (*ASC* 592), Ceawlin was driven out and within five years or so the much more Saxon sounding Coelwulf had established himself. Yet a generation later and the *Cerdingas* had regained dominance (supposedly in 626) only to lose it completely later to the family of Ecgberht. Russell asks whether it is possible that the Saxon dynasties of southern England were similarly established upon very British foundations.[37]

The Hwicce and Midland Britain

Another of the possible British elements subsequently absorbed into Anglo-Saxon origin stories like the Gewisse and also caught up in the saga of the formation of Wessex was a group called the Hwicce, mentioned by Bede and located in the south-west midlands and in the territory in which Bath lay, according to *Historia Brittonum*, which calls the city Badon.[38] The name Hwicce is a mutation of British *gwych* ('excellent'), through the *HB's Huich*. So a British origin, like the Gewisse, and indeed in what was supposedly Vortigern's family portion of Powis.[39] West of the Hwicce in the Midlands was the grouping called by the Saxons Magonsaete, who seem to have started out (by the implication of the name) in the *territorium* of Magnis (Kenchester, Herefords.) and may have even evolved from the northern portion of the British polity of Ercing, discussed briefly in Chapter 8. By the eighth century, both were still nominally independent kingdoms, the former dependent upon Wessex and the latter upon Mercia. It has even been suggested that King Penda of Mercia himself (or the territory he ruled) may have had British roots, although the origins of Mercia, more so than most, are clouded in obscurity. It may have emerged from a migrationary Germanic thrust out of East Anglia, perhaps coalesced on the *pagus* of the eastern Corieltauvian *civitas* originally around Margidunum, but later continued to expand west, severing Letocetum (*Luitcoed* = Wall, Staffs.) from greater Powis before, at the end of the seventh century, advancing to the Severn and absorbing Wroxeter, possibly by treaty (see Chapter 8).

Mercia seems early on to have consisted of a number of smaller entities, apparent most strikingly in the *Tribal Hideage*, a document over which much debate rages, thought to date from anywhere between the early seventh to the later eighth century.[40] Examination of these arguments tend to confirm the impression that coherent political units approximately co-extensive with the *civitates* seem to have emerged (or continued) in lowland Britain as central authority weakened, their identities submerged in the wholesale re-naming which followed Saxon settlement, much along the lines already suggested. It has already been shown that Deira and Bernicia emerged as British polities in the north-east (perhaps as a division of Brigantia) prior to being taken over by the Anglian élite. Lindinis (later Lindsey) to the south is an analogous case, although here again, the Anglian dynasty begins with people of British nomenclature.[41] Lindsey was absorbed by Mercia, along with the Middle Angles, the Magonsaete, the Hwicce and others, as it expanded and managed to escape from the domination of Northumbria and the western British, with both of whom King Penda had allied himself in the 620s and 630s. If we could learn even some details of the obscure origin of this important polity, we could adduce so much more about the break-down and collapse of British control over much of the lowland Britain from the sixth century.

British *imperium*

Throughout this study, a proposition has been put forward that Britain, after 409, remained under the control of some form of autonomous imperial system, characterised by Roman historians as *tyranni* (usurpers), and we can be reasonably certain that amongst their number were Vortigern/Vitalinus, Ambrosius the elder and Ambrosius Aurelianus. If we could pin the period of the final breakdown of central authority over lowland Britain down to somewhere in the mid-sixth century (and perhaps part of a process continuing piecemeal for a century), it would follow that there were people other than the three named exercising similar authority in the intervening century and a half.

As long as this central control was exercised, we can assume that something resembling the late Roman administrative structure must have remained in being, despite the inexorable diminution of Roman material standards. We hear nothing, unlike in Gaul, of the assumption of such powers by local magnates or bishops, although this has been proposed for the longevity of Viroconium. The final breakdown of this central control, at least in respect of its exercise by the Romano-British, was most likely triggered by the climate events of 536-541 and provided with final, fatal impetus by the onset of the Late Antique Little Ice Age, which seems to have set in from the middle of the seventh century.[42] This period is marked by an entry in the *Annales Cambriae*:

537 [*sic*] Gueith Camlann in qua Arthus et Medraut corruerunt et mortalitas in Brittannia et in Hibernia fuit.

544 dormitatio Ciarani

547 Mortalitas magna in qua pausat Mailcun rex Genedotae ... Tunc fuit wallwelen[43]

537 The Battle of Camlann in which Arthur and Medraut fell: and there was a plague in Britain and Ireland.

544 The sleep [ie. death] of [St] Kieran

547 A great death in which Maelgwyn, King of Gwynedd died ... This was the yellow plague.

Thus we observe a decade-long period of plague beginning with a great battle in which two notable people died (it does not say they fought *against* each other, though), the death, probably also through plague, of a very notable Irish saint and the death of a king Gildas describes as: 'the dragon of the Island ... exceeding many in power and simultaneously in malice, more liberal in giving, more excessive in sin, strong in arms ... Maglocunus.'[44]

Here was a king, Maelgwyn Gwynedd, renowned for strength and power, although quite how far his writ ran is quite unclear; to the east perhaps as far as the Peak, even well into Lancashire. 'Of the island' might suggest Britain as a whole, but Bromwich and others believe it refers only to Anglesey; more likely it was merely hyperbole. Yet he was clearly prominent enough to attract the opprobrium of Gildas as well as to have merited an obituary notice in the *Annales*. What little we know of him, apart from his sins (in Gildas's eyes) is given in *Historia Brittonum*, which tells us (as we now believe, erroneously) he was descended from Cunedda who came from the north.[45]

This plague seems to have been caused by either the impact of a small asteroid or an unidentified volcanic eruption and it was particularly drastic as, combined with persistent cold weather and rain, the consequences lasted a decade, one such being usually described as the Justinianic Plague, as it affected the Roman empire particularly badly, if we are to believe Procopius. If then, the Battle of Camlann, only known to us in later legendary sources and numerous mentions in the Triads, was a result of tensions generated by the climate event and marked the dissolution of effective central control, which also carried off several notable people, then we might be getting close to being able to date when the breakup of central control really began post-Badon, although we need to bear in mind that it still to some extent pertained when Gildas was writing, at about this time. Thereafter though, it seems to have been all downhill.

It is possible that some of the old provinces gained governors under central authority who were in fact leaders of locally stationed German *foederati*, the case of Hengist being appointed by a treaty formulated under Vortigern/Vitalinus to replace Gwynangon in Kent being a striking example. Hengist's alleged son Oisc (supposedly father of Ochta, whose namesake we encountered in Chapter 10) has been proposed as the antecedent of the Saxons of Kent, having been identified as the Ansehis of the *Ravenna Cosmography* who had led the Saxons to Britain from Old Saxony.[46]

In a similar way it may be that under the pressure of continual confrontation with Germanic settlers, the essentially civilian late Roman positions gradually became permanently militarised. As regards the overall control of the diocese, Bede tells us that at a period when British control had almost evaporated in lowland Britain, Aethelberht of Kent was providing military leadership (= *imperium*) over all the Germanic polities outside the north as *Bretwalda*, a style which on that basis could easily have applied to the *tyranni* ruling Britain before him. Indeed, the term may derive from or owe its origin to whatever style by which those shadowy holders of post-Roman *imperium* were acknowledged – they were, when all is said and done, claiming rule over all of Britain, whereas those Saxon rulers to whom the term *Bretwalda* was later applied ruled only a (large) part of what we now know as England.

Bede then goes on to list further kings who held similar *imperium*, although his choice seems subjective, as no Mercian is included. Later, several Mercian

Kings like Offa and Aethelbald had held astonishingly wide control over the former diocese, and king Coenwulf I, even describes himself as *imperator* in a document of 798, setting something of a precedent.[47] Aethelbald, of Mercia (716-757), thought to be the king depicted in *bas relief* on the Repton stone (a massive high cross shaft), appears as a typical Frankish warlord/late antique *magister militum*, his long hair and moustache contrasting with a *lorica squamata*, pleated skirt, armed with a *spatha* and brandishing a *caetra* (small targe). His mausoleum, now the crypt below the Saxon chancel of St Wystan's parish church at Repton in Derbyshire is stylar and groin-vaulted, very much late antique rather than Romanesque.[48]

Owein 'son of Maxen'

The title *bretwalda*, meaning either 'Britain-ruler' or 'broad-ruler', an epithet remarkably close to Gildas's supposed later reference to Vortigern as 'wide ruler', shows that Bede and the compliers of the *Anglo-Saxon Chronicle* were well aware that such a thing had existed in the past; the Germanic kings from the seventh century knew that control over the whole island/diocese had been a feature of days gone by and that being acknowledged to enjoy it conferred considerable prestige. Morris considers that 'The concept of a single government of Britain lingered feebly until the middle of the seventh century.[49]

This kind of awareness need not be attributed to shadowy memories of the Roman Empire and its British diocese; it surely reflected the post-Roman actuality. As has been stressed, there can be little doubt that Britain was from 409 governed as a discrete entity by home-grown strong men, the *tyranni*, locally based rulers over the entire diocese who had, for over a century (bar the hiatus of the Saxon revolt of the 440s) kept the burgeoning Germanic migrants in check, mainly by negotiation, settlement on under-populated land, and subsidy (in the shape of *annona*). The island had been reasonably united and prosperous enough to have been able to despatch a military expedition to Gaul under Riothamus in support of the imperial authorities, despite the rapidly changing material situation: dwindling cash supplies, urban decay and rural change.

Latest investigations have established continuity of land use throughout this period, enabling our *tyranni* to levy taxation in kind and to summon people in subsidiary authority to direct them in what they should do, or try to do. At this stage, post-revolt, Germanic occupation of land as demonstrated by archaeology did not necessarily mean independent control by the settlers' native leaders. At first, at least during much of the fifth century, these expanding Anglo-Saxon enclaves may have been subject to British central control under their own leaders as prefects or even *subreguli*, or with some other prestige-bearing title and taxed in kind accordingly. Only gradually would they have gained first effective independence and later full autonomy.

It has been tentatively proposed above that the shadowy 'son' of Maximus, Owein/Eugenius was the first person to consolidate rule over the diocese after Constantine III's *annus horribilis*, and the ejection of his place-men, perhaps echoed two entries in the Triads:

TYP 11: Three chief officers of the Island of Britain:
Caradoc son of Brân
and Cawrdaf son of Caradawg
and Owein son of Maxen Wledig.

TYP Appendix I: The Names of the Island of Britain:
There should be held therein a crown and three coronets. The Crown should be worn in London and one of the Coronets at Penrhyn Rhionydd in the North, the second at Aberffraw and the third in Cornwall.[50]

These may reflect a knowledge of the fifth or early sixth century when there was still a central authority in Britain, headed by one man with imperial authority (*imperium*). The British word in the Triad is *cynweissyat,* close in meaning to *tywyssog* (= 'prince', 'ruler'). Here we have someone who apparently held *imperium* over the island of Britain with at least nominal suzerainty over three subsidiary but semi-autonomous polities in Galloway (presumably), North Wales and Dumnonia, a situation remarkably close to that which we have seen emerging, probably under Maximus's instigation, from the 380s.

Bearing in mind the temporal scale indicated by Owein's supposed father, then we might well have, transmitted over far too many centuries to be incontrovertible, a possible name for the person who took command after the events of 409: the Saxon-Scots-Pictish incursion, the betrayal of Gerontius and the expulsion of Constantine III's appointees. One of Iolo Morgannwg's collection of Triads tells us that Owein 'refused to pay tribute to Rome', which, however dubious the source, chimes with Zosimus's evidence of 'taking up arms' and 'throwing off' imperial control.[51] It would take a person wielding considerable authority to do this, perhaps with the advantage of actually being *en poste*. In the reference from the Triad Appendix 1, we have set out those responsible for three areas of semi-autonomous control as suggested by various 'sons' of Maximus in the preceding chapters. Needless to say, the names of these subsidiary centres bear more up-to-date names than those of the fifth century, but nevertheless they are the same general areas. Aberffraw, for instance, was the epicentre of the House of Gwynedd, from the ninth century ruled by the former dynasty of Man and descended from a 'son' of Maximus, Anthun/Dunawt. Penrhyn Rhionydd was encountered as a possible early seat of the same dynasty in Chapter 9, while the relevance of Dumnonia (by the time of the transmission of the material incorporated in the Triad, reduced to Cornwall) is set out in Chapter 10.

In four sources, Owein is repeatedly described as a son of Magnus Maximus: the *Vita Cadoci* (at *c.* 1100 the earliest, and free from the obnubilatory tendencies of the post-Geoffrey of Monmouth sources), the *Vita Peiblici*, *Bonedd y Saint* 63 (of which MSS C & F endow Owein with the epithet *Finddu* ('Black lips'), and one Triad. One might also throw in Iolo Morgannawg's Triads 17 and 41 too, but the four less problematic sources surely suffice to convince us that the relationship was then very well established.[52] As the most reasonable assumption must be that Owein was highly unlikely to have actually been a son of Magnus Maximus, the question is why did he become so attached to these three genealogies and the one Triad? The inference of the analysis carried out in the three preceding chapters is that Maximus was a person well-remembered as having initiated a number of polities re-organised on the frontier zones of the diocese in alliance with the empire. And that the effectiveness of the settlement he made led to bardic genealogical pedigrees proudly beginning with his name as a founder, but in which frequent subsequent repetition allowed this place of honour to mutate into a first generation of a king-list, later embellished in the re-telling and written down more of less as we have them today.

That a similar process grafted Owein onto Maximus seems considerably less likely. There were twenty-one years between the demise of Maximus and the collapse of direct imperial rule, a whole generation if one measures the latter from the likely elevation of Maximus five or more years before 388. Yet the likelihood is that Owein must have been at least widely perceived as having in some way succeeded Maximus, or as a man who had been put in place by him. It is difficult to envisage quite how that might have been in practice, however. It may be that, on his move to the Continent in 383 (or before his advance to Milan in 387), Maximus had left behind in Britain an appointee as *vicarius* or as *magister militum* or *comes*. We noted in Part I that Britain appears to have remained quiet (or off the radar of contemporary chroniclers) at least until the rise of Stilicho, and probably until the usurpation of Marcus in 406, so it may be that this appointee turned out to have been highly effective and quite probably well-liked as well – the one by no means always being a consequence of the other. One might even suggest that he was British, too.

If we further propose that some time before the resumption of trouble in 406, this person had retired in his fifties, perhaps to an estate, we might envisage that on the ejection of many of Constantine III's appointees he was summoned (or interposed himself) to take control in order to lead the efforts to clear the diocese of raiders and set things up to avoid a repetition. If we further suppose that this person was a man called Eugenius, and that his efforts met with considerable success, we see how he might have become so firmly established as in Maximus's mould as to be associated with him in people's memories and hence become established in time as Maximus's son.

A later Iolo Triad claims that he was the 'unanimously agreed' ruler of Britain, while yet another tellingly informs us that Owein 'resumed sovereignty from the Roman emperor'.[53] It is a tragedy that we cannot provenance these snippets from before the time they were written down by Iolo. Were we able to push them back further, to a time *before* Geoffrey of Monmouth, we might be able to identify Owein/Eugenius much more positively as the missing *tyrannus*, who seized control in 409 and was ultimately succeeded by Ambrosius the elder or Vitalinus/Vortigern. Only a sequence of events like those propounded above could surely have explained the sudden subsequent popularity of the name Owein, especially amongst most of the early British dynasties that have come down to us. One can hardly imagine, for instance, that the two years of rule by the short-lived emperor Eugenius from 392 to 394 as having been likely to inspire an outbreak of naming in emulation.[54]

Unfortunately, we know precious little else about Owein 'son' of Maximus, except that he was believed by later chroniclers to be the progenitor of saints, which is probably the only reason that his name, unlike those of some of his supposed successors, has become transferred into the genealogies of the frontier princes. That his name was the Latin Eugenius, there seems little doubt. It may be that this somewhat hypothetical character may be identified with someone already recorded in the annals of the empire, but the only possible candidate is a *comes* Eugenius who left an inscription recording that he had restored the baths at Jerusalem. The date is, however, vague in the extreme, he can be pinpointed no more accurately than fourth or fifth centuries.[55] There is no reason why Owein/Eugenius could not have been a *comes* of Theodosius in the east, having perhaps taken up an appointment later under Maximus, but we cannot be sure.

Clearly, Owein was considered an important figure even in the periphery of the diocese, in that the genealogies later dressed up his ascendancy with British heroes, as with one of the sections in the Jesus College MS, which gives his posterity in order to provide a descent for a saint, before adding his supposed antecedents back to Cassivellaunus (but without nearly enough intervening generations). In this particular genealogy we are presented with the name of Owein's mother, and therefore supposedly Maximus's elusive empress. The source calls her Keindrech, daughter of Reiden ap Eledi, which, in a more modern rendering, might be *Ceindrech verch Rhydion ap Eidol*.[56] The potential empress's name would therefore Latinise as *Caniod[r]icea*, but actually translates as 'of beautiful form, or appearance'. Normally, Latin names are transliterated into British, as with Owein/Eugenius, but some, like *hael* = Liberalis (Chapter 9) seem to be actual translations. In the case of Ceindrech, her Roman name would therefore translate as either Speciosa or Formosa, of which the former is well attested in the fifth century, if not so much in the fourth. The western consul of 496 was a Speciosus, probably a member of the Anicii and a kinsman of the short-lived emperor Olybrius, himself a possible descendant of Maximus's daughter (Chapter 5), if one accepts the persuasive suggestions of Mommaerts and Kelley.[57] He was thought in turn to have been a close kinsman of a Speciosa, a notably religious aristocratic lady living at the end of the fifth century.[58]

The Jesus College source being late, the information may be vitiated, especially as Ceindrech's father and grandfather would appear to be legendary kings. Nevertheless, the particular genealogy seems untainted by either the *Dream* or Geoffrey of Monmouth and, apart from the former's Helen, it is our only clue as to Maximus's pious wife, especially as a Helen has already been more or less ruled out. But we cannot have our cake and eat it: having rejected Maximus as the actual parent of Owein, it is hardly reasonable to promote the latter's supposed mother as the emperor's wife!

Owein also had a daughter, according to *Historia Brittonum* (unnamed), who married Pascent[ius], son of Vortigern.[59] Were we able to trust the Pillar of Eliseg completely, this would mean that Maximus's grandson through Severa married the emperor's alleged granddaughter, demonstrating once again the sheer ubiquity in these genealogies of Maximus's name. The alliance seems plausible enough, both in terms of credibility and chronology. While commentators urge us not to cherry-pick from these fragmentary sources, they are our only hope of any degree of elucidation of events; most of these names will have had a genuine origin, that any were completely invented seems unlikely even at this remove.

The only other event attributed to Owein is his participation in a supposed battle with a giant at Dinas Emrys ('the fort of Ambrosius', near Beddgelert, Gwynedd). The giant in one version of this tale (written down very late, from an unknown tradition) is called Urnach and this is where Owein is again given the epithet *Finddu*.[60] It is just possible that the giant-slaying tale (in which both combatants die) represents a dim memory of a tradition of Owein taking on the 'giant' of a triple incursion of barbarian tribes, perhaps that of 409, which might have propelled him into power or being killed at some later point fighting a further incursion; or even in an internal challenge to his authority, the giant surely being a symbolic, wicked opponent. The fact that his daughter might have been married to a son of Vortigern is suggestive, however, bearing in mind the 'wide ruler's' uneven reputation. It was not for nothing that Vortigern was later as apprehensive of attack by Ambrosius as by the barbarians.

Apart from the one daughter and the issue set out at the beginning of Chapter 9, we only know that a descent from Owein was claimed by St Cadoc, but the intervening generations all appear to bear resolutely British names, rather than Roman ones. A very similar ascendancy is also ascribed to St Petroc until one reaches Nor, who is called *filius Protector* rather than *ap Owein* – but could *protector* perhaps have been a style adopted by Owein himself?[61] That Owein should be fighting a giant magnifies his significance; to fight a giant, he must have been somebody pretty memorable in the first place and someone whose fame must have arisen from tackling seemingly formidable opponents.

There seems to be a plausible case to be made that Owein was the person holding *imperium* after 409 in the mould, at least, of Maximus. He could have used a title like 'consul' or 'protector' or have been remembered as such; the latter epithet seems to have survived in the genealogy in lieu of the proper name of some putative forebears. Amongst Owein's descendants Glinguis/Gliws/Glwys emerges elsewhere as Glywys ap Solor, but is given the epithet 'Cernyw' ('Cornish') which is anachronistic – unless the Cornovii of Powis and their possible assignment to sort out the Irish in western Dumnonia is intended, but to locate Glywys in Cornwall seems highly improbable.[62] However, in *Bonedd y Saint,* one Clemens appears as a 'prince (*tywyssauc*) of Cornwall' and is given as St Petroc's father, suggesting that he is perhaps to be identified with Glywys, the locale notwithstanding.[63]

Central authority after Owein

The legendary sources leave us in no doubt that by 425 or so, Vortigern, identified with the Vitolinus/Vitalinus of the Battle of Wallop in 436 or thereabouts, was the person wielding *imperium* in Britain, and we have speculated that his period in control may have ended with that same battle, with Ambrosius, of whom Vortigern had been 'afraid' at an unspecified earlier time, prevailing. Perhaps Ambrosius had been the designated successor of Owein, whom Vortigern had somehow deposed and exiled Wallop (today three villages, then probably a locality), is on the eastern edge of Salisbury plain, ten miles south-east of Amesbury, which we have noted as a place possibly to be associated with Ambrosius.[64] What had caused this enmity is lost to us utterly. A rift between these two men – who may have been close kin, if the reconstructed family of the Aurelii set out in the previous chapter can be accepted – may have arisen over the use of Saxon *foederati*, and the treaty Vortigern is said to have made with them, or even the legendary fall-out from it, as set out in *Historia Brittonum*.[65] Having ousted Vortigern (terminally, as the *Historia Brittonum* would also have us believe) we assume that Ambrosius took over.

That he made some kind of settlement emerges in the entry in the *HB* in which we are told that Ambrosius 'who was the great king of all the kings of the British nation' who had the authority to grant Pascent, Vortigern's son, Buellt and Gwerthrynion (perhaps, as we have seen earlier, his patrimonial estates), implying that despite the deposition of Vortigern, a measure of harmony prevailed through the prudent exercise of *clementia*.[66] Ambrosius's time in the sun appears to have ended with the Saxon Revolt in the 440s, with the consequences as adumbrated by Gildas, although one can detect much hyperbole; he was, it must be remembered, writing an events-based diatribe, not a chronicle. Nevertheless, the hastening of the decline of the towns and the transformation of life in the countryside could well have been a consequence. Gildas states that the cause of the revolt was that the *annona* was not paid. As we have observed, this could have been caused by a recorded climate change anomaly (the *Annales Cambriae* open in their year 447 with 'days as dark as night'), leading to a crop failure which would have killed off any hope of a surplus, leading to some catastrophic breakdown in negotiations. This event may have marked the end of the well documented 'Roman Warm Period'.[67] The result would appear to have been the death of Ambrosius in the revolt.

We are told that there was prolonged chaos, which may have lasted a decade or so. As we have seen, it may have resulted in the 'appeal to Aëtius' in 446-454 (which may have in fact been to Aegidius after 455). For a while, some of the Northern powerbrokers may have taken a hand, but at some stage Ambrosius Aurelianus seems to have emerged and gradually restored order, as Gildas informs us.[68] There is no hint of another Owein-type figure in the legendary material. Again, there must have been a considerable timespan involved if we can accept the Battle of Badon as having taken place in or around 490.[69]

The despatch of Riothamus to Gaul in 468/469 would rather suggest that even then, central authority in Britain must have been completely restored, otherwise it would have been impossible for so substantial a contingent to have been spared to cross the Channel. Sending Riothamus to assist Anthemius might have been a good way for Ambrosius Aurelianus (if it was indeed done on his initiative, rather than that of an unidentified predecessor) to get a potential rival or troublemaker out of the way, or simply to help the Gallic authorities in their hour of need, in the hope that such a favour might be returned when called upon. That is unless, like Léon Fleuriot, one inclines to identify Riothamus with Ambrosius Aurelianus himself. After all, he argues, Riothamus and Aurelianus were contemporaries and the latter was the only British leader who is identified, according to the usual much later sources, as having *imperium* ruling Britons perhaps even on both sides of the Channel. Who might have had the authority to send him, though, is unclear. In support of his contention, Fleuriot suggests that the name *A[m] bros* in Breton genealogies is a regional mutation of Ambrosius, as *Emrys* is in Welsh. Ambrosius, so the theory goes, having pacified Britain, must have led his *comitatus* across to Gaul but defeated, returned to Britain. The idea would work if one were to accept Riothamus as a British title, cognate with 'vortigern', meaning 'supreme ruler' rather than a name.[70]

One possible drawback is that Riothamus appears to have spent nearly four years apparently not going anywhere much in Gaul after the unfortunate encounter with the Goths; not something such a leader would have countenanced had he authority to wield in insular Britain as well. After all, we do not know whether he even made it back to Britain after having received Sidonius's letter. Yet the incursion of Aelle, identified by Dr Russell as possibly being Ambrosius Aurelianus returning from Gaul, and even that of, say, Cerdic, were not Saxons turfed out of northern Gaul by Syagrius and Clovis at all, but could instead have been groups of disaffected returnees from Riothamus's forces, trying to impose themselves on central insular authority. Yet, if Gildas is right, the Battle of Badon, won by Ambrosius Aurelianus, ushered in a generation or more of peace.

Gildas fails to mention who had succeeded Ambrosius – Aurelianus – for he seems too busy attacking peripheral figures, unless the hard-to-pin-down Aurelius Caninus *was* the central authority following Aurelianus, as proposed in the previous chapter, for the other four princes who attract his disapprobation were all securely rulers in the periphery. Against Caninus, Gildas thunders,

> Hast thou not by thy hatred of thy country's peace, as if it were a deadly serpent, or by thy iniquitous thirst for civil wars and repeated spoils, closed the doors of heavenly peace and repose for thy soul? Left alone now, like a dry tree in the midst of a field, remember, I pray thee...[71]

This would suggest the succession (after a generation, presumably) of a lesser man than the paragon which emerges in what little we know of Aurelianus. Apart from being accused of fomenting civil wars for profit, the simile of a dry tree in a field does to some extent portray the centre as failing to hold in the midst of increasing pressures; it also suggests land that is waste, bringing us back to the role of climate anomalies in the collapse of central authority in Britain.

It is the lacuna in any possible narrative in the aftermath of the victory at Badon that is the oddest phenomenon. If we adhere to our assumption that Badon *was* fought *c.* 490, and Aurelius Caninus *was* earning Gildas's wrath forty years later, there must surely have been someone claiming power in Britain in between. Geoffrey of Monmouth actually does manage to suggest Caninus in this role, but if he was here drawing on some lost tradition, as Dr Miles has established that he occasionally seems to have done, then we cannot know it for sure.[72]

The problem of Arthur

It is within this historic void, of course, that Arthur may belong, if only we could get a handle on him and disentangle him from the elaborations of sources like the *Historia Regum Britanniae* and those deriving therefrom. There are numerous fairly oblique references to him in pre-Galfridian sources, but none are remotely verifiable. *Annales Cambriae* twice mention him, although the dates may be a couple of decades later than perhaps intended. There, this enigmatic figure is said to have 'carried the cross of Our Lord Jesus Christ for three days and three nights on his shoulders' at the battle of Badon. This does not say he *led* the forces of the Britons, though; it has been established that Ambrosius Aurelianus did. He was merely present in a prominent capacity – perhaps as *signifer*, standard bearer, or as a *comes*. That he was a doughty soldier emerges from early references, for instance in *Y Gododdin*, referring, according to John Koch, to events in the north of *c.* 570. One of the combatants, Gwawrddur,

> ... fed black ravens on the rampart of a fortress
> Though he was no Arthur
> Among the powerful ones in battle
> In the front rank, Gwawrddur was a palisade[73]

'Arthur's men' are also alluded to as present when Gereint was killed at Llongborth, mentioned in Chapter 10. It also appears in late Welsh sources that he was relatively ubiquitous and not always appreciated. No less than twenty-three Triads mention him and they are full of bizarre incidents and allusions. The *Historia Brittonum* attributes twelve battles to him (including Badon) but never calls him king, rather *dux bellorum* – clearly little divergent from a *magister militum* or the *duces* in the *Notitia Dignitatum* – who fought alongside British leaders. Later, the same relatively early source calls him *Arthuri militis*, 'the warrior Arthur'.[74] Perhaps significantly, none of the Triads refer to the Battle of Badon at all, not even in connection with Arthur. This reflects a passage of William of Malmesbury, who states that Ambrosius (Aurelianus) became monarch after Vortigern [and] quelled the presumptuous barbarians by the powerful aid of the warlike Arthur'.[75]

William's work pre-dates Geoffrey and is important because of it; like so many others, he found himself baffled by the many and various tales of Arthur he had heard. Could these sources refer to a *tyrannus* holding *imperium*, central authority, in Britain and managing to assemble the leaders of the polities on the periphery to combat Germanic expansion, or to a supremely talented *dux* fighting in various theatres at the behest of central authority? If the latter, the eleven battles and Badon may have been fought as the *magister militum* of Ambrosius; it is notable that, bar Badon, they could all be interpreted as vaguely northern, or north of The Wash.[76] Caradoc of Llancarfan in his hagiography of St Gildas, which can be claimed with confidence as antedating Geoffrey of Monmouth, describes Arthur ('Arthus') as 'King of the whole of Britain', a remark which echoes that of Triad 11 about Owein, from which one might be tempted to recognise in him the successor to Ambrosius Aurelianus as the supreme central authority in Britain.

Yet all the earliest scattered pre-Galfridian evidence places him securely in the north, supported by at least four later Northern princes bearing his name, suggesting a desire to embody his fame through association.[77] Furthermore, there are no pre-Galfridian references to his parentage; he fails to show up in any but later genealogies, a quality he shares with Ambrosius, and which lack is beginning to look diagnostic of anyone holding central authority. He only receives a genealogy in Mostyn MS 117, in which Uther makes his appearance as the father and who is grafted on to the lineage of Dumnonia, and all others follow this, with variations.[78] The Arthurian references also, like others originating amongst the *Gwr y Gogledd*, became re-localised after the collapse of the British north, partly in Ergyng/Herefordshire and more strongly in Dumnonia, especially Cornwall, with Celliwig and Tintagel prominent. Both existed (assuming that Celliwig can be identified with Callington) as flourishing settlements in the sixth century. The only battle unequivocally associated with Arthur is that of Camlann, an unlocated disaster which may have been the climax of a vicious internecine dispute. It appears in its earliest reference in *Annales Cambriae*, but *sub anno* 537. The *Annales* put it twenty-one years after Badon, which seems, at *sub anno* 516, surely a trifle late on Gildas's calculation; somewhere around 510/515 might be nearer the mark (assuming that it was a real event at all). The Triads, interestingly, are packed with references to Camlann. Possibly this battle (whatever date to which it should be assigned) marked the spur for the composition of Gildas's *de Excidio,* for he seems to see the world falling apart around his ears, after two generations of post-Badonic peace (during which there must have been ample opportunity for intermarriage between British and Germanic populations), even if he fails to mention the confrontation itself – probably because it did not suit his polemical purpose or because its import only emerged with hindsight.

The Arthurian quest is of course more complex (and even more popular) that the search for Jack the Ripper. In *Artorius: The Real King Arthur*, Linda Malcor and John Matthews have no doubt that he was a Roman soldier of the late second century. Though remarkably enough this does not make a nonsense of all the foregoing. They do not have Artorius at the Battle of Badon! The authors observe that

> The Arthurian legends follow a developmental pattern that is well known to scholars of British legend.
>
> 1. The presence of an historical figure who did something that struck a chord with his contemporaries and caused some of them to transmit his story
> 2. The use of the hero's name by members of the transmitting culture after a gap in time during which the name is not used, and
> 3. The attraction of other bodies of folklore to the existing cycle to create a new form of the legend.

Some of this is relevant to the figure of Magnus Maximus.

Final post-Roman central disintegration

Quite apart from being unable to make any deductions to aid the development of a narrative as to the post-Maximus dispositions of Britain from so elusive, if illustrious, a character, so also we are unable to suggest just how the later Roman dispensation of a centre under a *tyrannus* and the frontier under planted polities finally fell apart, but clearly it did. From the defeat and death of Cadwallon of Gwynedd ('king of the Britons') in 634 (or earlier) to that of Gereint II of Dumnonia around 711, any suggestion of central control seems a dead duck. The British appear increasingly confined to the polities of the frontier and even then, their hegemony was still shrinking, Dumnonia becoming ultimately confined to Cornwall, York eliminated by a dynastic marriage, Rheged absorbed by Strathclyde, Powis' heartlands absorbed by Mercia, and Wales remaining fragmented – although centuries later it did achieve an unstable unity, not least under the prince Llewellyn ap Iowerth (Llewellyn the Great), the last unconquered province of the Roman West, prior to being extinguished by Edward I from 1282.[79]

With regard to Arthur, it was Geoffrey of Monmouth who endowed him with a crown and a kingdom. Miles Russell also points out how most of the legendary king's exploits seem to mirror uncannily those of the leaders of the Britons during the expeditions of Julius Caesar and the conquest by Claudius – even more so when compared with Geoffrey's own unique and colourful accounts of these events.[80] Following all the unlikely drama of Arthur and his exploits, Geoffrey ends his history lamely. To seek out clues to the last rulers of the old diocese, he alone gives us any names, but almost all are princes attacked by Gildas: Constantine of Dumnonia follows Arthur and, as we have seen, Aurelius Caninus bobs up after him. Then we get Vortiporius of Demetia, followed by Maelgwyn ('Malgo') of Gwynedd – complete with a reprise of most of Gildas's uncomplimentary epithets – and ending with 'Keretic' who 'fomented discord', internecine strife, and encouraged foreign invasions, leading to the virtual dissolution of Britain as a single entity.[81]

Thereafter, we are told that Cadfan of Gwynedd tried to undertake a revival, headquartered in Leicester (of all places), previously under the control of one Brochmail (clearly intended for Brochmael of Powis, perhaps not entirely improbable at that period), followed by a wonderfully distorted account of Cadwallon's campaigns against the Northumbrians, none of which inspires the slightest confidence.[82] Yet Keretic the fomenter gives us pause. As Russell has asked, is this not the same British leader as the man who appears in the *Anglo-Saxon Chronicle* as Cerdic, encountered above? It looks as though the ninth-century chronicler of the *ASC* grafted this half-forgotten British prince into his work in order to endow the Kings of Wessex with a credible origin story.[83] No wonder he embodied the swansong of British unity.

The general pattern, though, is clear: the continuity of a central diocesan authority from 409, under *tyranni*, or locally elevated emperors (or whatever they styled themselves) displacing *vicarii*, ruling the core of the diocese, aided by subservient frontier polities established prior to the loss of imperial control, seems to have continued in a recognisably Roman form for somewhat over a century before a final disintegration began. The central authority seems still to have relied upon a mounted force, presumably modelled upon an imperial-style *comitatus*, aided when called upon by the leaders of the frontier polities with similar mounted armed units loyal to them. These military units gradually mutated, in the heat of conflict, the constraints of a new economic order and the expediencies imposed by repeated emergencies, from an imperially based *comitatus* prototype into a mounted three-hundred strong *teulu* or warband. In the end, with central authority gone, war was waged solely by the frontier leader's *llys* (court) and his personal *teulu*. As St Gregory the Great (another member of the Anician family) put it in the context of the empire as a whole, 'the old eagle has lost his plumage...'

Dinas Emrys, from Thomas Pennant's *A Tour in Wales 1770* (London, 1778).

Conclusion

Expanding Maximus's *Vita*

Magnus Maximus has gone down in Roman history as one of a succession of Roman imperial usurpers who, over three centuries, came and went amidst the unfolding drama of empire, each leaving a legacy of varying consequences. Although Maximus gained imperial recognition from a reigning emperor and from the western senate and ruled competently, he was still labelled after the event by his cowed contemporaries as an usurper. He is also cited as the man who, by withdrawing unspecified numbers of troops from Britain, began the sequence of events which ultimately led to the diocese becoming detached from the empire, to the ultimate 'ruin and conquest of Britain' as Gildas titled his polemic.

In some insular sources and semi-legendary later material, while negatively remembered for stripping Britain of its defensive capacity, he is also celebrated as something of a hero and as the founder of several princely houses. He is also remembered in medieval romances, to some extent supported by fragmentary earlier material, which claim that he established, if only indirectly, Armorica as a sort of proto-British colony. His importance in tradition came by 'not only making Britain Roman but also by making the Roman empire British.'[1] Maximus is thus remembered for both negative and positive aspects of his rule, a challenging dichotomy that has to be addressed.

To re-evaluate his career and achievements, the ancient sources have been interrogated and by attempting to see beyond their prejudices and by trying to determine if there is anything of value to be derived from the later insular sources, an attempt has been made to assess how much of them might be deemed admissible. The re-assessment has, it must be admitted, hinged on the assumption that the relationship between Maximus and Theodosius I as kin was a reality, with all the consequences that flow from it, including close acquaintanceship and the long-term companionship generated and strengthened by their having been comrades-in-arms. It has also been suggested that, far from being passed over on Theodosius's virtual coup as the imperial replacement for the dead Valens, he may have been sent to Britain to deal with unrest there in the vulnerable north-west flank of the Western Empire, perhaps with enhanced rank, which, thanks to hostile accounts following his downfall, may have been elided from his record in order to downplay his importance (or the possible complicity of Theodosius). That he had previously served, seemingly with success, in Britain, may have been one reason for his appointment. That this task may have taken some years and Maximus was in Britain for some time before his coup (whenever that actually occurred), would seem likely, an assumption supported by the re-assessment of the actual chronology underlying the *Chronicle of 452*. That his coup may have been made with the tacit connivance of the eastern emperor has been canvassed where the narrative has seemed to suggest it, although this teeters on the edge of conspiracy theory.

It has also been suggested that although Maximus took with him to the Continent his *comitatus*, very likely strengthened by other units drawn from the British diocesan establishment, he had made what he hoped were long-term arrangements to settle the frontier regions of the diocese to ensure stability despite temporarily depleted manpower, and the fact that numerous British genealogies begin with his name supports this. Maximus is an almost ubiquitous presence as a forebear of several of the ruling dynasties established at about this time in these crucial areas. From this, it has seemed reasonable to postulate similar dispositions put in place by Maximus or by his associates, appointees or successors as part of the same strategy. The succession of Roman names at the start of other dynasties like the Coelings and the discrete groupings of North Wales are positive pointers.

Such an arrangement, of course, was not new. Ammianus attests that a similar stratagem had been employed by the Emperor Theodosius's father on the African frontier following his suppression of Firmus. He set about enlisting the support of the native groups on the southern border by a combination of stick and carrot, putting dependable *praefecti* in charge of each grouping.[2] Maximus, as we have seen, was on the spot and may have had an important role in enacting this policy. St Augustine a generation later mentions the approach, implying that the settlement then made was still holding. With such an exemplar before him, and with probable personal involvement, a successful settlement of the same kind in Britain – another equally volatile frontier – would seem eminently sensible; the insular sources seem to support such a supposition as emphatically as such material ever can.[3]

From analysis of the insular sources, then, it has also been possible to link Maximus with the settlement of an Irish grouping in Demetia, and with other similar arrangements made in Wales; in the area between the

Walls (which is here again proposed as being the enigmatic fifth province of Valentia) and possibly also those in north Wales and western Dumnonia. The arrangements he seems to have made with native and Irish leaders were in essence the creation of minor client states under treaty. The successful completion of these arrangements would have given Maximus the confidence to withdraw selected troops on his move across the Channel and indeed, intimates an overall well-worked out strategy. The long-term stability of the diocese of Britain was ensured, and a share of empire would appear to have been the aim *ab initio*. It also would explain the fact that the slightly later *Notitia Dignitatum* records no Roman army units in these very areas suggested as having been under treaty, although the dispositions on Hadrian's Wall may represent supplementary positioning of regular forces as *limitanei* to maintain a second line of defence should things go badly awry further north, or to act as *douaniers*. Their presence may also explain the evolution of the dynasty in the area we call the Coelings. The erection, at just this period, of signal stations along the north-east coast, in north Wales and the re-commissioning of forts at Cardiff, Caernarfon, Holyhead and Lancaster, combined with an apparent simultaneous retreat from inland forts in Wales and the north (rendered superfluous to requirements in the new dispensation) would seem to support the strategic picture which emerges. This arrangement seems to have held successfully for a long time (assuming the account of Stilicho's subsequent visit to the British diocese was largely the product of rhetoric rather than substance). Maximus's contribution to the strengthening of Britain was of considerable importance, especially as it relates to the history of post-Roman Britain, and his widely reported withdrawal of troops represented only half the story.

From the British sources, Maximus seems to have applied himself to a charm offensive in the northernmost province (Valentia) with the aim of consolidating the inter-wall tract of what today is lowland Scotland and the borders, by effectively recognising local dynasts and putting them under the normal Roman obligations of clientelage, or treaty. Recognition by the Roman authorities and the award of prestigious titles (as, it would appear in more than one instance, *protector,* and possibly of *tribunus*) as on the Continent from about this time, were sought-after enhancements to local prestige and a vital element in securing compliance.

The dynasties claiming Maximus as an ancestor surely fall into this category; thus, in the intervallate area, both Galloway and Alclud probably qualify. The profusion of Roman names amongst the founders of these and other polities, suggest that in many cases while the emergent ruling families were most likely of insular origin, they were more thoroughly Romanised, having probably served in the entourage of the *vicarius*, at the court of the Western Emperor or on the staff of one of the *magistri militum*. It is notable that it took more than one generation for such nomenclature to revert to mainly British idioms. And while the dynasties of Manau Gododdin and York – the alleged descendants of Coel – did not make any claims on Maximus as founder, they nevertheless appear thoroughly Roman in origin, although Coel himself might seem to date to a generation later than Maximus, suggesting his dynasty may have originated with a *dux Britanniarum* perhaps left high and dry *en poste* in, say, 409.

Likewise, in Wales, another area omitted entirely from the *Notitia*, we see an organised drive to garrison the western littoral using the self-same stratagem, although only Demetia and Powis claim any actual connection with Maximus, and Powis itself seems to have had no strategic value, for its connection evolved through a slightly later marital alliance, if we believe the inscription on the Pillar of Eliseg. We do not appear to be looking at any kind of frontier state at all, but an extensive and approximately coherent inland entity, probably fashioned from a series of typically extensive landed estates, as seems to have been the case with Brycheiniog. Powis appears to have been rooted in the *civitas* of the Cornovii, and the connection with Maximus genuinely dynastic and not part of the complex web of client entities elsewhere. Yet, even here, we seem to find in the British name for the tribal grouping a possible origin for Cornwall. An element of the *civitas* may have been recruited, quite possibly under Maximus or a little later, to move to western Dumnonia, possibly to control or drive out an incursion of Irish. This was, after all the migrationary era, and Ireland need not be viewed as any different from Europe east of the Rhine, the north-east bank of the Danube or anywhere else then applying pressure on the Roman *limes*.

The Irish are one of the most interesting elements in all this, quite apart from the spread of Christianity in Ireland at the hands of the very upper-crust Gallo-Roman Palladius and the very Romano-British Patrick. The former, a relative of the senatorial poet and former Prefect of the City of Rome, Rutilius Claudius Namatianus, was the son of Exuperantius, a Praetorian Prefect of Gaul who had previously put down some kind of trouble in Armorica, probably as *vicarius*.[4] He enjoyed the same sort of connections as St Germanus and was sent to Ireland by Pope Celestine in 416. Would that we knew more about the connections of Patrick's family, too. They may have been the same kind of high-level connections as those enjoyed by his precursor in crossing the Irish Sea.

The influence of the church there at this stage, however, was hardly a factor, as we see the Irish as very effective raiders of late Roman Britain in the shape of the Scotti and Attecotti, yet at the same time we find units of the latter flourishing in the late Roman army, as the *Notitia Dignitatum* strikingly demonstrates and it is suggested that this was due to the settlement negotiated by Maximus, or as a result of the dissolution of his *comitatus* following his demise. We also see them as settlers, notably in Demetia (with its offshoot to the north-east in Brycheiniog), where an Irish dynasty claimed descent from Maximus, strongly suggesting that here again, their settlement in south-west Wales to defend this part of Britannia Prima was brought about through him as a matter of policy. That there was also Irish settlement in north Wales seems less the result of an organised transfer and settlement as successful raiding on perhaps depopulated Ordovician territory, with consequent settlement, to which Einion and his 'brothers' may well have been sent by the *vicarius* or successor central authority partly to expel and partly to mediatise them, each leader (most of them bearing Roman names with the implication that they were regular imperial officers) supervising a separate *regio* (district). Again, the names of these men suggest that this change came about through deliberate policy.

In around 500 there was a further change in the tribal origin of the Irish in north Wales, a knock-on effect of drastic political changes in south-east Ireland. Again, this could have been brought about by whatever British authority held sway in the area to strengthen a declining population. The omission of Maximus's name attached to the genealogies concerned with Einion and his 'kin' might suggest the events there happened later, as these self-same genealogies were ultimately attached to the Votadinian grandee Cunedda (a man with three generations of Roman ancestors); any diagnostic connection might have been thereby obfuscated.

On the other hand, Einion might well belong to the age of Constantine III or his British successor, for those strategic settlements of the frontier regions that seem attributable to Maximus may well have set a workable precedent which successors were only too keen to emulate. Constantine III, in taking troops to the Continent, may also have wished to ensure that the frontiers continued to remain stable and so put in place similar arrangements in north Wales and, perhaps, western Dumnonia – or strengthened existing ones. Whether, therefore, the first Irish settlement in north Wales was anything to do with Maximus we cannot tell, but his involvement in the south-west of the Principality is indisputable and may have established a template for emulation. There is persuasive evidence of close contact across the Irish Sea at this date, and it would be rash to rule out Maximus from having made a foray there as a step towards the consolidation of his attempts to settle the western frontiers of Britain.

Mention of Dumnonia raises the thorny problem of the central south and south-west. Here again, there is no obvious link to Maximus (except a legendary marriage of a 'daughter'), but Dumnonia seems to have emerged in a similar way, which surely links it with the other polities that can be attributed to him, although only the part of the *civitas* which later became known as Cornwall could really be termed a frontier zone. It is also important to have looked at links with Dumnonia, south Wales and Brittany, simply because all three seem at times to have shared astonishingly close links in the insular sources and in those from Brittany itself. Also, the fact that Anglo-

Saxon chroniclers believed that the ruling dynasty of what later became Wessex (and was gradually to include Dumnonia) was descended from a line of leaders clearly bearing British names argues for the earliest of these having been somehow involved in the events of the period following 409. Brittany has its legendary link with Maximus and with the family with which he was endowed by the author of the *Dream of Maxen Wledig*, not to mention in the pages of Geoffrey of Monmouth. The *Dream* also endows Maximus with a link to Caernarfon, which is otherwise unprovable, except insofar as the genealogies provide him with a son or grandson who was a Christian saint there. The facts that the late Roman army included a unit recruited there and that the fort of Segontium was strengthened and supplemented at just the time when Maximus was active are also persuasive. Perhaps this was a case of the imperial government providing improved defensive infrastructure as a *douceur* towards the establishment of a treaty.

We also see political units like Brycheiniog emerge from what appear to be substantial *latifundiae*, securely in the hands of the ruling élite, with the Irish princes of Demetia acting as midwife. In examining the legendary connections of Vortigern/Vitalinus with Gloucestershire and with the clan to which Ambrosius Aurelianus appears to have belonged, another network of extensive landed aristocracy is implicit. These, too, have links with Britannia Prima, and by looking at the possible continuing political background to immediate post-Roman Britain, a much more distinctly Roman-rooted picture begins to emerge, far from the sort of brigandage of supposed Celtic self-determination rooted in a catastrophic collapse of society sometimes promoted.

For a long time, a surprisingly robust central authority allowed this state of affairs to continue. That no such arrangements were made for the defence of the east and south suggests that Germanic incursions were not anticipated in the 380s, or that the Shore forts were deemed adequate. All this was despite the drastic and perhaps inevitable fifth-century changes that affected people's way of life, with the decline of urbanism (not always that rapid, as Viroconium, Verulamium and others prove), rural change, the pressures of Germanic settlement and the trauma of the Saxon Revolt.

Elements of this Germanic expansion seem to have started with rebellions by men such as Hengist, already settled (as with the 'sons' of Maximus in the north), as a *magister militum, dux* or *phylarch*, who may well have been brought in to strengthen the island's defences but who rebelled, perhaps as a result of a natural disaster interrupting the supply of *annona*, with dire consequences. Further expansions, which ended up mutating later on into Anglo-Saxon kingdoms, probably based to some extent on the archaic boundaries of the *civitates,* seem in some cases to have had at their core some renegade British *condottiere,* as with Wessex, as a result of the efforts of Cerdic who may be indentifiable with Geoffrey of Monmouth's 'fomentor of discord', Keretic. Even the dynasty of Mercia has been canvassed as of possible British origin.[5]

While there is some fairly persuasive circumstantial evidence that those in control of greater Dumnonia in the early fifth century may have had links with the family or circle of Constantine III and his *magister militum* Gerontius, there is also, in characters like SS Paul Aurelian and Samson, with their Dumnonian and south Welsh connections, the suggestion of a powerful Romano-British dynasty, with links to Gaul, to what the genealogies tell us of the family of Vortigern and through him, it would seem, to Maximus. The more one examines these apparent family groupings (which groupings they surely are, even if the attempts to tabulate them are perforce largely speculative), the more a hyperlinked upper echelon of Romano-British society emerges, as in Gaul. This stratum of insular society enjoyed plenty of close links to Gaul, to Christian leaders like SS Martin, Ambrose and Germanus, all from the same social milieu as well-attested British-born men like Faustus of Riez, Riothamus and the monk Riocatus; instructively, all were later linked by the genealogies to the house of Vortigern and thus (thanks to the Pillar of Eliseg) to that of Powis (and Maximus).

If it is reasonable to attribute to Maximus a lasting settlement of the frontiers using federates, viceroys and treaty-bound native British and settlers, then his achievement can be reasonably viewed as considerable. If we can accept that this new dispensation prevailed successfully between the Walls, expanding the province of Valentia to the Forth-Clyde line (to some extent confirmed by the *Historia Brittonum's* list of British *civitates*, which includes Edinburgh), then he stands as a rare example of a Roman leader who successfully managed to extend the empire at a time when it was drawing in its horns. That he seems to have engaged with Ireland in the process seems incontrovertible, and that this *entente* continued, despite attacks by other groups from Ireland, into the mid-fifth century and probably beyond would seem to stand to Maximus's credit too, whether he actually crossed the Irish Sea himself or not. If we can accept that Maximus concluded a set of complex diplomatic arrangements with elements of the Irish élite, then a visit by him to Ireland might not seem quite so unlikely, especially if we allow him a presence in Britain from 379 and as having imperial authority from the following year, as suggested by the re-evaluation of *Chronicle of 452*.

Meanwhile, these dispositions on Britain's frontier zones aside, it has been contended that Maximus's *coup* was by no means impromptu, but was probably planned, almost certainly with the covert encouragement of the emperor Theodosius I, Maximus's kinsman. The frontier settlement goes a long way to corroborate this. As regards the acclamation itself, it seems to have possibly occurred three years before the generally accepted date of 383 and it emerges from the letters of St Ambrose that Maximus had not intended to have Gratian killed, but rather had planned to apprehend him and send him to Theodosius at Constantinople, which would certainly better accord with any such tacit collusion between the two emperors. After all, Maximus on his own admission was a recently baptised and enthusiastic Christian.

This further deepens the suspicion that Theodosius was always prepared to tolerate Maximus's elevation and rule – or welcomed it. Where matters began to unravel in this regard was Andragathius's murder of the deposed Gratian (typical of an associate's zeal in seeking to attract greater favour from his master), which would have compromised Theodosius's position, were he to be seen as complicit in Maximus's coup. Nothing suggests that this was actually Maximus's intention, as the later chorus of condemnation suggests. The callous act of brutality could only rebound eventually upon its perpetrators and was an act which held no possible advantage for the claimant himself.

For Theodosius to use a trusted lieutenant and kinsman to remove Gratian and, later, Valentinian II, both inexperienced, unsuitably young and callow representatives of the previous dynasty, catspaws of their generals, while keeping his distance should anything go awry, appears a coherent stratagem. While suggesting that the entire saga of Maximus's coup was a premeditated series of moves in pursuit of a specific goal can be challenged, but it would appear as not beyond the bounds of possibility, and that matters were derailed only by the murder of Gratian and later, following the toppling of Valentinian II, the happenstance of Theodosius's sudden infatuation with Aelia Galla, a believable irruption of human nature in the raw.[6] In this context, Theodosius' elevation of his young son to the purple does not contradict this suggested series of events, but could instead be viewed as an insurance policy on the eastern emperor's part, should anything go wrong. The elevation of Victor by Maximus appears in precisely the same light; they might well have regarded themselves as one and the same dynasty, as with Valentinian I and Valens.

It is impossible to find any convincing reason to believe that Maximuus's empress was called Helena; the plot of the *Dream* is a first-class romance, rather than a tract containing dimly remembered events, although a folk memory of entering Italy by the posterity of British-born members of Maximus's troops in 387 cannot be discounted as the inspiration of the fictional Maximus's siege of Rome. This also goes for Helen's family, Eudaf Hen, Conan and Gadeon, although the first may well have had some kind of memorable existence if the Breton sources have any weight – it's just that any attempt to put Eudaf in context seems fruitless given the paucity of any reliable sources.

As for Caernarfon as the seat of British power in the *Dream*, we can at least join with Nash-Williams and others in saying that in Wales, archaeological evidence points to a post-Roman occupation of a number of sites, including

Segontium, which, he felt, was expanded quite probably into an ordered late- and post-Roman centre of government.

Maximus's son Victor and attested (but unnamed) daughters aside, it seems prudent to discount entirely the legendary posterity – Owein/Eugenius notwithstanding – as being anything to do with the emperor's actual kin, with Severa perhaps excepted. In respect of the attested kin, though, a probable line of descent has been noted from a postulated marriage of one daughter into the unimpeachably grand Anician family, thanks to Procopius, a source much more reliable than most contemporary insular ones, especially as the necessary records and family traditions were still available to the well-travelled eastern chronicler. To dismiss the connection as idle speculation on Procopius' part is unreasonably dismissive. From this connection, one can argue that the emperor Petronius Maximus was probably the product, suggesting that there might have been a distinct element of revenge in his organisation of the murder of his cousin Valentinian III, a comeuppance for the elimination of Magnus Maximus, proposed as Petronius Maximus's maternal grandfather, by the maternal grandfather of Valentinian sixty-seven years earlier – a fanciful notion, but not beyond the bounds of possibility and in tune with the Roman mind-set of the age.[7]

From insular and much less secure sources we have noted Maximus's supposed other descendants. Two daughters appear, Severa/Sevira and Gratiana. The latter appears twice (once anonymously) in late sources as the wife of a prominent Dumnonian, but in order to be accepted as fact she would have to have remained in Britain after 383, as would Severa/Sevira; not impossible but perhaps less likely. She, too, bore a perfectly reasonable Roman name and is said to have married Vortigern.

A proposed identification of Vortigern, aided by the circumstantial evidence of his genealogy and his appearance fighting Ambrosius in 436, as Vitalinus, provides a credible link to an attested Roman family in the form of Bruttia Aureliana, whose *gentilicium* Bruttia just happens to re-manifest itself in the name of one of Vortigern and Severa's sons and whose *cognomen* is very common amongst recorded fifth-century Romano-Britons, both adjectivally and otherwise. Their progeny, possibly including bishop Faustus (if such he was), endow the later kingdom of Powis with a dynastic connection with our emperor, not to mention his possible granddaughter, married into an Irish ruling family of no small consequence. The far-spread social and familial links to Gaul and Ireland are typical of the topographical reach of the Roman élite of the age and emphasise, in this respect, that post-Roman Britain was no decaying Cinderella, isolated from the dramatic flow of events being played out all over the western empire, but remained under the strong, imperial-style control of a *tyrannus*, his standing technically recognised by the rescript of 410 (assuming this applies to Britain) and embedded in the milieu from which only its direct political ties and military subsidies had been lost.

These British sources provide us with a possible and perhaps more likely name for Maximus's wife, Ceindrech (perhaps in Latin originally Speciosa), who could well have been British and whom he could have encountered, even if not immediately espoused, during his posting to the British diocese in 367-368.[8] Severa and Gratiana then become chronologically convincing, and the former's marriage to a man who appears later to have been raised to power in post-Roman Britain as a memorable *tyrannus* is wholly in keeping with the practices of the age. These connections may well be fictional, but they certainly *could* have been amongst the children taken into the care of Theodosius's family after 388. Or were they left out of harm's way, perhaps with relatives, in Britain in 383 or 384?

The remainder of Maximus's supposed sons, Anthun/Antonius, Dunawt/ Donatus, Leo, Peiblic/Publicius, Kustennin/Constantine and Owein/Eugenius, we have detached entirely from their supposed parent and put forward as recipients of honours and treaties bestowed by Maximus to encourage them to man the periphery of the diocese while their 'father' pursued his imperial mission. That the scribes and bards of their descendants or successors should have appropriated the emperor as an ancestor seems to have been no more than one might expect in the centuries following, separated from the empire by the decay both of records and of record-keeping. The deployment of this policy of settling the frontier regions with reliable allies, its existence attested *ex silentio* by the *Notitia's* omissions, seems to have preserved these areas to evolve into British polities until the seventh century in the north, the eighth in Dumnonia, the ninth in Cornwall, the eleventh in southern Scotland, and in Wales until the thirteenth – a tribute we believe to Maximus's talents of diplomacy, organisation and strategic vision, not to mention the ability of the rulers and people of these polities to prosper, or at least function, through challenging times.

While some of the re-organising of the frontier zones could have been done by successors of Maximus, building on his foundations, both before and after 409, the overall settlement was surely undertaken upon his initiative, also made possible the continuance of passably effective central control over the diocese, even after the Saxon revolt in the 440s. Thus, it has been necessary to look at the way that authority seems to have progressed through well over a century, mainly from the later insular evidence. As John Koch says,

> ... during the fifth century, it might still have been possible to defend what had been Roman Britain as a whole with a carefully planned strategy... but interests founded in this period subsequently became fragmented and localized. In the sixth century they could not continue.[9]

This unexpected stability, not everywhere apparent on the continent of Europe at this time, would seem, on the admittedly equivocal evidence presented here, to have been to a large extent the result of a political and strategic settlement undertaken by Magnus Maximus in the period following his defeat of a serious incursion of Picts and Scots in 380/1 or just prior to 382/383, quite probably upon foundations laid in the aftermath of the Barbarian Conspiracy. That he may well have continued to work on Britain's defences after his accession would seem apparent from his 384 visit to Britain, and one cannot imagine a competent ruler of his calibre allowing such arrangements to drop off the map subsequently, and it has been suggested that a competent *vicarious/tyrannus* (conceivably Owein/ Eugenius) and senior military appointments would have seen to it that things remained shipshape.

Maximus may well have founded a substantial cathedral church in London at the same time, although whether he also established a metropolitan see there himself (as the Triads contend) is less likely.[10] The emerging evidence of some continuity in many of Britain's *civitates*, the revisions of the numismatic evidence, the re-thinking of life outside the towns, suggesting only a gradual decline in the money economy, and other recent discoveries, like the mid-fifth century mosaic-floored rooms at Chedworth villa, indicate anything but a catastrophic collapse of the Roman way of life post-409.[11] The suggestion that Roman Britain's towns instantly 'went down the pan ... the whole infrastructure structure of forts, towns and villas disintegrated', as Dr Faulkner so colourfully put it, can no longer be accepted.[12]

No ancient author appears to disagree that Magnus Maximus ruled his part of the empire extremely well, the criticisms of his allowing the death of Gratian, the execution of Priscillian and his alleged miserly tendencies notwithstanding. His mistakes were to have allowed his barbarian *magister militum* to have killed Gratian (especially in so devious a manner), to have deposed Valentinian II and allowed him to reach Constantinople (instead, perhaps, of keeping him on as a puppet) and to have underestimated the skill of Theodosius's commanders when it came to defending Italy in 388.

When one looks at other usurpers, like Maxentius, Magnentius, Valentinus or Firmus, he stands out as a paragon. Throughout Roman history there have been usurpers, of whom many were ephemeral. Not a few others started out as optimistic opportunists and survived to become household names, having triumphed and been recognised: Vespasian, probably Trajan, Septimius Severus, Aurelian, Probus, Diocletian and Constantine, to name a few. It is those who failed to survive who had obloquy heaped upon them by those left behind; in Maximus's case, eloquently orchestrated through Pacatus's panegyric to Theodosius, delivered, no doubt, as Symmachus was hastily burning copies of his own panegyric to the defeated rival. Theodosius, favourable spin having taken effect, was able to a large extent to guarantee the permanence of his dynasty on his own and guarantee through an obsequious senate his rival's *damnatio memoriae*.

Although his period in power ended in defeat, Maximus's rule over north-west Europe was exceptionally sound and, if anything of value has been rescued from the insular sources here, then his legacy in Britain was impressive; after all, no native British dynast prefaced his pedigree with the name of Stilicho, Theodosius or Constantine III. Thanks to Maximus's far-ranging and carefully conceived settlement of the frontier regions, his insular legacy was remarkably long-lasting, securing the former diocese's ultimate (if diminishing) independence until 28 June 1283.

Cerdic as imagined by the Jacobean cartographer John Speed.
(M. Craven)

Endnotes

Introduction

1. Omissi (2018) 306
2. Matthews (1983) 431
3. Johnson (1982) 143.
4. Sulp. Sev. *V. Martini* 20. Other pro-Maximus sources included Rufinus of Aquileia, and Sidonius Apollinaris in his panegyric on Majorian.
5. Orosius VII. 34, 9
6. Wijnendaele (2020) 330.

1 Britain before Maximus

1. Coin evidence
2. ILS 414, 415
3. HA *V. Albini* 6. 1-6. The ordinary consuls began the year and named it.
4. Birley (2005) 174-180
5. Eg Herodian, 3, 7, 7-8
6. Wacher (1978) 51; C. Martin in *British Archaeology* 6 (7/1995) 6, cc. 1-3.
7. Thought to be the *Horrea Classis* of the Ravenna Cosmography; it has been argued that it was originally established in the later 180s; Tibbs (2019) 147.
8. Craven (2019) 271-275
9. Pearson (2002) *passim.*
10. Drinkwater (1987) 97; PLRE I Postumus 2
11. *Ibid.* 26-27, 239 f. & 255.
12. Zosimus I. 66, 2.
13. *Op. cit.* 9, 17
14. PLRE I Proculus 1
15. PLRE I Bonosus 1 & Hunila based on HA *V. Firmi* 15, 2, 3 & 7.
16. ILS 608
17. ILS 615; Birley (2005) 371
18. Birley (2005) 372-373
19. Birley (2005) 372 & n.9
20. PLRE I Carausius. He was referred to as *archipirata* ('superpirate').

Endnotes

21. *Roman Inscriptions of Britain (RIB)* 2291/ILS 8928.
22. Coin evidence and portraits wearing the *trabea*, consular garb.
23. Shiel (1977) 191-192; RIC 1-2.
24. *Eclogue* IV. 1, cf. de la Bédoyère, G. M. T., in *Numismatic Chronicle* 158 (1998) 79f., cf. eg. RIC548, 571, 595.
25. Casey (1994) 115-126.
26. Craven (2020) *passim*. The date of Cardiff appears to be less certain.
27. PLRE I Allectus
28. Casey (1994) 127, 134.
29. PLRE I Asclepiodotus 3. He was consul in 292.
30. Admirably encapsulated by Casey (1994) 150
31. *Pan Lat.* VI (7) 7,4 to 8, 2. The system may well have survived, paid entirely in kind, beyond 409 (qv *infra*).
32. Hurley *et al.* (2006) 23 & n. 54.
33. He was deified by the senate: ILS652.
34. *Ep.* 41, 2-3.
35. Probus: Zosimus I. 68; Valentinian: *Amm Marc.* xxix, 4.7; Crocus: Johnson (1980) 90; Wood (2006) 77-82. The Bucinobantes were from the region around Mainz.
36. *HB* 25; Morgan Evans (2014) 174. NB Maximus's alleged grandson St Peblic founded a church at Caernarfon, see Chapter 9. Segontium (Old Welsh *Cair Segeint*) is the name of the Roman fort on the outskirts of Caernarfon.
37. Hurley *et al.* (2006) 23, 31, cf. Mann (1979) 147
38. ILS 8942
39. Birley (2005) 397-398
40. Rivett & Smith (1979) 260, 306, 396-398, where it is suggested that after 293 the city was given the honorific title of Caesarea, which was then bumped up to Augusta in 306, cf. Birley (1981) 316-317. Cirencester's pre-eminence: RIB 103.
41. In the western *Notitia Dignitatum*, upon which see below.
42. Wacher (1978) 55
43. There seems to have once been a list of the ancient [Arch]bishops of London, quoted by Stow (1603) from Jocelyn of Furness, *De Britonum Episcopum* (c. 1170) who renders Restitutus as Iltutus, an asssumed error but one strangely presaging the Breton apostle of Llantwit Major (see below Chapter 10) – unless Restitutus really *was* St Illtud's original name, subsequently abbreviated.
44. Birley (2005) 397 n. 3; the other bishops were Eborius of York (clearly having taken his name from his see) and Adelphius of Lincoln, the priest was (predictably) Sacerdos and the deacon Arminius; they each seem, between them, to have represented all four provinces with one man supernumerary.
45. Southern & Dixon (1996) 15-19, 33-37.
46. PLRE I Constans 3, where the possibility is expressed that his date of birth was actually 323, making him just 14 (rather than 17) when he acceded to power.
47. Johnson (1982) 120-121
48. Morris (1999) 171, 174; or were these, in reality, rather later?
49. Amm. Marc. 28.3, 3.
50. Birley (2005) 399-400.
51. Higham & Jones (1985) 121, Note that Johnson has suggested that it was the entire diocese of Britain that was renamed Valentia: *op.cit.* 127; this theory has failed to find favour, however.

52. PLRE I Magnentius
53. ILS 743, 744 & 742.
54. PLRE I Decentius 3.
55. Eutropius x. 12; Victor, *Epit.* 42,4.
56. Johnson (1982) 51
57. Salway (1984) 351
58. ILS747
59. *Numismatic Chronicle*, 3rd series Vol. VII (1887) 191 and cf. C.H.V. Southerland, *'Carausius II', 'Censeris', and the Barbarous* Fel. Temp. Reparatio *Overstrikes, ibid.* 4th series Vol. IV/V (1945). Birley (2005) 420 considers them poor forgeries.
60. Amm Marc. 14. 5, 6; PLRE I Martinus 2, Paulus 4.
61. Amm. Msrc. 15.5
62. Drinkwater (1998) 293
63. Casey (1994) 165-167.
64. PLRE I Vetranio; he retired to Prusa (Bursa, modern Turkey) and died in 357.
65. CIIC 393: Thomas (1994) 205; the inscription and its disposition contain much additional, coded information.
66. 'Iacit' for 'Iacet' is a common late Latin corruption, cf.Ch. 8 above and an MI at Vienne, France: Knight (2007) 104
67. Numbers: Amm. Marc. xvi, 12. 1
68. Johnson (1982) 116
69. Sutherland (1994) 47
70. Amm. Marc. 20.1,1
71. Rance (2001) 257; Casey (1979) 74. Spear butts: Russell & Laycock (2010) 157, 163: the other possibility is that they were the result of the incursion preceding Maximus's elevation.
72. Amm. Marc. 20. 2, 4, where his character is not given a very promising press. PLRE I, Lupicinus 6.
73. Fleming (2021) 18f.
74. Amm. Marc. 20, 9, 9.
75. Amm. Marc. 27.8, 1.
76. White (2007) Ch. 5.
77. *Hostilibus insidiis circumventum* although *circumventum* could be 'cut off', or even a euphemism for 'killed'.
78. Amm. Mrac. 28, 8.1ff; Casey (1979) 74 & n.
79. PLRE I Fullofaudes, Jovinus 6 (who was perhaps the grandfather of the Gallic imperial claimants Jovinus and Sebastianus in the early fifth century), Nectaridus. On the sequence of events, see Birley (1981) 337, following R. Tomlin in *Britannia* 5 (1974) 303ff.
80. Amm. Marc. 27.8.2-3. PLRE I Theodosius 3 & 4.
81. Who exactly the Attacotti were is still a matter of debate; recent opinion seems to be returning to the view that they also came from Ireland, cf. Birley (2005) 424 n. 43 & Rance (2000) 243ff.
82. Rance (2001) 249
83. Amm. Marc. 27. 8, 4. Note that the author was living in the east when the events he is describing occurred and he would have had to have been garnered information at a distance, which may explain the slightly confusing account; cf. Charles-Edwards (2003) 25.
84. Syme (1968) 14, cf. Morris (1973) 15 ff.
85. Hughes (2013) 60-61.

86. Johnson (1982) 123; these other sources are: Pacatus's Panegyric on Theodosius I (qv infra) and four extracts from Claudian, all honouring Theodosius's son Honorius.
87. Zosimus adds that he also took the *Herculani*. These were units raised as *comitatenses* under the Tetrachs and, ironically, previously commanded by Magnentius prior to his seizure of power: Zosimus *NH* II. 58 & III.89.
88. Amm . Marc. 27.8, 7-10; PLRE I Civilis, Dulcitius 4.
89. Zosimus *NH* IV.100; the name is an error, which can be corrected from other sources. St Jerome and the later Chronicler Jordanes also mention him and misspell him.
90. Amm Marc. 28.3, 3-5; PLRE I Valentinus 5.
91. Frere (1966) 88
92. *Areani*: Casey (1979) 74; Bastions: Salway (1984) 390; *areani* and security: *ibid*. 376, 385
93. *Not. Dig. Oriens* IX. 29; *Occidens* V 197 & 200, VII. 24, 74; Rance (2001) 247
94. Amm,. Marc. 28. 3, 8. As summarised in exemplary manner by Birley (2005) 439, cf. Salway (1984) 390 & Dornier (1982) 253 who attributes it to Wales.
95. *Pan. Lat.* VIII, 21.
96. Giot *et al* (2003) 102, hence the Welsh name *Llydaw* for Brittany.
97. As Zonaras, cf. PLRE I Fl. Magnus Magnentius.
98. Mason (2001) 208, quoting the *Notitia Dignitatum*, but see below.
99. Quoted by Will Bowden, University of Nottingham, 2019.
100. Amm. Marc. 29. 4, 7.
101. Pontifex maximus: Cameron (1968) 97; Rüpke & Glock (2008) 61-62 & No. 1685. He was probably the last emperor to have borne it, too.

2 Magnus Maximus: Before Empire

1. Pan Lat. II (XII) 24, 1; He was previously long accredited with the middle name Clemens, but this has now been established as a misreading of one of the ancient sources: Birley (1981) 348.
2. John of Nikiou, *Chron.* 83.14: 'And ... there arose an usurper named Maximus, of British descent.'
3. PLRE I Antonius 5, Honorius 2, Maria.
4. Aur. Victor *Epit.* 46.viii; Zosimus IV.47, 1, but see Chapter IV.
5. Theodosius came from Cauca, Gallaecia (Coca, near Segovia): Zosimus IV.35, 3; CIL II. 4911; Theodosius: Zosimus IV.24, 4, and was born c. 346, cf. PLRE I Theodosius 4; on the province, Birley (1981) 348 n. 4.
6. Ambrose, *Ep.* 40, 32
7. Chron. Pasc. I. 646, 7. Pan. Lat. XII (II) 31, 1; Zosimus IV. 35, 3, strengthened by Gregory of Tours' remark [I. 43] '... after achieving victory for the Britons, who were oppressed by tyranny', although the passage is more commonly translated as '... for he crushed them [the British provinces] by his tyrannical behaviour' the latter referring to his acclamation and rule, the former to his earlier military exploits in Britain.
8. Amm. Marc. 25. 6, 3, killed with Julianus & Macrobius, also tribunes, cf. PLRE I Maximus 18.
9. Amm. Marc.29. 5, 6 & 5, 21: We are not told who the Maximus who fought under Theodosius actually was, but it is generally accepted that his was Magnus Maximus.

10. PLRE I Firmus 3; Amm. Marc. 29, 5, 6
11. Amm. Marc. 28, 3, 4-6; 30. 7, 10; PLRE I. Romanus 3, Vincentius 4.
12. Scheid & Zink (2019) *passim*.
13. Amm. Marc. 29, 5. 35; Moffat (2010) 88-89
14. Zosimus 4. 13, 4; Birtley (2005) 440 who reminds us that Theodosius received baptism prior to execution.
15. Suggested by Matthews (1975) 96, 173, n. 1, cf. Amm. Marc. 31. 4, 9ff. & Orosius 7. 33, 11; PLRE I. Lupicinus 3; Maximus 24
16. Pacatus was writing a year or so later; Ammianus a few years later: Birley (1981) 349.
17. Wijnendaele (2020) 332
18. Birley (2005) 401-404
19. Reluctant emperor: Zonaras XIII.17, 1
20. Birley (2005) 401-404
21. *Mabinogion, The Dream of Maxen Wletic,* see below, chapter 7.
22. Gibbon II (1903) 162
23. Former: Matthews (1975) 175 n. 6; *dux*: Frere (1967) 404; discussed in Birley (2005) 448-449.
24. As also, Wijnendaele (2020) 332
25. Zonaras, IV. 35, 4.
26. Greg. Tours *HF* I.43
27. Frere (1966) 399 but subsequently challenged, most recently by Fleming (2021) *passim*.
28. Zosimus IV, 32.
29. PLRE I Antonius 5, where it is suggested that he was brother of Maria who married Theodosius' brother, Honorius (*ibid*. Honorius 2)
30. Craven (2019) 314-328
31. Greg. Tur. *HF*. 1. 43
32. Polemius Silvius *Laterculus* 78-79, quoted in Birley (2005) 455, although nothing specifically connects Servatus with Britain, and the implication is that he was under Honorius, cf. PLRE II. Servatus 1.
33. Matthews (1975) 175-176 for a good assessment of Maximus's motives.
34. Sulpicius Severus quoted in Knight (2007) 46.
35. *Pan Lat* II (XII) 2, 23-24.
36. Supicius Severus, V. Martini 20, 3f; cf. Orosius 7. 34,9.
37. Letter, Maximus to Siricius in *Collectio Avellana* 40.
38. Amm. Marc. 29.4,7; later events: see chapter 8.
39. PLRE I Andragathius 3
40. Birley (1981) 351; the revised (earlier) date: Cameron (1968) 97 quoting Grunel.
41. Jones & Casey (1988) 367f. and (1991) 212f.; contra: Burgess (1994) 240-243.
42. Casey (1979) 71-72, cf. Jones & Casey (1988) 367ff. & (1991) 212ff., *contra*: Burgess (1990) 185f.
43. RIC Magnus Maximus 1.
44. RIC IX. 004 and note by J W E Pearce.
45. Casey, *op. cit.* 74-75.
46. *Contra*: Dumville (1977) 173ff. Kent thought that the abandonment of the inland forts was the work of Stilicho, but without unequivocal support for such a notion: Kent (1979) 77.
47. PLRE I Arcadius 5

48. *Pan. Lat.* II (XII) 43, 4.
49. *Pan Lat.* II (XII) 23, 4.
50. Drinkwater (1998) 295; Sivan (1993) 138
51. Rance (2001) 243ff.
52. Casey (1978) 68.
53. CIL XI 6327, quoted in Birley (1981) 351.
54. Casey (1979) 68, cf. RIC IX No. 1 (gold) and 4 (silver)
55. Birley (1981) 374-375; numismatic proof: Casey (1979) 76. Of Maximus's responsibility for removing the diocesan forces, cf. Gildas DE 14.
56. Dornier (1982) 253.
57. Breeze (1982) 159
58. Webster (1991) 124; PLRE II Claudianus 5. Claudianus *On the Consulship of Stilicho* iii, 130-161.
59. *Notitia Dignitatum, Occ.* VII, 41,17, 42.22, 84; 100, 109 & 110.
60. Casey (1979) 79
61. Departure point attested by Pacatus, *Pan. Lat.* II (XII) 23f., but the most likely, in any event.
62. PLRE I Merobaudes 2. It is unclear what became of Vallio, recorded in (all hostile) sources as the *magister equitum* (C-in-C cavalry) under Merobaudes; he would have been replaced by Andragathius, and it would appear that he had committed suicide, but Pacatus (*Pan Lat.* II (XII) 26.4) claims Maximus killed him in lurid circumstances, while Ambrose concedes suicide but lards Maximus with the blame: Amb. *Ep.* 24.11.
63. Murder of Gratian, Zonaras XVII; Zosimus IV. 35.6
64. Amb. *Ep.* 24, 10; PLRE I Andragathius 3.
65. Zosimus IV 116

3 Emperor in the West

1. PLRE I Fl. Evodius 2; Russell & Laycock (2010) 168; see below for more on those who joined his administration.
2. Matthews (1975) 178-179; for 384: Banchich and Lane (2012) 260
3. PLRE I p.1045; the eastern consuls were Richomeres and Clearchus.
4. Casey (1979) 70.
5. PLRE Anonymus 30. Most unusually, this official was not a eunuch, suggesting that he was probably an old friend or ex-comrade of Maximus, drafted in on the acclamation. His successor, who received an embassy from St Ambrose in 385 certainly was: *ibid.*, Anonymus 31. Banchich & Lane (2009) 260.
6. Birley (2005) 450 & n 111; Casey (1979) 67.
7. ILS 787
8. Amb. *Ep.* 24, 9.
9. PLRE I Theodosius 4.
10. As Nixon & Rodgers (1994) 453 n. 18.
11. Orosius 7.33, 6-7.
12. *Année Epigraphique* (1967) 561.
13. PLRE I Victor 6
14. PLRE I Victor 14, esp. Aur. Victor, 48, 6 '... made Augustus whist still an infant'; Prosper Tiro *sub anno* 384; Greg. *HF* II.9; Zosimus IV.50, 5 cf. 47, 1.
15. ILS 788; PRE I Maximus 39.

16. ILS 780; six others have been noted elsewhere.
17. Casey (1979) 67
18. Name: Rivet & Smith (1979) 260; coin types and implications: Casey (1979) 69, 72-73
19. Sankey (1998) 78-81; Rogers (2011) 122 urges some caution in its identification as a church.
20. Denison, S., in *British Archaeology* 6/1995, Keys, D. in *The Independent*. London 3/4/1995 cf. Sankey (1998) 78–82.
21. Thomas (1981) 191-200.
22. Williams (1977) No. 62; of Morgannwg's third series of Triads, Bromwich (1979 xii) wrote: 'Iolo Morgannwg re-wrote many of the older Triads in an expanded form with the introduction of some fresh material', of which this is one. Here Maximus is clearly replacing Constantine.
23. Sulp. Sev. *Chron.* II. 49, 2.
24. Sankey (1998) 81-82. The six gates although much rebuilt, survived until 1761.
25. Kulikowski (2019) 105
26. Frere (1966) 88 where these works are attributed to the *comes* Theodosius' measures of 369.
27. Or *pharos* (at Dinas Dinlle), cf. below.
28. Nash-Williams (1954) 28-33, 96; Laing (1977) 57-59; Shotter, D. C. A., *Roman Lancaster: Site and Settlement* in White (2001) 3-31. Note Shore fort at Lancaster called by Camden *Caer Gwerid*: Camden (1594) 587, hence presumably the current name for the surviving fragment, the Wery Wall.
29. *Notitia Dignitatum* (west) V 65.
30. *HB* 66; *Breudwyt Maxen Wledig* also makes a claim for post-Roman re-use of Tomen-y-Mur, Trawsfynydd, wherein the fort is called Mur Castell (Castle Walls).
31. RIB 430
32. Margary (1957) II. 48, 81-82, respectively Nos.68, and 67c; the Sarn Elen is 69b.
33. Casey (1979) 77, Laing (1977) 57-58, although Kent advocated abandonment by Stilicho: Kent (1979) 22.
34. Casey *et al* (1993) passim; Boyle (1991) 191-212
35. An excavation of 2019-2020 by Ian Miller and the University of Salford, briefly reported in *Current Archaeology* 373 (4/2021) 9. 1st/2nd century pottery were found and substantial stone foundations.
36. Another allegedly Roman bridge, remarkably complete, with a single stone span over the Cadnant, a tributary of the Seiont, survives, just outside the settlement at Rhosbodrual.
37. *Bonedd y Saint* 63. The father was Owein Finddu, see Ch. 9.
38. British Listed Buildings, Cadw ID 3881 (LGI). See also Part II.
39. Davies (1996) 25 & Figs. 18 & 64.
40. The distinct raised platform of which has yet to be excavated: Coflein.
41. Nash-Williams (1954) 94-96 (occupation until end of 4th century); signal stations: Arnold & Clark 28-29, 243.
42. Collins & Breeze (2014) 64, referring to Amm. Marc. 27.8 & 28.3
43. Mason (2001) 211; Salway (1984) 404, 406.
44. Faull (1977) 3
45. Ottaway (2004) 140-143.
46. PLRE I. Iustinianus 1, cf. PLRE II. Iustinianus 1.

47. Johnson (1982) 125; Fleming (2021) 26-27
48. Alcock (1971) 97-98 – and possibly not at all prior to 409.
49. Salway (1984) 385, 403
50. *Pan. Lat* II (XII) 26, 1-2, cf Guest (2014) 122
51. Symmachus, Sivan (1993) 136-137; drops Ausonius: 140; Hesperius, 139
52. Sivan (1993) 138-139
53. Matthews (1975) 174; Sivan (1993) 140, 144. He took his revenge in a poem after Maximus's death.
54. Sivan (1993) 145.
55. Sivan (1993) 145
56. Amm. Marc. xxvii. 6, 1; CIL XIII. 921, cf. PLRE Julianus 37; Lupicinus 5; Sivan (1993) 145
57. PLRE I Anonymus 36, Maximinus 9
58. PLRE I Marinianus 2 cf. Anonymous 58, *ibid.* p. 1015. Another unnamed appointee took over the following year: PLRE I Anonymus 59.
59. CIL II. 4911
60. Birley (2005) 450-451.
61. Jesus College MS 20, 5, cf. BL Harl. MS 3859, *Historia Britonum* 8, *Vita Cadoci* 16(b) etc.
62. PLRE Marcellinus 11 & Marcianus 14.
63. Birley (205) 452 quoting Socrates, *Historia Ecclesiastica* VII, 12.1, cf. PLRE I Chrysanthus
64. PLRE II Victorinus 1; Birley (2005) 454.
65. PLRE Leucadius 1 and Bonosus 3.
66. Aur. Victor ix. 17; all other references to him are in the SHA and impossibly unreliable. Unexpectedly, the name appears to recur in the much later account of Vortigern's family, see Chapter VIII.
67. PLRE I. Artemius 4; Greg. Tours HF I.46. If the same man, he had been *vicarius* of Spain a decade before.
68. PLRE I, Nannienus had been appointed *comes* by Valetinian I in 370.
69. PLRE I, Evodius 2, Syagrius 2
70. Craven (2019) 477 & Table LIX(a)
71. PLRE I, Cynegius 3; Florus 1; Cassia 2; PLRE II Cynegius 1; the consul Fl. Claudius Antonius 5 may belong in this nexus, too, qv. *supra*.
72. PLRE I p. 1045.
73. PLRE I Florentinus 2; Minervius 1, 2, 3, Protadius 1 &2; Sivan (1993) 139

4 Trier, Rome and Aquileia

1. Greg. *HF* I.42
2. PLRE I Martinus 3; Sulp. Sev. *V. Martini* 2.1
3. Sulpicius Severus, *Chronica* II.46
4. Jerome *Ep.* 123, 3; apparently, Virgil's *Georgics* ii.325; Mathiesen (1989) 13-15.
5. Pope Damasus, (son of an Antonius no less) was, like Maximus and Priscillianus, according to the *Liber Pontificalis*, Spanish: *LP*. 39
6. Matthews (1975) 165-167; Livermore (1971) 110, 112.
7. Noted by Thomas (1994) 184.
8. Harries (1994) 118-119

9. Siricius nevertheless exiled 'Manicheans' from Rome, presumably meaning Priscillianists: *LP* 40.
10. PLRE I. Delphidius, Euchrotia, Latronianus 1 & Procula. Latronianus was probably the grandson of a proconsul of Africa under Constantine, Domitius Latronianus 2, and thus of distinguished family.
11. PLRE I Tiberianus 3 he eventually returned from exile.
12. Greg. *HF* X.31
13. Greg. *HF* V 18, 9.
14. Sulpicius Severus, quoted in Mathiesen (1993) 97.
15. Sulpicius Severus, 20.4: the year is fixed by Evodius's consulship.
16. Prosp. *Chron.* 7.12, reviewed in Drinkwater & Elton (1992) 32, 34.
17. Greg. *Life of the Fathers* (1991 II., pp. 12-13. Interestingly, Marius Artemius, Maximus's *vicarius* in Spain at this time, retired to Clermont after Maximus's death, setting a trend which became more common after the Praetorian Prefecture of Gaul's base was moved from Trier to Arles in 395: Mathiesen (1993) 59.
18. Sulp. Sev. *Dial.* 3, 11
19. Supl. Sev. *V. Martini* 20, 5
20. Pan. Lat. II (XII) 26-29, Haarer (2014) 167.
21. Birley (2005) 449 & n. 103
22. Reported in Zosimus VI.38-40, probably 386; Williams and Friell (1994) 44 treat this event as the trigger for Theodosius's recognition of Maximus, probably because Zosimus fails to make clear the result of the initial embassy to Constantinople in 383/4, yet, as we have seen, most indications would place it two years earlier.
23. Zosimus IV 48.4-50.1
24. Matthews (1975) 223
25. Matthews (1975) 177 & nn., 2, 4.
26. *Ibid.*, 178
27. Ambr. *Ep.* 24.7 especially.
28. Zosimus IV.42.6ff.; PLRE I Domninus 3, possibly to be identified with Domninus 2.
29. Sozomen, *HE* 7, 13.
30. *Causus belli*: Sozomen, *HE* 7. 13
31. Matthews (1975) 223, n. 4
32. Ptrocopius HB I, 4.16, cf. Mommaerts & Kelly (1992) 111-121; PLRE I Probus 5
33. He was of consular rank when appointed: PLRE I Celsus 9, replacing Herculius, *ibid.*
34. First consul, L. Ragonius L. f. Pap. Urinatius Larcius Quinctianus: PIR² R17 (ILS 1124); Consul of 289, PLRE I Quinctianus 3.
35. PLRE I Venustus 2
36. Zosimus IV.43.2-44.4
37. *ibid.* IV.28f.
38. Williams and Friell (1994) 61 who call Zosimus 'erratic and hostile'.
39. The empress, the Spanish Aelia Flaccilla, died early in the previous year.
40. Craven (2019) 447-450
41. Matthews (1975) 224
42. Pat. Lat. II (XII) 35
43. Pan. Lat. II (XII) 44. 2f,; Zosimus IV 46, 1f, 47.1.
44. Procop. *Bell. Vand.* 1. 4. 16; the date is sometimes given as 28th August, a date successfully challenged by Chadwick (1976) 122, n. 3.1; insular sources: see below, Chapter 7.

45. See Chapter 3.
46. Ambrose, *ep.* 40, 22-23.
47. Preceding a similar outbreak of Christian anti-semitism in Syria at Callinicum where Theodosius' initial response was successfully undermined by Ambrose: Matthews (1975) 232-233.
48. Ausonius *op. cit.* 64–72
49. Sulp. Sev. *V. Martini* 20. 4
50. Matthews (1975) 237
51. Drinkwater (2019) 93
52. Syvänne (2019) 154-155.
53. Ambrose, Ep. 40, 32.
54. Quoted in Morris (1972) 419.n 2.; see above Chapter III.
55. Proc, *HB* 1, 4.16. Mommaerts & Kelly (1992) 112 suspect that Probinus was, in his turn descended from an heiress of the Emperor Probus, always, like Maximus, held in high esteem by senatorial historians.
56. Mommaerts & Kelly *op. cit.* 118
57. PLRE II Maximus 22, Valentinianus 4
58. On the mother of 'Owein son of Maximus', Keindrech verch Reiden ap Eledi as his empress see Ch. 11.
59. See note above; Knight (2007) 66.
60. There are three in PLRE I (all members of the house of Constantine, however) and one Helenus, who was not. There is another Helena in PLRE II, but amongst humbler folk note 10 in ILS: Dessau (1979) IV.200
61. Johns (2010) 7

5 Aftermath

1. Properly, Colonia Claudia Ara Agrippinensium, but colloquially just Colonia.
2. Matthews (1975) 238 is inclined to believe Valentinian's suicide; Zosimus has him as publicly murdered: IV.54.3.
3. PLE I Eugenius 6; *vir clarissimus* signified senatorial rank.
4. Matthews (1975) 239; coins: reverses, Victoria Augustorum; Victoria AVGG and Victoria AVGGG (latter mainly bronze).
5. Craven (2019) 470-471.
6. PLRE II Stilicho; see suggested *stemma*, Chapter 3 *stemma* 1.
7. See *stemma* 1 above.
8. PLRE II. Claudianus 5; Claudian, *De Cons. Stil.* 2. 247–55
9. Procopius, *De Bello Gothico,* 416–18
10. Higham & Jones (1985) 126
11. Collins & Breeze (2014) 65. The Frigidus too, could have been the occasion of the transference of the *Seguntienses*, but much less likely than 388. The date 402 derives from the apparent end of new coin issues reaching Britain.
12. Birley (2005) 455 cf. PLRE II Marcus 2.
13. Soz, *HE.* IX, 11.2
14. Polemius Silvius *Laterculus* 78-79, quoted in Birley *loc.cit.* His list includes Magnus Maximus (expressed as two people), Maximus's son, Victor, Gerontius's man Maximus, the Gallic senators Jovinus and Sebastianus along with the totally unknown Servatus, referred to in Chapter 2 as the possible cause of Maximus's appointment to Britain after Adrianople, but in this sequence, seemingly a successor of Constantine III's rival Maximus.

15. Zosimus VI. 3,1. The consul Probus being father of Petronius Maximus and husband of Maximus's daughter.
16. Zosimus V. 27, 2
17. Birley (2005) 458 following Olympiodorus, fragment 12. Regarding coins: unless some extreme rarities still await the attentions of archaeology or metal detectors.
18. *Op. cit.* 455, quoting Sozomen, *loc.cit.*
19. cf. PLRE I, four examples & PLRE II also four, of whom Marcus 1 was a fairly senior serving officer under the Praetorian Prefect of the East just a few years before; was he assigned to Britain shortly afterwards?
20. Zosimus VI, 1, 1.
21. Orosius *loc.cit.* PLRE II Gratian 3
22. Birley (2005) 457 n. 127
23. As Drinkwater J. F. in *Britannia* 29 (1998) 272.
24. Orosius VII. 40, 4
25. Procopius *BG* III. 2, 31
26. PLRE II Constantinus 21; Drinkwater (1998) 269ff.
27. Fleming (2021) 23-24, 28
28. Was one of these the enigmatic Servatus, mentioned by Sozomen?
29. Four months: Olympiodorus Fr. 12, Soz. *HE* IX. 11, 2 and Zosimus Vi. 2, 2 (the latter pair probably taking their cue from the former); all agree on the reign's length.
30. Jerome, Ep. 133, 9.
31. Knight (2007) 48, n. 7. Constantine later filled two Gallic sees with Martinian favourites: Dark (1994) 527.
32. Mathiesen (1989) *passim*.
33. Greg. Tours *HF* I. 43
34. Collinson & Breeze (2014) 61-72. Fifth century garrisoning of Hadrian's Wall: Collins, (2004) 131.
35. Mathiesen (1989) 31 n. 19. Bishop Justinianus was elevated to Tours in 430, thus perhaps a nephew.
36. PLRE I Justianianus 1, PLRE II Justinianus 1 & Nebiogastes: the latter were therefore fellow officers with Constantine in Britain: Zos. VI. 2, 2.
37. Jerome *Ep.* cxxiii, 16
38. Drinkwater (1998) 284 ff.
39. NB Galba's Spanish 'senate' in 68: Suetonius, *Galba* 10.2; Knight (2007) 170.
40. Mathiesen (1989) 28-29
41. PLRE II Edobichus & Gerontius 5
42. PLRE I Gerontius 1
43. Mathiesen 31. Nantes was earlier called Condevincum.
44. PLRE I Nunechius; PLRE II Nunechia.
45. Carroll (2001) 143, 144
46. PLRE II Constans 1 & Julianus 7.
47. PLRE II Iovius 1; he was an aristocratic Gallic kinsman of St Paulinus of Nola.
48. Although apparently dead by the time the accord had been reached. Two others of the family escaped to Constantinople.
49. PLRE II Justus 1. The concordance in their nomenclature, as with Constantinus and Constans, is highly suggestive at this period.
50. Olympiodorus, Fr. 16; PLRE II Maximus 4. Olympiodorus, although an easterner, was a contemporary: Matthews (1970) 79f.
51. Zosimus VI. 5, 2-3

52. Zosimus VI. 10, 2
53. Argued most convincingly by Birley (2005) 461-462.
54. As Johnson (1982) 135, 138, 141 *et multis aliis*. Some authors have implausibly suggested a bacaudic style 'people's uprising' of anachronistic nationalist freedom fighters.
55. Procopius *De Bello Vandalico* 3. 2. & 31, 8
56. Gildas *DE* 18
57. Russell & Laycock (2010) 173,183.
58. Drinkwater (1998) 293, but somewhat contradicted further on, *ibid*. 296.
59. Thompson (1977) 316.
60. Owein (Finddu), invariably cited as a 'son' of Maximus, thus perhaps a *protégé*: see Chapter 9 below.
61. PLRE II Julianus 7
62. *HRB* VI. 5
63. Mathiesen (1989) 27, cf. PLRE II Iovinus 2; PLRE II Rusticus 9. He was a friend of Sidonius Apollinaris's family, and quite probably a close relative of the poet and politician Ausonius (consul in 379) whom Magnus Maximus had furloughed: Sivan (1993) 60 f.
64. Knight (2007) 48; Mathiesen (1989) 32 who points out the precedent here set in ordaining deposed emperors like Avitus in 456 and Glycerius in 475. Strong emperors tended to die; the more harmless were ordained. Constantine had been, perhaps, just a mite too effective.
65. Greg. *HF* II.9
66. Prosper, year 412, Zosimus 6, 3, both quoted in Knight (2014) 167.
67. Soz. IX.13
68. Cunliffe Shaw (1973) 103.
69. PLRE II Maximus 4 & Maximus 7.
70. Kulikowski (2000) 123 ff.
71. Livermore (1971) 85. Apart from losing most of Baetica to Justinian's forces in the mid-6th century; this outpost of empire lasted until 624, except for the Balearics which survived under imperial control for a further two centuries.
72. Johnson (1982) 152, cf. Ward (1973) 253; note that a modest supply of gold coinage arrived in SE Britain after 411, much from Italian mints – five hoards are known of largely unworn coins – a small supply arriving in issues of Jovinus (411-413) to Zeno (474-491). The earlier ones *could* suggest military pay.

6 The Long Fifth Century

1. As Barnwell (1992) 68
2. Analysed with comparable sites and well closures in Fleming (2021) 76-78, 110.
3. Zosimus VI. 5, 2-3. *Tyranni* = usurpers, powerful men usurping the power vested under the empire in the local *ordones* of the *civitiates* eg. as also used by Gildas: Thomas (1994) 211. On a possible name, see Part II, chapter 9.
4. Salway (1993) 357
5. Barnwell (1992) 69; Fleming (2021) *passim*.
6. Kent (1979) 19.
7. *Tyrannus* was very much the favoured & unequivocal term for an usurper in Roman sources: Neri (1996) 71ff.

8. Procopius *De Bello Vandalico* 3. 2. & 31. 8.
9. Kent (1979) 15; Morris (1980) 45 &n., 48 & n; *HB* 42: *unus de consulibus Romanicae gentis.* Constantine III's consuls: Kent, *op.cit.*, 19.
10. *Op. cit.* XV.2
11. Victor, *Cursus Paschalis Annorum* DXXXII, 31
12. Bede *HE* I. 12
13. Morris (1980) 1-3
14. *HB* 31, cf. Alcock (1971) 104-105; Bede *HE* I. 14; ASC *sub anno* 449.
15. *HB* 66
16. Higham (1995) 53
17. Kent (1979) 15
18. *HB* 31 PLRE II Ambrosius 2, Vortigern
19. Gildas *DE* 23
20. Halsall (2013) 191f., 215f.
21. Bromwich (1978) 131-139.
22. Gildas *DE* 21.4. Note also that in this sort of context, *reges* (kings) was shorthand for *tyranni* (usurpers):Fanning (1992) 288f.
23. Gildas, *DE* 25.
24. Dismissed by Johnson (1982) 155 and others as merely signifying nobility.
25. *HB* 42; As PLRE II Ambrosius Aurelianus 9, cf. Russell (2017) 241.
26. *HB* 66; Bromwich (1978) 136-137; for the place-name: Watts (2004) 646, British *cat* = 'battle'. PLRE II Vitalinus, to which spelling he is hereafter corrected.
27. Jesus College MS 20.14, 16, 18 etc.
28. *Itineraries*, St Benet Hulme, 1479, Corpus Christi Cambridge MS 210, cf. Triad 51 & *HB* 42. Ercyng was a sub-Roman statelet the name of which is thought to derive from Roman Ariconium (Weston-under-Penyard), Herefordshire; *Cloart* may be Little Doward, Herefordshire. Reference to Ambrosius as Aurelius may be a lingering clue to his full style, thus perhaps, Aurelius Ambrosius.
29. *HB* 49; the only other place a genealogy of Vortigern appears in Jesus College MS 20,15
30. Jesus College MS 20; Watts 253; Rivett & Smith (1979) 368.*Gwalltir* = 'thick (abundant) hair'. A completely differing ascendancy for Vortigern is, however, found in the very much later *Buchedd Bueno* ('Book of St Bueno') of c. 1346; Bartrum (1966) 30, where he is son of Rittegyrn son of Deheuwynt son of Avallach son of Amalech son of Beli son of Anna, taking us, at a gallop, into the mythical Iron Age.
31. Pretty (1989) 174
32. Eg. Alexander Berenicianus and Alexander Julianus, sons of C. Julius Alexander, king of Western Cilicia in AD72, successively suffect consuls in 116 and 117: PIR^2 I. 136, 141, 142, or C. Julius Sohaemus, suffect consul prior to being installed in 141 as King of Emesa and Armenia. British examples have simply escaped record. Contra: Russell & Laycock, (2010) *passim* which, overall, does not necessarily convince.
33. See genealogy in Ch. 8.
34. Ausonius *Epigrammata* 107-12: *De quidam Silvio Bono qui erat Britt* – shades of Asterix the Gaul's adversary Christmas Bonus! But note a western *vir spectabilis* Bonosus in the 380s, and a *dux* called Flavius Bonus in 392: PLRE I Bonosus 3, Bonus.
35. On dating: Sivan (1993) 148; accepted date, *op. cit.* 165. Bonus is likely to have been a satirical name, too.

36. PLRE I Vitalis 6, cf. CIL XI 830; PLRE II. Vitalis I, cf. Symmachus Ep. Viii.9.
37. Hurst (1975) 267–94
38. Gildas *DE* 23.3; cf. Charles-Edwards (2013) 217.
39. Fleming (2021) 61-63; 161-162, 16-169
40. Charles-Edwards (2013) 439-440
41. Going back to Myres (1986) 15
42. Salway (1984) 474. Auxiliaris was Praetorian Prefect in 436, supported by the future western emperor Eparchius Avitus as *Magister Equitum per Gallias,* in succession to Aëtius; PLRE II. Auxiliaris 1, Avitus 5.
43. Hawkins, J. in Stoodley & Cosh (2021) 204-211 and Konshuh C in *ibid.* 226-227.
44. His parentage is lost to us, although *Bonedd y Saint* 61 calls his father 'Ridicus', conceivably a copyist's error for something more likely, for instance Ruricus [PLRE II] or Rusticus [PLRE II, ten examples]
45. *De Vita Christiana* 3, quoted in Johnson (1982) 147.
46. Hull (2004) 119. The name Agricola also appears amongst the forebears of Cunedda (see Chapter 9).
47. PLRE II Germanus 1. He may have been the son of Rusticus of Auxerre and Germanilla his wife, which could connect him with the family of Constantine III's praetorian prefect Decimius Rusticus [PLRE II. Rusticus 9], himself a likely relation of [Decimius Magnus] Ausonius.
48. Thomas (1994) 269
49. *V. Germani* 14, 15, cf. Bede I. 19-20; burial: Brown, M. in *Antiquaries Journal* 55 (1975) 294f.
50. St Alban's place of martyrdom is only first clearly identified by Gildas; for some thorny problems arising from this, cf. Wood (2009) 123f., succinctly encapsulated by Biddle & Kjølbye-Biddle (2008) 12.
51. Lançon (2000)108
52 *Why Geraint committed the camp to Germanus*, part of a Welsh poem, *Angau Kyvyndawt* BT 21, 14, quoted by Morris (1989) 64 & n. 1, who points out that the source is a 'hotch potch of allusions to earlier, lost poems'. Note that Moel y Geraint, otherwise Barber's Hill, lies immediately to the west of Llangollen, although the antiquity of the place name is open to question.
53. *V. Germani.,* 17-18
54. Alcock (1972) 182ff.
55. *HB* 32-34, where the miraculous events might suggest a subsequent siege of an enemy in a fortification.
56. Kightley, C., *Dinas Brân Castle* (Denbigh 2003) *passim.*
57. Morris (1989) 63, 64
58. *V. Germani* 25, cf. Bede I.21
59. *V. Germani* 26-27
60. PLRE II Elaphius 2, 3. The name appears to have lived on into post-Roman Britain: an Elafius (as Elffin) son of Gwyddien and father of Erfryg (= Urbicius) appears as a landowner in Gwent c710/740: Llandaff Charters 180a, 188a, 189 (Davies (1979) 112, 161.
61. Charles-Edwards (2013) 618; Thomas (1979) 95.
62. *HB* 47, 32
63. It was argued in the 19th century that St Garmon, as a Welsh saint, was a separate person, but this is now doubted.
64. Charles-Edwards (2013) 439-440
65. Kent (1979) 19; PLRE II Hengist (with a dubit).

66. Knight (2007) 50
67. Charles-Edwards (2003) 27
68. Climate change at this period: Harper (2017) 167-172.
69. *HB* 36, 43-46; *Chron Gal. 453*, Gildas, *DE* 22-24; *ASC*; Charles-Edwards (2003) 25, 28 & (2013) 217.
70. Frere (1966) 98
71. *Chron. Gall. 453*, 126
72. PLRE II Apollinaris 6; Wood (1992) 10, 14. Faustus was considered of equal social standing to Sidonius and Avitus and thus of the highest nobility: Wes (1992) 260.
73. *HB* 48.2; Jesus MS 20. 18: latter compiled before 1200; as we have it, *c.* 1350/1400.
74. Gildas, *DE* 20, 1; author's punctuation.
75. Gildas, *DE* 25.
76. Gildas, *DE* 26.
77. Bede *HE* I. 13
78. Harries (1994) 86
79. See also MacGeorge (2002) 82-110.
80. PLRE II Aegidius
81. Fanning (1992) 296-297, cf. Kent (1979) 24. Both sources, of course, were much later.
82. Barnwell (1992) 70 which he reminds us was a somewhat elastic term, often used as equivalent of 'emperor'.
83. Last certain suffecti: Lampadius (396); unknown, who broke his leg falling from his carriage in his inaugural Games, 401: Cameron (2013) 204; Rufius Valerius Messala (409) and F[l]. Ovinius Paternus in 443, but the latter possibly a consul *designatus* who died prematurely.
84. Charles-Edwards (2013) 42
85. On his family connections and probable antecedents see Craven (2019) 526-535.
86. Galliou & Jones (1991) 130-131
87. *HB* 67.3; on the Hwicce cf. Chapter 11.
88. Bede I. 16. The late *Annales Cambriae* (BL Harleian MS 3859) give 516 but attribute the victory to Arthur.
89. Johnson (1982) 192, fig. 50.
90. Fleming (2021) 65, 72.
91. *ibid.* 86.
92. Higham (1992) 75
93. Bland (2018) 98, 101, 120.
94. Fleming (2021) 24
95. Higham, *loc. cit.*
96. For a much more gradualist interpretation, see Fleming (2021) 72: 'The transition was much less abrupt than we thought.'
97. Burnett (1984) 164-165; Moorhead, S. in *Current Archaeology* 220 (7/2008) 42.
98. Rahtz & Watts (1979) 193.
99. Moorhead (2009) 40-41, 42
100. Moorhead & Walton (2014) 101
101. *Ibid.* 102; such a copy occurred in the Ballintree Hoard, Co. Derry; Bland (2018) 113
102. Kent (1979) 21.

103. Kent, *loc.cit.*
104. Moorhead & Walton *loc.cit*, cf. Moorhead (2009) 41-42; Breeze (1982) 160
105. Moorhead & Walton (2014) 103-104, 114
106. Bland (2018) 118
107. Moorhead (2009) 43
108. *Loc.cit.*
109. Sear 20632, RIC 2
110. Higham & Jones (1985) 135; Catling, C., review of Oosthuizen, S., *The Emergence of the English* (Amsterdam 2019) in *Current Archaeology* 355 (10-19) 24
111. Fleming (2021) 96, 106; Rogers (2011) 149.
112. Rogers (2011) 125
113. Interestingly, a conference specifically on the actuality of Dyrham was held in April 2022.
114. Cosh & Neal (2005) 247–252, *Daily Telegraph* 8/11/2001, p.5. On villas generally at this juncture: Percival (1976) 166f.
115. The persistence of wheel-thrown pottery into the 5th century elsewhere: Fleming (2021) 60-65.
116. Report précis, *Daily Telegraph* 9/12/2020 5; *Current Archaeology* 373 (4/2021) 18-25; 5th/6th century imported Mediterranean pottery has also been found at other related sites.
117. Beeson in Nichol *et al* (2020) 41-72, esp. 8.36-37.
118. Beeson, A in *Current Archaeology* (1/2021) 41.
119. Nichol *et al.* (2020) *sub* 8.16-17 & p. 74. The last élite Caepio was T. Rustius Caepio, suffect consul in 173; PLRE II Fortunata 5th/6th century *clarissima femina*; no examples of what was once a relatively common name in PLRE I.
120. Withington: *Daily Telegraph* 3/1/2006, 5 & Finberg (1955) 4 f.; Turkdean *Daily Telegraph* 26/2/1999, 23.
121. As, only slightly less emphatically perhaps, Fleming (2021) 182-186
122. Johnson (1982) 184-185.
123. Davies (1979a) 153-161.
124. Thomas (1979) 90, 94-95
125. Johnson, *op.cit.* 171.
126. Fleming (2021) 91-93
127. Arnold & Davies (2000) 81, 158. His identity is lost to us.
128. Villa: Corney (2003) 9, 15, 17, 22; Christian burials were found outside the villa. Name: William of Malmesbury, *Historia Regum* I. 23, cf. Ch. 8.
129. Percival (1976) 174-176
130. Corney, *op. cit.* 24.
131. Percival (1976) 183-198
132. *Current Archaeology* 213 (2/2009) 35-39, cf. Percival (1976) 178 & *loc. cit.*
133. Aaron & Julius: Gildas, *DE* 8; Bede I. 7.
134. Thomas (1979) 95-96. Metropolitan: a bishop with pre-eminence over the other Bishops in a Roman diocese; archepiscopal status has been claimed for various post-Roman sees, but none are certain.
135. Higham (1995) 61, 164
136. Frere (1966) 98
137. Dark (2000) 97-104; Rogers (2011) 100, 176.
138. Rogers (2011) 10, 109

139. Salway (1984) 464-67, with a discussion of the implications of the man's rank; White & Barker (1998) 102-136; Niblett (2001) 131-146; Rogers (2011) 102; Biddle & Kjølbye-Biddle (2008) 15-18, 22-23: Amphibalus is merely a Latinisation of the Greek word for 'cloak'.

140. Not that St Paul-in-the-Bail can be treated with absolute certainty as Roman in origin: Rogers, *op. cit.* 120-121.

141. White (2007) Ch 6; Chester: Rogers, *op. cit.* 95; Cirencester, *ibid.* 80, 103. On the Ordovices, see also Ch. 9.

142. Mason (2001) 211, 212-215; Ottaway (2004) 140-149; McCarthy (2002) 134-150 & Cunliffe (2000) 149-50, strengthened by Gerrard, J. in *Antiquaries Journal* 87 (2007).

143. Frere in Wacher (1966) 91-97; Rogers (2011) 82 & n. 3, 83 & 95. Canterbury: Bede *HE* 1.26

144. *Ibid.* 470-495; note, though, that he was part of a long-lived Gallic dynasty: Craven (2019) 528-535.

145. Cool (2014) 20

146. Ferris (2011) 11-124, Craven (1988) 15-17; Fincham (2004) 156 & Jackson (2012) xiii, 251.

147. Charles-Edwards (2013) 214

148. As Moffatt (2010) 127; for a more pessimistic view, Fleming (2021) 108, 127, highlighting the scavenging of iron and bronze clamps from standing buildings as a result of an acute metal shortage, resulting in the collapse of many, rather as Constans III did on his visit to Rome in 663 with similar results.

149. Grave AX at Yeavering, early 7th century: Hope-Taylor (1977) 67-69; cf. Bede *HE* II.34.

150. Quoted in Moffatt (2010) 123

151. Collins & Breeze (2014) 61-62.

152. Charles-Edwards (2003) 25

153. *Current Archaeology* 368 (11/2020) 10.

154. Birley (2014) 204

155. Russel & Laycock (2010) 165

156. Nash-Williams (1950) 93; Laing (1977) 57. On a late 4th-century gold crossbow brooch from there: Arnold & Davies (2000) 33 & plate 6.

157. *Op.cit.* 58; Laing (1979) 57-58

158. Morris (1995) 140-143.

159. Arnold & Davies (2000) 143

160. Amm. Marc. 27.8, 28.3 & see above, chapter IV; Collins & Breeze (2014) 64

161. Hassall & Ireland (1979).

162. Henig (2004) 18

163. Fleming (2021) 72, 179.

164. Henig (2004) 19-20

165. Salway (1984) 376, 385, 404

166. Knight (2007) 178

167. Higham & Jones (1985) 126, cf. Jesus College MS20, 19: Bartrum (1966) 46. See chapter 9.

168. Cf. *Not. Dig. Occ.* V. 197, V. 200 & VII. 78. But note that their prefixes specifically refer to Honorius (395-423) rather than Maximus, a change that would have occurred post-388.

169. *loc. cit.*

170. Skene (1890) III.25

171. Procopius, *BG* IV. 20
172. Oosthuizen. *loc.cit.*
173. Russell (2017) 231-232

7 'Are these Men Real?' The Sources

1. Knight (2007) 175; Russell (2017) 230-231
2. Bromwich (1978) 454.
3. Koch (2013) 5 & n.12, 11-14, 16.
4. Although some later king-lists certainly do purport to extend to British pre-history too. McCarthy (2002) 144.
5. Charles-Edwards (2013) 625-650.
6. Gildas *DE* 34.4 cf. Charles-Edwards (2003) 198.
7. Koch (2013) 40
8. *Ibid.* 234
9. Thomas (1994) 82; Demetian rulers: see Chapter 8.
10. Mass diptychs: Thomas (1994) 150; Bretons: Giot *et al* (2003) 123.
11. Barnwell (1997) 170
12. Wiseman (2008) 236-241
13. *Ibid.* 239, 305
14. Wood H. J. T., *The Value of Welsh Pedigrees*, in *The Ancestor* IV (1/1903) 58, 60.
15. Matthews (1975) 175 & n. 3, where these connections are given little credence, although with caveats.
16. Stacey (2003) 234
17. Gildas *DE* 13-14
18. *Chron.* 83.14
19. Bede, *HE* I. 9
20. HB 26, 27 & 29.
21. Knight (2014) 168
22. Orosius VII, 34, 9, cf. Prosper, *sub anno* 388.
23. Charles-Edwards (2013) 404-409, 448
24. The genitive of 'son' mutates with context: *m[ab]*, *map*, *ap*; *map* = 'son of', abbreviated m (elsewhere as mutations, *mab*, *vab*, Welsh *ap*) and *merch* = 'daughter of', elsewhere Welsh *verch*.
25. Charles-Edwards (2013) 346. Here and below: *m[ap]* = son of, *merch/verch* = daughter of.
26. Bartrum (1966) 9.
27. *DE* 31.
28. Bartrum (1966) 31.
29. Charles-Edwards (2013) 328, 346
30. *Vita S Cadoci* 45, Bartrum (1966) 24-2. Knight (2014) 169
31. Bartrum (1966) 14
32. Bartrum (1966) 130 citing BL Harl. MS 1974 fol. 30r & 31r but written down as late as *c.* 1600.
33. *HRB* VI. 4-5
34. Tacitus, *Annals* xii, 33–38
35. Bartrum (1966) 41
36. Caesar, *BG* V, 8-23
37. Charles-Thomas (2013) 617
38. Bartrum (1966) *loc.cit.*

39. Knight (2014) 170

40. Where *vab* = son of. *Achau'r Saint* 24: Bartrum (1966) 70, replicating *Bonedd y Sant* 63 (qv).

41. Bartrum (1966) 100, 106

42. Davies (2007) 103-110

43. Charles-Edwards (1971) 295-296. There are echoes of Geoffrey of Monmouth in the tale.

44. Dream: Morris (1989) 418-420. Russell (2017) 230.

45. As *Bonedd yr Arwyr* ('pedigrees of the heroes') 33.

46. As *HB* 27.

47. Morris (1989) 418, 419

48. Morris (1989) 419; Sarn Elen: Margary No. 69a, *op.cit* (1955) II.85-89. Oddly, the Sarn Helen avoids Caernarfon, which is reached via Margary nos. 67c & 68.

49. *HRB* V. 9-15, VI. 1-2

50. This occurs earlier, *HRB* V. 6-8.

51. *HRB* V, 9

52. *Ibid.* V. 12-16, VI., 1

53. Russell (2017) 25, 41, 42

54. Bromwich (1978) 453

55. Knight (2014) 167

56. Repeated in Harleian 3859. 2 and Jesus College MS 20. 13.

57. Allowing 30 years per generation in Jesus College MS 20, four would make Cassivellaunus a contemporary of Septimius Severus's sons!

58. Jesus College MS 20.8

59. Bromwich (1978) 75, 377.

60. *Op. cit.* 452.

8 Maximus as Founding Father

1. Arnold & Clarke (2000) 144: into the late 4th century 'at least'.

2. Henceforth *ED*; Bodleian Library, Oxford, MS Rawlinson B. 502; it recurs in the *Third Branch of the Mabinogi: Manawydan*.

3. Bartrum (1966) 4

4. Irish settlement: *HB* 62; British pedigree: Harleian MS 3859.2

5. *op. cit.* 10, BL Harl. MS 3859.2.

6. Tacitus, *De Vita Julii Agricolae*, 24; Thomas (1994) 83.

7. Voteporigis CIIC 358; Clutorius CIIC 435 & Maglocunus CIIC 446; Thomas (1994) 81f.

8. *Achau Brenhinoedd A Thywysogion Cymru* 18(a): the descent is through the female line. One might suspect Kustenin represents Constantine III; Tryffin's father appears as Ewein (Owein).

9. CIIC 327

10. Thomas (1994) 123-124. I have restored Turpilio here rather than the early imperial Turpili[an]us [eg. PIR[2] P406/407] remembering the unfortunate successor of Stilicho as *Magister militum* (West), killed in 409: PLRE II. Turpilio. The name may, in consequence, have had some resonance in Britain.

11. Davies (1979) 96 Charter 125b. He was ruling Dyfed when St David was born if we may believe Rhygyfach ap Sulien, his hagiographer: Bromwich (1978) 515.

12. CIIC 358, now in Carmarthen Museum. Note that there are suggestions that these Latin/Ogham stones may be earlier than first thought: Rance (2001) 256 & n. 91.
13. Gildas *DE* 31
14. Rance (2001) 254-255 (& n. 85), 257, 263ff.
15. Charles-Edwards (2013) 175
16. Alcock (1971) 124
17. Thomas (1994) 55-56; Charles-Edwards (2013) 451; Rance (2000) 243 ff. It is interesting to note that Maredydd's other son, Rhun II whose son was called Triffyn, i.e. Triphun = *tribunus*, who died in 814 or 815: *ibid.* 662.
18. Rance (2001) 257-258; Roman coins were found on the site as long ago as the 1880s and pottery in 2018.
19. Rance (2001) 267
20. Arnold & Davies (2000) 146; a question posed by implication long ago by Cunliffe Shaw (1968) 54.
21. Charles-Edwards (2003) 32; Rance *loc. cit.*
22. *HB* 14
23. Rance (2001) 254
24. Thomas (1979) 84
25. Byrne (1973) 69f. The daughter is named in the Book of Armagh as Scotnoc or Scotnoë.
26. Morris 3 (1995) 66-67, 89. St Finnian was his pupil. The name remained popular for a while afterwards in Ireland.
27. Byrne (1973) 182-183
28. Morris 3 (1995) 172
29. A feminine of Carinus, cf. the *augustus* Carinus, deposed by Diocletian in 284.
30. Byrne (1973) 70-86; Carina: *ibid.* 76; *Annals*: M378-405. The latter date Fiortchurn and Patrick too early, so this date, too, cannot be taken as being particularly accurate although the 26 years seem suitably elastic.
31. EWGT 33 (34): *The Mothers of Irish Saints* 3. She appears in none of the other ten or so genealogies of the saint in that work.
32. Byrne (1973) 135: the poems are possibly fifth or sixth century in origin.
33. Byrne (1973) 132-133
34. Summed up neatly in *Current Archaeology* 202 (3/2006) 530-539, cf. Arnold & Clark (2000) 144f.
35. *British Archaeology* 6 (7/1995) 4, c 1-2
36. Thomas (1994) 51-61
37. Tacitus, *Agricola* 24. The implication is that Agricola physically crossed with the prince: Juvenal, *Satires* 2. 159-160, '... arms had been taken beyond the shores of *Iuverna* (Hibernia).'
38. Tuthmael = *Touto-maglos*, valid both sides of St George's Channel. BL Harleian MS 3859. 4; Ailred, *Vita Niniani* 4; Morris 3 (1995) 109-110. Another appears in Jesus MS20.10, 11, 19 & 26.
39. Byrne (1973) 54
40. Warner, R. B., 'Yes, the Romans Did Invade Ireland' in *British Archaeology* 14 (5/96) 8; another such hoard was found in Ballinrees, Co. Derry.
41. Wallace (2000) 33; Rance (2001) 261; Bland (2018) 124
42. Di Martino (2003) 92-110
43. Gildas *DE* 27
44. *Ibid.* 31

45. Thomas (1994) 132; *De Situ Brycheiniog* 10.
46. Marcella: even in the late empire, a common enough name: both PLRE I & II have three examples.
47. *Cognatio Brychan* 10
48. Annun Ddu also appears in British genealogies as Mark Antony, however: Harleian MS 3859.16; but as 'King of the Greeks' also in Jesus College MS 20.1 and *Plant Brychan* (the Children of King Brychan) 1.
49. PLRE I Gregorius 7, *en poste* in 313. The Thebaïd was southern Egypt, bordering the Red Sea.
50. Thomas (1994) 146 & n. 41. Britannia Prima as a praesidial province: *Not. Dig. Occidens* XXIII.5.
51. Cult of Matrona: Bromwich (1978) 458; as a name, cf. PLRE I Matronianus 2: *dux* and *praeses* of Isauria (S. Turkey) 382; others in PLRE II *sub nomine*.
52. *Bonedd y Sant* 44, 45
53. Occupation of Y Gaer: Davies (1996) 24 & n. 87
54. Crannog: a good review of the archaeology of this important structure: Catling, C. *The Palace in the Lake*, in *Current Archaeology* 364 (7/2020) 18-27, where a late ninth-century date is proposed. Paul[in]us: Doble (1971) 139, 152-153.
55. Preliminary announcement in the Society of Antiquaries Newsletter, *Salon* 22/6/2022.
56. Tomlin (1975) 68-72.
57. Thomas (1994) 146-147 & n. 42. Brycheiniog even boasted a later ruler called Awst (Augustus): Llandaff Charters 146,154 of *c.* 720.
58. *Ibid.* 144.
59. Davies (1996) 98 sets out the superabundance of (mainly legendary) evidence.
60. Knight (2007), 169, 177.
61. BL Harl. MS 3859.27; Bromwich (1978) 395, cf. Jesus MS 20.14, 16, 18.
62. *HB* 48; Ro[n]wenn (not named) *HB* 37; named: *TYP* 37R & *HRB* VI.12; on the former, see below.
63. *AC* 800; Wm of Malmesbury *loc.cit.* The reason for the association is utterly obscure, unless it relates to the large villa with fifth-century adaptations alluded to in Ch. 6.
64. As Lichfield, Koch suggests as the easternmost *pagus* of the Cornovii: Koch (2013) 237.
65. Charles-Edwards (2013) 16; Koch (2013) 69, 123-126.
66. Morris (1989) 63: cf. PLRE I Bruttius Praesens (*c.* 320); PLRE II Catellus (*c.* 523/540), Catella (*c.* 490).
67. PLRE I Aureliana 1, Marcellinus 6, Vitalis 6; Maximus, Ch. 3.
68. Alcock (1971) 124; on these possible connections see also see Ch. 10 below. They may be one and the same.
69. *Ibid.* 129
70. Thomas (1994) 223-224. This connection is explored further in Chapter 10.
71. As Bromwich (1978) 395
72. *HB* 34-3; Koch (2013) 134
73. White *et al.* (2013) 206. An isolated small bronze coin of Valentinian III from after 430 found there has an equivocal role diagnostically: Casey (1974) 383f.
74. Webster (1991) 134; White & Barker (1998) 117-136; *British Archaeological News* (3/1994) 6-9. The place and river name is 'pre-English': Gelling (1984) 12; possibly it mutated from Cwmddu (black valley) or even Cwmderw (valley of oaks).

75. Marwnad: NLW MS 4973, pp. 108a-109b; some Anglo-Saxon pedigrees make Merewalh third son of Penda, considered highly unlikely; Koch (2013)196, 233-234 & 291; Davies (1996) 101.
76. *The Book of Taliesin* XXIII.
77. Excavations of 1929-1931 and 2004; Mason (2001) 212-213; *Current Archaeology* 202 (3/2006) 517-524; on Catguallaun Liu (= rudder, thus 'leader/guider'): Koch (2013) 106 & n. 6, 129.
78. Richards (1947) 93; Mason (2001) 212-214
79. Koch (2013) 127-128
80. Davies (1979) 76. Cynddylan suggests Powis, cf. the later homonymous subject of the *marwnad Cynddylan,* while Cynfelin is only known as a ruler of the Votadini and a descendant of Coel Hen. Yet is the entire *marwnad* of Cynddylan misdated and misattributed: could it really have been about Dyrham?
81. Charles-Edwards (2013) 416-417. NB Harleian MS 3859.27 giving Cyngen's sister as Nest who married Merfyn Frych, King of Gwynedd & Man, and thus also an alleged descendant of Maxim Wledig: *op.cit.* 468.
82. Charles-Edwards (2013) 414
83. Eg. PLRE II Pascentius, a *comes* in Africa, early fifth century. Not necessarily a son of Vortigern as phrased on the Pillar of Eliseg, but certainly so in *HB* 48-49 & Jesus College MS 20.14.
84. Jesus Coll. MS 20 14, 18; *Achau Brenhinoedd a Thywysogion Cymru* 20 and *Hen Lwythau Gwynedd a'r Mars*, 2. *Llwyth Aelan* (MS f).
85. Harl MS 3859.16
86. Harl MS 3859.18; *Achau Brenhinoedd a Thywysogion Cymru* 9 (b)
87. PLRE I Asteria 1, Marcellinus 4 [=5/16, cf. ILS 8944], Musolamius 1. Musolamius' father, Flavius Gallicanus was also consul (in 330). Presumably his wife was a Bruttia, a distinguished early imperial patrician family going back to the first century AD and which produced Commodus' unfortunate empress, Bruttia Crispina, her second name indicating a descent from the Qunictii Crispini, of ancient patrician stock.
88. *Bonedd y Sant* 44, 45, NB upper-class Matronae 1, 2 & 3 in PLRE II.
89. Charles-Edwards (2013) 439-440, cf. *HB* IV. 14-21.
90. Russell (2017) 237-238; on Ronwen: *HB* 37 TYP 37R, but could the name be earlier? Bromwich (1978) 503.
91. Bede *HE* I.15.
92. *HB* 48 cf. 39
93. *HB* 44: *Cateyrn* at Episford, cf. *ASC sub anno* 455; Aylesford, and Vortimer after a battle 'by the inscribed stone at the seaside' a little later, cf. *ASC sub anno* 465: '... on their side a thane was slain whose name was Wipped.'
94. Charles-Edwards (2013) 199-200, cf. Sid. Ap. *Euchariston ad Faustum Episcopum,* carmen xvi; Faustus's friendship with Sidonius, once his pupil: Harries (1994) 52, 174.
95. *HB* 48; remainder of the genealogy (above): Bartrum (1966) 6-8 etc.
96. *Bonedd y Saint* 29, MS G, cf. *TYP* 66 (NLW Peniarth MS 47 version), 88; Bromwich (1978) 299-300, 564.
97. *HB* 31, 36-38, 39, 43-46, 47; *DE* 23-24
98. Bland (2018) 114. Ursicinus does not appear in PLRE under both names but could possibly be identifiable with Ursicinus I in PLRE II, who was western *comes rei privatae* in 405 and thus could easily have had an extensive British estate.

99. Davies (1996) 24 & n. 87
100. *Bonedd y Sant* 44, 45
101. The dynasty is fully analysed and provisionally allocated date-ranges in Davies (1979) 74, 75-77.
102. Penmachno (Gwynedd) stone 3; the father, Avitus, bore a typical western Roman name, popular in Gaul and born by the emperor of 456-457. Justin II celebrated a consulship on his accession and one other in 568, after which the years were counted as '*post consule Justini*': PLRE IIIa Justinus 5; Charles Edwards (2013) 237, 238. Iestin, cf. Davies (1979) 126, Llandaff Charter 253.
103. Doble (1971) 186
104. Doble (1971) 208 n. 3, cf. PLRE I & II several also two imperial princesses called Eudocia; two Gauls called Auxiliaris in PLRE II
105. Doble (1971) 119, cf. PLRE II. Regina and four called Reginus, also Rüpke & Glock (2008) No.2905.

9 The Men of the North

1. The names, for the sake of standardization, are given in the text in their modern form, as used by Bartrum (1966) in his index. On the diagram above, the MS spellings are used.
2. As suggested in Craven (2019) 636.
3. *Bonedd y Sant* 18; *Bonedd Gwr y Gogledd* 11. In the latter, Dyfnwal is also given as grandson of Ceredic Wletig, thought to have been identifiable St Patrick's Coroticus (of Alclud), presumably through a daughter.
4. CIIC 515; Genealogy of Nudd, Dyfnwal and Maximus: *Bonedd y Saint* 18, TYP 2; Bromwich (1978) 476.
5. Liberalis: PLRE II Cecilius; PLRE I: nine examples; PLRE II, only one.
6. *TYP* 56; the pedigree is given in NLW Peniarth MSS 127.95 & 128.56: Bromwich (1978) 403. The name, in post-Geoffrey of Monmouth MSS, was surely adapted to read *Uthyr* = Uther.
7. *TYP* 13. The suggested derivation of Owein from an Irish root (not wholly accepted) seems unlikely.
8. Jesus College MS 20.4.
9. Williams (1977) 41.
10. *Ibid.* No. 17, but cf. Bromwich (1978) 477-479, 560.
11. Jesus MS 20.4. where Maximus's great-great-grandson Gluis is the eponym of Glewyssing.
12. See note 4 above; Charles-Edwards (2013) 571-572
13. Collins (2004) 131
14. *Not. Dig. Occ.* V. 197 *Honoriani Atecottti Seniores* & *ibid.* V. 200 *Honoriani Atecotti Juniores* & again in *Not. Dig. Occ.* VII. 78 *Atecotti Juniores Gallicani* cf. Cunliffe-Shaw (1973) 46
15. Mann (1979) 145-146: needless to say, these forts were abandoned in the later 4th century.
16. Alcock (1979) 135-136; Mann (1979) 151.
17. BL Harleian MS 3859; Alcock (1971) 129.
18. Bernard & Atkinson (1989) II. 177; Cunliffe-Shaw (1973) 49, 145. Name: PLRE I has two, PLRE II has eleven and PLRE IIIb has no less than 23 Leos, by then an imperial name.

19. Mauricius: PLRE I has two examples and PLRE IIIb ten; Opilio: PLRE II has five and PLRE IIIb has two.
20. Bede *HE* 5; *HB* 56.
21. Koch (2013) 83, 84.
22. Koch (2013) 89
23. Charles-Edwards (2013) 385; on the Roman name of Corbridge: Rivett & Smith (1979) 323.
24. TYP 1; Bromwich (1978) 4. *Penrhyn Rhionydd* in the Appendix I of TYP: *op.cit.* 228-229. Dumfries has been another suggestion, the origin of the place name of which is much argued.
25. Charles Edwards (2013) 473; contemporary Manx issues also crop up in the *Annals of Ulster*. Maughold cross 69. The name is cognate with Latin Viriat[i]us (a name absent from PLRE but not from PIR²): Bromwich (1978) 396. Man was temporarily overrun by Eadwine of Northumbria in the early seventh century, and again when Ecgfrith sent an army to Ireland to attack Brega in the 680s, but with apparently no lasting consequences: Charles-Edwards (2003) 41, 43
26. *TYP* 29, cf. Bromwich (1978) 60
27. *TYP* 54. Rhydderch Hael was son of Tudwal Tudclyd, a son of Ednyvet, as Tutuvallus, healed and reformed by St Ninian according to the saint's *Vita* by Aelred of Rievaulx, IV.
28. ABT 1(a), echoed with variations inspired by *HRB* by *Hanes Gruffydd ap Cynan* (c. 1170) 2.
29. Amm. Marc,. 28. 6, 21, 28-29; PLRE Caecilius 1. The same Seissyllt appears above in the discussion of the Yarrowkirk stone.
30. Koch (2013) 45-46, 49-52
31. BL Harleian MS 3859.1
32. Koch (2013) 74
33. PLRE IIIa Florentinus 1, Gundulfus; cf. PLRE IIIb *stemma* 12, p. 1545.
34. PLRE I: three examples. Emperor, M. Claudius Tacitus, reigned 275-276. Morris connects him with Kent.
35. Paternus: PLRE I: twelves examples; Aeternalis, PLRE I. The name also occurs in Wales, on a stone inscription in Irish mode (with secondary Ogham), to *Ettern maqui Victor* (Aetern[ali]us son of Victor): CIIC 430, Clydai. Could the father's name reflect a continuing admiration for Maximus? TYP Ap. III.9 & V.5.
36. PLRE I Paternus 7.
37. Koch (2013) 58
38. Gildas *DE* 19
39. Koch (2013) 50, 53; Charles-Edwards (2003) 123.
40. *HB* 62
41. His son Dunawt (Donatus) was king of Elmet: BL Harl. MS 3859.9 & 11. A stone inscription in Wales identifies a person as from Elmet: Arnold & Davies (2000) 152. The kingdom was snuffed out by Edwin of Northumbria. Higham re-dates this to 626/630 by Edwin's building of a church at his palace of *Campodunum*, usually thought to be Leeds but which perhaps really, on place name evidence, should be Doncaster: Higham (1995) 77 & n. 13, 83; *HB* 63; Bede *HE* IV. 23.
42. Koch (2013) 68
43. Arnold & Davies (2000) 152
44. Charles-Edwards 180-181. Ennianus is a perfectly reasonable adjectival form of the Roman *nomen* Ennius, albeit scarce at this date; a handful of Ennii show up in ILS for the third century: eg. 6597, 8247.

45. Charles-Edwards (2003) 33 & *ibid*. (2013) 178-180

46. Koch (2013) *loc.cit.*

47. Dornier (1982) 258, arguing that *Caer Leon* in the *Dream of Maxen Wledig* is intended for Chester.

48. Koch (2013) 69, 72

49. The plague was *Yersinia Pestis*, which appeared in the west from 541: Harper (2017) 202; Climate event: *New Scientist* 14 (6/1994) 5; the devastation of the land in this cataclysm might have inspired the wasteland in the Grail legends: Baillie (1998) and the theme recurs also in the *Third Branch of the Mabinogi, Manawydan*.

50. Bromwch (1978) 557; Gildas *DE* 33-36, in which his career seems even then to have been a longish one to have crammed in so much wickedness!

51. BL Harl. MS 3859.32

52. BL Harl. MS 3859.18; PLRE I has eight examples; PLRE II only one.

53. PLRE I Tiberianus 2

54. PLRE II, five examples; NB Marianus 5, a *vir perfectissimus* and prefect of the fleet in an unknown part of the empire, late fourth century.

55. Romanus: PLRE I has 15 examples, Vol. II has 9; Donatus: PLRE I has 7 examples, with 5 in Vol. II.

56. *Vita Carantoci* 2 EWGT 26; In which context note Aíbell, a mother goddess: Byrne (1973) 166.

57. CIIC 361-2

58. PLRE II Potentinus

59. University College, London CISP No. MWROG 1, cf, the centurion M. Carantius Macrinus *c*. AD 90: ILS 2118.

60. Laing (1979) 57-58

61. Laing (1979) 59

62. Russell (2017) 28ff.

63. Koch (2013) 76-77

64. PLRE II. Coelius

65. Cunliffe-Shaw (1973) 138; J. Morris in *Essays Presented to Eric Birley* (1965) 149.

66. Eg. the earliest genealogies mentioning him: BL Harleian MS 3859.10 and the *Vita Cadoci*.

67. Bromwich (1978) 504; on Dyfnwal, see above.

68. Morris (1989) 54

69. Cole: the rhyme was first published in 1708 by William King, cf. Birley (1979) 160; Helen: *Bonedd y Sant* 14(a); Gwreic verch Gadeon: Jesus College MS20.7.

70. *HRB* V. 6; this would, in *Dream* terms, make Coel a nephew by marriage to Maximus: too convenient, surely.

71. *Bonedd yr Arwyr* 27(a), but in Jesus College MS 20 as Wawl (= 'wall')

72. Chadwick (1949) 137; Note also PLRE I Decimius Germanianus 7, possibly a brother of Ausonius: Sivan (1993) 57, 60 and C. Artorius Germanianus [PLRE I. Germanianus 2], a fourth-century senator at Rome, whose *nomen* at least ought to excite the Arthurians!

73. Meirchiaun may have been located in Cumbria if the place names Maughanby (6 mls. NE of Penrith), and Powmaughan are any guide. See also the suggested *stemma*.

74. *HB: Bellum Arnetid*, cf. *AC, sub anno* 573, cf. Moffat (2010) 127-131.

75. McCarthy (2002) 142, 144, 150; Higham (1995) 162.

76. Suggesting that its British name remained current here until Norse settlers in the 9th century added a uniquely Norse suffix.
77. Watts (2004) 503 disagrees (Rochdale).
78. McCarthy (2002) *loc.cit.* & 147, 151; Cunliffe Shaw (1969) 150.
79. *Myrwnad* of Owain ap Urien. Cunliffe-Shaw (1973) 156; Watts (2004) again demurs (Levens) 371 but agrees concerning Lyvennet: *op.cit.* 391.
80. The great preponderance of Norse and Norman names holding land in Craven in 1086, unlike areas further east, would seem to suggest little Saxon penetration in this rugged area between the collapse of the greater British polity and the Norse settlements in the 9th century and later.
81. Higham (1993) 84, 101. The plague of 547 may have damaged the Britons more than the Saxons, empowering the nascent Saxon polities on the north-east littoral. The name Craven, which survives as an extensive locality, is British, either from *craf* = wild garlic: Watts (2004) 166, or perhaps better *crai* = fresh water + *fan* = peak, or even a mutation from *cribyn* = crest. On *Eccles* names see also Chapter 9.
82. Bede *Vita S. Cuthberhti* (*c.* 715) 27; its existence implies continuing maintenance of acqueducts.
83. McCarthy (2002) 137
84. Elmet from British *Elfed*; Leeds probably from the archaic name of R. Aire, *Llawd*: Watts (2004) 213, 367.
85. His epithet was *mwynvawr* ('the wealthy') or perhaps more correctly *vawr* ('great').
86. Koch (2013) 225; Bromwich (1978) 503, cf. *HB* 57
87. Faull (1977) 2-3
88. Marriage: HB 57 (her father was Royth ap Rhun), cf Kirby (1991) 78, 90; McCarthy (2002) 144; Cunliffe-Shaw (1969) 166; Higham (1993) 111 & Faull (1977) 22.
89. Camden (1594) 587: Jesus College MS 20.17, 19
90. Named in *TYP* 80 and the identity generally accepted: Bromwich (1978) 351.
91. Charles-Edwards (2003) 42
92. Bede *HE* IV.26, cf. Moffatt (2010) 209.
93. *HB* 57; *Liber Vitae* of Durham, 9th century, possibly copied in part from a 6th century MS; Cunliffe-Shaw (1969) 152, cf Joliffe, J. E. A. in *English Historical Review* XLI (1926), 1-42. Rieinmelth's name seems to mean 'Queen of Lightning': Moffat (2010) 209.
94. Chadwick (1949) 149; BL Harleian MS 3859.5; Thomas (1979) 91, who proposes a date of *c.* 450-475.
95. Tibbs (2019) 75
96. *HB* 66a
97. PLRE I Clemens 1, 2; Quin[c]tilius 1-4 & Quintillus 1-2.
98. Charles-Edwards (2013) 481; on the boundaries of Stratchclyde: Moffat (2010) 242.
99. *Ibid.* 571-572
100. cf. Halsall (2013) 219
101. Bede *HE* III.1. Excepting Elmet, eliminated more than a decade earlier, although no doubt briefly 'liberated' once Penda and Cadwallon's *drang nach Norden* got under way.
102. Barnwell (1997) 169. And, of course, Caedwalla (Cadwallon) appears later also as a king of Wessex, see below Chapter 11.

10 South-west and Beyond

1. BL Harl. MS 2414 f. 68v; the reader must excuse my attempted translation.
2. Note on *De Situ Brecheniauc* 14: Bartrum (1966) 130 who quotes BL Harl. MS 1974 ff. 30r, 31r (written down *c.* 1600).
3. Thomas (1994) 162, n. 64
4. Koch (2013) 69, 123-126
5. *HB* 14; *Cormac's Glossary*: quoted in Charles-Edwards (2013) 181.
6. Morris (1973) 69
7. Pearce (1978) 143
8. Thomas (1966) 76. Tamar valley: identified by LiDAR and excavation by Chris Smart of Exeter University, 2020., *Current Archaeology* 365 (8/2020) 10.
9. Thomas (1994) 210
10. ASC 658, 825; Charles-Edwards (2013) 22, 428-431; Pearce (1978) 168-169.
11. Collins & Breeze (2014) 64, referring to Amm. Marc. 27.8 & 28.3.
12. Thomas (1994) 211, 214
13. Dark (2000) 169-170
14. Thomas (1994) 211-212
15. Pearce (1978) 143
16. CIIC 373 (Newchurch), CIIC 472 (St Breock): Thomas (1994) 42.
17. Mostyn MS 117.4 cf. *Achau Brenhinoedd a Thywysogion* 11. As a descendant of Sevira and Vortigern, Seferus might be regarded as well named after his ancestor.
18. *Vita Brioci* 50-52.
19. Genealogies: *Ach Morgan ab Owain*, Jesus College MS 20.10, *Vita* St Winnoc & *Bonedd y Sant* 76; Giot *et al* (2003) 128, 144 who also notes the *Vitae* of SS Guénolé & Guénaël, where Rhiwallon is described as *dux* emphasizing how late must have been the copyists' practice of adding regal titles to these leaders.
20. Charles-Edwards (1023) 22, 24
21. CIIC 476, Thomas (1994) 269-270
22. Doble (1971) 183-184 quoting *V. Teilo*; Bromwich (1978) 359; Gerrans, admitted by Watts (2004) 249.
23. *TYP* 14
24. The name seems Roman, although absent from PLRE II; perhaps originally Polemius or Paulacius; the former [PLRE II Polemius] was a Praetorian Prefect of Gaul 471/472 and a friend of Sidonius Apollinaris, providing a link to SS. Germanus and Faustus. Poulentius/Paulentius as it stands might seem acceptable.
25. *V. St Illtuti* BL Cotton MS Vespasian A xiv, 1-2, cf. Doble (1971) 56-86.
26. *V.* St Cadog, 19, cf. Doble (1971) 103; Olson (2017) 6f.
27. No fewer than 12 examples in PLRE II. The name was originally of Egyptian origin, subsequently Romanised but NB Sowerby, in Olson (2017) 35 considers this a biblical name and attributes such an origin to other relatives' names.
28. Wrnonoc, *V. St Pauli*, written c. 884, Doble (1971) 146ff.
29. *HRB* I. 1; Roberts (1971) xxiv-xxxi
30. *HRB* V. 15-16 where rendered Dionotus.
31. Russell (2017) *passim*.
32. Jesus College MS 20.11, *Bonedd y Saint* 76; Arthurian: *Bonedd yr Arwyr* 30b, Mostyn MS 117.5

33. Custennin as 'Fendigeid': TYP 51 (but endowed with accents of *HRB*): Morris 3 (1995) 154

34. As proposed in Craven ((2019) 489, table LX. Custennin Fendigaid is identified with Custennin Gorneu and both with Gildas's Constantine of Dumnonia by Bromwich, however: Bromwich (1978) 358.

35. Sozomen IX. 13 (not in PLRE II); PLRE II Maximus 4 & Maximus 7.

36. Giot *et al* (2003) 125

37. See Craven (2019) 636, Appendix II, Table LVIII(b). The British sources: Jesus MS 20, 10-11 & *Bonedd y Saint* 26.

38. *Buchedd. Llawddog* EWGT 31: Eleri was a descendant of Antonius/Donatus, 'son' of Maximus, cf. chapter 9.

39. Jesus MS 20. 26 & 27, cf. desc. from Eudaf: *ibid*. 11. PLRE I has four men called Urbanus, while *Gerneu* can alternatively translated as 'best' = Lat. maximus. In later tradition (eg. *HRB*, *TYP*[3] 52) he becomes a cousin of Arthur.

40. Watts (2004) 478, 479

41. National Library of Wales (NLW) Peniarth MS 1, cf. Pearce (1978) 142; Thomas (1994) 212.

42. Watts (2004) 360

43. *Y Gododdin* I. 1042, cf. Bromwich (1978) 357.

44. Bromwich (1978) 359

45. See chapter 8.

46. HRB V 8-11

47. Jesus MS 20.4, *Bonedd y Saint* 63; Jesus MS 20.7, 11 cf. *Bonedd yr Arwyr*: 27a, 33; Arthurian: 30b, 31.

48. Giot et al (2003) 126, 132

49. Letaviam/Llydawc = Brittany

50. Bromwich (1979) 548.

51. *Vita* St Docco 1-3; *Bonedd y Sant* 20, cf. *Achau Sant* 1.

52. PLRE I Arborius I; Veria Liceria. She was a daughter of Eusebius of Nantes: Sivan (1993) 60.

53. PLRE II Licerius, Lupicinus 3

54. PLRE II Constantinus 21, Constans 1, Gerontius 5, Julianus 7, Nunechia; Alanus: Sozomen IX.13.

55. CIIC 461, cf. Thomas (1994) 283-284.

56. Morris 3 (1995) 69-71. He does not necessarily suggest kinship.

57. Eagles (2018) 46, n. 58

58. Jesus MS20. 9, 10; Craven (2019) 489

59. Patrick: Morris 3 (1995) 114, all his family bore Roman names; stone: CIIC 1402; PLRE I Potitus 1 a *vicarius* of Rome in 380 and a likely Valerius, a family then for the second time reviving archaic nomenclature; Thomas (1994) 288. Cf. Chapter 9 for a derivative name commemorated in North Wales, Potentinus.

60. CIIC 1209: Thomas (1994) 281 who prefers 'Publicius', a *nomen* less often found in the fourth and fifth centuries; PLRE I & II: two examples each as 'Publicola', yet the 'Poplicola' spelling was still favoured in the 250s: ILS 1190. One would prefer (St.) Peiblig (cf. above) as a British rendering of Publicius.

61. CIIC 465

62. Thomas (1994) 265. There is no shortages of senatorial Anicii in any volume of PLRE.

63. Mommaerts & Kelley (1992) *passim*.
64. The family was an ancient one, from Praeneste; the Anicius Ingenuus an army MO buried at Vercovicium (Housesteads, on the Wall) in the late second century was clearly a member, although unlikely to have been a forebear of the person commemorated on the stone. Some Anicii settled in Africa.
65. Gerontius, *Vita St Melaniae*, 18.
66. PLRE I Melania 1 & 2, Potitus 1, Poplicola 2 (& II. 2), cf. *stemmata* 20, 30.
67. Jesus MS 20.26, 27. He also appears in *Culhuch and Olwen* in *The Mabinogion* (also very late) but Rachel Bromwich thinks his name is merely a copyist's error for *Gorneu* as in Custennin Gorneu: *op.cit.* 365.
68. Morris (1989) 158; he appears as Cador in *HRB*; *Bonedd y Saint* 26, 27. Peredur and Theudu occur in Jesus College MS 20.10; Morris 3 (1995) 167-171 considers Theudu to have been a king specifically of Cornwall, although perhaps too early, given the passage of generations from Gereint and the lack of certain references to Cornwall before *c.* 700.
69. Gildas *DE* 28.1; *Annales Cambriae, sub anno* 589.
70. Giot *et al* (2003) 131; one version would abbreviate the descent: Riwal ap Cadovius ap Geraint ap Urbian, which in some ways is chronologically more satisfying.
71. *Vitae* St Winnoc & St Brioc 50-52 quoted in Giot *et al, loc.cit.*; Jankulak in Olson (2017) 175 & n. 71.
72. *HF* iv. 4
73. Pearce (1978) 141; Giot *et al* (2003) 125.
74. *TYP* 14, note Bromwich's full discussion: Bromwich (1978) 445-448.
75. *Vita* of St Hervé, quoted by Giot *et al.*; *V. Prima* of St Sampson 1, 53.
76. Charles-Edwards (2013) 67. 74
77. CIIC 487
78. Place names: Watts (2004) 345: 'unexplained', but Holmes (2005) 16, 23 agrees with Bromwich (1978) 193, 446. *TYP* 73 implies that Drustan was heir of March, not specifically son or nephew.
79. Compare the survival of Roman names in Vandal Africa and beyond: Conant (2015) 248-250, 282-283 & 290.
80. Gildas *DE* 30.1
81. Davies (1996) 215 accepts the early (7th-century) date for this vita, noting that its author used an account on 'an ancient' who had known the saint and information from Samson's mother transmitted via an uncle.
82. Giot *et al* (2003) 130; Gildas *DE* 25.3; dissenting: Thomas (1994) 180 cf Jesus MS 20.5: Kynvarch mab Meirchawn mab Gwrgust Letlwm map Cenew map Coyl Hen.
83. Thomas (1994) 223-224
84. Salway (1994) 140-141, 135 n. 67; Conant *loc.cit.*, but cf. C. Priscius Nemesianus, a sixth century (?) prefect of the vigils at Rome, CIL VI.783.
85. Giot et al (2003) 127.
86. PLRE I Carausius. A possible second usurper of the same name was mentioned in Pt. I ch. 1.
87. He was a friend of the British-born bishop, Faustus of Riez, and of Sidonius Apollinaris: PLRE II Felix 21. Magnus Felix was very plausibly also a descendant of Magnus Maximus himself: Mommaerts & Kelley (1992) *loc. cit.*
88. Fleuriot, quoted in Giot *et al* (2003) 130; Jordanes *Getica*, XLV 237, 238; Greg. Tours *HF* II. 18.

89. Sid. Ap. *Ep*. III.9; the *territorium* of the Bituriges roughly approximates to the later Duchy of Berry, cf. Harries (1994) 210: Eagles (2018) 16, Charles-Edwards (2013) 59-60.
90. As most recently, Eagles (2018) 16
91. Syagrius as *tyrannus*, a typical usurper: Greg. Tours *HF* I. ii. 27; Barwell (1992) 70 & Fanning (1992) 296f.
92. Galiou & Jones (1991) 132, 139
93. Proc. *HB* V. 12, 18-19
94. *Giot et al* (2003) 61-62, 253
95. Russell (2017) 258-259. Bede calls Aelle the first *bretwealda*, which certainly fits Aurelius Ambrosius. Kirby notes that he inhabits a chronological vacuum and that his three alleged sons bear names derived from Sussex coastal locales and that they are therefore probably invented: Kirby (1991) 56; Williams *et al* (1991) 16.
96. *ASC sub anno* 491; Russell, *loc.cit.*
97. Paul Aurelian: Doble (1971) 146-153; Ambrosius: Gildas *DE* 25.4
98. Doble (1971) 152-153; Notolius and Potolius look like a scribal 'double', and garbled to boot; the names are challenging: Notolius could derive from Natalis: Doble *op.cit.* 152 & n. 11, cf. PLRE I. Natalis; Potolius as a scribal error for, say, Potamius (PLRE I & II) is possible and Leonorius for the much more common Leontius (PLRE I = 23 examples, II =30 examples).
99. Giot et al (2003) 129; *Vita Cadoci* 45, fo. 37r, EWGT 24.
100. For example, Umbrius Felix, a junior official in Mauretania in 408: PLRE II Felix 23. Later tradition has Umbraphel a son of Budic of Brittany and endows him with sons St Maglor[ius] and Henwg.
101. In *HRB*, Afrella and Anna become daughters of Vortimer.
102. Giot *et al* (2003) 127, 129. The nature of this link is difficult to elucidate.
103. *HB* 41, 42. Vortigern's paganism: Charles-Edwards (2013) 443. See above on the possible use of 'consul' post 409.
104. Ambrose, *de Excessu Fratris Satyri* I. 32
105. Halsall (2013) 209, cf. PLRE I Ambrosius 1 & 3, Marcellina 1, Satyrus & Uranius 2.
106. PLRE I. *Stemma* 27
107. Morris (1989) 99-100
108. See above; PLRE II. Ecdicius 3 cf. *ibid.*, *stemma* 14
109. PLRE I Philagrius 4; Umbrii PIR[1] V.569, cf. PLRE I Primus 4.
110. Gelling (1984) 98, 150; Glover (1975) 5, Gelling (1953) I. 161, cf. Watts (2004) 12, 13.
111. Morris (1989) 155 arguing that these places had an *ambros-* element in their pre-Saxon names, and that they acquired new suffixes after the Saxon overrun; Watts (2004) 12, 13, not forgetting the river Amber in Derbyshire, listed as 'uncertain': *loc.cit.*
112. Higham (1994) 205, but with the proviso that H. argues that Gildas wrote *c.* 480s, rather than 530s; Fleming (2021) 72.
113. The name Ellefi sounds strangely cognate with that of the Elafius whose child St Germanus healed, although it would be stretching credibility to move this essentially metropolitan incident to south Wales.
114. Swift (2000) 99-101
115. Doble (1971) 205 & n.137 & 206: dedications and place name evidence.
116. Gildas *DE* 25: 'others repaired to parts beyond the sea, with great lamentations...'

117. Charles-Edwards (2013) 74
118. Galliou & Jones (1991) 130-131
119. Sarn Elen: Margary (1955) II. 85-89, route 69a; it does not touch Caernarfon, but the latter is joined to it by Margary 67c & 68.
120. *HRB* V.9; Bromwich (1978) 342: Segontium appearing in the Dream due to the patronage of Llewellyn Fawr ap Iorwerth of Gwynedd (1173-1240), where Arfon was an especially favoured locale.

11 'Owein son of Maxen' and Lowland Britain

1. Roberts (2014) 183; Isaac[i]us: PLRE II, five examples.
2. Harl. MS 3859.17, corrected by Jesus MS 20.40; *Achau Brenhinoedd* 27 omits Einyawn, however.
3. *HB* 34
4. Alcock (1971) 133
5. Frere (1966) 93; Thomas (1979) 97; Norwich (1985) 313; Glover (1976) 65, although interpreted by her as from *Aecclesse* in 975 = 'meadow of the Oak', *aec+ laes.*
6. Stoodley & Cosh (2021) 84-85, 181-182
7. In Stoodley & Cosh *op. cit.* 204-206
8. Glover (1975) 51, but deriving from the unattested personal name *Eccel or *Ecca. St Martin's, in use in 597: Bede *HE* I. 26. Nobody questions the British element in the Derbyshire Ecclesbourne river.
9. Coates (1989) 70
10. Russell (2017) 234; Faull (1977) 19
11. Bede *HE* I.26
12. Dark (2000) 97-104; Rippon (2018) *passim.* but note Cadrod Calchfyvydd, apparently a Votadinian prince and a Coeling: *Achau Brenhinoedd A Thywysogion Cymru,* 9a
13. Frere (1966) 96
14. Hoard: *Current Archaeology* (1/2013) 10; now in the local Museum.
15. Niblett (2001) 132; Frere (1966) 99-100.
16. JC.4; *Vita Cadoci* .45
17. *HB* 66a.3
18. Germanus: Bede *HE* I.17-18; Niblett, *op.cit.* 135, 139-140, 143, 146.
19. Rivett (1966) 109
20. Poundbury: Sparey-Green (2004) 109-110; Charles-Edwards (2013) 22-23 Thomas (1994) 218; cf Eagles (2018) 139-140; CIIC ii.1061-1064. One wonders what other, perhaps more dramatic inscriptions lie buried in cherished ancient buildings.
21. Davey (2004) 52-53
22. Cunliffe (2000) 146; Fleming (2021) 127, Gerrard (2007) 148-164.
23. Fleming (2021 26-27, 72, 165-167, 179.
24. Higham (1995) 159-160; Kirby (1991) 223-224
25. *HE* III.67
26. Higham (1995) 154
27. Russell (2017) 239; El[e]sa is also probably British, being cognate with Elise/ Eliseg eg. in Eliseg's Pillar, Bartrum (1966) 187.
28. Attested as a 'grandson' of Caradog Vreichvras.

29. Bede *HE* I.20, III.1, IV. 12, 15; Kirby (191) 223-224, Figs. 3-4. Names: examples: Bartrum (1966) 182, 178, 213, 174, 178, 176² & 182 respectively. Note Cynwrig ap Rhiwallon ap Dingad, supposedly a descendant of Vortigern: Bartrum 103, *ABT* 9b. Note also that Caedwalla died in Rome, 688 whom Geoffrey of Monmouth confuses with his somewhat earlier British namesake Cadwallon of Gwynedd.

30. Kirby (1991) 49-50, 54-55

31. by Dr Bonner of Cambridge.

32. Alcock (1971) 116, 118

33. Alcock (1971) 112

34. But doubted by Bromwich (1978) 290

35. Matthews (2012) 99, save the chronology; on Caradoc Vreichvras: *Bonedd y Saint* 29, 43, 51, 52, 69, 88, 89; cf. TYP1, 18, 38, 71, cf. Bromwich (1978) 299-300.

36. *HRB* XI 8

37. Russell (2017) 295-296. There was probably a further dynastic change around 784, leading to the accession of Ecgberht in 802, from whom all subsequent Wessex kings descend.

38. *HB* 67.3

39. Bede *HE* II. 2; Russell (2017) 239 & cf. Chapter 8 above.

40. Kirby (1991) 9 & n 44.; in Mercia: Hunt (2016) 19-21, Whitehead (2018) 52 & Zalucky (2001) 13-17.

41. Stenton (1971) 48, e.g. Caedbad.

42. Harper (2017) 208f., 255

43. BL Harleian MS 3859, cf. Morris 8 (1980) 45/85.

44. *DE* 33.1

45. *HB* 62.2; TYP 1, 42, 46, 69; full references in Bromwich (1989) 437-441.

46. Kirby 15 & n. 85

47. *HE* II. 5; Kirby (1991) 18; Charles-Edwards (1013) 426 & n. 71; Morris (1989) 329-330.

48. Cross excavated by Martin Biddle and the late Birthe Kølbye-Biddle in the 1980s and now in Derby Museum.

49. Koch (2013) 167; Morris (1989) 331

50. *Llyfri Gwyn Rhydderch*, fo. 600. 4: Bromwich (1978) 228-229.

51. Smith (1977) Nos. 21 & 34; Zosimus IV 5, 2-3.

52. *V. Cadoci* 45 & Jesus Coll. MS20.4 (Cadoc); *Bonedd y Saint* 63 MSS C, F. (Peblic). TYP 11.

53. Smith (1977) No. 34· but cf. Bromwich (1978) 477-479, 560.

54. Possibly thirty examples of Owein: Bartrum (1966) 207. That Owein was really a 'son' of the emperor Eugenius seems even more unlikely; the name was relatively common in the wider empire.

55. PLRE II. Eugenius 3

56. Jesus College MS 20.4.

57. Chapter 4.

58. PLRE II. Speciosa, Speciosus 1. The latter had previously been thrice prefect of the City of Rome: Mommaerts & Kelley (1992) 111-121.

59. Bartrum (1966) 6-8. Another Ceinrech, daughter of Eliffer Gosgordvawr (= Eleutherius of the Great Army), ruler of York, and a Coeling, appears in one version of *TYP* 70: Bromwich (1978) 307, 344-345, cf Coeling *stemma* in Chapter 9.

60. Full references in Bromwich (1978) 477-479.

61. *V. Petroci*: Bartrum 29-30; *V. Cadoci, ibid*. 24-25.
62. *Cognatio Brychan* 15(1); Jesus MS 20.4, 5, 9; *Achau'r Saint* 4; *Plant Brychan* 3a.
63. *Bonedd y Saint* 39 cf. *Achau'r Saint* 48. Note a Clemens as an antecedent of the first dynasty of Alclud, Chapter 9.
64. Chapter 10
65. *HB* 37-38, 45-46
66. *HB* 48
67. *AC*, MS B, *sub anno* 447.Cimate anomaly: McCave (1999) 515-517, but under (not wholly unanimous) challenge.
68. *DE* 25.2
69. Bede, *Chronica Majora,* dates Badon to the reign of Zeno (474-491).
70. Fleuriot (1980) 170; but as Sidonius addresses him as Riothamus, it seems reasonable to assume that this was his hypochoristic, not a title.
71. *DE* 30.2
72. *HRB* XI.5, there rendered as 'Aurelius Conan'.
73. Line 1241-4; Koch (1997) xxiii-xxxiii.
74. *HB* 56,73.2, the latter reference referring to the killing by Arthur of his son Amr (= Ambrosius) and his burial by a spring in *Erging* (Archenfield, Herefs., from Roman Ariconium, by Weston-under-Penyard).
75. *Gestum Regum Anglorum* I.9
76. Russell (2017) 282
77. Bromwich (1978) 382, 409; on Arthur (a helpful *résumé*) 274-277.
78. Mostyn MS 17.5: the ascendancy ends with Llyr Lletieith, 'King Lear'.
79. Saving a brief and turbulent revival under Owein Glyndŵr.
80. Russell (2017) 277-281
81. *HRB* XI.3-8
82. *Ibid*. XII.
83. Russell (2013) 283-286.

Conclusion: Expanding Maximus's Vita

1. Jankulak (2010) 54
2. Amm. Marc. 29, v. 35
3. St Augustine's letter quoted in Morris (1989) 18 & n.
4. PLRE II Exuperantius 2, Namatianus and Palladius 2.
5. Eg. Whitehead (2018) 14
6. Casey (1979) 67.
7. PLRE II Valentinianus 4
8. Perhaps a vestige of such may be detectable in *HRB* V. 6-8 & 9.
9. Koch (2013) *loc.cit.*
10. Smith (1977) No. 62
11. Chedworth, see now *Current Archaeology* 371 (1/2021) 8 and www. nastionaltrust.org.uk/chedworth. Fifth- and sixth-century Mediterranean pottery has also been found on site and at other villas.
12. Letter, *Current Archaeology* 371 (1/2012) 7.

Bibliography

Primary texts and abbreviations

Ambrosius, *Epistulae, The Letters of St Ambrose of Milan*, translated by anonymous clergy with notes and indices (Oxford 1881); Amb. *Ep.*

Ammianus Marcellinus, *Roman History*, books 14-31, trans. Hamilton, W. (London 1986); Amm. Marc.

Annales Cambriae ed. & trans. Morris, J. (Chichester 1980) 85-91; AC

Aurelius Victor, Sex., *Liber de Caesaribus;* Aur. Vict. *Caes*

Aurelius Victor, Sex., *De Caesaribus Libri Epitome;* Aur. Victor *Epit*

Ausonius, Magnus Decimus: *Ordo Urbium Nobilium*

Bartrum, P. C.(ed.) *Early Welsh Genealogical Tracts* (Cardiff 1966) but mainly noted above by individual original sources; EWGT

Bede, *Historia Ecclesiastica Gentis Anglorum*, Sherley-Price L (trans.) ed. Farmer, D. H. (London 1990); Bede *HE*

Breudwyt Macsen Wledig trans. & ed. Davies, S. (Oxford 2007) 103-110

Brut y Brenhinedd, ed. & trans. Roberts, B. F. (Dublin 1971)

Chronica Gallica ad an. CCCCLII ed. T. Mommsen, T. in: *Chronica Minora* (Berlin 1892, repr. 1961) I. 629-666

Chronicon Pascale 284-628 AD trans. Whitby M & Whitby, M. (Liverpool 1989)

Corpus Inscriptionum Insularum Celticarum, ed. Macalister, R. A. S (2 vols., Dublin 1945. 1949); CIIC+no.

Corpus Inscriptionum Latinarum; CIL+vol.+no.

Epitome de Caesaribus ed. & trans. Banchich, T. M. (Buffalo 2018); *Ep.*

Eusebius, *Vita Constantini*, ed. & trans. Cameron, A. & Hall, S. G. (Oxford 1999)

Gildas, *De Excidio et Conquestu Britanniae* trans. Winterbottom, M. *The Ruin of Britain and other Documents* (London 1978); Gildas *DE*

Geoffrey of Monmouth *Historia Regum Britanniae,* trans. Evans, S. (London 1912); HRB

Gregory of Tours, *Historia Francorum* trans. Lewis Thorpe (London 1974); Greg. *HF*

Gregory of Tours, *Life of the Fathers* (trans. James, E. (Liverpool 1991)

Hydatius, Burgess, R. W. (ed. & trans.) *The Chronicle of Hydatius and the Consularia Constantinopolitana* (Oxford 1993)

Historia Brittonum ed. & trans. Morris, J. (Chichester 1980) 50-84; HB

Inscriptiones Latinae Selectae (ed. Dessau, H.) 5 vols. Chicago (1979); ILS+no.

Liber Pontificalis, trans Davis, R. (Liverpool 1989); *LP*

Malmesbury, William of, *Gesta Regum Anglorum* trans. Stevenson, J. (Lampeter 1989); GR

Notitia Dignitatum, ed. Seeck, O. (Berlin 1876, reprinted Cambridge 2019); *Not. Dig.*

Orosius, Paulus, *Historia Adversus Paganos;* Orosius

Panegyrici Latini ed. & trans., Nixon, C. E. V. & Rodgers, B. S., (Berkeley & Oxford 1994); *Pan. Lat.*

Procopius *Historia Bellorum*, Vols 5-8 *de Bello Gothico,* ed. & trans. Dewing, H. B. (Harvard 1961); Proc. *HB*

Prosper of Aquitaine, *Epitoma Chronicon;* Prosp. *Chron.*

Roman Inscriptions of Britain, ed. Collingwood R. G. & Wright, R. P., Vol. 1 (Oxford 1965); RIB+no.

Socrates, *Historia Ecclesiastica*; Soc. *HE*

Sozomen, *Historia Ecclesiastica* (written 436); Soz. *HE*

Sulpicius Severus, *Diologus*; Sulp. Sev. *Dial.*

Sulpicius Severus, *Vita Sancti Martini*; Sulp. Sev. *V. Martini*

Trioedd Ynys Prydein/Welsh Triads ed. & trans. Bromwich, R. 2nd edn. (Cardiff 1979); TYP+no.

Tysilio, *Chronicle of the Kings of Britain*, trans. Roberts, P. (London 1811)

Victor of Aquitaine, *Cursus Paschalis Annorum DXXXII* (457)

Vita S. Germani Noble R., & Head, T. (trans.), in: *Soldiers of Christ: Saints' Lives from Late Antiquity and the Early Middle Ages* (Pennsylvania 1994) 75-106

William of Malmesbury, *Gestum Regum Anglorum* ed. & trans. Mynors, R. A. B., Thomson, R. M. & Winterbottom M., 2 Vols. (Oxford 1998 & 2002); *GRA*

Zonaras, *The Histories*, trans. Banchich, T. M. & Lane, E. N. (London & NY 2009)

Zosimus, *New History*, trans & ed. Ridley, R. T. (Canberra 1982); Zos. *HN*

Secondary sources

Alcock, L., *Arthur's Britain: History and Archaeology AD 367-634* (London 1971)

Alcock, L., 'By South Cadbury is that Camelot...' The excavation of Cadbury Castle 1966-70 (London 1972)

Alcock, L., 'The North Britons, the Picts and the Scots' in Casey, P. J. (ed.) *The End of Roman Britain: Papers Arising from a Conference, Durham, 1978*, BAR British Series Vol. 71 (Oxford, 1979) 134-142.

Arnold, C. J. & Davies, J. L., *Roman and Early Medieval Wales* (Stroud 2000)

Baillie, M. G. L., *Exodus to Arthur: Catastrophe Encounters with Comets* (London 1999).

Barnwell, P. S., *Emperors, Prefects and Kings: The Roman West 395-565* (London 1992)

Barnwell, P. S., *Kings, Courtiers and Imperium: The Barbarian West 565-725* (London 1997)

Bartrum, P. C. (ed.), *Early Welsh Genealogical Tracts* Cardiff (1966)

Bernard, J. H. & Atkinson, R, *The Irish Liber Hymnorum* 2 Vols. (London 1898)

Biddle, M, & Kjølbye-Biddle, B., *Alban* in Herbert, A., Martin, P., & Thomas, G., *St Albans Cathedral and Abbey* (London 2008) 11-31.

Birley, A. R., *The People of Roman Britain* (London 1979)

Birley, A. R, *The* Fasti *of Roman Britain* (Oxford 1981)

Birley, A. R., *The Roman Government of Britain* (Oxford 2005)

Birley, A. R., 'Brigomaglos and Riacus: A Brave New World' in Haarer, F. K. et al, eds, *AD 410: The History and Archaeology of Late and Post-Roman Britain* (London 2014) 195-205

Bland, R., *Coin Hoards and Hoarding in Roman Britain AD43-c. 498* British Numismatic Society Vol. 13 (London 2018)

Bibliography

Boon, G. C., *Segontium Roman Fort* (London 1963)

Bowen, E. G., *Settlements of the Celtic Saints in Wales* (Cardiff 1956)

Boyle, S. D. *Excavations at Hen Waliau, Caernarfon, 1952-1985*. Bulletin of the Board of Celtic Studies 38 (1991) 191-212

Breeze, D. J., *The Northern Frontiers of Roman Britain* (London 1982)

Bromwich, R., Jarman, A. O. H., & Roberts, B. F., *The Arthur of the Welsh* (Cardiff 1991)

Burgess, R. W., 'The Dark Ages Return to Fifth-Century Britain: the 'Restored' Gallic Chronicle Exploded' in *Britannia* 21 (1990) 185-195

Burgess, R. W., 'The Gallic Chronicle' in *Britannia* 25 (1994) 240-243

Burnett, A., 'Clipped *Siliquae* and the End of Roman Britain' in *Britannia* XV (1984) 163-168.

Byrne, F. J., *Irish Kings and High Kings* (London 1973)

Camden, W., *Britannia* 3rd edn., (London 1594)

Cameron, A. 'Gratian's Repudiation of the Pontifical Robe' in *Journal of Roman Studies (JRS)* LVIII (1968) 97f.

Cameron, A., 'The Origin and Context and Function of Consular Diptychs' in *JRS* CIII (2013) 174-207.

Carroll, M., *Romans, Celts and Germans: The German Provinces of Rome* (Stroud 2001)

Casey, J., 'A Coin of Valentinian III from Wroxeter' in *Britannia* 5 (1974) 383-386

Casey, P. J., 'Magnus Maximus in Britain: a Re-appraisal' in Casey, P. J. (ed.) *The End of Roman Britain: Papers Arising from a Conference, Durham, 1978,* BAR British Series Vol. 71 (Oxford, 1979) 66-79.

Casey, P. J., Davies J. L. & Evans J., *Excavations at Segontium (Caernarfon) Roman Fort 1975-1979* CBA Research Report 90 (Oxford 1993)

Chadwick H. M., *Early Scotland: The Picts the Scots & the Welsh of Southern Scotland* (Cambridge 1949)

Chadwick H. M., *Priscillian of Avila: Occult and the Charismatic in the Early Church* (Oxford 1976)

Charles-Edwards, T. M., 'The Date of the Four Branches of the Mabinogi' in *Transactions of the Honourable Society of Cymmrodorion* (Part 2, 1971) pp. 263–298

Charles-Edwards, T. M., *After Rome* (Oxford 2003)

Charles-Edwards, T. M., *Wales and the Britons 350-1064* (Oxford 2013)

Cleary, S. E. *et al* (eds.) *Chedworth Roman Villa* (London 2022)

Coates, R., ed., *The Place-names of Kent* (London 1989)

Collins, R. 'Before "The End", Hadrian's Wall in the fourth century and after' in Collins, R & Gerrard, J. (eds.) *Debating Late Antiquity in Britain AD 300-700* BAR British Series Vol. 365 (Oxford 2004) 123-132

Collins, R. & Breeze, D., '*Limitanei* and *Comitatenses*: Military Failure at the End of Roman Britain' in Haarer et al, eds, *AD 410: The History and Archaeology of Late and Post-Roman Britain* (2014) 61-72

Collins, R. & Gerrard, J., *Debating Late Antiquity in Britain AD300-700* BAR British Series Vol. 365 (Oxford 2004)

Conant, J., *Staying Roman: Conquest and Identity in Africa and the Mediterranean 439-700* (Cambridge 2015)

Cool, H., 'Which 'Romans', what 'Home'? The Myth of the End of Roman Britain' in Haarer (London 2014) 20f.

Cornery, M., *The Roman Villa at Bradford-on-Avon: The Investigations of 2002* (Bradford-on-Avon 2003)

Cosh, S. R., & Neal, D. S., *Roman Mosaics of Britain, Vol 2: South-West Britain* (London 2005) 247–252.

Craven, M. A. J. B., *The Complete Imperial Families of Ancient Rome* (Stroud 2019)

Crow, J., *Housesteads: A Fort and Garrison on Hadrian's Wall* (Stroud 1995)

Cunliffe, B., *Roman Bath Discovered* (Stroud 2000)

Cunliffe-Shaw, R., *The Men of the North* (Leyland, 1973)

Dark, K. R., 'A Sub-Roman Defence of Hadrian's Wall?' in *Britannia* XXIII (1992) 111-126

Dark, K. R., *Civitas to Kingdom; British Political Continuity 300-800* (Leicester 1994)

Dark, K. R., *Britain and the End of the Roman Empire* (Stroud 2000)

Davey, J., 'The Environs of South Cadbury in the Late Antique and Early Medieval Period' in Collins, R. & Gerrard, J., *Debating Late Antiquity in Britain AD300-700* BAR British Series Vol. 365 (Oxford 2004) 43-54

Davies, W., 'Settlements and Post-Roman Estates in South East Wales' in Casey, P J (ed.) *The End of Roman Britain: Papers Arising from a Conference, Durham, 1978,* BAR British Series Vol. 71 (Oxford, 1979a) 66-79.

Davies, W., *The Llandaff Charters* (Aberystwyth 1979)

Davies, W., *Wales in the Early Middle Ages* (Leicester 1982)

Di Martino, V., *Roman Ireland* (Cork 2003)

Doble, G. H., ed. Evans, D. S., *Lives of the Welsh Saints* (Cardiff 1971)

Dornier, A., 'The Province of Valentia' in *Britannia* 13 (1982) 252-260

Doyle, C., *Honorius: The Fight for the Roman West AD 395-423* (London 2019)

Drinkwater, J. F., *The Gallic Empire; Separatism and Continuity in the North Western Provinces of the Roman Empire AD 260-274* (Stuttgart 1987)

Drinkwater, J. F., 'The Usurpers Constantine III (407-411) and Jovinus (411-413)' in *Britannia* 29 (1998) 269-298

Drinkwater, J. F., *Nero: Emperor and Court* (Cambridge 2019)

Drinkwater J. F. & Elton, H. (eds.) *Fifth-Century Gaul: A Crisis of Identity?* (Cambridge 1992)

Dumville, D. N., 'Sub-Roman Britain: History and Legend' in *History* 62 (6/1977) 73-92.

Eagles, B., *From Roman Civitas to Anglo-Saxon Shire: Topographical Studies on the Formation of Wessex* (Oxford 2018)

Edwards, N, 'Rethinking the Pillar of Eliseg' in *Antiquaries Journal* 89 (2009) 143-177

Evans, D. M., *Legacy Hunting and Welsh Identities* in Haarer (London 2014) 173 f.

Faulkner, N., *The Decline and Fall of Roman Britain* (Stroud 2000)

Faulkner, N, 'The Case for the Dark Ages' in Collins, R. & Gerrard, J., *Debating Late Antiquity in Britain AD 300-700* BAR British Series Vol. 365 (Oxford 2004) 5-12

Faull, M. L., 'British Survival in Anglo-Saxon Northumbria' in Laing, Ll., (ed.) *Studies in Celtic Survival* BAR British Series Vol. 37 (Oxford 1977) 1-55

Ferris, I, *Vinovia: The Buried Roman City of Binchester in Northern England* (Stroud 2011)

Finberg, H. P. R., *Roman and Saxon Withington: A Study in Continuity* (Leicester 1955)

Fincham, G., *Durobrivae: A Roman Town Between Fen and Upland* (Stroud 2004)

Fleming R., *The Material Fall of Roman Britain, 300-525 CE* (Penn State 2021)

Fleuriot, L., *Les Origines de la Bretagne: l'Émigration* (Paris 1980)

Frere, S. S., *The End of Towns in Roman Britain* in Wacher, J. S. (ed.), *The Civitas Capitals of Roman Britain* (Leicester 1966) 87-106

Frere, S. S., *Britannia: A History of Roman Britain* (London 1967)

Galliou, P, & Jones, M., *The Bretons* (Oxford 1991)

Gelling, M. *The Place Names of Oxfordshire* English Place Name Society Vol. XXIII (Cambridge 1953)

Gelling, M., *Place Names in the Landscape* (London 1984)

Gerrard, J. 'The Temple of Sulis-Minerva at Bath and the end of Roman Britain' in *Antiquaries Journal* 82 (2007) 148-164.

Gibbon, E., *History of the Decline and Fall of the Roman Empire* 7 Vols. (Oxford 1902-1906)

Giot, P.-R., Guigon, P & Merdrignac, B., *The British Settlement of Brittany: The First Bretons in Armorica* (Stroud 2003)

Glover, J, *The Place Names of Sussex* (London 1975)

Glover, J, *The Place Names of Kent* (London 1976)

Green, T., *Britons and Anglo-Saxons: Lincolnshire 400-650* (Lincoln 2012)

Guest, P., 'The Hoarding of Roman Metal Objects in Fifth Century Britain' in Haarer (London 2014) 115-129

Guy, B. 'Constantine, Helena, Maximus: on the Appropriation of Roman History in Medieval Wales, *c.* 800-1250' in *Journal of Medieval History* 44 issue 4 (2018) 381-405

Haarer, F. K. et al, eds, *AD 410: The History and Archaeology of Late and Post-Roman Britain* (London 2014)

Halsall, G., *Worlds of Arthur: Facts and Fictions of the Dark Ages* (Oxford 2013)

Harper, K., *The Fate of Rome: Climate, Disease and the End of an Empire* (Princeton and Oxford 2017)

Harries, J., *Sidonius Apollinaris and the Fall of Rome AD407-485* (Oxford 1994)

Hartley, E., Hawkes, J., Henig, M. & Mee, F. (eds.), *Constantine the Great: York's Roman Emperor* (York 2006)

Hassall, M. W. C. & Ireland, R. (ed.) *De Rebus Bellicis* in British Archaeological Reports, International Series (Oxford 1979) Vol. 63 part 2.

Henig, M., 'Remaining Roman in Britain AD 300-700: The Evidence of Portable Art' in Casey, P. J. (ed.) *The End of Roman Britain: Papers Arising from a Conference, Durham, 1978,* BAR British Series Vol. 71 (Oxford, 1979) 13-23

Higham, N. J., *Rome, Britain and the Anglo-Saxons* (London 1992)

Higham, N. J., *The Kingdom of Northumberland AD350 -1100* (Stroud 1993)

Higham, N. J., *An English Empire: Bede and the Early Anglo-Saxon Kings* (Manchester 1995)

Higham, N. J., *Britons in Anglo-Saxon England* (Woodbridge 2007)

Higham, N. J. & Jones, B., *The Carvetii* (Stroud 1985)

Holmes, J., *One Thousand Cornish Place Names Explained* (Truro 2005)

Hope-Taylor, B., *Yeavering: An Anglo-British Centre of Early Northumbria* (London 1977)

Hughes, I., *Imperial Brothers: Valentinian, Valens and the Disaster at Adrianople* (Barnsley 2013)

Hull, D., 'Religious Heresy and Political Dissent in Late Antiquity: A Comparison Between Syria and Britain' in Collins, R. & Gerrard, J., *Debating Late Antiquity in Britain AD300-700* BAR British series Vol. 365 (Oxford 2004) 113-133

Hunt, J., *Warriors, Warlords and Saints: the Anglo-Saxon Kingdom of Mercia* (Alcester 2016)

Hurst, H. R., 'Excavations at Gloucester', third interim report, 1966-75, in *Antiquaries Journal* 55 (1975) 267–94

Jackson, K. H., *Language and History in Early Britain: A Chronological Survey of the Brittonic Languages, First to Twelfth Centuries* (Edinburgh 1953)

Jankulak, J., *Geoffrey of Monmouth* (Cardiff 2010)

Jankulak, K., *Present yet Absent: the Cult of St. Samson of Dol in Wales* in Olson (2017) 163-180

Johns, C., *The Hoxne Late Roman Treasure: Gold Jewellery and Silver Plate* (BM London 2010)

Johnson, S., *The Roman Forts of the Saxon Shore* (London 1976)

Johnson, S., *Later Roman Britain* (London 1982)

Johnston, D. E. (ed.), *The Saxon Shore* CBA Research Report 18 (London 1977)

Jones, M. E. & Casey, J., 'The Gallic Chronicle Restored: A Chronology for the Anglo-Saxon Invasions and the End of Roman Britain' in *Britannia* 19 (1988) 367-398

Jones, M. E. & Casey, J., 'The Gallic Chronicle Exploded?' In *Britannia* 22 (1991) 212-215

Kent, J. P. C., 'The End of Roman Britain: The Literary and Numismatic Evidence Reviewed' in Casey, P J (ed.) *The End of Roman Britain: Papers Arising from a Conference, Durham, 1978,* BAR British Series Vol. 71 (Oxford, 1979) 15-28.

Kirby, D. P., *The Earliest English Kings* (London 1991)

Knight, J. K., *The End of Antiquity: Archaeology, Society and Religion AD235-700* (Stroud 2007)

Knight, J. K., 'The Afterlife of Tyrants: Roman Emperors in Early Medieval Wales' in Haarer (London 2014) 165-172

Koch, J. T., *The Gododdin of Aneurin: Text and Context from Dark-Age North Britain* (Cardiff 1997).

Koch, J. T., *Cunedda, Cynan, Cadwallon, Cynddylan: Four Welsh Poems and Britain 383-655* (Aberystwyth 2013)

Kulikowski, M., *Imperial Tragedy: From Constantine's Empire to the Destruction of Roman Italy AD 363-568* (London 2019)

Laing, L., (ed.) *Studies in Celtic Survival* BAR British Series Vol. 37 (Oxford 1977)

Livermore, H. V., *The Origins of Spain and Portugal* (London 1971)

Malcor, L. A. and J. Matthews *Artorius, The Real King Arthur* (Stroud 2022)

Mann, J. C., 'Hadrian's Wall: The Last Phases' in Casey, P. J., (ed.) *The End of Roman Britain: Papers Arising from a Conference, Durham, 1978,* BAR British Series Vol. 71 (Oxford, 1979) 144-151

Margary, I. D., *Roman Roads in Britain* 2 Vols. (London 1955)

Martindale, J. R., Jones, A. H., M. & Morris, J. (eds.) *The Prosopography of the Later Roman Empire* 3 Vols (Cambridge 1971, 1980, 1992); PLRE

Mason, J. P., *Roman Chester: City of the Eagles* (Stroud 2001)

Mathiesen, R. W., *Ecclesiastical Factionalism and Religious Controversy in Fifth-Century Gaul* (Washington 1989)

Mathiesen, R. W., *Roman Aristocrats in Barbarian Gaul: Strategies for Survival in an Age of Transition* (Austin 1993)

Matthews, J. F., 'Olympiodorus of Thebes and the History of the West (AD407-425)' in *JRS* LX (1970) 79-97

Matthews, J. F., *Western Aristocracies and the Imperial Court AD 364-425* (Oxford 1975)

Matthews, J. F., 'Macsen, Maximus and Constantine' in *Welsh History Review* 11, 4 (12/1983) 131-148.

Matthews, R., *Ceawlin: The Man who Created England* (Barnsley 2012)

Mattingly, H. *et al.*, *Roman Imperial Coinage* 10 vols. (London 1923-1994); RIC

McCave, I. N., 'Holocene periodicity in North Atlantic climate and deep-ocean flow south of Iceland' in *Nature*, 397 (2/1999) 515-7.

McCarthy, M. *Roman Carlisle and the Lands of the Solway* (Stroud 2002

McGeorge, P., *Late Roman Warlords* (Oxford 2002)

McGill, S., Sogno, C & Watts, E., *From the Tetrarchs to Theodosius: Later Roman History and Culture 284-450 CE* (Cambridge 2010)

Moffat, A., *The Faded Map: Lost Kingdoms of Scotland* (Edinburgh 2010)

Moorhead, S., *Numismatic Enigmas* in *Current Archaeology* 220 (9/2009)

Moorhead, S. & Walton, P., *Coinage and the End of Roman Britain* in Haarer (London 2014) 99-116

Morris, J., *Arthurian Sources, Vol. 8, Nennius' British History and the Welsh Annals* (Chichester 1980)

Morris, J., *The Age of Arthur: A History of the British Isles from 350-650* (London 1989)

Morris, J., *Arthurian Sources Vol. 3 Persons* (Chichester 1995)

Morris, J., *Arthurian Sources Vol. 5 Genealogies and Texts* (Chichester 1995)

Morris, J., *Londinium: London in the Roman Empire* (London 1999)

Myres, J. N. L., *The English Settlements* (Oxford 1986)

Nash-Williams, V. E., *Early Christian Monuments of Wales* (Cardiff 1950)

Nash-Williams, V. E., *The Roman Frontier in Wales* (Cardiff 1954)

Neri, V., 'L'usurpatore come Tiranno nel Lesico Politico della Tarda Antichità' in Paschoud, F. & Szidat, J. (eds.) *Usurpation in der Spätantike* (Stuttgart 1996) 71-86.

Niblett, R., *Verulamium: The Roman City of St Albans* (Stroud 2001)

Nichol, M., et al., *Mud Hole Villa, Boxford, West Berkshire: The Results of the 2019 Excavation* (Cirencester 2020)

Norwich, J. J., 2nd Viscount, *The Architecture of Southern England* (London 1985)

Olson, L. (ed.), *St. Samson of Dol and the Earliest History of Brittany, Cornwall and Wales*, Studies in Celtic History XXXVII (Woodbridge 2017)

Omissi, A., *Emperors and Usurpers in the Later Roman Empire: Civil War, Panegyric and the Construction of Legitimacy* (Oxford, 2018)

Oosthuizen, S., *The Emergence of the English* (Leeds 2019)

Ottaway, P., *Roman York* (Stroud 2004)

Pearce, S. M., *The Kingdom of Dumnonia: Studies in History and Tradition in South West Britain AD 350-1150* (Padstow 1978)

Pearson, A., *The Roman Shore Forts: Coastal Defences of Southern Britain* (Stroud 2002)

Pearson, A., *The Construction of the Saxon Shore Forts,* BAR British Series 349 (London 2003)

Percival, J., *The Roman Villa* (London 1976)

Petts, D., 'Christianity and Cross-Channel Connectivity in Late and Sub-Roman Britain' in Haarer (London 2014) 73-90.

Pretty, K., 'Defining the Magonsaete' in Basset, S. (ed.) *The Origins of Anglo-Saxon Kingdoms* (Leicester 1989) 171f.

Rahtz, P. & Watts, L., 'The End of Roman Temples in the West of Britain' in Casey, P J (ed.) *The End of Roman Britain: Papers Arising from a Conference, Durham, 1978,* BAR British Series Vol. 71 (Oxford, 1979) 15-28.

Rance, P, 'Attacotti, Deisi and Magnus Maximus: the Case for Irish Federates in Late Roman Britain' in *Britannia* 32 (2001) 243-270

Richards, R, *Old Cheshire Churches* (London 1947)

Rippon, S., *Kingdom, Civitas and Country: The Evolution of Territorial Identity in the English Landscape* (Oxford 2018)

Rippon, S., Smart, C. & Pears, B., *The Fields of Britannia: Continuity and Change in the Late Roman and Early Medieval Landscape* (Oxford 2015).

Rivett, A. L. F., 'Some Historical Aspects of the *Civitates* of Roman Britain' in Wacher, J. S., ed., *The Civitas Capitals of Roman Britain* (Leicester 1966) 101-113

Rivett, A. L. F. & Smith, C., *The Place Names of Roman Britain* (Cambridge 1979)

Roberts, I., 'Rethinking the Archaeology of Elmet' in Haarer (London 2014) 182-194

Rogers, A., *Late Roman Towns in Britain* (Cambridge 2011)

Round J. H., 'The Origins of the Carews' in *The Ancestor* V (4/1903) 47.

Rüpke, J. & Glock, A., (trans Richardson, D. M. R.) *Fasti Sacerdotum* (Oxford 2008)

Russell, M. & Laycock, S., *UnRoman Britain: Exposing the Great Myth of Britannia* (Stroud 2011)

Russell, M., *Arthur and the Kings of Britain* (Stroud 2017)

Salway, B., 'What's in a Name? A Survey of Roman Onomastic Practice from c. 700BC to AD700' in *JRS* LXXXIV (1994) 124-145.

Salway, P., *Roman Britain* (Oxford, 1984)

Salway, P., *The Oxford Illustrated History of Roman Britain* (Oxford 1993)

Sankey, D. (1998) 'Cathedrals, Granaries and Urban Vitality in late Roman London' in Watson, B. (ed.) *Roman London: Recent Archaeological Work*. Supplementary Series 24 *Journal of Roman Archaeology* (1998) 78-82

Scheid, J. & Zink, M., *Les Sociétés Tribales en Afrique de Nord, IXe Journée d'Etudes Nord-Africaines* (Paris, 2019)

Settipani, C., *Continuité Gentilice et Continuité Senatoriale dans les Familles Senatoriales Romaines a L'époque Imperiale: Mythe et Réalité,* Vol. II (Oxford 2000)

Shiel, N., *The Episode of Carausius and Allectus* BAR 40 (Oxford 1977)

Sivan, H., *Ausonius of Bordeaux: Genesis of a Gallic Aristocracy* (London 1993)

Skene, W. F., *The Four Ancient Books of Wales* (Edinburgh 1868)

Skene, W. F., *Celtic Scotland: A History of Ancient Alban*, 3 vols., 2nd edn. (Edinburgh 1886/1887/1890)

Smith, M. (ed.), *The Triads of Britain Compiled by Iolo Morganwg* (London 1977)

Southern, P. & Dixon, K. R., *The Late Roman Army* (London 1996)

Sowerby, R., *A Family and its Saint in the Vita Prima Somsonis* in Olson (2017) 19-36

Sparey-Green, C., 'Living Amongst the Dead: From Roman cemetery to Post-Roman Monastic Settlement at Poundbury' in Collins, R. & Gerrard, J., *Debating Late Antiquity in Britain AD300-700* BAR 365 (Oxford 2004) 103-111

Stacey, R. C., 'Texts and Society' in *After Rome* ed. Charles-Edwards, T. (Oxford 2003) 221-257

Stenton, F., *Anglo-Saxon England* (Oxford, 1971)

Stevens, C. E., 'Magnus Maximus in British History' in *Études Celtiques* III (1938) 86

Stoodley, N. & Cosh S. R., *The Romano-British Villa and Anglo-Saxon Cemetery at Eccles, Kent* (Oxford, 2021)

Stow, J., (ed. Kingsford C. L.) *Survey of London* 2nd edn 1603, 2 Vols (London 1927)

Sutherland, E., *In Search of The Picts: A Celtic Dark Age Nation* (London 1994)

Swift, E., *The End of the Western Roman Empire: An Archaeological Investigation* (Stroud 2000)

Syme, R., *Ammianus and the Historia Augusta* (Oxford 1968)

Syvänne, I., *The Reign of Gallienus: The Apogee of Roman Cavalry* (Barnsley 2019)

Thomas, C., 'The Character and Origins of Roman Dumnonia' in Thomas, C. (ed.) *Rural Settlement in Roman Britain* CBA Research Report 7 (London 1966) 74-98.

Thomas, C., 'St Patrick and Fifth-Century Britain: an Historical Model Explored' in Casey, P. J. (ed.) *The End of Roman Britain: Papers Arising from a Conference, Durham, 1978,* BAR British Series Vol. 71 (Oxford, 1979) 81-101

Thomas, C., *Christianity in Roman Britain to AD500* (London 1981)

Bibliography

Thomas, C., *And Shall these Mute Stones Speak? Post-Roman Inscriptions in Western Britain* (Cardiff 1994)

Thomas, C., *Christian Celts: Messages and Images* (Stroud 1998)

Thompson, E. A., 'Britain AD 406-410' in *Britannia* 8 (1977) 303-318

Tibbs, A., *Beyond the Empire: A Guide to the Roman Remains in Scotland* (Ramsbury 2019)

Tomlin, R. S. O., 'A Sub-Roman Gravestone from Aberhydfer near Trecastle' in *Archaeologia Cambrensis* CXXIV (1975) 68-72

Toolis, R. & Bowles, C., *The Lost Dark Age Kingdom of Rheged: The Discovery of a Royal Stronghold at Trusty's Hill, Galloway* (Oxford 2017)

Turner, S., 'Coast and Countryside in Late Antique South West England *c*. AD 400-600' in Collins, R. & Gerrard, J., *Debating Late Antiquity in Britain AD300-700* BAR British Series Vol. 365 (Oxford 2004) 25-32

Wacher, J. S. (ed,) *The Civitas Capitals of Roman Britain* (Leicester 1966)

Wacher, J. S., *Roman Britain* (London 1978)

Wallace, P. F., *A Guide to the National Museum of Ireland* (Dublin 2000)

Ward J. H., 'The British Sections of the *Notitia Dignitatum*, an Alternative Interpretation' in *Britannia* IV (1973) 253f.

Watson, B. (ed.) *Roman London: Recent Archaeological Work* (Portsmouth RI 1998)

Watts, V., *The Cambridge Dictionary of English Place Names* (Cambridge 2004)

Welsby, D. A., *The Roman Military Defence of British Province in its Later Phases*: BAR 101 (Oxford 1982)

White, A. (ed), *A History of Lancaster* (Edinburgh 2001)

White, R., *Britannia Prima: Britain's Last Roman Province* (Stroud 2007)

White, R. & Barker, P., *Wroxeter: Life and Death of a Roman City* (Stroud 1999)

White, R. H., Gaffney, C. & Gaffney V. L., *Wroxeter, the Cornovii and the Urban Process*, Vol. 2 *Characterizing the City* (Oxford 2013)

Whitehead, A., *Mercia: The Rise and Fall of a Kingdom* (Stroud 2018)

Wijnendaele, J. W. P., 'Ammianus, Magnus Maximus and the Gothic Uprising' in *Britannia* 51 (2020) 330-335

Williams, A., Smyth, A. P. & Kirby, D. P., *A Biographical Dictionary of Dark Age Britain: England Scotland and Wales c. 500–c. 1050* (London 1991)

Williams, I., *Early Welsh Poetry* (Dublin 1954)

Williams, S. & Friell, G., *Theodosius: The Empire at Bay* (London 1994)

Willmott, T., *Birdoswald Roman Fort: 1800 Years on Hadrian's Wall* (Stroud 2001)

Wiseman, T. P., *Unwritten Rome* (Exeter 2008)

Wood, I. N., 'Germanus, Alban and Auxerre' in *Bulletin du Centre d'Études Médiévales d'Auxerre* 13 (2009) 123-129.

Wood, I., 'The Crocus Conundrum' in Hartley, E., Hawkes, J, Henig, M & Mee, F (eds.), *Constantine the Great: York's Roman Emperor* (York 2006), 77-82

Zalucky, S., *Mercia: the Anglo-Saxon Kingdom of Central England* (Eardisley 2001).

Index

Cities/Towns are listed under Latin name (where known) first; some are cross-referenced with their modern equivalents. **Romans** are listed under their familiar names; **Britons** are generally listed under their British/Welsh names followed by the Latin version where known. (**E**) and (**W**) indicate the eastern and western parts of the empire. A distinction has been made between the British Kingdom of Powis and the modern county of Powys. **Saints** are listed under their names, but locales named after saints, are listed under 'St.'